BLOOMSBURY'S OUTSIDER

BLOOMSBURY'S OUTSIDER

A Life of David Garnett

SARAH KNIGHTS

BLOOMSBURY READER

LONDON · OXFORD · NEW YORK · NEW DELHI · SYDNEY

This edition published in 2015 by Bloomsbury Reader

Bloomsbury Reader is a division of Bloomsbury Publishing Plc,

50 Bedford Square, London WC1B 3DP

First published in Great Britain in 2015 by Bloomsbury Reader

ISBN: 9781448215454

eISBN: 9781448215447

Visit www.bloomsburyreader.com to find out more about our authors and their books.
You will find extracts, author interviews, author events and you can sign up for
newsletters to be the first to hear about our latest releases and special offers.

You can also find us on Twitter @bloomsreader.

Printed and bound by CPI Group (UK) Ltd, Croydon, CR0 4YY

For Tony and Rafael

Contents

Part 1

Constance

Chapter One

'Alas and alack, I have married a Black.'
'Oh damn it, oh darn it, I have married a Garnett.'[1]

This interchange between Constance (née Black) and Edward Garnett, David Garnett's parents, was more than affectionate banter. They both believed there was such a thing as a 'Black' or a 'Garnett' with definable characteristics. David remarked: 'My father believes in heredity and has a passion for explaining people by their grandparents. "That's the old Willoughby horse-thief strain coming out in her," he will say [...] when some female guest has walked off with a book.'[2] David inherited this belief, and like Edward, perceived regional influence upon character. It seemed entirely logical to him that the famous 'Garnett obstinacy' hailed from the Yorkshire Garnetts, that his passionate disposition stemmed from the Irish Singletons and that his earthy

---

[1] Richard Garnett, *Constance Garnett: A Heroic Life* (London: Sinclair-Stevenson, 1991) p. 78.
[2] David Garnett, 'A Whole Hive of Genius', *The Saturday Review of Literature* (New York), Saturday 1 October 1932.

rationalism was acquired from the Scottish Blacks.

Like Edward and Constance, David considered himself a congenital outsider, attracted to experimental living, to life beyond the mainstream. He liked to define himself in terms of genetic inheritance and evolution: nature as opposed to nurture. Darwinism was a highly convenient belief system, rational and scientific, and if one had inherited certain *surviving* characteristics, then good or bad, one couldn't do much about them. Although David despised organised religion and did not believe in any afterlife in the religious sense, he did believe there was another kind of life after death:

> We have reason to believe that every living creature is a fresh permutation of ancestral genes which determine its individuality. Half of the possible genes are passed on to the new individual from each parent, half are discarded. The heredity constitution which results is infinitely more important than education or experience.[3]

Thus David's forebears were a source of considerable pride. His mother's paternal grandfather, in particular, was much admired. Born in Scotland in 1788 to a family of fishermen, Peter Black commanded the first regular steam-packet to St Petersburg, built two steamships which sailed between Lübeck and St Petersburg, and was to embark on a career in the Russian navy when he died in 1831. Constance was the daughter of his son, David Black, a dour Brighton solicitor, who had married Clara Patten, a sweet-natured and well-read young woman. The sixth of their eight children, Constance was born in 1861.

---

[3] David Garnett, *The Golden Echo* (London: Chatto & Windus, 1953), p. x.

Constance was earnest, wore steel spectacles over her pale blue eyes, had a fair complexion and light brown hair worn in a bun on top of her head. According to David Garnett, she was 'conscious of being more intelligent than the majority of people and, all her married life, of being more intelligent than my father'.[4] Constance gained the equivalent of a First in Classics from Newnham College, Cambridge in 1883 (when women were not formally awarded degrees). She was extremely literal, firm in her convictions, independent and adventurous; she disliked luxury or ostentation and loved the countryside. An active Fabian, she narrowly avoided being proposed to by George Bernard Shaw, who was at the time too poor to marry.

David also inherited many Garnett characteristics, the most obvious being his grandfather's slow, deliberate vocal delivery. Dr Richard Garnett was the grandson of a Yorkshire paper manufacturer and son of the Reverend Richard Garnett, philologist, who in 1838 became Assistant Keeper of Printed Books at the British Museum. Despite an almost complete lack of formal education, Dr Richard Garnett (as he was called to distinguish him from his father) was a considerable scholar; he became Superintendent of the Reading Room in the British Museum, contributed significantly to the *Dictionary of National Biography*, and his poem 'Where Corals Lie' was set to music by Elgar. He is best remembered for *Twilight of the Gods*, tales of pagan fantasy imbued with dry humour. Such was Dr Garnett's stature that his obituary in *The New York Times* stated: 'No one was better known to the English writing world.'[5]

---

[4] David Garnett, 'Memoir of Constance Garnett', unpublished MS [Northwestern].

[5] Quoted in James Fergusson, *David Garnett's Family Books: The Property of the Estate of David Garnett* (London: James Fergusson Books and Manuscripts, 2009) p. 71.

David Garnett's paternal grandmother, Olivia Narney Singleton, was of Anglo-Irish protestant stock, from what David called a line of 'warm-hearted, passionate, lavish, open-handed libertines'.[6] Six years younger than Constance, Edward was born in 1868, and with his five surviving siblings, was raised in an atmosphere of Victorian respectability combined with complete liberality of opinion. Edward was a tall, lanky, curly haired man who loved to tease and was always amused by anyone taking themselves too seriously.

Far from being a stereotypical Victorian couple, Constance and Edward lived together before their marriage in 1889. David felt no need to rebel against his parents: he had no reason to counter Victorian mores because they had done it for him. Instead, he felt immensely grateful to them not only for bestowing upon him what he believed to be their innately remarkable qualities and values, but for giving him unconditional freedom and love. 'I was lucky enough', he commented, 'to find very little in my parents' beliefs which I had to jettison.'[7]

Edward early revealed his metier as an exemplary and inspirational publishers' reader. His grandson Richard (who knew him) considered Edward 'a congenital outsider, never accepting received opinions and original in all his literary judgements'.[8] As his career progressed, Edward's discernment and advice was invaluable to many talented writers, including D.H. Lawrence, Joseph Conrad, John Galsworthy, W.B. Yeats and H.E. Bates.

While Edward worked in London, Constance remained in the country at Henhurst Cross near Dorking in Surrey. There

[6] DG, *Echo*, p. xi.

[7] DG/Frances Partridge, Charry, 22 December 1972 [KCC].

[8] RG, *Constance*, p. 50.

she began to learn Russian, inspired in this endeavour by her friend Felix Volkhovsky, the Russian revolutionary and man of letters. From these beginnings Constance launched a distinguished career translating Russian literary classics into the English language.

Constance worked at Russian throughout her pregnancy. From her parents' house in Brighton where she had temporarily moved to be attended by the family doctor, she wrote to Edward in February 1892 expressing her hope that the child would be free from 'Black coldness' and 'Northern Garnett obstinacy'. Instead she wanted him (for she seemed certain it would be a boy) to be a 'warm-blooded impulsive romantic independent muddle-headed boy – full of spirits and sympathetic – nearly all his father with only the smallest grain of his mother'.[9]

David Garnett was born on 9 March following a long labour and difficult delivery in which chloroform and forceps were employed. He was a large baby, weighing 9¾ pounds. The nurse commented: 'I've known bigger babies & prettier babies, but never such a cute one, as soon as he was born he lifted up his head & looked about him.'[10] Dr Richard Garnett (who wrote about astrology under the anagrammatic pseudonym 'A.G. Trent') lost little time in commissioning a horoscope for his grandson. It recommended that David should refrain from public life, live in Brighton and take as an occupation something relating to the sea. It did not, however, predict his life-long sea-sickness.

Edward's sister Olive Garnett declared her nephew 'a pretty little fellow & very "manly" [...]. He has the most innocent and

---

[9] Quoted in RG, *Constance*, p. 76.
[10] CG, unpublished memoir [Northwestern].

confiding & altogether winning smile I ever saw in a baby.'[11] David was a pretty little fellow, blond-haired and blue-eyed. But some months after his birth Constance noticed something wrong with his eyes. Perhaps resulting from the forceps delivery, David had defective eye muscles which prevented him from looking out of the corners of his eyes. As an adult, this was one source of his charismatic charm, for he would turn his head sideways, bestowing his full focus on whomever he was with. 'Many people', remarked his son, Richard, 'found his candid gaze most attractive.'[12]

The infant David liked to tease, alarming Constance by pretending to pick up a pin and clench it in his fist. She tried to make him relinquish it, only to find his hand empty. Little David was so enamoured of Randolph Caldecott's illustration of Baby Bunting in his rabbit-skin cap that a rabbit-skin cap was made for him. In consequence, the village boys called him 'Bunny', and the name stuck. It was used by almost all his friends and relatives, a name which suited him in all stages of his life. Rather than compromising his masculinity and dignity, or infantilising him, it seemed to grow with him, softening his stature, gravitas and occasional pomposity.

On New Year's Eve 1893, when Bunny was twenty-one months old, Constance left him in the care of Edward's sister, May, while she travelled to Russia. There were several reasons for this momentous journey, but it stemmed from Constance's and Edward's friendship with Sergey Stepniak, to whom they had been introduced by Volkhovsky shortly after Bunny's birth. Having arrived in England in 1884 as a political refugee, in 1890

---

[11] Barry C. Johnson, ed., *Tea and Anarchy! The Bloomsbury Diary of Olive Garnett 1890–1893* (London: Bartletts Press, 1989), p. 72.

[12] RG, *Constance*, p. 77.

Stepniak founded the Society of Friends of Russian Freedom. He was a powerful and charismatic figure, committed to ending Russian autocracy and the iniquitous exile system. Moreover in 1878 he had assassinated General Mezentsev, St Petersburg's repressive and cruel Chief of Police. Despite a sometimes fierce countenance, Stepniak had a gentle charm and affectionate nature, and was greatly taken with Bunny, who liked to carry his toys and pile them upon Uncle Stepniak's knee. When Edward whimsically commented that Stepnaik was the offspring of a goddess and a bear, Bunny exclaimed, ' "That bear that was Uncle Stepniak's Dad was a good bear" '.[13]

Stepniak encouraged Constance in her translating, and she began to experience a sense of vocation for both translation and Russian literature. In consequence, she wanted to see Russia herself and to get a feel for the language and atmosphere of the country. As her grandson and biographer Richard Garnett suggests, Constance's decision to visit Russia may have been of underlying benefit to Stepniak, who 'had need of innocent-looking emissaries to carry letters and books that could not safely be sent through the censored mails and perhaps also to take money [...] to help Russian political prisoners and exiles to escape'.[14]

Her bravery and fortitude in undertaking this expedition cannot be exaggerated. Not only was she a woman travelling great distances alone, to a remote country (and on potentially subversive business) but she had a weak constitution. Throughout her childhood tuberculosis of the hip confined Constance to long periods in bed. She suffered from migraine and was extremely short-sighted. Though physically frail, she was emotionally and

---

[13] CG, unpublished memoir.
[14] RG, *Constance*, p. 106.

intellectually robust, and like her grandfather, Peter Black, some-thing of a pioneer. As she hoped, her Russian expedition enhanced her strengths as a translator, leading Joseph Conrad to conclude: 'Turgeniev for me is Constance Garnett and Constance Garnett *is* Turgeniev.'[15]

Later, Constance questioned how she had the heart to leave Bunny for almost two months at that young age. While she was away he would take out her photograph from the drawer, murmur-ing, as he kissed it, "My mummy gone Russ".[16] But he was always proud of her work and influence, and told her, during the Great War: 'You have probably had more effect on the minds of every-body under thirty in England than any three living men. On their attitude, their morals, their sympathies […]. I think [Dostoevsky's] *The Idiot* has probably done more to alter the morals of my gener-ation than the war or anything that happens to them in the war.'[17]

Constance coped with travelling, propelled by 'a passionate longing for adventure', but passion, in the sexual sense, had fallen from her marriage after Bunny was born.[18] Constance seems to have accepted that her libido would not return and that, as her doctor informed her, she must 'expect to feel middle-aged'.[19] A few weeks after Bunny's birth, running for a train, she experienced what was probably a prolapsed uterus. She was told to rest and prescribed an internal 'support'. Feeling that 'one

---

[15] Edward Garnett, ed., *Letters from Conrad 1895–1924* (London: The Nonesuch Press, 1928), p. 269.

[16] CG, unpublished memoir.

[17] Constance's translation published 1913; DG/CG, Charleston, n.d. 'Sunday' [1917] [HRRC].

[18] CG, unpublished memoir.

[19] RG, *Constance*, p. 79

side of my passion seems to have died away', she worried that Edward would doubt her love. In an astonishingly compassionate and understanding letter, she effectively released him from the ties of conventional faithfulness: 'I want to make you happy without clogging you and hampering you as women always do. I know and see quite clearly that in many ways we must get more separate as time passes but that need never touch the innermost core of love which will always remain with us.'[20]

If physical passion no longer bound them, Edward and Constance were united in their affection for both Bunny and The Cearne, the isolated and idiosyncratic house they created. With the aid of a bequest from Constance's father, The Cearne was designed by Edward's brother-in-law, Harrison Cowlishaw, an architect working in the Arts & Crafts tradition. Edward and Constance independently viewed potential sites, and to their surprise found they both selected the same spot. They were attracted to a rather remote and inaccessible plot near the village of Limpsfield, on the Surrey-Kent border, offering a magnificent view to south and west. Shielded by woodland, it also provided privacy and solitude. Bunny later recalled visiting the site, carried aloft on Stepniak's shoulders, from where he saw the building's great rafters, bare against the sky.

The Cearne was constructed in an L-shape, with immensely thick walls, heavy, hinged wooden doors and enormous inglenook fireplaces. D.H. Lawrence perspicaciously described it as 'one of those new, ancient cottages',[21] and perceived 'something

---

[20] CG/EG, n.d. 'Thursday' [1892] [Northwestern], quoted in RG, *Constance*, p. 80.

[21] James T. Boulton, ed., *The Letters of D.H. Lawrence*, Vol. 1 (Cambridge University Press, 1979), p. 314.

unexpected and individualised' about it.[22] Although in ethos it complied with Arts and Crafts traditions of simplicity in design and integrity in materials, it didn't quite fit the Arts and Crafts mould. It was too simple in style, too medieval, too cold and too uncompromisingly stark. It had the benefit of an upstairs bathroom (though the water closet was housed outside the back door), but generally lacked in comfort, causing Edward and his guests to draw their chairs deep into the inglenook to warm themselves against ever-present draughts. Bunny adored The Cearne: 'How I love the place! I love every twig, every stone, everything', he later eulogised. 'How well the place fits me!' 'Coming home is like slipping on an old pair of downtrodden slippers.' He roamed the surrounding countryside which became an extension of the house itself: 'There is nothing I don't know when I'm at home about the place, it is all absolutely familiar. I know the surface of the ground, the stones the roots, even the molehills. When I go into the wood I know all the trees.'[23]

As a boy, Bunny was solitary but not lonely, spending hours contentedly wandering the countryside, absorbed in flora and fauna. Even so he was conscious that he and his parents were 'outsiders', set apart from the villagers and from village life. Instead, the Garnetts both attracted and were absorbed into a growing community of like-minded free-thinkers, which gradually drifted into the neighbourhood and whom Bunny later labelled 'the Limpsfield intelligentsia'.[24] Among this remarkable group were John Atkinson Hobson, the radical social theorist

---

[22] Boulton, ed., *Letters of D.H. Lawrence*, DHL/CG, Broadstairs, Friday [11 July 1913], p. 33.

[23] DG/RAG, The Cearne, n.d. [1920] [Northwestern].

[24] DG, *Echo*, p. 73.

and economist, his wife, Florence, a campaigner for women's rights, and Edward Pease, secretary of the Fabian Society. The community also attracted Constance's circle of Russian exiles, who settled nearby at what was to become known as 'Dostoevsky Corner'.

Having moved into The Cearne in February 1896, Constance and Edward filled the interstices of their marriage in different ways. Constance was fulfilled in her role as a mother and by her work as a translator. But Edward, who spent much of the week in London, needed more: he required someone to supply the physical love which Constance no longer gave. He had fallen in love with the artist, Ellen Maurice 'Nellie' Heath, who, by 1899, had become his mistress (though they did not live together until 1914). While this label reflects Nellie's social position, it does not adequately represent the place she occupied in the hearts of Bunny, Constance and Edward. Constance seems to have positively encouraged the association – Nellie later told a friend that it was she who first mentioned the possibility of a relationship with Edward.

Nellie, who had been raised in France by her widowed father, Richard Heath, a devout Christian Socialist, came to England to study painting under Walter Sickert. Bunny said of her: 'The first impression was of extraordinary softness, a softness physically expressed at that time in velvet blouses and velveteen skirts; a softness of speech and a gentleness of manner and disposition.' He added that the softness was underpinned by 'an iron will-power', a necessity given Nellie's social position as Edward's lover.[25] Bunny's cousin Rayne Nickalls recalled receiving a warning from her father, Robert, about Edward and Nellie living

---

[25] DG, *Echo*, pp. 49–50.

together 'in open defiance of the conventions'; 'people talked and he would not like me to be mixed up in anything of that kind'.[26]

Bunny loved Nellie almost as much as his parents. He was troubled neither by the way his parents conducted their lives, nor by the disapproval that their lifestyle sometimes elicited. He never felt, as he might have done, that Constance had been betrayed in any way by his father or by Nellie. For Bunny, the triumvirate of Connie, Edward and Nellie exemplified conjugal contentment, familial warmth and fulfilled creativity. It was a pattern he would continue to seek as an adult, with variable success.

---

[26] Rayne Garnett Nickalls, extract from memoir, 'The Time is Past and Gone' [Caroline White].

Chapter Two

'Perhaps I am exceptional in feeling the horror of institutional life so strongly.'[1]

In December 1895 Constance and Edward had a terrible shock: Stepniak had been killed by a train. Perhaps he hadn't heard the engine's approach, as he had learnt to block out sound in prison. Constance had barely recovered from this loss when Edward became seriously ill with typhoid. She nursed him until he eventually recovered, but meanwhile Bunny was sent to his uncle and aunt, Ernest and Minnie Black, in Brighton. There he found the atmosphere very different from that of The Cearne. Sitting one morning upon his chamber-pot, the four-year-old was accosted by Uncle Ernest who protested that such a position was unmanly, instructing Bunny to either stand up or to kneel before it. Bunny did what he was asked, but even at that age, contemptuous of convention, he considered his uncle a fool.

Bunny was a bright child, composing his first story aged three, about a little horse which became lost and was found by a big

[1] DG/T.E. Lawrence, Hilton, 20 May [?1929] [Northwestern].

horse which carried it home in its mouth. Already sharp-eyed and inquisitive, Bunny ran to Constance excited that their neighbour's sow had twelve piglets, ' "And how could there be room inside her for all of them?" ' he enquired, having evidently absorbed the rudimentary facts of life.[2] He learned to read aged four, but with reluctance, determined that once he had mastered reading, he would never do it again. His writing at that age, both as script and narrative, was already assured, although unpunctuated. 'Dear Grannie', he wrote to Narney, 'Will you come down to see me on Saturday Mother is coming to London tomorrow and will tell you your train.'[3]

Narney had given Bunny a fine wooden rocking horse, which he called Chopper. He and Constance composed a poem about Chopper which opens a delightful window into the nursery world they shared, revealing that pleasure in words and composition was part of their relationship.

When Daddy-Dumdy-Dee is cross
And Mum's at work or ill
I saddle Chopper my good horse
And ride off to Leith Hill.
We trot along the roads so fast
That people cry as we go past
'I never saw a horse go faster,
I wonder who's that Gee-gee's master.'
'I'm David Garnett, Chopper's master!
I shout and gallop on the faster [...][4]

---

[2] CG, unpublished memoir.
[3] DG/Olivia Narney Garnett, 21 October 1896 [Eton].
[4] CG/Olive Garnett, quoted in RG, *Constance*, p. 144.

16

In October 1897 Constance wrote to her father-in-law: 'The great household event is David's going to school', and that this 'so far has been a great success. He likes it & is reported as good & intelligent.'[5] The school was at Limpsfield and there five-year-old Bunny was immediately broken of writing with his left hand. It was also there that Bunny began a lifelong friendship with a handsome little daredevil, Harold Hobson, J. A. and Florence Hobson's son. According to Bunny the friendship was cemented when he took Harold to a nearby field to watch a pair of geldings mate.

The 'great household event' did not last. As Bunny's initial enthusiasm rapidly diminished, Constance decided to teach him herself, though immersed in translation she often left him to study alone. Nellie's brother, Carl Heath, was drafted in as tutor, and Bunny was joined in his lessons by Harold Hobson and his sister Mabel, and by the four daughters of Sydney and Margaret Olivier, who had recently settled nearby. (Olivier had returned from the post of colonial secretary of British Honduras and would later become Governor of Jamaica.) Sydney Olivier believed in imperial reform and had written *Fabian Essays on Socialism* (1889); he and Margaret fitted perfectly into the political and intellectual community around The Cearne.

The Olivier sisters were ideal companions for Bunny. These beautiful, intelligent and untamed girls loved the outdoors, were experts at cricket, champion hut-builders and practised tree-climbers. According to Bunny, 'coming to the row of beech-trees that divided Limpsfield Common from the High Chart, one would see them in white jerseys and dark blue knickers, frocks or skirts discarded, high above one's head'.[6] Margery, the eldest,

---

5 CG/Dr Richard Garnett, The Cearne, 11 October 1897 [HRRC].
6 DG, *Echo*, p. 99.

was tall, brown-eyed and brown haired, impulsive, but with an underlying vulnerability. Brynhild was a great beauty, with fairer hair than the others, and 'starry eyes that flashed and sparkled'.[7] Daphne was dark and rather dreamy. It was with Noel, his exact contemporary, a pretty girl with a serious expression and steely determination, that Bunny had a particular bond, for they shared a fascination with wildlife, collecting animal skeletons, stuffing birds and skinning rabbits together.

This circle of playmates was occasionally joined by Edward and Marjorie Pease's sons, Nicholas and Michael. The boys were never part of the inner circle of Oliviers and Hobsons and did not inspire Bunny's loyalty. His tepid feelings might be explained by a passage in his draft autobiography, scored through and with the word 'OMIT' added, where Bunny recounts walking, one day, near The Cearne, with Michael Pease. On seeing Nellie with Edward, Pease denounced them to Bunny as 'immoral persons'.

Edward delighted in Bunny's friends, writing plays for the children to perform. In 'Robin Hood', with a cast comprising the Olivier girls, Harold and Mabel Hobson, and Bunny's cousin, Speedwell Black, nine-year-old Bunny was padded out and topped with a bald pate, as Friar Tuck. The play was performed at The Cearne before an audience which included George Bernard Shaw and the writer E. V. Lucas.

As an only child, Bunny enjoyed the avuncular friendships of his parents' circle, including Constance's Russian émigrés and Edward's stable of writers, first among them, Joseph Conrad. One windy day at The Cearne, Conrad made Bunny a sailing boat, tying a sheet for a sail to the top corners of the

---

7 DG, *Echo*, p. 31.

18

clothes-prop. Conrad sat in a linen basket, steering the 'boat' and issuing orders to Bunny to take in the sail. A frequent guest at The Cearne, Conrad was particularly fond of Bunny, signing off his letters to him 'Your affectionate friend'. For Christmas one year he sent him three volumes of James Fenimore Cooper's *Leather-Stocking-Tales* with an accompanying note: 'I read them at your age [...] and I trust that you, of a much later generation, shall find in these pages much at least of the charm which delighted me then and has not evaporated even to this day.'[8]

For a time Ford Madox Hueffer and his wife Elsie rented a cottage near The Cearne. On one occasion Bunny went with them to visit Stephen Crane, accompanied by Henry James riding a bicycle. It was with W.H. Hudson that Bunny had a particular affinity, for both were absorbed in the natural world, and Hudson admired Bunny's youthful skills as a naturalist. The tall man and young boy went on excursions together, once crouching uncomfortably in a gorse hedge, where Hudson mimicked birdsong and called the birds towards them. Hudson gave Bunny books, including his own *British Birds*, which Bunny always treasured, although he was less keen on J.M. Barrie's *Little White Bird*, which he had the effrontery to return to his benefactor.

A regular visitor to The Cearne, John Galsworthy always remained calm in the face of a crisis, and there seemed often to be a crisis when he visited. On one occasion he captured a savage cat which had torn Bunny's brow, and on another he remained calmly detached when the dog, Puppsie, brought a stinking maggot-ridden rat indoors. Galsworthy removed the offending

[8] Joseph Conrad/DG, Stanford, Kent, 22 December [1902] quoted in David Garnett, *Great Friends* (London: Macmillan, 1979) p. 18.

object, which he buried, afterwards washing his hands and then dusting his knees with an *Eau de Cologne* scented handkerchief. Bunny rewarded Galsworthy's unfailing kindness with the honorary title 'Running Elk'.

Although Bunny's schooling remained limited he nevertheless acquired considerable learning, but his knowledge was idiosyncratic, based upon the accidents of influence rather than benefiting from any formal curriculum. He had a precocious knowledge of Russian literature, an unusually deep understanding of natural history, a taste for English and French literature, but otherwise great gaps in his education. At the age of seven he either read, or more likely had read to him, Constance's translation of Turgenev's *A Desperate Character*, which, Edward informed Conrad, prompted Bunny to exclaim: ' "I love him. I ENVY him", and on the maternal warning that a D[esperate] C[haracter] came to a bad end he remarked scornfully "Yes, at the end, we all come to a bad end!" '9

Bunny loved to be taken to London, which for him consisted of 'hansom cabs and the galleries of the British Museum'.10 Here, under his grandfather's supervision, he pored over illustrated books in the King's Library and was let loose in the galleries. His grandparents lived in a house within the museum which opened directly into the Manuscript Department and Bunny considered it a great privilege to have such immediate access from the domestic to the public sphere. On being taken to the forecourt of the museum by his grandfather, Bunny was

---

9 Inscription EG to Joseph Conrad in a copy of CG's translation of Turgenev's *A Desperate Character*, information supplied to the author by Helen Smith.
10 DG, *Echo*, p. 40.

thrilled by the saluting porter in his gold-laced top-hat. He felt a particular *frisson* when his Grandpapa led him into the Reading Room, for he knew it was forbidden to anyone under the age of twenty-one. 'I kept close to him, and we passed the policeman, but he made no move to stop me.'[11]

From the outset of the Boer War in October 1899, Constance and Edward were pro-Boer, as was J.A. Hobson, Harold's father. The two boys shared their parents' sympathies in this respect, and in consequence were stoned by village boys on Limpsfield Common, where they were pursued by angry cries of 'Krujer!' Bunny noted ruefully: 'Having to run the gauntlet to get to Carl Heath who lived unfortunately only a 'stone's throw' from Limpsfield elementary school.'[12] A year later, walking through the woods, Connie invented a game in which she and Bunny were a Boer mother and son, escaping a farm burned, under the 'Scorched Earth' policy, by General Roberts. Bunny was being educated to think independently, an education he might not have received at school.

With Edward's encouragement, Bunny undertook his first paid work aged eleven, drawing a map of the 'NEW SEA and the BEVIS COUNTRY', to illustrate Richard Jefferies' *Bevis*. The map was labelled with the legend 'D.G. FECIT', and the publisher George Duckworth paid Bunny five shillings for his labours. If this made him feel grown-up, he was brought sharply down to earth when Constance sent him to Westerham Prep School, some five miles from The Cearne, the fees paid by Edward's father. Bunny travelled to school by archaic means even for those times, riding high upon a Bantam, a diminutive

---

[11] DG, *Echo*, p. 42.

[12] DG, Synopsis, Draft Autobiography, Vol I., [Northwestern].

version of a Penny-farthing, which had been ridden by his uncle Arthur Garnett as a boy. 'It was typical of my family,' Bunny later commented: 'Mounted on this museum specimen and wearing a French beret over my untidy mop of hair, I presented myself to the critical inspection of the other little boys and was at once christened "Onions".'[13]

It was not, however, the boys who bullied Bunny, but a master, Mr Hunt. When Bunny employed the words *sarcasm* and *irony* in an English essay, Hunt sneeringly suggested to the class that Bunny did not know what he was writing about. Too clever by half, Bunny replied that 'sarcasm was making fun of people, as he was making fun of me, but that irony was when the truth was funny, because it was quite different from what people pretended'. Hunt caned Bunny, who, furious at this affront, 'begged so hard' that Constance and Edward agreed not to send him back to school.

Freedom from the constraints of the academic year made possible other educational adventures. In May 1904 Constance promised her father-in-law: 'I will be careful that not a word of criticism shall be heard from David or me that could wound the most sensitively patriotic and orthodox ears in Russia.'[14] The promise was occasioned by Constance's decision to visit Russia, this time with twelve-year-old Bunny. She felt the need to reassure Dr Garnett and Edward, who were concerned that she had chosen to go at a politically sensitive time, after the outbreak of the Russo-Japanese war and when typhoid was endemic. They would stay in St Petersburg then spend a few days in Moscow, before setting out for Yablonka, in Tula Province, south of

---

[13] DG, *Echo*, p. 94.
[14] CG/Dr R. Garnett, 9 May 1904, quoted in RG, *Constance*, p. 120.

Moscow, to stay with Constance's old friend Sasha Shteven with whom she had travelled in Russia on her first visit. Sasha (Baroness Aleksandra Alekseeva Shteven) had since married a landowner called Yershov, of whom Constance knew little. Finally, she and Bunny were to stay in Tambov Province further away to the south-east, with the family of Aleksandr Ivanovich Ertel, an estate manager whom they had not previously met.

On 11 May they sailed from Hull in a Finnish boat, Bunny carrying a treasured pocket compass and magnifying glass, which Conrad had given him. For the first twenty-four hours, both Connie and Bunny were seasick, too ill to undress at bedtime. Reaching calmer waters, Bunny spent his time on deck with his telescope and admired the sailors' Finnish knives. At Copenhagen where they remained on board while the ship took in cargo, Bunny was enthralled by the cranes and mechanics of cargo-loading, although once again afloat and sea-sick, he declared he would 'give all to possess the sight of a beech-leaf!'[15] They reached Helsingfors on 16 May, where they waited twelve hours to find a train to St Petersburg with sleeping accommodation. This afforded Bunny the opportunity to buy a little Finnish knife, and to practice his Russian by purchasing fruit from a Finn who spoke less Russian than he did. On the train, the lack of ventilation made Bunny so faint that Constance stood him at an open door at the end of a carriage. They arrived at St Petersburg the next day, relieved to find Constance's friend Madame Lavrov waiting on the platform.

In St Petersburg they stayed with Madame Lavrov's daughter, Madame Sliepstov, in a fine flat with huge rooms overlooking the Neva. Unfortunately Constance was instantly plunged into

---

[15] CG/EG, 'Polaris', Monday morning [16 May 1904 ns] [Northwestern].

confusion and uncertainty: she found a letter from Sasha waiting, informing her that Sasha's daughter had typhoid. Constance was torn by her desire to see her friend and her need to protect Bunny. She wrote to Edward asking him to ascertain whether it was possible to protect against typhoid by drinking only boiled water and by avoiding butter, milk and raw vegetables. 'It will be a cruel disappointment', she added, 'to have come to Russia & not to be able to see Sasha!' 'Don't be anxious', she reassured him, 'If you knew how I feel the responsibility here every moment of the boy, you would not be afraid of my doing anything silly.'[16] Constance was reassured when a physician explained that typhoid was not infectious but contracted by drinking polluted water and that all would be well if their water was thoroughly boiled.

Bunny wrote to Edward, telling him, excitedly, that he had seen some Cossacks and had crossed the Neva in a river steamer and was soon to go to the Hermitage. Later he recalled that: 'Of the many things which impressed me, the most exciting was seeing a fashionable lady driving down the Nevsky Prospekt, in an open troika with an enormous bearded coachman on the box, while beside her on the seat of the carriage was a large bear cub, about half-grown.'[17]

Bunny kept hugging himself with delight, exclaiming "How I love it! It's like a dream!" Constance found him an ideal travelling companion, 'always catching every impression & sensation & eager & interested in every detail'.[18] But Bunny could not fail to

[16] CG/EG, Chez Madame Sliepstov, Wednesday [18 May 1904 ns] [Northwestern].

[17] DG, *Echo*, p. 75.

[18] CG/EG, Chez Madame Sliepstov, Friday 20 May 1904 [ns] [Northwestern].

notice signs of disorder and military bustle everywhere. In St Petersburg his chief impression was of soldiers and uniforms: 'The streets were thick with officers in white blouses, peaked caps and epaulettes, high boots of Russian leather, jingling spurs, sabres worn in the Russian manner, back to front, and rolled grey overcoats worn slung round the body like bandoliers. There were Cossacks, Circassians, Generals of enormous size, military of all arms and all ranks, and the saluting was incessant.'[19] He was too young and impressionable to understand the implications of the military presence which had been called in to control escalating civil unrest in the face of rising prices, poor working conditions and the Tsarist government. Watching a review of cavalry before the Winter Palace, Bunny longed to handle the sabres and revolvers, but knew better than to confess this to his mother.

In St Petersburg, according to Constance, Bunny 'had fallen in love with more than one new friend'.[20] He was so enamoured of a bearskin in Madame Lavrov's apartment that he wielded his handy Finnish knife to secretly lop off its smallest claw as a souvenir. After St Petersburg they stayed a few days in Moscow before leaving not as planned to visit Sasha, but to take the longer journey by rail to Morshansk in Tambov Province, to meet the unknown Ertels.

The journey was tedious. Owing to the war, 'the lines were crowded with trains of wagons filled with men and horses and hay – trains which bumped along at ten miles an hour interminably while we waited for an hour in one siding, and an hour in another, watching them go past'.[21] At Morshansk Constance and Bunny

---

[19] DG, *Echo*, p. 75.
[20] CG/EG, in the train to Moscow, Tuesday [24 May 1904 ns] [Northwestern].
[21] DG, *Echo*, p. 77.

were met by the Ertels' carriage, which conveyed them the half-day drive to the estate where Ertel lived with Marya Vasilievna (his wife in all but name), and their teenage daughters Natalie (Natasha) and Elena (Lolya), an adopted daughter Elena Grigorievna Goncharova (Lenochka), Miss Haslam the English governess, and Kirik Levin, a young man whom they had found as a baby, lying in the road. The Ertels lived in a large, white, brick and wood house, with a green-painted roof. Bunny and Constance immediately felt at home, comfortable in the company of a family with whom they formed an instant, affectionate, rapport.

Bunny enjoyed the extended-family intimacy the Ertels afforded, and he introduced a particularly British pastime to his new friends, one which rather perplexed them: a paper chase. As he later commented, 'The Russians were a good deal astonished at people running on a hot summer's day of their own free will and without an object'. A few days later the Ertels were paid an unexpected visit by the District Commissioner, who had received reports that they had been scattering revolutionary leaflets all over the countryside.

Ertel gave Bunny a pony, Moochen, which he quickly learnt to ride. He wrote to Edward:

I am having a very jolly time riding every day on a pony called Moohen I am going to have a knout [whip] which is a lovely thing [...]. All the stable-boys are so nice that one wants to hug them [...]. It looks like a picture in the Boys Own paper sometimes when I ride up to one man and 5 other men gallop up & all the horses rub noses. It is worth seeing them crack their knouts, they ride as they were centaurs.[22]

---

[22] DG/EG, [Kludovo] [June 1904] [Northwestern].

Bunny soon befriended the stable-hands and the ten or so boys, aged between eight and fifteen, who herded the horses. He spent his afternoons with them, noting that the boys were utterly responsible, all the while watching for any straying beast. On one occasion some horses escaped, resulting in an unforgettable corral in which Bunny took part:

> My pony was for a time completely out of my control, and horses were on all sides of me, their manes tossing, their eyes rolling in mischief, the earth trembling under us, Kolya, ahead of me, cutting out and heading off a chestnut two-year-old, and Vanya, who was only about ten and riding bareback with rope reins on his old bridle, passing me on the right, going like the wind and performing prodigies with the twelve-foot lash of his stock-whip.[23]

Bunny and Constance moved from the main house to a wooden summer-house in the garden, comprising a spacious room opening onto a verandah on which was a solid table where Constance worked. Their day began with breakfast at the main house after which they returned to the hut, where Bunny spent the morning working on a Russian exercise or translating Tolstoy. It was an idyllic time, but the war encroached. Two weeks after their arrival, mobilisation was proclaimed – many of the village men were called up. Constance described the impact on the village: 'The proclamation arrived at 3 o'clock in the night on Sunday & on Wednesday morning early 40 men from the village & 6 from the estate were marched off followed by the whole village, weeping & mourning as though at a funeral.' She told

---

[23] DG, *Echo*, p. 81.

Edward that Bunny 'was much upset & had a good cry the previous evening over the sadness of all his friends, usually so smiling & cheerful'.[24] Bunny was further upset when his beloved Moochen was commandeered and taken to Morshansk with many other local horses. Fortunately it had a wall-eye, was found wanting, and returned.

On 24 June Constance sent Edward a postcard, proclaiming: 'I am in danger of getting too fat & David of getting spoiled!'[25] They were fed very well, not least at the numerous dinner parties given by the Ertels, which Bunny remembered typically consisted of:

> soup accompanied by little pies, always filled with delicious and unexpected delicacies – minced cockscombs, sweetbreads, mushrooms and sour cream. Then there was caviare in large dishes and hot toast; a couple of roast sucking pigs, stuffed with buckwheat kasha, which drank up the fat; new peas, thin pancakes with sharp cranberry sauce and thick layers of sour cream, and lastly a vast ice pudding, stuffed with grated pistachio nuts and fragments of candied peel and angelica.[26]

It was as well that food was copious, as there would be little in the way of nourishment on the next stage of their odyssey. On 28 June they set out for Tula Province to visit Sasha. Although Constance still had misgivings about the visit, she felt compelled to see her friend, who had by then been summoned to care for a

[24] CG/EG, Saturday 18 June [1904 ns] [Eton].
[25] CG/EG, Hludovo, 24 June [1904 ns] [Northwestern].
[26] DG, *Echo*, p. 84.

sick relative, with only a few days remaining before her departure. Arriving in Tula, Connie and Bunny were surprised to find no carriage waiting, and no other means of accomplishing the fifteen mile journey to the Yershovs. After two hours, a carriage eventually arrived, Yershov having at the last minute decided to send a conveyance. He was not happy about their visit, and in consequence Constance and Bunny had to lodge in the local school mistress's house. Although they found Sasha warm and welcoming, her husband was unsmiling and opinionated. They hoped to visit Tolstoy, at Yasnaya Polyana less than twenty miles away, but Yershov disapproved of Tolstoy and would not make available his carriage.

At Sasha's there was no boiled water except at tea-time; nor was there sufficient food. One day they waited until four o'clock for some barely edible bread. There were no shops: they could eat only what they were given. The food was covered in flies, leading Yershov to ask Constance whether flies were such a problem in England. (Diplomatically she replied that flies weren't, but wasps were.) Constance could not sleep, for their room had no blinds and it was light all night. Eventually Bunny procured some nails from a local boy, and hung a rug at the window. Connie felt insecure, worried lest either of them became ill, and anxious about getting sufficient boiled water for Bunny, who, she told Edward, 'was always thirsty & kept his promise to you heroically'.[27] She regretted not leaving Bunny behind with the Ertels, as Madame Ertel had urged her to do. Having endured this ordeal for five days, Constance decided to return to the Ertels, where she hoped Bunny would recoup the weight he had lost. 'David is awfully glad to get back to all his friends', she told

---

[27] CG/EG, Sunday midday 3 July [1904 ns] [Eton].

Nellie, 'all the kind dear men & boys on the estate. Everyone there seems really to love him.'[28]

Constance was relieved to spend a further month with the Ertels, though she had begun to count the days to home. However, two weeks after their return from Tula, Constance became ill with recurrent diarrhoea. She and Bunny were alone, the Ertels away for a week. Constance could not have managed without Bunny's devoted care. He was her comfort, 'so good & responsible', getting up every night to warm milk for her. While Constance recovered, they heard that Vyacheslav Plehve, the Minister of the Interior, had been assassinated (on 28 July). Mindful of the censor, Constance could only tell Edward that this news 'produced an immense sensation as you can imagine'.[29]

On 6 August Constance and Bunny began their journey home. 'We felt so sad at parting from everyone', she wrote to Edward, 'The boy shed a few tears when he said goodbye to the men & lads in the stables & one or two of them cried too'.[30] This time they travelled almost entirely by train, arriving in England on 13 August. Five months later, Russia was overcome by the turmoil of massacre and revolution which followed Bloody Sunday, 22 January 1905. The peasants turned on their masters' property, burning houses, palaces and farms. Ertel's property was left unscathed; in his absence, Yershov's house burnt to the ground.

---

28 CG/EMH [July 1904 ns] [Eton].
29 CG/EG, Friday 29 July, 'Saturday morning' [1904 ns] [Northwestern].
30 CG/EG, Sunday [7 August 1904 ns] [Northwestern].

Chapter Three

'At times I feel as if I were born for the salvation of the world – at times as if I would never be more than a travelling tinker – never anything in between– That I suppose is youth.'[1]

Constance turned her attention again to the question of Bunny's education. He had a genuine abhorrence of school, hated feeling that he had to conform, that he was being controlled, that he couldn't do as he pleased. What mattered most was freedom. Children, Bunny said later, 'have to get right away from parents and schoolmasters and safeguards and to have nobody to consider but themselves'.[2] Bunny believed he was different from other people and that the rules governing them did not apply to him. As a child, he acquired self-resilience, intellectual independence and a disregard for convention. As an *only* child, he had no sense of deference to his parents or their generation but engaged

---

[1]   DG/CG, Uplands, Letchworth, n.d. [?January] [1910] [HRRC].
[2]   David Garnett, 'Books in General', *New Statesman and Nation*, 5 December 1936.

with them equally. This was perhaps unusual, but it enabled him to see the world uncompromisingly on his own terms and shaped a powerful will and an expectation that he could do as he liked.

In May 1905 Edward told Galsworthy that the thirteen-year-old Bunny 'reminds me extraordinarily of what I was at 13 – his expression, and gait, and everything bring back my boyhood to me. He is interested in *everything*, and never *does* anything!'[3] This idleness would not last, as in September Bunny was sent to University College School on Gower Street in London, not far from the British Museum. Constance and Edward changed places, Edward basing himself at The Cearne, while Constance rented a flat at 19 Grove Place, Hampstead. As Bunny put it, they exchanged the 'confusion and muddle of The Cearne' for the 'Spartan amenities of a workman's flat in Hampstead', an inexpensive area only recently integrated into London, inhabited by artisans, artists, writers and musicians.[4]

'Every day', Bunny later wrote, 'I went to my hated school on a horse drawn tram through streets which were absolutely empty of any of the things I found interesting. At thirteen, I did not like looking at human beings, or shops, or buildings.'[5] He found his new school dreary and intellectually dull; he hated the institutional smell, and a self-conscious outsider, felt excluded by his peers. Worse, he had to participate in the school cadet force. A few days after starting school he suffered the humiliation of wetting himself on a prolonged march. Unused to school-boy

---

[3] EG/John Galsworthy, The Cearne, 8 May 1905, in Edward Garnett, ed., *Letters from John Galsworthy 1900–1932* (London: Jonathan Cape, 1934), p. 60.

[4] DG, *Echo*, p. 105.

[5] DG, 'Books in General', *New Statesman and Nation*, 11 June 1938.

banter and unable to withstand bullying, this indignity overshadowed his school career. Finding he could no longer exert control over his life, Bunny's placid nature gave way to angry outbursts.

Relief came at weekends and holidays at The Cearne where he continued the independent and solitary education he enjoyed. On one occasion he walked ten miles by footpath from The Cearne to Sevenoaks Weald, to visit Edward Thomas and his family. At this time Thomas was not yet a poet, but a writer of fine, lyrical prose. Bunny found him beautiful in countenance and demeanour. They got on well, partly through a shared admiration for Richard Jefferies and partly because Thomas was interested in Bunny's conversation and they always found things to talk about. They both loved the natural world, and walking in the countryside with Thomas, Bunny began to see it through his older friend's eyes.

After two years at University College School, Bunny seemed to have made no academic progress. Constance decided, therefore, that he should attend a crammer, University Tutorial College in Red Lion Square, near High Holborn. Bunny was delighted: 'I was a free agent, out of the clutches of tyrants, no longer to be facetiously insulted in public by the masters or tortured in private by the boys. If I played truant and spent the afternoon looking at the mummies in the British Museum, nothing would happen.'[6] At college Bunny valued being treated as a rational being, and disliking the enforced camaraderie of institutional life, was glad there was no attempt at social life outside the classroom. He was inspired by the zoology teacher, 'Flatfish' Cunningham, and it was in zoology and botany that Bunny excelled, and where he found what he believed to be his vocation. He was good at French, but as he acknowledged, 'Mathematics and English were the

---

[6] DG, Memoir of School, unpublished MS [Northwestern].

trouble'. It is surprising, perhaps, that such a well-read young man, with access to his parents' libraries and to the conversation of respected writers, should find English a difficult subject. But his approach was instinctive and aural; he found grammar a waste of time and was always an eccentric punctuator.

In Hampstead, Bunny's neighbours were writers, artists and intellectuals. He met the poets Ernest and Dollie Radford and their son Maitland, who introduced Bunny to the ballet, taking him to see Anna Pavlova perform. Maitland was a socialist and a doctor with a well-developed sense of the injustices heaped on the poor in London's East End. Others among the talented younger Hampstead generation were Godwin Baynes, a trainee doctor, who later became Jung's assistant, and his sister Ruth; the brothers Clifford and Arnold Bax, writer and composer respectively; Rosalind Thornycroft, a gifted artist, daughter of the sculptor, Hamo Thornycroft and cousin of Siegfried Sassoon; and the Farjeon siblings, Harry, Joe, the poet Eleanor, and Herbert (Bertie), later a famous dramatist and theatre critic. As with the Hobsons and Oliviers in Surrey, Bunny had found a conducive set of friends. As time passed the two sets overlapped and sometimes merged. Bunny introduced Godwin Baynes to Edward Thomas and Godwin treated Thomas for depression.

Rosalind Thornycroft recalled that during the summer they would 'get up at about six o'clock to the sound of pheasants calling, walk through the woods, bathe naked in the lakes; climb trees, Godwin reaching the topmost branches to sway in the wind.'[7] Ten years Bunny's senior, and at the centre of the group, Godwin Baynes combined physical strength with an aesthetic

---

[7] Quoted in Diana Baynes Jansen, *Jung's Apprentice: A Biography of Helton Godwin Baynes* (Einsiedeln: Daimon Verlag, 2003), p. 32.

sensibility. Handsome, intelligent and charismatic, he inspired devotion in all his followers. According to Bunny, Godwin 'was about six foot three in height, so broad-chested and strongly built that he did not seem a tall man but a well-proportioned hero of antiquity'.[8] Looking back, Bunny observed that Godwin 'had become an enthusiastic neo-pagan and I myself was just ripe for the neo-pagan revelation'.[9]

Bunny was to remain a Neo-Pagan until the Great War suspended youthful idealism and slaughtered youthful idealists. But in 1907, when the term 'Neo-Pagan' had yet to be coined by Virginia Woolf, these young, creative, utopian, socialistic idealists enjoyed conversation and friendship, much of it outdoors. They channelled their physical vigour into swimming, diving and tramping the countryside, and revelled in beauty. But if such appreciation was sexual, this was (for now) sublimated to maintain the illusion of young men and women sleeping or swimming naked together, as brothers and sisters under the stars. Eleanor Farjeon expressed this apparent innocence in her poem, *Pan-Worship* (1908) where she describes the young Apollo (Godwin/Bunny/Maitland?):

With limbs like light and golden locks toss'd back
On a smooth ivory shoulder[10]

Eleanor called Godwin a 'sun-god', and Bunny echoed this sentiment in relation to all of them: 'We live the life of pagan Gods

---

8   DG, *Echo*, p. 166.
9   DG, *Echo*, p. 166.
10 Eleanor Farjeon, *Pan-Worship and Other Poems* (London: Elkin Mathews, 1908), p. 10.

in a heaven we have all created.'[11]

Rosalind commented that they 'were taken up with the idea of the freedom of natural life', and, under Bunny's influence, adopted the habit of carrying a back-pack and sleeping bag, ready to sleep outside.[12] Godwin often visited The Cearne, where he slept out in the woods with Bunny and Harold Hobson. He later recalled passing 'the most beautiful night of my life' with Bunny by his side, sleeping beneath the fir trees 'on a great mound of sun-dried bracken'.[13] At the time Bunny described that very night: 'We were like two Chrysalids in our bags. Friendly Chrysalids, side by side [...]. We were so ecstatic we tried to hug each other.'[14] Despite protestations to the contrary, there was a sexual sub-text to this 'natural life', and one that was inevitably sometimes homo-erotically charged.

Bunny still struggled academically, mathematics and English a persistent problem. As he repeatedly failed to matriculate, he remained at the Tutorial College where he began to be drawn into a distinctly shadowy world of darkened rooms, dim halls and clandestine meetings. This began at a revision class of three students where he noticed an 'exotic brown man' with curly black hair. Having established that his new friend's name was Sukhasagan Dutt and that he was a Bengali, Bunny invited him to lunch at the ABC in Southampton Row, where they got on so well that they agreed to meet the next day at Holborn Baths, for a swim. On 10 March 1909, the day after his seventeenth birthday, Bunny brought Dutt to Hampstead, to meet Constance.

---

[11] DG/Brynhild Olivier [September 1909] [KCC].

[12] Quoted in Baynes Jansen, *Jung's Apprentice*, p. 49.

[13] Godwin Baynes quoted in Baynes Jansen, *Jung's Apprentice*, p. 46.

[14] DG/Brynhild Olivier [September 1909] [KCC].

Like his mother, Bunny was always curious about people from other parts of the world; he was neither susceptible to casual racism nor prone to imperialist arrogance. On the contrary, just a few weeks previously, he had copied out a passage from Robert Drury's journal of his captivity in Madagascar, which culminated with the words: 'if an impartial Comparison was to be made of their Virtue, I think the Negroe Heathens will excel the white Christians'.[15]

Dutt soon became Bunny's closest friend, introducing the young Englishman to his Indian friends whom Bunny discovered were 'lively and innocent young men, always full of jokes and leg-pulls, little excitements and enthusiasms'.[16] It was not long, however, before he encountered a less frivolous side. Dutt believed he was under surveillance as his brother had been imprisoned in India for making the bomb thrown at an English magistrate at Midnapore, resulting in the deaths of two English women. Although Dutt was training in London for the Bar, as a result of his brother's activities he realised it was unlikely he would ever practise, and, according to Bunny, decided to become an actor. In his autobiography, Bunny asserts that Dutt was against terrorism, but it was Dutt who first took Bunny to attend a meeting at India House, in Highgate, the London base of Indian nationalism, a 'powerhouse for every kind of sedition.'[17] Here he was introduced to Vinayak Damodar Savarkar, the charismatic Bengali leader of the Indian nationalist movement in Britain.

---

[15] DG, 'journal and notebook', quoted in RG, *Constance*, p. 241.

[16] DG, *Echo*, p. 140.

[17] Lawrence James, *Raj: The Making and Unmaking of British India* (London: Little, Brown, 1997; Softback Preview, 1998), p. 429.

In 1905 Lord Curzon, Viceroy of India, oversaw the partition of Bengal between Muslims and Hindus. In the intervening four years agitation against partition and for Indian self-government had gathered momentum, especially in Bengal and among young, educated Hindu Bengali men who established networks of revolutionary cells within India and in London and Paris. According to Lawrence James, 'Indian self-government was an essential part of a process of spiritual advancement which would transform the country into a moral force capable of influencing the entire human race'. Thus 'Hindu theology rather than western political thought offered a basis for national identity and the struggle against an alien, and, it was stressed, unholy government. Violent opposition to the Raj, even the murder of its officials, was justified because it was a tyranny which violated the motherland.'[18]

Savarkar had arrived in England in 1906 to study for the Bar. At twenty-six, he was nine years Bunny's senior, 'small and slight in build, with very broad cheekbones, a delicate aquiline nose, a sensitive, refined mouth and an extremely pale skin'.[19] Bunny was dazzled by him. On the occasion of their first meeting, Savarkar had been reading to a group of students from his history of the Indian Mutiny, *The Indian War of Independence of 1857 by an Indian Nationalist*. Afterwards, the speaker and his audience adjourned to a room where Indian music was played on a gramophone. One bright spark decided to play Harry Lauder in mock deference to their blond-haired blue-eyed guest, but to Bunny's relief a 'Byronic young man' came to his rescue and changed the music back.

---

[18] James, *Raj*, pp. 427–8.
[19] DG, *Echo*, p. 143.

On 1 July 1909 Sir Curzon Wyllie, a senior official at the India Office, was shot dead as he was leaving a meeting in London. The perpetrator was an engineering student, Madanlal Dhingra, the same Byronic figure who had rescued Bunny from Harry Lauder. Bunny speculated that Dhingra had mistaken Wyllie for Lord Curzon, as a result of the similarities in their names. But this was to underestimate the Bengalis' sophistication: Sir Curzon Wyllie had been identified in Indian nationalist circles as an enemy of India.

Bunny was not thrown by his friends' association with terrorism. Quite the contrary:

> I was able to accept acts of murder & violence with sympathy bordering on admiration, since I had all my life been familiar with terrorism in Russia & had in fact known & liked two eminent assassins, who were respected friends of my parents [...]. But in any case I should have felt it particularly disgraceful to resent the murder of Englishmen by Indians since I was myself English and to some extent shared the guilt of British Imperialism.[20]

Bunny had now found his own cause, a cause neither inherited from his parents nor inculcated in the nursery. 'I felt exhilarated. I had embarked on an adventure of my own finding.'[21] To what extent *he* found this adventure, and to what extent it found *him*, is difficult to determine. Certainly, his eagerness for a cause of his own and boyish enthusiasm for other cultures may have obscured his judgement.

---

[20] DG, unpublished MS [Northwestern].
[21] DG, *Echo*, p. 144.

Dhingra was arrested and his request to make a statement at his trial was refused. When Savarkar asked Bunny to get Dhingra's statement published, Bunny did not hesitate to take it to his parents' friend, Robert Lynd, a journalist at the *Daily News*, wherein it appeared the following morning. Dhingra was nevertheless convicted of murder and hanged. At this point Dutt unexpectedly left college. This begs a series of questions: did Dutt leave because he had achieved what he set out to do in befriending Bunny? What was a Law student (turned actor) doing in Bunny's revision class? Had Bunny been targeted by these Bengali revolutionaries – perhaps because of his parents' known sympathies with Russian terrorists? It was certainly unusual for the young men of Savarkar's circle, with their known anti-British sentiments to befriend English boys. Bunny had naively embarked on what he thought a romantic adventure, a potent combination of a *Boys' Own* story with real life. What he didn't understand at this stage, was how dangerous real life could be. For now he had done what he could to help his Bengali friends. But he would be of further use to them in months to come.

Meanwhile, Bunny was looking to the future as he hoped to go to the Royal College of Science (now Imperial College) to study Botany. (Cambridge was discounted as his parents could not afford to send him there.) Even so, Constance pondered how they would finance Bunny's studies. At this time she earned about £10 a year from royalties (£575 in today's terms) and Edward earned a relatively meagre £15 a month from Duckworth, for whom he was now working as a publisher's reader. With this income, they had to run both The Cearne and the Hampstead flat. A solution seemed to have been found when in January 1910 Constance learned that she had been awarded a Civil List Pension of £70 a year in recognition of her work as a translator. Unfortunately this good news met with outrage from Edward, who not only believed people would think he was living off his wife's pension, but also found it insulting to be beholden to the establishment. Although Constance countered that the sum was exactly what she calculated Bunny would cost as a student, Edward insisted she decline the pension. It was only after Bunny wrote his father a diplomatic letter, contrasting the Black versus Garnett temperament, that Edward was encouraged to change his mind.

Bunny wrote disconsolately to Constance in January 1910: 'It seems quite possible I may never take to science or settle down to a respectable life', but later that month he learnt that he had finally passed the London Matriculation examination.[22] But how should he fill his time until starting university in October? It was decided he should receive further tuition, but Constance did not want Bunny loitering in London. Instead, he would stay with his Aunt Lucy and Uncle Harry Cowlishaw at Letchworth and receive lessons from a local schoolmaster.

Ostensibly working on his maths and physics, Bunny was reading library books on Indian topics. He considered organising a meeting on the subject of India in Letchworth and hoped to persuade Dutt to join him there. Bunny carried a portrait of Savarkar, and remarked to Constance: 'All I want now are photographs of Sergey & John Mitchell & Parnell to have a revolutionary gallery of the three countries in which I (& you) are most interested.'[23]

Fearing arrest, Savarkar left London for Paris, returning on 13 March 1910 only to be promptly arrested at Victoria Station.

---

[22] DG, Uplands, Letchworth, n.d. [January 1910] [HRRC].
[23] DG/CG, c/o Mrs Cowlishaw, Uplands [1910] [HRRC].

Bunny rushed from Letchworth to London, going directly to Bow Street where Savarkar was up before a magistrate. Here he discovered that Savarkar was to be sent to Brixton Gaol. The next morning Bunny proceeded to Brixton, writing afterwards to Edward: 'You may be surprised to find that I am in London. Savarkar has been arrested [...] & I came up to see what I could do.'[24]

The British authorities did not want to charge Savarkar for in Britain he would receive a relatively lenient sentence. Instead, they hoped he could be charged with offences in India, to where he would be extradited and thus subjected to a heavier penalty. Eventually the Indian authorities applied for extradition on the basis of speeches which Savarkar was alleged to have made some years previously. Bunny was incensed at the iniquity of this situation, writing to the Editor of the *Daily News* a letter published under the strap-line 'Past Offences', enquiring why Savarkar had not previously been prosecuted for these speeches. 'By thus holding back a charge', Bunny maintained, 'the police have a powerful threat, tantamount to blackmail. They might threaten a man with prosecution in order to guarantee his behaviour in the future. Is this in the public interest? I think not.'[25]

Visiting Savarkar in Brixton Gaol Bunny found him calm and unruffled. The prisoner requested only that Bunny should bring him some clean collars, size 13½. But Bunny wanted to do more, and with his mother's support decided to raise funds for Savarkar's defence. Edward was concerned about his son's involvement with Savarkar but Constance observed astutely: 'The fact is he loves him with that first rush of romantic devotion and adoration – it

---

[24] DG/EG [March 1910] [Eton].
[25] 3 May 1910.

is the first time he has felt this.' 'Remember how you felt', she urged Edward, 'and what it would have meant to you at 18, if this awful thing had happened to the person you adored.'[26]

On 31 May Savarkar wrote to Bunny to thank him, in a roundabout way, for raising funds to pay for his defence. Savarkar said he hoped his appeal *would* succeed, but stressed that if it did not, it was the effort which mattered. He would sacrifice everything for the cause. He ended by stating that he would be serving the Motherland and God even if destined for the Andaman Islands.[27]

As Constance so touchingly perceived, Bunny's interest had shifted from the political onto Savarkar as an individual. It was now Savarkar the romantic hero who mattered and for this reason, Bunny decided to become a romantic hero too. He informed Savarkar he had devised a plan to spring him from gaol and Savarkar agreed to go along with it.

The plan centred on Brixton Gaol's system of double-gates. Bunny had noted a perceptible weakness in the time-lag between opening one set of gates and closing the other. Every week Savarkar was remanded at Bow Street, to where he was conveyed not by Black Maria, but in a taxi. Bunny proposed that someone would watch the gates to observe at which point the outside set opened whilst the vehicle remained stationary inside before leaving with the prisoner. At that moment, a car would drive in containing supposed visitors, who, armed with bags of pepper and truncheons, would leap out and overpower the detectives guarding Savarkar. (Bunny had contacted Constance's friend, Florence Dryhurst, the mother-in-law of Robert Lynd, to ask whether she

---

[26] CG/EG, n.d. [1910] [Eton].
[27] V. Savarkar/DG, Brixton Prison, 31 May 1910 [RG].

43

thought any of her Sinn Fein contacts would be willing to create a diversion at the prison, but he later abandoned this idea.)

The visitors or rescuers, two men willing to sacrifice their freedom for Savarkar, would be supplied by Virendranath Chattopadhyaya, otherwise known as 'Chatto', a prominent Indian nationalist who had recently moved to Paris having been expelled from the Bar in London as a result of his support of Savarkar. The rescuers would arrive from France by boat, be driven to Brixton, rescue Savarkar, drive him back to the boat, and then sail with him to France, Chatto providing the car for the round-trip. The boat was to be obtained in France by V.V.S. Aiyar, a prominent Indian nationalist and loyal supporter of Savarkar, who had also studied for the Bar in London, and fled to France following a British warrant for his arrest.

Not content with masterminding this exploit, Bunny was also to take an active role as he would go to Paris to collect the rescuers, remain in the car while the rescue took place, and then act as their guide for the return journey to the coast. In preparation, and as though from a scene in *The Great Escape*, Bunny spent days at a time bicycling here and there to identify the safest route, avoiding level crossings and towns. Like a character in a Le Carré novel, Bunny rendezvoused with Chatto 'on the Kensington end of the Serpentine', where they came alongside each other in hired boats.[28] He purchased a woman's motoring hat and veil, which, together with a cloak, the fugitive would don the moment he entered the get-away car, and speed off resembling Toad in *The Wind in the Willows*.

For the first time Bunny deceived his parents, informing them that he was leaving London for Letchworth. Instead he crossed

---

[28] DG, *Echo*, p. 155.

to Dieppe, reaching Paris the following morning after a sleepless night. There he met Aiyar as arranged. Although the rescuers were at the ready, Aiyar had taken no steps to hire a boat. Too exhausted to register the implication of this omission, Bunny took a train to Le Havre where he eventually found someone willing to charter a smack. In Paris, Bunny returned to Aiyar's hotel where he was handed a note and informed that Edward had turned up looking for him and was going to the French police. The note, which Bunny later discovered had been penned by the Irish nationalist Maud Gonne, conveyed a message from Mrs Dryhurst: 'Don't let the ship sink for a ha'porth of tar.'[29]

Constance and Edward had learnt of Bunny's plans from the Hobsons, who had been informed of the matter by their daughter Mabel, who had been told of Bunny's intentions by Mrs Dryhurst. Before leaving for France, Edward wrote a note to Nellie: 'I am on my way to Paris. D is there, engaged in a wild romantic scheme – which may have most serious consequences.' 'The poor boy is living in pure romantic cloudland: swept off his feet by his affection for S., and perhaps the tool of others.'[30]

Bunny returned to England with Edward. After sleeping for hours he sent a message to Chatto saying the rescue was off. Then he went to Brixton to apprise Savarkar of the situation. Bunny believed he had been betrayed by Aiyar though he did not understand why. Had the escape plan been taken seriously, it is unlikely that Aiyar would thus betray Savarkar (and Chatto), especially as Aiyar headed a committee to secure Savarkar's release. Perhaps there was no intention of adopting Bunny's

---

[29] DG, *Echo*, p. 158.
[30] EG/EMH, 8 o'clock [29 May 1910] [Northwestern], quoted in RG, *Constance*, p. 244.

plan: Savarkar had earlier hinted to Aiyar that Marseilles (rather than Dieppe) might be significant in an attempted escape.[31] Had Bunny been duped? Was he, as Edward feared, a tool of others, a pawn in a more elaborate scheme? Or were these young revolutionaries merely content to string him along as he *had* been of use, and might yet be so? For all Bunny's talk of Russian terrorists, he was still a wide-eyed innocent, unaware of the scale of the drama in which he played a minor role.

Savarkar was put on a ship to India where he was to stand trial. At Marseilles he jumped ship, slipping, slight of figure, through a porthole; he was immediately recaptured. Although there was an outcry at his being returned to the British while on French soil, he was taken back to India, where he received a fifty years' sentence, and, according to his prediction, was sent to the Andaman Islands. In 1921 he was removed to mainland prison, released in 1924 and then re-interned until 1937. On his eventual release he entered politics. Despite his long years in prison, Savarkar was and remains an extremely important figure in the movement for Hindu nationalism; his portrait now hangs (not without controversy) in the Indian Parliament alongside the great men of the country. Chatto was shot in Moscow in 1937 on Stalin's orders; Aiyar drowned in 1925 in circumstances which remain contentious.

What would have happened to Bunny if he had carried through his plan or had been caught in the process of his aborted endeavours? If the offence had been regarded as high treason Bunny would have received the death sentence. If it had not

---

[31] www.savarkar.org/en/centenary-epic-leap-1%E2%80%99affaire-savarkar.

been regarded as such, it would have fallen within the scope of the Treason Felony Act (1848), a provision designed specifically to prevent conspiracy with overseas agents or governments from overthrowing the state. For this, the sentence was life imprisonment or transportation. Perhaps, given Constance and Edward's class position and influential friends, Bunny would have received some leniency with regard to his youth, but he had, unwittingly, been involved in committing what would have been considered a most heinous crime.[32]

Reflecting on the episode, Bunny penned a poem to 'V.D.S':

I feel no passion now, nor pain, nor grief.
What is there left? The flame of joy has gone.
It burnt me quickly like an autumn leaf
That gives one curl of flame and then is done
Leaving no sparks to slowly linger on.
Only the cold philosophies now hold
What has been beaten fire and brilliant joy.
What little ash there is, is icy cold,
It is the ultimate. You cannot change it, or destroy
The lasting image of a fiery boy.
I gave my heart to free a man in chains,
Alas it proved a very sorry file [sic].
It spilt itself, and left some sanguine stains
Which now are rusting in an Indian isle.
I was quite blind with anger all the while.[33]

---

[32] I am indebted to Professor Nicola Lacey and to Jawaid Luqmani for advice on this matter.

[33] DG, 'TO V.D.S.' [Savarkar], London 1910 [Northwestern].

Chapter Four

'The companionship of flushed cheeks, sparkling eyes and lovely, rippling tresses of dark hair [...] was happiness'.[1]

In June 1910 Bunny submitted his application to study for an Associateship (the equivalent of a BSc) in Botany at the Royal College of Science, one of three constituent colleges of Imperial College, London.[2] Bunny's form reads as if he was applying to study the humanities rather than science. Outlining relevant experience per scientific topic, he wrote variously, 'very little'; 'six weeks', and 'none'. The form took on a more optimistic tone under 'Any Additional Information', where Bunny asserted his knowledge of English Literature was 'above average' and of 'Standard & Modern Authors' 'fairly wide'. He added that he had lived in Russia and planned to spend the summer in Germany.[3]

---

[1] DG, *Echo*, p. 181.

[2] The colleges had merged, but retained somewhat separate identities at this time.

[3] Imperial College Archives.

If his application was successful, Bunny would be expected to attend college every weekday, to work long hours in the laboratory, go to lectures, work in a team and to maintain a disciplined schedule. Would this romantic revolutionary be able to adapt to a highly regimented life, to institutionalisation and to no longer being sole master of his destiny? Surprisingly, the answer to this question was 'yes', for Bunny was able to apply himself to something if he was interested in it *and* if there was sufficient diversion, variety and stimulation in other areas of his life. Indeed, while experiencing the excitement and emotional tension of his involvement with Savarkar, Bunny was also periodically living a contemplative Neo-Pagan existence. Henceforward, he would be able to divide his life into entirely separate compartments, and like someone changing uniform, adapt his persona to the particular moment.

And so, throughout the Savarkar affair and between bouts of industry at Letchworth, Bunny led a carefree existence, roaming the countryside in the company of his Neo-Pagan comrades. The late spring of 1910 saw the first of a series of organised camps, usually including one or more of the Olivier sisters but now with a progressively expansive and shifting cast.

This first camp, on the Norfolk Broads, arose through Bunny's friendship with Rupert Brooke, whom he came to know via Noel Olivier, with whom, despite the six-year age difference and Noel's then schoolgirl status, Rupert was infatuated. In May 1910 Brooke wrote to Bunny inviting him to Grantchester, near Cambridge, promising swimming and bucolic fun. Noel warned Rupert not to make his guest 'angery [sic] about anything' adding that 'he is very dangerous when enraged and more than once has nearly Killed people who have agravated

[sic] him'.[4] Bunny bicycled from Letchworth to the Old Vicarage, where he found Rupert welcoming and delightful. Together they read Rupert's poems and at midnight bathed naked in Byron's pool. Bunny considered Rupert beautiful, 'tall and well built, loosely put together, with a careless animal grace and a face made for smiling'.[5] But Bunny also found him strangely inscrutable. That weekend he was introduced to some of Rupert's Cambridge friends, including Geoffrey Keynes, who had known Rupert since their schooldays at Rugby, and with whom Bunny would enjoy a lifelong friendship.

Rupert wrote to Noel to say how much he liked Bunny, and to reassure her that his new friend had not become 'angery'. They had gone on from Grantchester to the Norfolk Broads where they were joined for a week aboard a wherry by Brynhild, Godwin and Rosalind Thornycroft (now Godwin's girlfriend). Bunny felt particularly close to Rupert at this time, the two young men sharing a cabin and what Bunny called 'a certain lazy warmth.'[6] But this closeness remained chastely Neo-Pagan, even though Rupert's first consummated sexual encounter had taken place only months before, with a young man whom, he acknowledged, closely resembled Bunny.[7]

Later that summer, Bunny attended a camp at Penshurst, in

[4] Noel Olivier/Rupert Brooke, The Champions, Limpsfield, Thursday [5 May 1910], in Pippa Harris, ed., *Song of Love: The Letters of Rupert Brooke and Noel Olivier* (London: Bloomsbury, 1991) p. 36.

[5] DG, *Echo*, p. 169.

[6] DG, *Echo*, p. 222.

[7] Rupert Brooke/James Strachey, The Old Vicarage, 10 July 1910 [but re autumn 1909], in Keith Hale, ed., *Friends and Apostles: The Correspondence of Rupert Brooke and James Strachey 1905–1914* (New Haven, CT: Yale University Press, 1998), p. 251.

Kent, which included the Olivier sisters, Harold Hobson, Godwin Baynes, Rupert Brooke and his friend Dudley Ward. They went bathing in the dark, placing a bicycle-lamp on the riverside to illuminate the water.

> Then one after another, we took running dives into the unseen river. It was exciting – the moment of doubt before one struck the water, and then swimming rapidly out of the next diver's way. The smell of new-mown hay, of the river and weeds, the curious polished smoothness that fresh river-water leaves on the skin [...]. Soon we were sitting round the blazing fire, Noel's eyes shining in welcome for the new arrivals and the soft river-water trickling from her hair down her bare shoulders.[8]

Harold and Bunny bathed naked in the moonlight, leaping from a springboard into the river, afterwards racing each other along the banks to get warm and dry. Bunny said that what he loved best at this time was 'to fall asleep within a yard or two of a lovely girl without a thought of trying to make love to her'. 'It was simply part of the social climate in which I was brought up and had nothing to do with innocence or its reverse, not a matter of morality but of manners.'[9] But neither sleeping in a barn with a pretty woman, nor lying beneath the stars with a handsome man, was an entirely innocent pastime, as part of the enjoyment was the sublimated sexual *frisson* engendered by such intimacy, reflected in Bunny's lingering descriptions of bare shoulders and smooth skin.

---

[8] DG, *Echo*, pp. 169–70.
[9] DG, *Echo*, p. 179.

The idyll was interrupted in July when Bunny went to Germany. Fearing that he was idling away his time, with the assistance of Ford Madox Hueffer, Constance found Frau Heider, a Prussian widow, with whom Bunny would lodge in the town of Boppard on the banks of the Rhine, some twenty-five kilometres south of Koblenz. There he would learn German. Before his departure, Bunny received a letter: 'My dear boy', it began, 'You have come to an age when new instincts & feelings may at any time put you in a position of the greatest temptation and danger.' The letter warned against 'a moment's want of self control' which might cause 'the biggest regret & misery for the rest of your life'. In essence, it counselled vigilance against syphilis. 'You may', the letter began, 'within the next few years be led by real love into intimacy with some girl, as I was with your mother before our marriage.'

As you know, I don't look at these questions from the usual man of the world standard, & such a relation is in reality what I should most wish for your happiness. But you have no right to risk <u>parentage</u> before you are ready for responsibilities. By the use of certain protective coverings – called Malthusian sheaths – this risk can be avoided, & every young man ought to know this & to make it an absolute rule of conduct never to allow himself to be led into sexual intercourse with any woman <u>without this precaution</u>, which eliminates risk of motherhood, & greatly minimizes the risk of contracting disease.[10]

In its surviving form and ostensibly from Edward, the letter is in Constance's hand, and seems to have been a draft, perhaps – as

---

[10] CG/DG, n.d. [1910] [Eton].

it included a number of question marks – for Edward's comments, or perhaps for Edward to sign as seeming more fitting from father to son. But whichever parent was the originator, this letter was astonishingly liberal in wishing Bunny the same degree of sexual freedom they had enjoyed, whilst counselling against unprotected intercourse. Constance had another reason to impart this advice: as Richard Garnett has pointed out, 'she believed her father's terminal illness was locomotor ataxia – by then known to be a consequence of syphilis'.[11] Bunny obviously received the letter in some form, for having arrived at Boppard, he replied to Constance, saying how sweet it was 'to have a mother one can talk to'.[12]

'Everything is very nice', he stiffly informed Constance, although there were discouraging signs, including a celluloid crucifix over his bed.[13] The Heider household comprised Frau Heider, her two sons, Wilhelm and Ferdinand and an aged grandmother. Both young men were soldiers of a precise military bearing whom Bunny abhorred for their supercilious treatment of the servant girls. He soon concluded that a month with the Heiders was long enough. Their worthiness grated, they never stopped asking intrusive questions and he found their formality unbearable. Worse, the Heiders were devout Catholics who said grace before and prayers after every meal, and were intent on getting Bunny into church. 'Various things', Bunny told Constance, were '*verboten*', and his hosts insisted on informing him that he was under the scrutiny of the 'all-seeing eye of

[11] RG, *Constance*, p. 247.

[12] DG/CG, Boppard, n.d. [1910] [HRRC].

[13] DG/CG, Bei Frau Heider, Boppard, Germany, n.d. 'Saturday night' [c. 22 July 1910] [HRRC].

God'. The Heiders could not understand Bunny's lack of Christian faith and so concluded he must be Jewish. He gladly went along with this. As he explained to Constance, 'they seem to think my name Jewish. David is Biblical – Garnett they regard as Jewish as they should Diamond or any other jewel'.[14]

Consumed with homesickness, Bunny yearned for the easy informality of his English friendships. Thankfully, relief appeared in the shape of Ford Madox Hueffer and Violet Hunt, visiting Ford's great-aunt nearby. Bunny was glad to be in convivial company, and on the receiving end of Ford's customary affection. This interlude was extended by the arrival of Maitland Radford with whom Bunny embarked on a walking tour of the Moselle, where they climbed high above the vineyards bordering the Rhine into forests and upland pastures, spending their nights lodging in a forester's house. Bunny wanted to see more of the country, but both his allotted time in Germany and money were running out. He decided that Constance might agree to his remaining if he could persuade her that his German would further improve, but he needed to devise a plan which released him from the Heiders. He wrote to Constance explaining that he wanted to stay another three weeks, adding that he hoped Ursula Cox, a cousin of the Oliviers, would join him for a week on her way to Russia. 'If you see Ursula kiss her for me', he instructed his mother, '& tell her she is a dear & that I am very fond of her'.[15] Whether at the prospect of Bunny's increased fluency or the thought of young love blossoming, Constance agreed. However, Ursula did not take up Bunny's invitation, aware that he might be developing feelings she could not reciprocate. At this

---

[14] DG/CG, Boppard, n.d. [August 1910] [HRRC].
[15] DG/CG, Boppard [August 1910] [HRRC].

time his emotional state found expression in his writing anguished poems entitled 'The Agonies of Eighteen' and 'Love is a Bird – But What a Fowl is Love'.

Alone again and released from the Heiders' shackles, Bunny became reckless, spending money he could not afford on hiring rowing boats and 'expensive dinners & a knife & an automatic fire-machine [a pistol] & picture postcards & another book and coffees & then another coffee & then a seat to hear the band & then tipping a waitress magnificently because she smelled like Bryn'.[16] Connie must have been horrified to learn of such extravagance and that her son had resorted to borrowing money from a bookseller. Although Bunny had what his daughter Henrietta Garnett called 'a Spartan streak' which 'made him scorn anything approaching luxury,'[17] he also had what his sister-in-law Frances Partridge identified as a streak of recklessness, and it was this which led him, in Germany, to uncontrolled expenditure.

Bunny travelled up the Rhine 'seeing castles and castles and robber holds & keeps & castles'. 'Everyone should travel', he informed Brynhild, 'it is so educating. It wakes one up. I feel quite different from the sleepy David I was in England.'[18] Now broke, he slept in a doss house at Freiberg, and resorted to sleeping out in the forest 'with my hand on my pistol & my hair bristling.'[19] By the time he was due to return home, he was

---

[16] DG/CG, Hotel Bayerischer Hof, 24 August 1910 [HRRC].

[17] Henrietta Garnett, 'Aspects of My Father', *Telegraph Weekend Magazine*, 9 April 1989.

[18] DG/Brynhild Olivier, Felberg, Black Forest, Monday 29 August [1910] [KCC].

[19] DG/Lenotchka, n.d. [August 1910] [Eton] [this is probably a draft or unsent letter].

penniless, sending Constance an alarming telegram requesting funds. Fortunately, he was 'temporarily relieved by dear Ford' whom he had also wired.[20]

In early September, Bunny returned to England. Despite its weaknesses, his university application had been a success, and in October he began his course of study in Botany and Zoology at the Royal College of Science in South Kensington. Bunny was fortunate in the calibre of the professors by whom he was taught and for whom he would, ultimately, undertake research. J.B. Farmer was a pioneering botanist in the study of cell structure, who contributed to extending the boundaries of the Darwinian hypothesis of pangenesis (by which cells were understood to share in the transmission of inherited characteristics). In contrast, while both Adam Sedgwick and Clifford Dobell were leading figures in British zoology, neither was in favour of evolutionary theory, but both made vital contributions in their fields. Sedgwick, a one-time colleague and friend of Darwin, rejected his concept of natural selection because he felt it denied God's will. Dobell was an agnostic, but nevertheless believed evolutionary theory inapplicable to proto-zoology.

Bunny was still hankering after Ursula Cox whom he had come to know when, together with the Ertels' adopted daughter Lenotchka, she had visited the Oliviers in 1910. Bunny's ardour was further inflamed by rumours that now in Moscow, Ursula was in love with the Ertels' adopted son, Kirik Levin. When Bunny announced that he wanted to spend his Easter vacation in Moscow, his parents somehow managed to fund the trip.

Bunny found a room in the apartment block where Ursula and her mother lodged with the Ertels. He was taken to a supper

---

[20] DG/CG, n.d. [Germany, postmark 29 August 1910] [HRRC].

party where he encountered his competitor, Kirik Levin and realised he was no threat. Bunny's letters to Constance were filled with long talks with Mme Ertel, visits to the opera, excursions to estates, expeditions to horse shows and tours of the Kremlin. 'Oh this is a divine city!' 'What a jumble this place is – what a mixture of riches & poverty – of luxury & disease & misery – of civilization and of Barbarism – and of order & anarchy. It has the best and the worst of everything in the world.'[21] His letters were full of everything except Ursula.

Bunny had said nothing to Ursula about his feelings and thought she was unaware of the reason for his visit. Outside on a wintry evening after a party, when Bunny eventually confessed love, Ursula gently replied that she was not in love with him. He felt the rejection strongly, although writing to Connie he assumed a brave face: 'I can't tell you anything about my feelings [...]. Because I don't want to tell anyone how I feel & because whenever one sets anything on paper it becomes false & exaggerated [...]. So all I can say is that I am very lucky & happy in seeing Ursula at all and that I don't regret having come to Moscow in the least.'[22] Bunny returned to London in time to begin the new term on 25 April, having resolved to throw himself into his work. He did well that term, easily passing the end of year exams and coming second in the first class, though scrutinising the results list, he automatically searched for his name in the second class, and not finding it, assumed he had failed.

Bunny was tall for a man of his generation – nearly six foot – good looking – but as photographs reveal, he still had a full, rather chubby face and a figure as yet un-moderated by both the

---

[21] DG/CG, Bozgsbiskehka 4.38, 'Tuesday' [April 1911] [Eton].
[22] DG/CG, Bozgsbiskehka, 4.38, Mockba, 'Wednesday' [April 1911] [Eton].

vanity and vigorous exercise of years to come. Bunny looked young for his nineteen years and it was perhaps this boyish gaucheness which brought out a little more than the maternal instinct in Antonia Almgren, a thirty-one-year-old woman who sought refuge from an unhappy marriage that summer, at The Cearne.

Tony Almgren was 'thin and a little worn by her experiences, with huge dark eyes and a slight peculiarity in speech – a difficulty in pronouncing her r's, which being overcome gave them too much emphasis'.[23] When Bunny flew off his bicycle, cracking an elbow and spraining a wrist in the process, Tony was at hand to provide relief in the form of vibratory massage, which involved her leaning across him in order to manipulate his elbow. As Bunny remarked, healing one kind of inflammation only gave rise to another. After several physiotherapy sessions, he took the pragmatic step and plucked up courage to ask whether he could become her lover. Permission was granted, on condition that he obtained contraceptives. These he procured, naturally enough, from a 'bicycle tyre and hot water bottle shop'.[24] And so began Bunny's first sexual relationship. It was not a love affair, for he never felt love for Tony, recognising that she did not love him. Nevertheless, while a dutiful college student during the week, Bunny found it gratifying to think of his weekends as the lover of a married woman. Gradually he saw her less often, and then not at all. He thought that Constance, perhaps, had nudged Tony towards him. Afterwards he vowed never to become involved in a sexual relationship unless he was in love. Bunny thought it curious, at the time, that his uncle, Arthur Garnett, a friend and

---

[23] DG, Draft Autobiography [HRRC].

[24] DG, Draft Autobiography [HRRC].

confidant of Tony's, said he thought Bunny had 'managed very well to break off with her'.[25]

Some time in 1911, dressed as an Indian prince, Bunny attended a fancy-dress party in aid of Women's Suffrage at Crosby Hall, Chelsea. Although there were several people there whom he knew, including Maitland Radford, Godwin Baynes and the Olivier girls, he felt ill at ease. He recognised that the party consisted of 'one big family' whose 'members can gossip with each other until outside contacts are made, or shyness has worn off'. In contrast, he observed, the only child 'walks awkwardly across the slippery floor, simply because he is too embarrassed to stand still any longer'.[26] Bunny attempted conversation with lantern-jawed Adrian Stephen, whose sister Virginia, standing next to him, rushed across the room to greet a friend. Bunny was transfixed when James Strachey and his sister Marjorie danced a *pas-de-deux* down the centre of the hall. It was all so exotic and unfamiliar. Bunny's old friends were beginning to pair off, but not with him. The gauche science student did pluck up courage to dance with a shy young woman with wide spaced brown eyes, dark hair and an olive complexion. He was rather taken with her, but it would be ten years before he encountered her again.

---

[25] DG, Draft Autobiography [HRRC].
[26] DG, *Echo*, p. 208.

Chapter Five

'Work and love – they are curiously intermingled & neither can be complete without the other.'[1]

Looking back upon his time at university, Bunny recognised that he 'longed not for one friend, or sweetheart even, but a whole roomful who would provide a feast of intellect, a flow of soul, fountains of love. Of course at twenty I believed that I wanted love […] But I didn't. I wanted what I might have had if I had been educated at Cambridge and which I missed at South Kensington. To live among a lot of people who are open and intimate with each other.'[2]

As the Neo-Pagan companions of Bunny's youth grew up, they were absorbed into the social circle Bunny had encountered at Crosby Hall, where Bloomsbury and Cambridge merged with Hampstead and Limpsfield. James Strachey embodied this amalgamation: he was a member of the Bloomsbury Group and a Cambridge Apostle, in love with Rupert Brooke but loved by Noel Olivier. Five years Bunny's senior, James was studious

---

[1]   DG/AVG, Charry, evening, 8 January 1974 [KCC].
[2]   DG, 'For the Memoir Club', n.d., unpublished MS [Northwestern].

looking and bespectacled, the youngest of the ten Strachey siblings. He would later translate Freud's published work into English, but at this time he was assistant editor of the *Spectator*. At Crosby Hall, Bunny had looked shyly upon the Stracheys and Stephens, and it would be a while before he felt comfortable in their presence. But in March 1912 James Strachey began to court twenty-year-old Bunny, showering him with invitations to the theatre, concerts, parties, dinners and the country; some were accepted, others politely declined or evaded with excuses of headaches or over-work.

Bunny came across variously as boyishly exuberant, shy, charming, affectionate and demonstrative. It was a fetching mix. But he had no idea of how attractive others found him. In James's company, he readily adopted the characteristic and contagious 'Strachey voice', with its arch expressions of sexual innuendo, without realising the implications of such mannerisms. 'I want you to tell me things', he wrote to James in Strachey-ese, 'And later on we must have some orgies. Yes orgies – with Noel and so on.'[3] Quite apart from the fact that Bunny knew such a proposal was preposterous (Noel was studying medicine at the London School of Medicine for Women and was not the type to indulge in orgies), he seemed not to comprehend the impact he had on people and sometimes unwittingly conveyed the wrong message. James told Rupert that he was enjoying 'the usual mild flirtation with Bunny'.[4] Perhaps Bunny was uncertain what message he wanted to convey as his feelings for Godwin Baynes, though unacknowledged, were clearly more than platonic.

---

[3] DG/James Strachey, n.d. [postmark Hampstead 27 September 1912] [BL].

[4] James Strachey/Rupert Brooke, Wednesday [13 March 1912]. In Hale, ed., *Friends & Apostles*, p. 227.

Bunny was fond of James, but felt the need to proceed cautiously, as James was obviously interested in him in a way which Bunny found confusing. On the one hand he delighted in James's company, but on the other he periodically retreated from it. Having already missed a trip to the theatre with James, Bunny could not refuse a weekend with him in Surrey. Writing afterwards, Bunny admitted: 'I was very stupid all the time but it is a mood which has almost become a habit with me.'[5] The stupidity might have been a matter of high spirits, for which Bunny was becoming well known. Equally it may have arisen from confusion about his sexuality or embarrassment over James's expectations. Having had neither the advantage of a public school or a Cambridge education, Bunny did not come from a male-oriented background where homosexual relationships were relatively common. It was difficult for him to acquire the casual familiarity and easy intimacy of this coterie, to become one of those people who 'are open and intimate with each other', which he yearned to be. But Rupert Brooke and James Strachey opened windows onto an appealing fraternal Cambridge world of intellectual camaraderie quite different to that of Imperial College, a world, moreover, of clear sexual undertones for those who knew the code.

The Neo-Pagans were growing up. In 1912 Brynhild Olivier was the first to break away when she married the art historian Hugh Popham. Bunny felt it was time that he fell in love, but could not decide with whom. His gaze alighted upon Godwin's fiancée, Rosalind Thornycroft. While Godwin was in Dresden, Bunny planned to take Rosalind on an expedition up the Severn. His hopes were thwarted when they were joined by that earlier

5   DG/James Strachey, n.d. [pmk Hampstead 27 September 1912] [BL].

object of his unrequited love, Ursula Cox and by Theodore Williams, a Jamaican friend of the Oliviers. Bunny's diary is full of the colour of sinking boats, high jinks and camaraderie, all nuanced with the shade of nostalgia. 'When? when shall it ever be again?' he asked rhetorically. 'Oh how I love those three companions.'[6] It was as though Bunny wanted to escape adolescence but at the same time could not quite make the leap into adulthood.

That summer Bunny travelled to Munich to attend a course of botanical lectures. He had arranged to meet Harold Hobson there, but pending Harold's arrival, Bunny was alone, although he attended a fancy dress party, in the now obligatory guise of an Indian prince. He was delighted to receive a letter from D.H. Lawrence, inviting him to Icking, some sixteen miles south of Munich, where Lawrence was living with Frieda Weekley. Bunny looked forward to meeting Lawrence as he was one of Edward's authors, and both Lawrence and Frieda had stayed with Edward at The Cearne in Bunny's absence. Lawrence had earlier written to Edward: 'We should *love* to see David [...]. Send him to see us here.'[7] He also wrote to Bunny, explaining 'I am living with a lady who is not my wife, but who goes as my wife down here in Bavaria'. He assumed Bunny would find him easy to recognise at the railway station, because 'I look frightfully English, and so I guess do you, so there is no need for either of us to carry the Union Jack for recognition'.[8]

---

[6] DG, 'Expedition up the Severn July 1912, Party of Ros, Ursula, Theodore & Bunny', unpublished MS [RG]

[7] DHL/EG, Icking, 18 July 1912, in Boulton, ed., *Letters of D.H. Lawrence*, p. 426.

[8] DHL/DG, Icking [23 July 1912] in Boulton, ed., *Letters of D.H. Lawrence*, p. 428.

On 24 July Bunny arrived and was met at the station by a man with 'the most beautiful, lovely, blue eyes.' Bunny described Lawrence as 'slight in build, with a weak, narrow chest and shoulders', but with a 'fair height', and light movements which 'gave him a sort of grace'. In the crowded station, Bunny, who always liked to compare people to animals, thought him 'a mongrel terrier among a crowd of Pomeranians and Alsatians, English to the bone'. He was charmed by Lawrence's sparkling eyes, which, he felt, seemed to invite him to join in some fun: 'I could no more hold out against it than a well-behaved spaniel can resist the mongrel terrier's invitation to slip off poaching.'[9] The two men hit it off immediately.

This was a difficult time for Lawrence as Frieda desperately missed her children in England. Her estranged husband would not let her see them, and as a result Lawrence felt vulnerable, fearing Frieda would leave him. On top of this, his manuscript, 'Paul Morel' had just been rejected. Bunny's arrival, therefore, was a welcome diversion, and he certainly cheered them up. He told Edward: 'Lawrence & Frieda are delicious. They fight & swear the whole time & their position is so tragic that they can't help laughing when they realise it.' He thought Frieda 'a heroic figure – I mean she belongs to the heroic ages', while of Lawrence Bunny remarked: 'well you know what Lawrence is. He is so much a genius that it makes one distrust him – He is quite uncanny.'[10] As Bunny would later discover, this was a prescient observation.

While Bunny thought Lawrence a mongrel terrier, his host considered him an 'adorable' 'lucky dog', telling Edward that

---

[9] DG, *Echo*, pp. 241–2.
[10] DG/EG [Munich] [late July/early August 1912] [Eton].

Bunny was 'awfully like you, in a thousand ways – his walk, his touch of mischief and wickedness, and nice things besides […]. We are awfully fond of him.' Bunny had changed physically in recent months, shedding the puppy fat and developing a more athletic physique. Like Edward, he was a strong swimmer, and Lawrence admired his strength and gusto. 'You should see him swim the Isar', he wrote to Edward:

He simply smashes his way through the water, while F[rieda] sits on the bank bursting with admiration, and I am green with envy. By Jove, I reckon his parents have done joyously well for this young man. Oh but you should see him dance Mordkin passion dances, with great orange and yellow and red and dark green scarves of F's, and his legs and arms bare; while I sit on the sofa and do the music, and burst with laughter, and F. stands out on the balcony in the dark, scared. Such a prancing whirl of legs and arms and raving colours you never saw: and F. shrieks when he brandishes the murderous knife in my music-making face; and some-body calls in German from below: 'Go and trample somewhere else,' and at last he falls panting. Oh the delightful Bunny![11]

Bunny had evidently been inspired by Mikhail Mordkin, a dancer with the Ballets Russes, which took London by storm in 1911.

On 5 August Lawrence and Frieda set off to travel to Italy, their first destination Mayrhofen, over the border in Austria. On

[11] DHL/EG, Icking, Sunday 4 August 1912, in Boulton, ed., *Letters of D.H. Lawrence*, p. 429.

the 22nd Lawrence informed Edward, 'Bunny is here – we are fearfully happy together.'[12] According to Lawrence's later, fiction-alised version of events, *Mr Noon* (published posthumously in 1934), Bunny appeared wearing 'a homespun jacket and flannel trousers and an old hat and a rag of a tie'.[13] Instead of staying with Lawrence and Frieda, he took a room across the road, as he was expecting Harold to join him. Now an engineering student at King's College, London, Harold was good looking, tall, thin and muscular, and according to Bunny, full of nervous energy.

On 26 August the four of them set off to trek as far as Sterzing. In the hot sunshine, Harold and Bunny stopped to bathe in the icy mountain streams. While Bunny and Lawrence sought alpine flowers for Bunny's collection, Harold and Frieda slipped into a hay-hut where they had sex. As Lawrence's biographer John Worthen explained, Frieda 'wanted Hobson, he wanted her – and it was a certain way of proving that she might be walking in Italy with Lawrence, but was still decidedly her own woman'.[14] Although Bunny had taught Harold the facts of life in long-ago Limpsfield, Harold had evidently eclipsed Bunny in that depart-ment, at least for now. On the third day, ten kilometres from Sterzing, Bunny and Harold parted company from Lawrence and Frieda to catch a train home.

In January 1913, Bunny wrote to James Strachey expressing remorse for having been a 'beastly person just recently', adding,

[12] DHL/EG, Mayrhofen, 22 August 1912, in Boulton, ed., *Letters of D.H. Lawrence*, p. 442.

[13] D.H. Lawrence, *Mr Noon*, ed. Lindeth Vasey (Cambridge University Press, 1984), p. 255.

[14] John Worthen, *D.H. Lawrence: The Early Years (1885–1912)*, (Cambridge University Press, 1991), p. 428.

'It is something wrong with my nerves'.[15] Lawrence, who thought Bunny sounded 'a bit unhooked' in his letters at this time, commented to Edward, 'manhood comes hard to him evidently', suggesting that Bunny needed to break away from his mother (a veiled reference to Lawrence's anxiety about Bunny's mixing with homosexuals).[16] Bunny's labile state stemmed partly from his yearning for what might have been had he been educated at Cambridge; partly it was frustration at dividing his life between the science laboratory and that coterie of friends with whom he felt he was in his natural environment. Mostly he yearned to find someone with whom to fall in love.

In May 1913 Bunny found her. She was Ruth Baynes, Godwin's younger sister. Like Godwin, Ruth was tall and powerfully built, but unlike him, she was shy and retiring. By June Bunny had become a regular visitor at Bethnal Green, where she lived with Godwin and Rosalind, now married. 'I like her very much', Bunny informed Edward. 'She is quiet and rather dignified and amusingly like Godwin sometimes.'[17] As an only child, Bunny often sought a shared intimacy between people who were connected to each other through family or friendship. It was as though he endeavoured to appropriate that kinship to create an extended family for himself. First Godwin had been the focus of Bunny's youthful adoration; then Bunny wanted Rosalind; now he had Ruth. This is made explicit in the last verse of 'To Ruth', a poem in which Bunny celebrated his love:

---

[15] DG/James Strachey, 4 Downshire Hill, 'Tuesday night' [postmark 15 January 1913] [BL].

[16] DHL/EG, Villa Igéa, 11 March 1913, in Boulton, ed., *Letters of D.H. Lawrence*, pp. 526–7.

[17] DG/EG, The Cearne, 2 July [1913] [Eton].

Was it old Godwin who with spiderly arts
Bound us together with those blessed bars
And, playing Vulcan to your Venus and my Mars,
Snared in intimacy our unconscious hearts?

Bunny was always welcome at Bethnal Green, where he found the light hearted atmosphere most agreeable. But Godwin was part of the attraction, and as an example of masculinity, he exerted a powerful influence upon Bunny. Now twenty-one, and relatively inexperienced, Bunny looked up to thirty-one-year-old Godwin, who, the previous year had written passionate love letters to Brynhild Olivier, undeterred by the fact of her engagement to Hugh Popham or of his own engagement to Rosalind. In one letter he stated: 'I am not disturbed when I think of Rosalind and then of you, I see you both so clearly and know I can be faithful to both. One cannot put a padlock to one's heart and give it to one woman.'[18] A few years later, these words could have been written by Bunny.

In the summer of 1913 Bunny gained his Associateship at Imperial College. Realising he had only one more year of study, he decided to try for a scholarship. There was no requirement to sit an exam but he would need to shine at interview and to be supported by the recommendations of his professors. In preparation, Bunny spent long hours in the Natural History Museum, where he met John Ramsbottom, Keeper of Botany, who became something of a mentor to Bunny, sharing his knowledge with him and allowing him to use the library's collection of slides. It was particularly helpful that Ramsbottom had a special interest in fungi, a subject which formed part of Bunny's syllabus.

---

[18] Quoted in Baynes Johnson, *Jung's Apprentice*, p. 49.

Bunny continued to participate in Neo-Pagan camps, but the idyll was beginning to fade. They were growing up, some had even married; allegiances, once collective and innocent, now became individualised and intimate. The Garden of Eden had finally given way to the Garden of Earthly Delights. If the Neo-Pagan summer was drawing towards a close (or if Bunny had outgrown it), an exciting new prospect beckoned. Bunny discovered Bohemia, and he was taken there by the poet Anna Wickham. The Garnetts had moved, the previous autumn, from Grove Place to Downshire Hill in Hampstead, where Anna Wickham was a close neighbour. At twenty-nine, she was eight years older than Bunny, married with two sons and at this time trying to forge ahead as a poet against extreme opposition from her husband, who at one point incarcerated her in a private asylum.

Anna was tall and striking, with beautiful eyes and a forthright expressive countenance. Bunny felt sympathy for her predicament and read and admired her poems. Moreover, as Jennifer Vaughan Jones, Anna Wickham's biographer commented: 'Anna's story had all the elements that he was highly susceptible to: a beautiful woman, an evil conspiracy, the chance to rescue, and the chance to be admired.'[19] If Anna did not altogether discourage Bunny from becoming infatuated, her life was too complicated to allow for an affair with an exuberant young man. But she found Bohemia an escape from her stultifying marriage and introduced Bunny to the delights of the Café Royal. There he found a potent mix of people from the worlds of politics, literature, music, art and sport rubbing shoulders with the

---

[19] Jennifer Vaughan Jones, *Anna Wickham: A Poet's Daring Life* (Lanham, New York & Oxford: Madison Books, 2003), p. 106.

models, actresses, night-club singers, drug dealers and others of the *demi-monde*. It was a place where respectability was a dubious virtue and it seemed a thousand miles from microscopes and labs. If Imperial College ruled Bunny's days, then the Café Royal conquered his nights. They were different worlds.

Located on Regent Street, the Café Royal was dominated by a famously ornate saloon resplendent with gilt caryatids, red plush banquettes, marble tables and a sawdust floor. At this time, many artists' models congregated there. Some were fresh from the country, hoping to catch the eye of an Epstein or Augustus John; some were well-established and regularly employed; others were of uncertain status, relying on casual prostitution to fund cocaine habits. Nearby, the Cave of the Golden Calf was the nightclub of choice for those moving on in the early hours. Here the entertainment was provided by Lillian Shelley (known as 'Shelley'), a vivacious and pretty woman with glossy curly hair. One evening, at the Cave of the Golden Calf, Bunny lost three pounds at poker, a sum which he could ill afford. Afterwards Shelley invited him over, 'her breast heaving, her eyes blazing'. As Bunny recorded in his diary:

> She welcomed me & made me sit by her and held my knee all the time. Presently she said:
> "Garnett – get me a liqueur brandy – don't let them see."
> I spent my last shilling on it – and then drank half of it – so people should think it was mine so that wild creature shouldn't get any more drunk. Finally I succeeded in getting her to go home.[20]

---

[20] DG, notes in The Eclipse Exercise Book [1913–14] unpublished MS [Northwestern].

If Bunny was gallant, he was still naïve. But his capacity to fill every minute and to live life at an extraordinary pace was now manifest. He could burn the midnight oil in Bohemia and work hard in college all day.

In December 1913, in the course of a college fieldtrip to Silchester Common, Hampshire, Bunny found a minute species of mushroom nestling in the moss under gorse, which he did not recognise, or at least he found it unrecognisable in such a diminutive form. He took it to John Ramsbottom, who reported in the Journal of Botany that the fungus was a new species, 'distinguished from its allies by the exceptionally small size of the apothecia.'[21] The fungus was officially named *Discinella minutissima* (Ramsb.et Garn.) and its discovery remained an achievement of which Bunny was justifiably proud.

W.H. Hudson wrote teasingly to Edward that he hoped Bunny would not confine himself to mushrooms and toadstools and disappear into obscure reaches of academia. But already, aged twenty-one, Bunny was not someone who would confine himself to anything restrictive, professionally or personally. He enjoyed college because he was interested in his work, but also because there was a lot going on outside it. Bunny could never be confined to one kind of life; he needed variety. The Limpsfield intelligentsia, the Neo-Pagans and now Bohemia, were all examples of Bunny's attraction to experiencing life away from the mainstream. He had such a capacity for experience that he wanted it in as many forms as possible. When in July 1914 Bunny was awarded the Marshall Scholarship, his dual life twixt college and Bohemia was consolidated for another year.

---

[21] J. Ramsbottom, 'A New Species of Discinella', published extract from *The Journal of Botany* (London: West, Newman & Co.) [August 1914], pp. 215–16.

To be nearer to Imperial College, the Garnetts moved to a modest maisonette at Pond Place, off the Fulham Road, in Bohemian Chelsea. At this time a young man entered Bunny's life who would become one of his closest friends. Bunny met Francis Birrell (known as Frankie) at a party given by the Pophams and did not immediately take to him. In contrast, Frankie instantly fell for Bunny, trailing behind him like a devoted dog. Three years Bunny's senior, Frankie worked in the textiles department of the Victoria & Albert Museum. He was the son of the politician and essayist Augustine Birrell, and had been educated at Eton and King's College, Cambridge. Frankie was small, tousled-haired and bespectacled, with a face like an impish schoolboy. He was loved by everyone for his keen intelligence and quick wit, his tendency to exaggeration, enormous enthusiasm and a stoicism which belied his myopic gaze and small frame. It only took a second meeting for Bunny to be charmed.

According to Bunny's journal, it was after drinking large quantities of the potent Sutton's cocktail (six parts gin, 3 parts Curacao, 2 parts brandy, 1 part orange bitters) that, his 'relations' with Frankie began. On leaving a nightclub, he and Frankie took a taxi to Chelsea, where Frankie lived at Elm Park Gardens, around the corner from Pond Place. In the taxi Bunny put his arm around his friend's shoulders and began kissing him. 'I kissed him & held him in my arms all the way home & then went off saying goodbye rather coldly lest the policeman should hear.' As a result of this rather mixed-message, Frankie rushed off to Hugh Popham to whom he declared his love for Bunny. As Bunny recorded in his journal: 'Hugh immediately told Bryn who assured Francis [...] that it had been like that with me & Godwin & she knew absolutely certainly that I should never

never copulate with him.'[22] It is interesting that Bunny felt the need to record this reported conversation in his private journal, as if he was trying to prove something to himself. Perhaps he needed reassurance that he did not have homosexual feelings for either Godwin or Frankie. It was as though he could not resolve his own conflicted sexuality.

Such confusion was not unusual. Although James and Frankie were at home with their sexualities, others of Bunny's generation and class shared his feelings of confusion, while adding to the confusion by adopting the demonstrative and flamboyant language then in vogue among some homosexuals. In 1913 or 1914 the Neo-Pagans were briefly joined by Vernon Mottram, a former grammar-school boy some ten years Bunny's senior, who had gained a scholarship to study science at Cambridge, later enjoying a distinguished career as a physiologist and nutritionist. It is difficult to gauge, from his few surviving letters to Bunny, whether his affection for his friend was as profoundly loving in reality as expressed on the written page. 'My dearly beloved Bunny', one letter began, 'Know of a soft corner in my heart kept swept & garnished for you if you ever want to occupy it'.[23]

Many years later, in an unpublished autobiography written for his sons, Mottram described a thread running through his life, 'the experience of sex by a person who is ambivalent'. He said that as a schoolboy he had fallen in love with another boy, explaining that at school he had been 'restricted to boys', 'and, of course, it became much more striking at Cambridge'.[24] But he

---

[22] DG, Journal 1914, unpublished MS [Northwestern].

[23] Vernon Mottram/DG, Caterham School, Caterham Valley, 12 August 1914 [Northwestern].

[24] V.H. Mottram, unpublished autobiography [Wellcome Library].

emphasised that while many people of his acquaintance had 'professed homosexuality' most went on to marry. Mottram turned to psychoanalysis to remedy his 'ambivalence'.

Such 'ambivalence' might also have been fuelled by fear of discovery and arrest as homosexual acts were illegal in England until 1967, hence Bunny's cold goodbye to Frankie, 'lest the policeman should hear'. Unlike Mottram, Bunny would not need to seek a 'cure' for homosexuality. The more homosexuals he came to know the more he realised that it was the individual to whom he was attracted, irrespective of gender.

Part 2

Duncan

Chapter Six

'Since liberty, Nature for all has designed,
A pox on the fool who to one is confined.'[1]

At what would be his final Neo-Pagan camp, in Cornwall in
August 1914, Bunny was blissfully unaware of the momentous
events unfolding in Europe, barely registering the assassination
of Archduke Franz Ferdinand in Sarajevo on 28 June. On 4
August Britain declared war on Germany. Assuming Bunny
would face pressure to enlist, Constance urged him to begin
medical training as an alternative to fighting. Again and again
she encouraged him to opt for non-combatant service, asserting
that this was not the cowardly option: 'They say the ambulance
work is quite as dangerous, so you need not feel you are shirking.'[2]
Bunny considered training as a bacteriologist and joining Rupert
Brooke's friend, Geoffrey Keynes, in the Royal Army Medical
Corps. But Bunny had recently become acquainted with
Geoffrey's brother, John Maynard Keynes, who assured him that

---

[1]   Thomas Shadwell, *The Libertine*, 1675.
[2]   CG/DG, Friday 7 August [1914] [KCC].

the war would last no longer than a year or eighteen months, on which basis he returned to college in October 1914 for his scholarship year.

For Bunny's generation the idea of war was no more than an abstract: in Britain there was no *memory* of conflict, except that of the Boer War, fought in distant lands. Moreover participation in the war was widely opposed and many people questioned Britain's involvement. Even so, the atmosphere in London rapidly changed. When Bunny gave a dinner party at Pond Place for the newly married Lawrences, one of his guests called down to Frieda, bidding her farewell in German. A few days later Bunny received the first of a succession of visits from plain-clothes policemen enquiring how many Germans lived in the flat.

But life went on, and Bunny remained determined to extract every ounce of pleasure from it. To which end, in September 1914 he and Frankie Birrell established the Caroline Club. Its name was doubly appropriate as it was formed primarily for the reading of Restoration drama, much of it written in the Carolingian period, and meetings were held (every Tuesday) at the Pophams' home, 5 Caroline Place. Restoration drama had been out of fashion since the late 18th century, but its bawdy wit provided a wonderful antidote to wartime concerns. The club's members were drawn from Bunny's and Frankie's now largely overlapping circle of friends. The Olivier sisters and James Strachey were soon joined by Adrian Stephen, whom Bunny had first met at Crosby Hall. Their friendship had been consolidated in early 1913 when Bunny received an invitation from Adrian to take tea at Brunswick Square. Bunny had since attended Adrian's poker parties held in the big first-floor drawing room. As Bunny's limited and rather shabby wardrobe did not lend itself to such occasions, he wore evening dress, his only smart attire. He thought it would make him seem sophisticated, as if he had come from an elegant dinner party.

It was some time, however, before Bunny felt entirely comfortable among Adrian's friends, many of whom were members of the Bloomsbury Group, a circle which in London centred on Adrian and his sisters Virginia Woolf and Vanessa Bell, but which had largely been forged from members of the elite but secret Cambridge intellectual society, known as the Apostles. The Bloomsbury Group rejected conventional authority or conventional morality, believing personal relationships were paramount, and that in such relationships truth and honesty were more important than exclusivity. It was a close-knit group of people who knew one another very well, and who tended to have intimate relationships with those already in the fold. For this reason, there was a certain amount of recycling.

In September 1914 the Caroline Club entertained Rupert Brooke, now a Sub-Lieutenant in the RNVR, and admitted five of Adrian's Bloomsbury friends: John Maynard Keynes, Gerald Shove, Clive Bell, Saxon Sidney-Turner and Duncan Grant. A fortnight later Vanessa Bell and her husband Clive were in attendance, and in November James Strachey's brother, Lytton, came along. There were more and more people with whom Bunny could take tea, have dinner and visit the Café Royal. According to a young acquaintance, Michael Fordham, Bunny was at this time 'very beautiful and seemed to me like a god'.[3] Suddenly he found himself much in demand.

But war could not be kept at arm's length indefinitely. It impinged upon Edward's income: his employer, the publisher

---

[3] Michael Fordham, *The Making of an Analyst: A Memoir* (London: Free Association Books, 1993), pp. 24–5.

George Duckworth, announced he would publish nothing for three months and could pay only a basic £15 per month. There was no guarantee of Edward receiving any extra for reviewing or of Constance obtaining translation work. In November she and Edward received a circular communication from the Parliamentary Recruiting Committee instructing them to supply the 'names of those of your household [aged between eighteen and thirty-eight] who are willing to enlist for the War'. Further, the letter stated:

> In order to maintain and reinforce our troops abroad and to complete the new Armies which we hope within a few months to throw into the field, we need all the best the Nation can give us of its youth and strength [...]. Every man, therefore, who is eligible, will ask his own conscience whether, in this emergency, it is not his duty to hold himself ready to enlist in the forces of the Crown.[4]

The pressure to enlist was mounting, but Bunny either decided against or was discouraged from doing so. The latter seems likely, as in a letter from Edward Thomas to W.H. Hudson, the former reported that he had heard Edward Garnett say that Bunny 'had been dissuaded from enlisting'.[5] For the meantime, conscription remained voluntary and Bunny's status as a science scholar meant he had *bona fide* work to occupy him. But as more and

---

[4] Parliamentary Recruiting Committee circular [Constance and Edward Garnett], 12 Downing Street, London, November 1914 [Northwestern].

[5] E. Thomas/W.H. Hudson, c/o Robert Frost, Ryton, Dymock, Gloucester, 26 November 1914, in R. George Thomas, ed., *Edward Thomas: Selected Letters* (New York: Oxford University Press, 1995), p. 101.

more young men enlisted, those that did not became progressively visible exceptions.

If Bunny needed proof of his growing popularity, it came in December 1914 in the form of an invitation from Lady Ottoline Morrell, the extravagantly dressed and elaborately coiffed *grande dame* of literary and artistic London, who held court at her weekly salons in Bedford Square. Ottoline knew *everyone*. According to his diary, Bunny's first attendance at Ottoline's began awkwardly. But he soon relaxed sufficiently to perform an Apache dance with the French actress, Valentine Tessier.

Later that month, Bunny embarked on a weeklong walking tour with Frankie Birrell from Yatton in Somerset to Lockeridge, near Marlborough, in Wiltshire. Their destination was a cottage called 'The Lacket', the country residence of Lytton Strachey, who had invited Bunny and Frankie to his Christmas party. Bunny was relieved to be out of London as he had been confined to the laboratory for several weekends. They arrived on 23 December to find Noel and Daphne Olivier, James Strachey and the Bloomsbury artist Duncan Grant already there. As the cottage was too small to accommodate everyone, Bunny and Frankie took rooms, as the season demanded, at the local inn. When, on Boxing Day, Bunny, Noel, Daphne, Frankie, James and Duncan set out for a walk, Noel and James paired off, as did Frankie and Daphne, leaving Bunny and Duncan together. With half an eye on Daphne, with whom Bunny fancied himself in love, he did not register the momentousness of the occasion. Looking back he recognised it as a turning point, a moment which 'marked an epoch in my life'.[6]

On 2 January 1915 Bunny received an invitation from Maynard Keynes, requesting 'the pleasure of the company of

---

[6] DG, *Flowers*, p. 18.

Mr Bunny at dinner at the Café Róyal at 7.30 pm on Wednesday January 6, before Mrs Clive Bell's party.' Bunny was instructed to dress in 'any clothes, the fancier the better or as you like it'.[7] There is no record of whether he dressed as an Indian prince, but he did record that at dinner Maynard placed him between Duncan and Vanessa. There were seventeen to dinner, including Clive Bell, Leonard and Virginia Woolf, the critic Desmond MacCarthy and his wife, Molly. Afterwards Bunny found Vanessa's party most impressive, with 'dances & songs & Gerald Shove very drunk with roses in his hair'. Overcome with sentiment, Bunny told Maynard he was a dear, to which Maynard replied that he would kiss Bunny if there weren't so many people present.[8] As the party drew to an end, Maynard and Frankie drifted off together and Bunny left with Duncan. To Bunny's surprise, Duncan declared love. Bunny walked home with him, and spent the night, chastely, in Duncan's studio, Bunny on the bed, Duncan on the floor clasping Bunny's dangling hand.

Duncan was seven years Bunny's senior. Like many, Bunny discerned something special in Duncan: not only was he exquisitely beautiful, with large eyes shaped like those of a classical sculpture, lovely bone structure and full, sensual lips, but he had a particular warmth and teasing humour which no one could fail to be charmed by. He also had a singular ability to live absolutely in the moment, whether absorbed in the act of painting a picture or in the company of friends. He had fallen in love with Bunny during their Boxing Day walk, and soon afterwards sent Bunny a straightforwardly polite invitation to dinner or tea. But he had

---

7 JMK/DG, 10 Great Ormond Street, 2 January 1915 [HG].
8 DG, Journal, Thursday 7 [January 1915] [Northwestern].

chosen not to send another missal, rapidly scribbled in pencil, which read:

> Bunny You don't realize how much I love you. Why should you? You are happy old creature. I am so glad.
>
> My heart aches to see you & to tell you I care for you more than you can possibly imagine.
>
> [...] Don't think I'm complaining, can't you see I want to be with you? It's <u>miserable</u> without you.[9]

In fact Duncan had first been attracted to Bunny almost two years earlier. In January 1913 he had written to Bunny, inviting him to a party he was hosting jointly with Adrian Stephen. On the back, Bunny later inscribed: 'Earliest letter inviting me to one of Adrian's parties.' So it was Duncan who was responsible for drawing Bunny into Bloomsbury, and it was Duncan who issued that first important invitation.

In January 1915, after the night at the studio, Duncan wrote asking Bunny whether he was 'always just simply kind to everyone', warning him that such kindness 'is very dangerous for poor people like me'. He told Bunny, 'You mustn't go on unless you don't mind my wanting to see you much oftener than you want to see me', adding, 'But, oh! But, oh! [...] if you see me again you must be VERY KIND but honest as the DAY.'[10] Two days later Bunny recorded in his journal, 'went to Duncan's & spent

---

[9] D. Grant/DG, unsent letter [late December 1914/early January 1915] enclosed with D. Grant/DG, Wilmington House, Nr Dartford, Kent, Sunday 18 July 1915 [HG].

[10] D. Grant/DG, C/O Mrs Primmer, The Beeches, Bank, n.d. [c. 6 January 1915] [HG].

the night there'. This time there was no reticence, Bunny feeling inspired with a passion 'borne partly of curiosity about this darling strange creature so like an animal & so full of charm'.[11]

Two weeks later, Vanessa Bell came to tea at Pond Place. She was thirty-six, thirteen years older than Bunny, but he found her extremely beautiful, tall and striking, with a 'lovely, sensitive mouth' and 'strangely innocent grey-blue eyes'. Later, when Bunny knew her better, he considered her unique for her ease in male company, unselfconscious ribaldry and gay humour.[12] Bunny recorded in his diary:

> She was altogether charming & talked to me – I said I had thought the best thing to do would be to be brutal to Duncan but I had found it impossible ...... And she said she was glad I had. She was in love with Duncan but couldn't feel jealous of a man. Duncan always had been in love with a man – Adrian for a long time, Maynard at one time [...] She thought we could have nice times together. I said I had been much more falling in love with her than Duncan & that I was a womanizer.[13]

Bunny was still hedging his bets, but so was Vanessa. She knew Duncan was homosexual, but the two of them had a particular bond which she did not want to lose. To keep Duncan close, she needed to be close to his lover, and so a few weeks later, Vanessa took Bunny into her confidence, speaking intimately of her former love affair with Roger Fry. She soon embarked on a

---

[11] DG, Journal, Friday [8 January 1915] [Northwestern].

[12] DG, *Flowers*, p. 26.

[13] DG, Journal, Monday [18 January 1915] [Northwestern].

charm offensive, telling Bunny she and Duncan often talked of him, and when talking of his looks, 'decided that we liked looking at you & after all what more can one say of anyone?'[14]

While it might be assumed that Frankie Birrell preceded Duncan into Bunny's bed, this seems unlikely, as Bunny's diary records no more than the kiss in the taxi. Bunny knew Frankie was in love with him, but felt unable to reciprocate. He later rationalised his relationship with Frankie as 'sentimental love on his part and a flattered readiness to experiment on mine'.[15] Or, as he explained, Frankie 'was physically attracted by me, but I was unable to respond, and during our friendship [...] I was quite incapable of returning his early "falling in love with me".[16] But for several years Frankie would continue to send Bunny highly emotional letters to which Bunny could not reply in the same tone. Even so, he loved Frankie with a combination of amused affection and fraternal protectiveness. When Frankie's mother died in March 1915, it was Bunny who comforted him, tenderly kissing his tear-swollen eyes, before endeavouring to buoy him up with gossip. Frankie occupied a special place in Bunny's heart, and Bunny worried that he would be hurt with Duncan on the scene. Bunny noted in his journal, that when Frankie found out about the relationship, he 'prophesied unhappiness for all of us'.[17]

Beneath the darkening shadow of war, friendships intensified and the London social whirl gained an electric momentum.

---

[14] VB/DG, Eleanor House, West Wittering, Monday [in DG's hand '12 April, 1915'] [HG].

[15] David Garnett, *Great Friends* (London: Macmillan, 1979), p. 90.

[16] Quoted in Boulton, ed., *Letters of D.H. Lawrence*, Vol. II (1982), p. 320.

[17] DG, Journal [24 January 1915] [Northwestern].

There were countless parties, some given on the eve of departure by those who had enlisted, like Maitland Radford (in the RAMC). Bloomsbury dinner parties were followed variously by dancing, puppet shows, masquerades, charades and impromptu revues. At one party the artist Barbara Hiles's fervent dancing gave Bunny a swollen black eye. It was as though everyone was grabbing at life, ignorant of what lay around the corner. Bunny had finally attained his wish 'not for one friend, or sweetheart even, but a whole roomful'. One evening Daphne and Noel Olivier invited him back and they chatted to him while he had a bath, and he chatted to them while they bathed, and he felt it was 'jolly sitting with them naked & unashamed'.[18] A few days later, in Daphne's bed, he admired her beautiful body. 'I never want to see a man again & speak to one', he concluded, adding 'How sick I am of all this dull sodomitical twaddle!'[19]

Bunny's desire for fountains of love did not go down well with Duncan who responded with emotional outbursts. Bunny decided to keep away for a few days, returning to Pond Place, where he received a note from Duncan, promising to stop being jealous. 'All I want to say my angel is that I'm not going to be selfish & spoil your life, I really want you to do what you want. Be happy & love as many people as are worth it & remember that this is my real point of view.'[20]

Duncan's possessive behaviour was unusual. His affairs with Lytton, Maynard, Adrian and James had all been relatively short lived, following the same pattern of a period of intensity cooling

---

[18] DG, Journal [26 January 1915] [Northwestern].
[19] DG, Journal, Saturday [6 February 1915] [Northwestern].
[20] D. Grant/DG, n.d. [25 January 1915] [HG].

gradually into affectionate friendship. Moreover Duncan did not appreciate anyone behaving possessively over him. But despite his protestations to the contrary, he wanted an exclusivity which Bunny could not provide. The underlying cause of Duncan's possessiveness was an inability to cope with Bunny's relationships with women. Had Bunny wanted other men, it might have mattered less; Duncan may perhaps have felt less threatened. But Bunny made it clear that he could only love Duncan in the context of being free to love women as well.

Bunny saw Frankie almost every day, enjoyed weekends with Duncan and still found time to rendezvous with Ruth Baynes in the country. After one of Ottoline's parties one evening, Bunny was strolling past Harrods with Lytton Strachey, when Lytton turned and kissed him on the lips in full view of the street. Bunny dashed into a taxi, a prudent measure at a time when homosexuals were hounded and routinely harassed by the police. He reflected that it was less a matter of his 'minding being kissed', than of 'disliking being kissed in the street by a *bearded* man'.[21] In fact Bunny was ready for any number of new experiences. Depressed about college work, he sought consolation with a prostitute, 'Rose Dolces', who assured him that she was fresh from the country, had a series of connections with married men, and rarely went on the streets.

In February 1915 Duncan moved temporarily to Eleanors, a farmhouse at West Wittering, near Chichester in West Sussex, which Vanessa had taken as an escape from London. When Bunny joined Duncan there towards the end of the month, the two men were blissfully happy, on one occasion raiding the cellar of the artist Henry Tonks's adjacent studio, drinking

---

[21] DG, Journal, Thursday [18 February 1915] [Northwestern]; my italics.

wine in the sunlight, and fighting 'drunkenly & lustfully', before enjoying 'the sweet lassitude of sleeping in each other's arms'.[22] But in London Bunny found himself in a situation reminiscent of that which he had experienced with James Strachey in 1912. This time it was James's older brother Lytton who endeavoured to court Bunny, bombarding him with invitations. Although Bunny enjoyed Lytton's clever, witty and risqué conversation, he kept a distance, which Lytton did not fail to notice, writing: 'It sometimes occurs to me that my persistent invitations may be too much for you; but at other times I fancy that you are very indulgent [...] in spite of your not writing to me.'[23]

Bunny and Frankie spent a weekend, that spring, with D.H. and Frieda Lawrence at Greatham, East Hampshire. Lawrence evidently found Bunny so changed by his Bloomsbury friends that he wrote to Ottoline suggesting there was 'something wrong' with Bunny. 'Is he also', Lawrence asked, 'like Keynes and Grant [?]' He said they made him dream 'of a beetle that bites like a scorpion', a beetle, moreover, which he was able to kill.[24] According to John Worthen, Lawrence's biographer, Lawrence's feeling of revulsion arose because he '*knew* this feeling, which was why he found it so disturbing. It was a revelation to him of the way in which he himself might be homosexual, and did not want to be.'[25] Lawrence wrote to Bunny the same day, imploring him to break free of his homosexual friends:

---

[22] DG, Journal, Saturday [20 February 1915] [Northwestern].

[23] GLS/DG, 6 Belsize Park Gardens, Friday 7 May 1915 [Princeton].

[24] DHL/Lady Ottoline Morrell, Greatham [19 April 1915], in Boulton, ed., *Letters of D.H. Lawrence*, Vol. II, p. 318.

[25] Worthen, *D.H. Lawrence*, p. 162.

It is foolish of you to say that it doesn't matter either way – the men loving men. It doesn't matter in the public way. But it matters so much, David, to the man himself [...] that it is like a blow of triumphant decay, when I meet Birrell or the others. I simply can't bear it [...]. Why is there this horrible sense of frowstiness, so repulsive, as if it came from deep inward dirt – a sort of sewer – deep in men like K[eynes] and B[irrell] and D[uncan] G[rant].

[...] Now David, in the name of everything that is called love, leave this set and stop this blasphemy against love.[26]

The letter came as a shock to Bunny, for he had written to Edward about the weekend, commenting on Lawrence's good spirits. Eleanor Farjeon, staying in a cottage nearby, recalled a light-hearted weekend, with cricket and croquet.[27] But Bunny stood his ground with Lawrence regarding the 'men loving men' question. Consequently, in Lawrence's eyes the vigorously masculine Bunny whom he had loved in Germany, was no more. Now he was David and beyond redemption. After this, Bunny saw Lawrence only once more, by accident, on the evening of Armistice Day. But he wrote and told him how much he admired *Lady Chatterley's Lover*, and received a warm letter in reply. Bunny later reflected that Lawrence 'could charm every human creature who attracted or interested him and at first meeting almost every fresh separate person did attract him. He did, however, use up his human attachments rather fast.'[28]

---

[26] DHL/DG, Greatham [19 April 1915], in Boulton, *Letters of D.H. Lawrence*, pp. 320–1.

[27] Eleanor Farjeon, *Edward Thomas: The Last Four Years* (Oxford: Oxford University Press, 1958; paperback edition 1979), p. 133.

[28] DG, 'A Whole Hive of Genius'.

In May Vanessa wrote to Roger Fry, stating she felt 'happier about Duncan and Bunny because I see that Bunny really does care a good deal for him'. Refuting Fry's contention that she might have feelings for Bunny herself, Vanessa explained that 'he likes I think to be demonstrative to everyone he likes, but he's not in love with me.'[29] Although Bunny and Duncan had latterly been very happy together, Duncan's jealousy periodically resurfaced. He conceived a notion that Bunny was in love with Maria Nhys, a young woman in Ottoline's employ. Leaving the Morrells' Bedford Square house one afternoon, Bunny was confronted by Duncan rushing towards him white-faced and apparently unable to speak. Duncan seemed so unhinged that Bunny feared he was out of his mind. A few weeks later, after an evening at Ottoline's, Bunny went back to Maynard's Gower Street rooms, where, the worse for whisky, he kissed Maynard in bed. Hovering suspiciously on the threshold, Duncan witnessed the event and became extremely agitated. The situation was compounded by Duncan's prolonged absences at Wittering, where he had too long to speculate about what Bunny was doing and with whom.

Bunny was always ready for an adventure, and when, one evening at the Café Royal, he was given the nod by a lovely young artists' model, he quickly acceded to her request to obtain cocaine from a chemist. Betty May was extremely pretty with an olive complexion, and deep-violet-blue eyes set wide apart. She was only five feet tall, but with her fierce and feisty disposition, was known as 'Tiger Woman'. Bunny assumed she was eighteen, but at twenty-two, she was only one year younger than him. At

---

[29] VB/Roger Fry, Eleanor Farm, West Wittering, Sunday [?9 May] [1915], in Regina Marler, ed., *Selected Letters of Vanessa Bell*, introduction by Quentin Bell (London: Bloomsbury Publishing, 1993, paperback 1994), pp. 179–80.

Pond Place he lit a fire, they undressed, and in order to show willing, Bunny took some cocaine. Under the influence, Betty started a row, to which Bunny responded angrily, telling her that he did not regard her as a prostitute, 'but as a human being full of lust like myself'.[30] Later they talked, and Bunny, who had decided to reform her, insisted that Betty give up drugs, which she promised to do. The next morning, according to Bunny's journal, Betty was 'full of love' for him, so he gave her ten shillings. And so began a relationship in which Bunny furnished Betty with occasional hand-outs for the next sixty years.

[30] DG, Journal Monday [31 May] 1915 [Northwestern].

Chapter Seven

'My opinions had been formed by what I had seen of the war and by the people I had been working among.'[1]

Bunny's university career ended in June 1915. Constance worried that he would enlist, as Bunny oscillated between enlisting and following her advice not to. But Bunny made a surprising decision: he elected to join Frankie Birrell and undertake reconstructive work for the Friends Relief Mission in France. Thus he could contribute to the war effort without having to fight. Although he could not tolerate organised religion, even in the pared down contemplative form which the Friends' worship took, he believed he could be of practical use building accommodation in villages which the Germans had destroyed.

There may have been another underlying motive for Bunny's decision. His love life had taken a complicated turn, as there had been a development in his relationship with Lytton Strachey. Lytton had redoubled his pursuit, repeatedly inviting Bunny to the Lacket. Bunny obviously capitulated, as before leaving for

---

[1] DG, *Flowers*, p. 93.

France, he wrote to Lytton asking him to 'Give me your blessing my dear', adding, 'don't lets wrangle each day seriously who first shall post off the message of his love. I love you – I was innocent & you were a long while letting my pride and my love for you quarrel with each other.'[2] Lytton replied, imploring Bunny to come to the Lacket one more time. 'Of course', he added, 'I know that I must ask you to forgive me a great deal. The difficulty is one cannot wear one's heart on one's sleeve for daws to peck at.'[3]

Aware that he could be summoned to the Quakers any day, Bunny threw himself into a whirlwind of activity, attending parties, dining with friends, visiting his mother, and upsetting Duncan by having sex with Betty May in his studio. On 30 June he wrote in wobbly handwriting, atop a double-decker bus, to thank Lytton for sending him his poems, which Bunny carried with him, on the first stage of his journey to France.

The previous day Bunny had lunched with his father. Over a carafe of wine Edward began to clear his throat with what appeared to be embarrassment. Remembering the parental advice proffered before his trip to Germany, Bunny felt sure he was to be given a similar homily, but was delighted when his father's hand opened to reveal a pocket corkscrew. Thus armed, and garbed in the Quakers' grey uniform with the emblematic red and black star on cap and sleeve, Bunny and Frankie set off for the Marne, in Northwestern France. In the train en route, they found themselves at the receiving end of a lecture from a Scottish Quaker about the supposed immorality of French women. This did not augur well, and on arriving at Sermaize where the Friends were based, the all-pervasive air of piety did little to raise their spirits.

---

2   DG/GLS, 19 Pond Place [15 June 1915] [BL].
3   GLS/DG, The Lacket, 16 June 1915 [Princeton].

The two young men were soon confronted with the realities of war. They boarded a lorry, and set off on an unforgettable drive through a blasted landscape which became so engraved on Bunny's memory, that he was able to describe it twenty years later with absolute clarity:

The white dust rose behind us and we were carried through chequered light under over-hanging trees – some of which had oddly splintered branches – and all the way along [...] and in and out of the shadows of the aspens there were tawdry, decorated scratchings up of earth, over which trico-lours fluttered and medals jingled from the wooden crosses. For this road was the extreme limit to which the French army had been pressed back upon itself and from which it had, against Joffre's orders, rebounded like a coiled spring upon the Boches. In some places the graves were strung out as much as fifty yards apart, in others they lined the road a dozen deep. French soldiers were buried where they had fallen and the country of the Marne was like a large-scale map dotted with little flags that showed the course of battle. All through the district we were entering there were fresh graves dotted along the roads, in the fields and at the edges of the woods.[4]

What Bunny saw before him were the scars left by the Battle of the Marne and by the German invasion of September 1914. He not only encountered a shattered landscape, scattered with

[4] David Garnett, 'War Victims' Relief', in *We Did Not Fight: 1914–18 Experiences of War Resisters*, edited by Julian Bell (London: Cobden-Sanderson, 1935), pp. 131–2.

wooden crosses, but the fragmented lives of the survivors, mostly women, the elderly and children, who had lost their homes and loved-ones.

As pacifists, members of the Friends' War Victims' Relief Organisation were not involved in active work which might be construed as validating or supporting war, but their role was to assist the victims of war. Thus Bunny and Frankie were part of a team responsible for erecting temporary housing to provide shelter for the people and their livestock, so that normal life and livelihoods might, as far as possible, be resumed. Bunny was overwhelmed by the stoicism of the French and their determination to rebuild their lives. He sent a postcard to Edward which, he said, gave 'a vague idea of the ruins. The houses are rubbish heaps – the gardens perfectly spick and span – a strange contrast.'[5]

Initially based at Nettancourt, Bunny and Frankie worked in nearby Sommeilles, a hilltop village overlooking the Argonne Forest, where only two houses remained standing. As Bunny recalled:

When I first saw the village, it created a strange impression. The roof of the church had been knocked in by shells and burnt; and there was nothing left of the Town Hall but a pair of smiling stone lions, a flight of steps and a handsome portico; up the main street there was one little house standing between the rows of burnt-out walls which stretched up to the top of the hill. Yet if one went in between the walls, one saw behind them neat cultivated gardens, rows of

[5] DG/EG, Carte Postale, 'Bataille de la Marne', postmark 3 July 1915 [Northwestern].

watered lettuces and bean-sticks, the climbing haricots just in flower; bees going in and out of the hives, and chicks running to shelter under the hen's wing.[6]

At Sommeilles Bunny and Frankie assembled pre-fabricated wooden frame-houses which varied according to the size of the family, usually consisting of between one and three rooms. Once the frames, joists and planks had arrived by lorry, the Quakers bolted the frames together, laid joists and floors, nailed on the walls, bolted gables and rafters and covered them with planks before finally tiling the roofs. This did not require particular skill, but was physically demanding. Bunny relished this work, revelling in his strength and enjoying the result of his manual labour.

Bunny, Frankie and the hut building contingent soon split off from the main body of Nettancourt Quakers, moving to Sommeilles, where in late July they built themselves a hut. This had one big room and a kitchen; relics of a previous dwelling had been brought in to furnish stone steps and seats on either side of the doorway. In the hot, high summer, the weather was extremely pleasant, 'the people smile at us & the cherries are thick on the trees'.[7] Photographs of Bunny at this time show a muscular bronzed young man, his arms bare in rolled up shirt-sleeves, his hair a tousled sun-bleached thatch. The men lived largely out of doors, washing and shaving in front of the hut, a mirror nailed to the boards. In good weather they slept outside, but while Frankie, the eternal public schoolboy, relished

6   DG, 'War Victims' Relief', pp. 133–4.
7   DG/Ottoline Morrell, Équipe Anglaise, Nettancourt, Meuse, 3 July [1915] [HRRC].

the proximity of so many young men, Bunny found the all-male environment trying.

They established a routine which began at 4.45 in the morning, when after a cup of tea and with cigarettes clamped between their teeth, they began work. At 7.30 they breakfasted on coffee, porridge and omelette, stopping for lunch at noon. At 5.30 the working day ended, and they would be given a substantial dinner and wine. As Bunny remarked to Lytton, 'we live like kings & Mr Cadbury pays for it'.[8] Bunny and his co-workers were fortunate because although the houses had been demolished, the gardens and cellars remained intact, from which the generous French could supply wine and vegetables, a welcome replacement for the Quaker rations of tinned fish and chocolate. But the war, which raged only twenty miles away, was ever-present in the continuous thudding of heavy guns and the noise of aeroplanes passing overhead. At night they were often woken by the sound of a heavy bombardment, which rattled the window panes, and sometimes they could see the black puffs of exploding shells above the Argonne tree-tops.

Bunny was profoundly moved by the dignity of his French friends. One story which he could not forget was that of the Germans throwing a wounded French soldier into a burning house, where they left him to die. In an act of courage and defiance, a thirteen-year-old boy, Georges Raiwot, raked through the hot embers to retrieve the ashes of the soldier, which he carried to the cemetery to be buried. Bunny became fond of this young man, as he did of many of the villagers, in particular Georges Leglais, a former pilot who had retired after losing his right arm. It was impossible not to love these people, who despite

---

[8]   DG/Lytton Strachey, Mission Anglaise, La Fontaine, Sommeilles, 29 July [1915] [BL].

terrible privations were nothing but kind and hospitable to the Englishmen living among them.

While the sun smiled upon Bunny in France, in England, as Vanessa reported, 'a profound gloom has settled on us – on Duncan particularly'. 'I wish', she said, 'you could come twinkling out from behind the great ilex. How everything would change & what a nice excited furry little bear would be rolling about on the lawn instead of the rather pathetic quiet caged creature sighing beside me.' Vanessa evidently now saw Bunny as integral to her life, or at least, in being integral to Duncan's happiness, necessary for hers too: 'Please write again my dear creature', she concluded, 'you're so much wanted by the other members of the trio who often talk & always think of you.'[9] Duncan wrote telling Bunny that he missed him more and more, and was 'absolutely determined to love you till the end of time'.[10] He also sent, by way of a love token, that first, unsent, letter in which he had declared his feelings for Bunny.

Letters from home afforded a window into the habitual society and gossip which continued in England, or at least in Gordon Square. Bunny loved Lytton's tantalising dispatches, designed to taunt the Censor, in which he offered to do all manner of things to Bunny in a series of '----'s. Bunny had also embarked on an epistolary flirtation with Barbara Hiles, the crop-headed former Slade student whose dancing had given him a black eye.

Although Frankie relished living in an all male society, Bunny found the insularity claustrophobic. He began to feel restless, a restlessness compounded by being made to attend Quaker

---

[9] VB/DG, Garsington Manor, Oxford, 12 July [1915] [HG].

[10] D. Grant/DG, 46 Gordon Square, Bloomsbury, Thursday 15 July [1915] [HG].

meetings. There was no variety, nowhere to go, no escape, nothing except the guns going 'thud, thud, thud […] without stopping for five seconds altogether'.[11] As someone who sought diversity, Bunny did not enjoy being confined, and felt cornered by the watchfulness of the Quakers. Mostly he missed the company of women and disliked having to live a chaste life on a rather public platform under the scrutiny of both villagers and Quaker brethren.

To fill their spare time, Bunny and Frankie collaborated in writing a play, ostensibly based on their lives in France. Frankie could not resist introducing 'one rather moving evening scene with all the young men getting into bed under the stars by a tenuous lamplight'.[12] But Bunny was finding enforced intimacy with Frankie progressively difficult. As a result of Frankie's inability to sublimate his feelings, Bunny began to plan a holiday in England and decided he might not return to Sommeilles, although he expected to continue to work for the Friends in some capacity. Frankie later acknowledged that the 'surrounding Quakerism' combined with his unrequited love for Bunny made them 'unable to continue living in close proximity'. Frankie's love for Bunny was such that three years later he told him, 'I show no signs of falling in love with anybody else'.[13]

Meanwhile, in August 1915 Edward arrived in Italy, where he was stationed above the River Isonzo with a British Red Cross ambulance unit. Constance seemed less concerned for his safety than for Bunny's. She feared Bunny would soon complete the

[11] DG/D. Grant, Mission Anglaise, Nettancourt, Meuse, 'Tuesday' [postmark 14 July 1915] [HG].

[12] F. Birrell/J.M. Keynes, Mission Anglaise, La Fontaine, Sommeille par Nettancourt, Meuse, Friday 11 August [1915] [KCC].

[13] F. Birrell/DG, 53 Rue de Rivoli, Paris, 21 December [1918] [Northwestern].

work in Sommeilles and might attempt something more adventurous and dangerous. She mounted a campaign to ensure his safety, inveigling Nellie to elicit the help of friends. Nellie wrote to Louise Bréal, asking her to use her influence to see if Bunny could obtain work at the Pasteur Institute or in the Red Cross Hospitals in France. 'You will probably say', Nellie acknowledged perspicaciously, 'why doesn't he go with Edward? He might – but Connie of course would give anything to keep him away from the fighting line.'[14]

Although Bunny normally shirked leadership, he had been made Corporal, directing the building work, assigning duties, prioritising those in need of houses, ordering materials and arranging transport. He felt incompetent faced with such responsibility, but was obviously considered capable, for Edmund Harvey, the Liberal MP leader of the Friends' War Victims' Relief Mission, subsequently appointed him *Chef d'Equipe*. This involved even more responsibility, including dispatching progress reports, keeping accounts and, as Bunny wryly commented, reading the Bible at breakfast 'to prevent debauchery & license among the members'.[15] To his surprise, Bunny enjoyed himself. He informed Constance that he proposed to remain in Sommeilles until work there was finished, which he anticipated would be at the end of October. Afterwards, he would come home for a holiday. 'Whether I go back to France, or to Italy, or

[14] EMH/Louise Bréal, c/o Mrs Pitman, The Chestnuts, Shipham, Somerset, 1 September 1915 [Martin Brunt].

[15] DG/CG, La Fontaine, Sommeille-par-Nettancourt, Meuse, France, 6 September 1915 [Eton]; this is written in Constance's hand, presumably, as was her custom, in order to send a copy of Bunny's letter to Edward, while retaining the original herself.

Russia, or Mesopotamia', he said, 'or whether I stay in England depends on all sorts of things.' To Constance's consternation he added: 'But I am much attracted by Italy.' 'Driving a motor would be sickening but I don't think more dangerous.'[16] As photographs show, Bunny had some experience of driving in Sommeilles, and he felt that with a month or so of training, he would be equipped to drive an ambulance or work as a chauffeur.

Alarmed, Constance wrote anxiously to Edward: 'I wish it could turn out to be possible for him to do hospital or orderly work only & no driving.' 'I think', she added, 'he is distinctly less fitted in anything wanting sight & judgment of distance than most people.'[17] She explained that an oculist had discovered Bunny's focussing muscles were defective, causing him to turn his head to see things at the side. 'If he has to meet me at the station, I see him moving his head to & fro hunting about & not seeing me till long after I have seen him.'[18] She had a point: Bunny's driving was always a nerve-racking experience for his passengers.

Vanessa wrote to tell Bunny how glad it would make her to see him again, but she could not resist communicating her happiness in having Duncan to herself. 'I have been extraordinarily selfishly happy lately', she wrote:

I sit out or in & paint with the animal & he takes me for walks in the evening & he's there when I wake up & when

---

[16] DG/CG, La Fontaine, Sommeille [September 1915] [Northwestern]; in Constance's hand.

[17] CG/EG, The Cearne, 23 September 1915 [HRRC].

[18] CG/EG, The Cearne, 30 September [1915] [HRRC].

I go to bed & sometimes in between too (which in between can be read either way) & he's been so extraordinarily charming & odd in his ways & speech & so unlike any body or anything else in this world & so amazingly nice to me that I have been about as childishly happy as one can be.[19]

When Bunny returned to London for his holiday, Duncan was so overwhelmed at seeing him that he needed a day to recover his composure. Lytton wrote addressing Bunny as 'Darling, darling creature', asking 'How have you managed it, dearest David, to be … just what you are?'[20]

After only two weeks, Bunny returned to France where he hoped work at the Pasteur Institute might materialise as it would enable him to be with Duncan, who had been invited to Paris with an offer of design work by Jacques Copeau, the influential theatrical producer. On 3 November 1915 Bunny and Duncan left together for Paris, but at Dieppe they became separated; Bunny continued alone, assuming Duncan would join him later. Although Duncan had obtained prior approval from the Foreign Office to work in Paris, he was subjected to intensive questioning. As his answers proved unsatisfactory, neither the French nor the English authorities would allow him to proceed to Paris or to remain in France. And so, as he wrote to Bunny, 'I am being shipped back […] like any bloody undesirable alien'. 'When shall I see you again?' he asked. 'It is too beastly.'[21]

Alone in Paris, Bunny trailed about the boulevards, as he told Lytton, 'a pale bloated lonely figure like the last stages of Oscar

---

[19] VB/DG, The Grange, Bosham, 22 September [1915] [HG].

[20] GLS/DG, 6 Belsize Park Gardens, 22 October 1915 [Princeton].

[21] D. Grant/DG, SS Arundel, Dieppe [?4 November] [1915] [HG].

Wilde'.[22] He felt life would be intolerable without Duncan, and worried how he would survive without money. Vanessa sent him £5, and wrote suggesting that as it seemed doubtful Duncan could go to Paris, Bunny should return to London. 'You know of course that I'm not simply disinterested in suggesting this but apart from what it would mean to me wouldn't you both really be happier in London?'[23]

Conscription appeared increasingly probable. As the war continued, fewer men were enlisting, the initial patriotic influx long over, and the impetus of Kitchener's call to arms ('Your Country Needs You') on the wane. The voluntary system could no longer cope with a continuing war and mounting casualties. But Bunny's sojourn in France with the Quakers had once and for all settled the question of whether to enlist. As he later explained: 'My experience at Sommeilles had given me confidence in myself and had also turned me into a pacifist.' He read Clive Bell's pamphlet *Peace at Once* (1915) and agreed with his argument that war should be ended as soon as possible by a negotiated peace. As a result of the devastation he witnessed in France, the destruction of communities and desecration of life, he could not believe that war was justified. Conscientious objection was the only rational option.

Edward's return to England in November 1915 coincided with bad news. As a result of wartime privations, Duckworth had terminated Edward's employment. He and Constance would have very little income and this would mean they could not afford to support Bunny financially if he remained in Paris.

<hr>

[22] DG/GLS, Hotel de L'Elysée, 3 Rue de Beaume, Paris [November 1915] [BL].

[23] VB/DG, 46 Gordon Square, 'Friday' [November 1915] [HG].

Bunny decided to return to Sommeilles to see everyone there one last time. Before doing so, he wrote to Frankie's father, Augustine Birrell MP. Bunny had heard from Lytton that D.H. Lawrence's novel *The Rainbow* had been banned as obscene and burnt by the police. Bunny wrote asking Birrell to intercede. Like Edward, Bunny disapproved strongly of censorship, believing it undermined artistic freedom and truth. Birrell replied dismissively that the book was 'a stagnant pool of dull water collected at the bottom of a disused Quarry'.[24]

Back at Sommeilles Bunny found the weather vile and the personnel changed. He could no longer talk easily to Frankie, for there was a 'silent listener at every conversation between Francis & me'.[25] There Bunny received a letter from Maynard, written very much with Duncan in mind: 'Why don't you come back?' 'If you come back here, either you get a job or you have a very good excuse for leading what life you like and an opportunity you may never have again of seeing if you can write. It's really absurd to stay out there and quite against reason. Lastly its here Duncan is.' 'My dear Bunny', he added, 'do come back; on my word its good advice.'[26] Vanessa wrote too, imploring Bunny to 'make your two allies happy by coming for there are also lots of quite unreasonable reasons, such as thinking how happy we three should be [...] & altogether how absurd it is in this life not to snatch at any obvious happiness one can get even at some risk'.[27]

Bunny replied to Maynard, explaining that if he came home he would be unable to support himself. With impecunious

[24] Augustine Birrell/DG, 16 November 1915 [Northwestern].

[25] DG/GLS [Sommeilles, late November/early December 1915] [BL].

[26] JMK/DG, 3 Gower Street WC, 28 November 1915 [Northwestern].

[27] VB/DG, 46 Gordon Square, Monday 29 November [1915] [HG].

parents and no prospect of a job: 'I shall have to come back to do what? … Live upon my friends in one way or another – borrow from Nessa, come to breakfast with you, and take sixpence off the mantelpiece.'[28] But between them, Maynard, Vanessa and Duncan were determined Bunny should return. Vanessa wrote, 'You can live rent free here & food won't come to much however you come by it'.[29] Duncan reasoned: 'Bunny you know perfectly well I could afford to provide fodder for 2 & you would have no rent to pay. And you know or you ought to know that I should be happier with you, than anything that could happen.'[30]

Bunny returned at the end of December 1915. It was wonderful to see Duncan again, to visit Constance at his beloved Cearne and to stay at Asheham, in Sussex, where Vanessa had rented a house. Here he found himself 'in an almost forgotten heaven' with Vanessa, Duncan, Clive, Lytton and Maynard.[31] In the first few days of 1916, reunited with his closest Bloomsbury friends, Bunny roamed the Sussex Downs, exhilarating in his new-found freedom. They discussed the proposed conscription bill, and could only savour the moment, uncertain what the future would bring. The last twelve months had seen extraordinary changes in Bunny's life. He had grown up, was no longer an idealistic Neo-Pagan but now determined to be a conscientious objector. He had discovered Bloomsbury, and no matter that he thought himself a womaniser, he had a male lover at the centre of his life.

[28] DG/JMK, La Fontaine, Sommeille, 6 December [1915] [KCC].

[29] VB/DG, 46 Gordon Square, 7 December [1915] [HG].

[30] D. Grant/DG, n.d. 'Friday' [December 1915] [HG].

[31] DG, *Flowers*, p. 103.

Chapter Eight

'One is a pawn in a game of chess played by people who don't know the moves.'[1]

On 27 January 1916 the Military Services Act enforced conscription for all men aged between nineteen and forty-one who were unmarried, widowed or without dependent children. On the face of it, this would impact hard on Bloomsbury: many of the men were within this age bracket, and those who were homosexual were 'single' and free of dependents. Exemptions were made for those deemed medically unfit, undertaking work of national importance and for conscientious objectors. But conscientiously objecting was no easy matter and was subject to the approval of Local Tribunals, a quasi-judicial system of local bigwigs wholeheartedly behind the war.

Bunny joined the No-Conscription Fellowship where he worked as a volunteer alongside Duncan, Adrian, Vanessa, Clive Bell and James Strachey, the latter having been sacked from the *Spectator* for his pacifist beliefs. Based on Bride Lane, between the

---

[1] DG/F. Birrell, Wissett Lodge, 20 September [1916] [Northwestern].

Farringdon Road and Fleet Street, the N-CF had been established earlier in the war to campaign against conscription and assist men who did not want to fight. Howard Marten, a Quaker member of the N-CF singled out a particular group of 'artistically minded' volunteers, whom he remarked 'had a terrific repugnance of war which could only express itself individually'.[2] This was true of Bloomsbury, where conscientious objection was endemic. As Bunny put it, they were 'pacifists almost to a man and woman during the First World War and put personal relationships higher than patriotism or success.'[3]

Although Lytton Strachey and Clive Bell were deemed unfit to serve on health grounds, they nevertheless went before the Tribunals to gain exemption. Even Maynard, eligible for exemption as a result of his position in the Treasury, applied to be a conscientious objector. Duncan opted for conscientious objection, despite considerable family pressure to follow in the military footsteps of his father, Major Bartle Grant. (Bunny thought that Major Grant blamed him for Duncan's failure to enlist, as in conversation with Duncan, Major Grant always referred to Bunny as "Your friend Garbage".[4]) Within Bloomsbury, only Ralph Partridge enlisted, but this was before he joined the fold; he later resigned his commission on moral grounds. But Bloomsbury was unusual. Conscientious objectors were a small minority of the population, numbering only 16,000. Most of Bunny's non-Bloomsbury friends enlisted including Bertie Farjeon, Maitland Radford, Godwin Baynes and Geoffrey

---

[2] Quoted in Felicity Goodall, *A Question of Conscience: Conscientious Objection in the Two World Wars* (Stroud: Sutton Publishing, 1997), p. 4.

[3] DG interviewed by James Mellen, 1 March 1971 [BL: Sound Archive].

[4] DG, *Flowers*, p. 112.

Keynes. Edward Thomas and Rupert Brooke lost their lives.

Bunny was prepared to face 'whatever penalties I may be subjected to and however much I may suffer by incurring the contempt of brave & honourable men'.[5] In his 'Answers to Questions of Objection to Combatant Service', he explained that he held 'a genuine conscientious objection' which extended to undertaking any form of military service, and that he had inherited these values from his parents. In answer to the stock-question concerning whether he would defend people to whom he was attached, he replied: 'I should have no hesitation whatso-ever in resorting to violence. My objection to being a soldier is not that I might have to kill but that my being a soldier involves delegating my right of moral judgment to commit me to support-ing the prosecution of war.'[6]

Conscientious objectors displayed considerable courage. In many respects they were pioneers: in the absence of conscription in Britain before 1916, conscientious objection had been both unnecessary and unknown. Without a working model, the conchies had to make it up as they went along and were forced to cope with increasingly draconian treatment by the State and a derisive public image. As Bertrand Russell explained, the great-est challenge for a small minority 'was the purely psychological one of resisting mass suggestion, of which the force becomes terrific when the whole nation is in a state of violent collective excitement.'[7] The threat of imprisonment loomed over conchies

---

[5] DG/CG, 15 February [1916] [Northwestern].

[6] D. Garnett, 'Answers to Questions of Objection to Combatant Service', unpublished MS [Northwestern].

[7] Bertrand Russell, 'Some Psychological Difficulties of Pacifism in Wartime', in *We Did Not Fight*, p. 329.

at the mercy of largely unsympathetic tribunals. Adrian Stephen, who worked for the N-CF as an observer at tribunals, found them singularly biased and undemocratic. He observed that 'it would have been asking much of half a dozen grocers, haberdashers and retired colonels, to rise above the general body of mankind to such a height as to behave with reasonable tolerance'.[8]

More than six thousand conchies were refused exemption, court-martialled and sent to military prisons. There they endured considerable privation. They slept on plank beds in tiny cells, were prohibited from communicating with their fellow prisoners and from sending or receiving letters; rations were meagre and lacked nutrition. Some prisoners became mentally ill; others, including Clifford Allen, one of the founders of the N-CF, died prematurely, weakened by years in prison. Faced with potential imprisonment, far from being cowards, conscientious objectors exhibited strength of purpose and commitment to a moral cause.

Bunny could have applied for exemption on medical grounds. As Connie observed, his eyesight was compromised and he had to turn his head in order to look to the side. This would probably have disbarred him from active service or even ambulance work. But there is no evidence that this course of action occurred to him. It is characteristic that he would, like Maynard, have chosen to make a stand for what he believed in, and that as an 'outsider' this choice would represent the minority view.

The early months of 1916 were filled with uncertainty: when would Bunny receive his call-up papers? When would he go before the tribunal? Would he be sent to prison? Constance faced renewed anxiety about her son. But Bunny and Duncan decided the best scheme was to get on with life, and they soon had a

---

[8] Adrian Stephen, 'The Tribunals', in *We Did Not Fight*, p. 384.

vague plan to become fruit farmers, and thus, as they thought, fall into the category of undertaking work of national importance. The fruit farm, located at Wissett, near Halesworth in Suffolk, had belonged to a cousin of Duncan's mother. She died in 1915, and as a result her executor, Duncan's father, was looking for a tenant.

In the meantime, Bunny sent his application for military exemption to his local tribunal at St Pancras and began writing a story based on his experiences at Sommeilles. Beginning to make positive plans for the farm, Bunny informed Constance that he proposed to keep poultry but asked her for general instructions regarding when to sew crops. He had always been keen on growing vegetables and foraging for food, but had no experience as a fruit grower and smallholder. Duncan had no idea at all. It was Maynard who influenced their decision to become farmers, for he assured them they stood a better chance of exemption if they were working on the land. Aware that he would have to rely on Duncan and Vanessa to finance the enterprise, Bunny determined to do the lion's share of work in return for his keep.

Wissett is a small village situated within a river valley. It consists of a single main street occupied by cottages and a church, although when Bunny and Duncan lived there, it also had two public houses. Wissett Lodge is located half a mile from the village, on a ridge overlooking the valley. According to the present owners, the house dates back to the sixteenth century, but to Bunny it seemed like an early Victorian house, for it contained numerous small, dark rooms, the windows masked by both a magnificent wisteria and an enormous ilex. From the outset, his plans were grandiose: he proposed growing several hundredweights of potatoes, keeping a large flock of geese and a hundred hens.

While making Wissett Lodge habitable, Bunny stayed nearby at the Swan Inn. Suffering from a cold, Duncan was, at Vanessa's insistence, temporarily confined to bed in London. Meanwhile, Constance had again embarked on a frenzy of activity on behalf of her son, writing letters to anyone whom she felt could be of influence as a character witness at the tribunal. This irritated Bunny so much that he wrote what was for him an unusually tetchy letter, telling Constance that Sydney Olivier would not be the faintest use and that no one would have heard of J.A. Hobson. He added, 'I think your [sic] more likely to spoil my chances by making me nervous than wake me up to the seriousness of my position'.[9]

While Duncan languished in London, Bunny was happily employed. Having moved into the Lodge, he set about restoring the neglected farm. The currants had suffered from lack of pruning and been attacked by mites. The numerous empty bee hives, in which the previous incumbents had been left to die, required thorough disinfecting. Bunny was particularly content as he had been joined by Barbara Hiles, the petite bobbed-haired artist with whom he had started a flirtatious correspondence in France. Although she spent the nights at the local inn ('to keep the right side of the village gossips'), her days were spent with Bunny at the Lodge.[10] This low-key romance marked the beginning of a lifelong friendship in which they would casually pick up the strings of their love affair from time to time. With typical Bloomsbury candour, Bunny felt the need to communicate his various *amours* to Duncan, announcing that Barbara was

---

[9] DG/CG, The Swan Inn, Wissett, 'Thursday' [?March] [1916] [HRRC].
[10] DG/CG, Wissett Lodge, 'Sunday' [March 1916] [HRRC].

presently ensconced and at Easter he expected Ruth Baynes to appear. Bunny loved Duncan dearly, but he needed women, was fascinated by them, and his ego required the regular burnishing that only a new love affair could bring. Duncan hoped that when he moved to Wissett, he would have Bunny to himself.

Women liked Bunny because he admired them and valued their intellects. According to his daughter, Frances Garnett, his seduction of a woman 'would happen in a very romantic way – around actually talking ideas'.[11] He was also physically attractive, strong and muscular. But it was the singular way in which he focussed on the object of his attention which was particularly beguiling. One former lover told him that the reason women found him so attractive was 'the rapid turn of your head!'[12] As Frances Partridge observed, when Bunny looked at someone, 'it was characteristic of him to turn his whole head and blue gaze swiftly towards them, until his chin touched his shoulder'.[13] He not only dazzled women with his blue gaze, but also, and perhaps unusually for a man at this time, sought to take care with what he liked to call 'the lineaments of satisfied desire', an echo of William Blake's lines: 'What is it women in men require? / The lineaments of gratified desire.'[14]

Duncan eventually arrived at Wissett in March 1916 and in early April Vanessa came accompanied by her children, Julian

---

[11] Frances Garnett interviewed by the author, May 2008.

[12] Barbara Mackenzie-Smith/DG, King Edward VII Hospital for Officers, Beaumont Street, London, 4 December 1972 [Northwestern].

[13] Frances Partridge, *Everything to Lose: Diaries 1945–1960* (London: Victor Gollancz, 1985; Phoenix paperback edition, 1997), p. 118.

[14] DG, *Flowers*, p. 19; the words are misquoted from William Blake's poem 'The Question Answered'.

and Quentin, and the servants, Blanche and Flossie. With the farm to manage and an uncertain future, they decided the best philosophy was to assume they would be installed for the duration. Bunny and Duncan discovered their tribunal would be held at Halesworth rather than in London. Thus, decisions regarding their requests for exemption were further delayed, giving cause for optimism. As Bunny told Constance, 'Every delay is so much to the good as the best informers believe the War will be over this autumn or late summer'.[15] At Wissett, however, war seemed closer than in London. One starlit night they saw a Zeppelin looming over the house; on another occasion, hearing a low whining noise, Bunny jumped out of bed and rushed out onto the lawn, where he saw a long dark outline in the sky and subsequently heard bombs dropping nearby at Wangford.

'What an amazing book I could make out of the Wissett episode', Bunny wrote to Constance a year later. 'Duncan dyeing the fowls blue, & then the time when we picked 60 bunches [of daffodils] containing twelve flowers & packed them up & cycled 20 miles to Norwich, sold them with the greatest difficulty for 4 shillings, had a lunch which cost us six shillings, & the innkeeper charged us 2/ – for the use of the bicycle'.[16] In some respects this period at Wissett was idyllic, despite the military tribunals overshadowing them. Their happiness derived from relative independence, so that Bunny could indulge a nascent passion for farming and Duncan and Vanessa could continue to paint. Even their inexperience as farmers did not get them down. Bunny spent hours poring over Board of Agriculture manuals to little avail. In cold weather they brought all the rabbits indoors,

---

15 DG/CG, Wissett, 3 April [1916] [HRRC].
16 DG/CG, Charleston [c. late June] [?1917] [HRRC].

creating chaos. One of the doe rabbits was found to have a penis, but no testicles, their new puppy had nits, and Bunny was covered with a rash, resulting from a plague of fleas. The farm seemed to grow before their eyes: they discovered additional orchards in corners of the village which they didn't know existed and the numbers of blackcurrant bushes threatened to overwhelm them. Fortunately Constance came to stay, full of valuable suggestions about poultry and vegetables. Edward visited too, pronouncing Wissett a jolly place.

They received a continuous stream of visitors, Wissett becoming a country outpost of Bloomsbury. Clive Bell and his mistress, Mary Hutchinson, visited finding the fleas intolerable. They also received an improbable visitor in the shape of Ottoline Morrell, who found the house 'dark and damp and exceedingly untidy', although she assumed a brave face, resolving that 'untidiness in sunshine does not matter'. She noted that Bunny 'has quite the look of a farm labourer now'.[17]

Finding it depressing to have twenty empty bee hives, Bunny set about purchasing bees, asking Constance to give him the bee-keepers bible, Simmins's *Modern Bee Farm* for his birthday. To his horror, on his twenty-fourth birthday Bunny found all his bees dead from Isle of Wight disease. He spent the day dejectedly burning the frames and dead bees. Later that summer, with financial help from Maynard, Bunny purchased Italian bees, 'lovely yellow banded creatures', and informed Constance that he seriously considered going in for bee farming after the war. 'I believe I have a natural aptitude', he told her. Bunny became increasingly absorbed in bee-keeping, enjoying practising

---

[17] Robert Gathorne-Hardy, ed., *Ottoline at Garsington: Memoirs of Lady Ottoline Morrell 1915–1918* (London: Faber and Faber, 1974), p. 123.

scientific methods and learning a new discipline. But as the months passed, mounting anxiety about whether they would be allowed to remain at Wissett and constant exhaustion began to take their toll. 'You know what the evenings are', he wrote to his mother, 'one yawns writes down how many eggs were laid & stumbles off to bed by 10 o'clock.'[18] Bunny's temper began to emerge, partly as a result of his taking on the bulk of labour, but also because it was impossible to make long-term plans for the farm, which affected its viability. At this time Bunny took refuge in Constance's translation of *War and Peace*. 'I'm absurd', he wrote, '& live among that society as much as among my own friends.'[19]

Eventually they learnt that they would go before the Halesworth Tribunal on 4 May. Constance and Edward expected to attend, but Bunny kept them at arm's length. He was an adult; in the past twelve months he had grown up enormously and was full of resilience and independence. Moreover, Bunny did not want to appear tied to his mother's apron strings. He had marshalled his own support from influential people among his friends. He did not need his parents' associates to intercede on his behalf: Maynard Keynes, Adrian Stephen and Ottoline's husband, the MP Philip Morrell, would more than suffice. Nevertheless, at the last moment Constance asked Nellie to garner the support of her brother Carl, now an influential Quaker. She also wrote to Galsworthy, who sent in a letter testifying to Bunny being a conscientious objector 'of the most complete kind'.[20] Assuming he would be sent to prison, Bunny

---

[18] DG/CG, Wissett, 1 June [1916] [HRRC].
[19] DG/CG, 'Tuesday' [1916] [HRRC].
[20] DG/CG, Wissett, 'Monday night' [May 1916] [HRRC].

wrote to Edward, 'don't worry, don't worry, don't worry'. 'Nothing that one is afraid of is likely to hurt me.'[21]

A few days later Bunny wrote again to Edward describing the tribunal as 'a farce'.[22] His application had been turned down and now he had to prepare to appeal. As Vanessa told Virginia Woolf, 'The Tribunal consisted of perfectly bovine country bumpkins, whose skulls couldn't be penetrated at all. They would hardly listen to anything and one felt at once that it was quite hopeless.'[23] From the outset, the parochial farmers on the Tribunal were suspicious because Bunny and Duncan had only recently moved to Suffolk. Moreover, when Adrian mentioned that Bunny's mother was a lifelong pacifist and had visited Tolstoy in Russia, the Tribunal was nonplussed, assuming Tolstoy was a Russian town.

Their futures unresolved, Bunny and Duncan continued to work under the suspicious eyes of the locals. They tried not to draw attention to themselves: 'Yesterday was Sunday & we observe it by not working in the big orchards near the village.'[24] In the countryside, suspicion of outsiders prevailed, and spy stories proliferated, particularly in coastal areas. The previous year, when Duncan and Clive had stayed at Wittering on the Sussex coast, they had been pursued by local police, following reports that they spoke in a foreign tongue. Duncan and Bunny had both been required to produce their birth certificates to prove their indigenous status. At Henham, just a few miles from

---

[21] DG/EG, Wissett Lodge, 1 May [1916] [HRRC].

[22] DG/EG, Wissett Lodge, [May 1916] [HRRC].

[23] VB/Virginia Woolf, Wissett Lodge, 10 May [1916] [Berg], Marler, ed., *Letters of Vanessa Bell*, pp. 196–7.

[24] DG/CG, Wissett Lodge, 'Monday night' [1916] [HRRC].

Wissett and close to the sea, the schoolmaster had been persecuted under suspicion as a German agent, on the flimsy premise that his son had entertained a German friend in previous years.[25]

The appeal took place at Ipswich on 19 May. This time the atmosphere was entirely different. Maynard arrived looking extremely purposeful, clutching a large bag emblazoned with the royal cipher. He demanded their cases be heard as expeditiously as possible, 'as he had left work of the utmost national importance in order to attend'.[26] Philip Morrell also gave evidence on their behalf, and Bunny submitted a letter from the Prefect of the Marne praising his work with the Quakers. They were awarded non-combatant service: they would be soldiers, but would not have to fight. Although Maynard appealed immediately, the response would take several months in coming. Uncertainty and tension prevailed.

In June Lytton Strachey arrived for a weekend. Bunny felt sure that Lytton's visit was 'as much to see me as to see any of the others'.[27] Initially feeling rather excluded from the tightly-knit triangular *ménage*, Lytton pondered whether it was 'their married state that oppressed me?' 'But then', he added, 'were *they* married? – Perhaps it was their *un*married state.' Lytton's record of the weekend is preserved in an autobiographical fragment in which one particular passage suggests that his relationship with Bunny had hitherto progressed beyond flirtation. 'Perhaps if I could have lain with Bunny', he reflected, 'and then I smiled to think of my romantic visions before coming [to Wissett] – of a

[25] See Pamela Horn, *Rural Life in England in the First World War* (Dublin: Gill & Macmillan, 1984), p. 37.

[26] DG, *Flowers*, pp. 122–3.

[27] DG, *Flowers*, p. 118.

recrudescence of that affair, under Duncan's nose'.[28] Certainly Lytton found Bunny most attractive, and his recollections reveal something of the sexual potency which Bunny exuded. As Lytton chattered with Bunny outside, he found himself wanting to 'take hold of his large brown bare arm. *That* I knew was beautiful.' Feeling progressively melancholy, Lytton later walked with Bunny in the dusk: 'He was so calm and gentle, and his body was so large, with his shirt (with nothing under it) open all the way down – that I longed to throw myself onto him as if he were a feather-bed.'[29]

Lytton also captured the complexity of Bunny's character, the mixture of animal-magnetism and shyness, 'his charming way', 'his sympathy' his ability to amuse, and 'how shy and distrustful of himself he was in company'. 'Without any difficulty', Lytton continued, 'I stretched out my hand and put it into his breast [...]. We came nearer to each other, and with a divine vigour, embraced [...]. We kissed a great deal, and I was happy. Physically, as well as mentally, he had assuaged me. That was what was so wonderful about him – he gave neither too little nor too much'.[30] This encounter occurred in the context of Lytton's own confused state: he had fallen in love with the artist Dora Carrington (always known as Carrington), and felt unable to share his feelings with anyone except Bunny, to whom he confided in the garden at Wissett. Like others later on, Lytton turned to Bunny certain of his innate sympathy. Bunny expressed

---

[28] Lytton Strachey, 'Monday June 26th 1916' in Michael Holroyd, ed., *Lytton Strachey by Himself* (London: William Heinemann, 1971; Abacus, 2005), p. 185.

[29] Ibid., p. 201.

[30] Strachey, 'Monday June 26th 1916', p. 204.

this sympathy in a way in which he knew Lytton would understand. 'The darling!' Lytton recalled, 'How beautifully he had smoothed me down!'[31] 'You are a blessed creature to find in this world', he wrote to Bunny afterwards.[32]

Between comforting friends and harvesting blackcurrants, Bunny snatched moments to write, although reading *War and Peace* he despaired of ever achieving anything satisfactory. On 19 September Bunny wrote to Constance: 'All has been chaos & confusion.'[33] The Board of Agriculture man (Mr Watling, a local farmer) had visited Wissett to assess whether they could be considered to be undertaking work of national importance. He subsequently sent a damaging report refusing to recommend the continuation of their work at Wissett to the Pelham Committee, a committee established to assist the Tribunals in selecting suitable work for the applicants. He concluded that Bunny and Duncan were doing the work of two women, although the farm had been worked by two men, a boy and a woman before the war. 'The mysterious atmosphere of one of Conrad's tales has descended on us', Bunny told Frankie. 'The whole Pelham Committee & Central Tribunal believe that we were mysterious young men of means who had established themselves in a large country house with ten footmen and two mistresses apiece & spent our time shooting pheasants and entertaining the upper classes with champagne at breakfast [...]. The whole thing is typically English isn't it?'[34] But as Bunny informed Constance, a resolution had been found. Vanessa had taken a house at Firle in

---

[31] Strachey, 'Monday June 26th 1916', p. 204.

[32] GLS/DG, 67 Belsize Park Gardens, Hampstead, 1 July [1916] [Princeton].

[33] DG/CG, Wissett Lodge, 19 September [1916] [HRRC].

[34] DG/F Birrell, Wissett Lodge, 20 September [1916] [Northwestern].

Sussex, where Bunny and Duncan would work for a local farmer. Ever the optimist he added, 'I have a thousand plans of course already'.[35]

---

[35] DG/CG, Wissett Lodge, 19 September [1916] [HRRC].

Chapter Nine

'The diary habit has come to life at Charleston.' (Virginia Woolf)[1]

Vanessa had taken on the lease of Charleston Farmhouse, an attractive four-square building sitting beneath Firle Beacon on the Sussex Downs. She left Wissett in September 1916, taking the children back to London, while Duncan cleared up the Suffolk house and Bunny set off for Charleston accompanied by Barbara Hiles and Carrington. In his distinctly civilian yellow corduroy coat and breeches, he felt self-conscious on the train to Lewes, surrounded by uniformed men. The three companions decided to walk from Lewes to Charleston, but as dusk fell they turned off to Asheham to seek the hospitality of Leonard and Virginia Woolf. Finding the house in darkness and its inhabitants away, they decided nevertheless to spend the night there. Bunny shinned up a drainpipe, letting himself in through a back window.

---

[1] Anne Olivier Bell, ed., *The Diary of Virginia Woolf Volume I: 1915–19* (London: The Hogarth Press, 1977; Penguin Books 1979), p. 93; entry for Thursday 3 January 1918 but referring to Christmas 1917.

The trio thought nothing of snuggling into the same bed for warmth, Bunny in the middle. Although he and Barbara were lovers, Bunny also fancied himself in love with Carrington. But she was in love with Lytton Strachey and afterwards wrote to Bunny deflecting his declarations of love: 'I am sorry to be so solidly virtuous', she said, 'But I still maintain it is quite impossible to talk seriously, or make love with another person in the same bed'.[2] In an 'autobiographical fragment' Bunny alleged that he and Carrington later became lovers, but there is no evidence of this, and at different times he furnished conflicting accounts on the subject.[3]

Barbara and Carrington returned to Lewes, and Bunny settled into a temporary, but solitary existence, at the Ram Inn, at nearby Firle. Alone at Wissett, Duncan was miserable: everything reminded him of Bunny. He was also remorseful, apologising to Bunny for having been selfish during their last days together, presumably because Barbara had been there as well. Bunny was lonely too. 'The longer I am away from you', he

---

[2] D. Carrington/DG, 3 Gower Street, London, 'Tuesday evening' DG gives as 11 October 1916 but the Tuesday was in fact 10 October], in David Garnett, ed., *Carrington: Letters and Extracts from Her Diaries* (London: Jonathan Cape, 1970; Oxford University Press 1979) p. 45.

[3] For example, in 1966 he told Diana Mosley that he had been in love with Carrington (Diana Mosley/Deborah Duchess of Devonshire, Temple de la Gloire, Orsay, 7 April 1966, in Charlotte Mosley, ed., *The Mitfords: Letters Between Six Sisters* (London: Fourth Estate, 2007; Harper Perennial ,2008), p. 456), whereas two years later he told Frances Partridge he had not (DG/Frances Partridge, Moby Dick, 12 March 1968 [KCC]). In an interview in 1972 he stated, 'I was rather in love with her to start with but she had too many other fish to fry' (DG Interviewed by James Mellen, 1 March 1971 (BL: Sound Archive).

wrote to Duncan, 'the more I feel that even temporary absence from you is intolerable.'[4]

Having assumed their trespass at Asheham remained unde-tected, Bunny was surprised to receive a letter to the contrary from Carrington. They had been seen by a local resident who reported to the Woolfs that their house had been broken into. According to Carrington, 'Virginia was in rather a panic as strange people had broken in, eaten all the food and *moved the beds*!!!!' 'Of course', she added, 'I knew at once it was a fabrication about the beds being moved.'[5] Bunny, whose tenacious adherence to the principle of truth often backfired, compounded the situation by confessing his involvement to Virginia, raking up the dust after it had settled and thus blotting his copybook with her for some time.

From the outset Bunny loved Charleston, but he had little time to execute his plans to cultivate the garden and tend bees, as he began work for Mr Hecks straight away. He soon discovered that working for someone else was entirely different to working for oneself. He was employed pulling mangels, a gruelling and back-breaking job involving hours stooping in muddy fields. Although Hecks was only four years Bunny's senior, their relations remained formal. Whilst Bunny was clearly a 'gentleman', Hecks's attitude was that of a yeoman farmer towards his labourer. He made it clear that he was 'anxious to keep the conscientious objector rather quiet'. 'I am', Bunny explained, 'a young man come to learn farming.'[6]

The arrival of a strong young farm-hand might well have aroused suspicion, especially as there was only a tiny minority of

[4] DG/D. Grant, The Ram, Firle, [October 1916] [HG].

[5] D. Carrington/DG, 'Friday' [13 October 1916], in DG, ed., *Carrington*, p. 45.

[6] DG/CG, The Ram, Firle, 'Friday night' [6 October 1916] [HRRC].

conscientious objectors working in agriculture. Moreover, in Sussex the war was omnipresent, military camps proliferated and gunfire could be heard across the Channel. Families were losing their men-folk to war and anti-conchie feeling was rife. The views of the headmaster of the village school at nearby Fletching were typical: 'the papers are full of the applications for exemption that are coming before the Tribunals and the miserable excuses put forward make one's blood boil to think Englishmen are so degenerate.'[7] Bunny and Duncan kept a low profile, travelling the back lanes from Charleston to work. At the farm they were periodically scrutinized by plain-clothes policemen, checking they were not shirking their labours.

Initially, the triangular bond between Vanessa, Bunny and Duncan held reasonably firm. Bunny became fond of Vanessa's boys, establishing lifelong friendships with both. He gave Julian a copy of Richard Jefferies' *Bevis* for his ninth birthday, containing the map which he had drawn in 1904. Julian's younger brother, Quentin, when teased by one of the servants about 'Uncle Bunny', retorted: 'Now you know Trissie Bunny isn't really my uncle quite well', adding, 'Do you know what he is? He's my bosom friend.'[8] Quentin later described Bunny at this time as a 'shy youth but very attractive'; 'a tall, rather clumsy, but very athletic-looking young man', referring to 'the sculptural splendour' of his body.[9] Farm work helped Bunny to achieve this

[7] Caroline Dakers, *The Countryside at War 1914–18* (London: Constable, 1987), p. 106.

[8] D. Grant, Diary, Thursday January [1918] unpublished MS [HG].

[9] Quentin Bell, obituary of David Garnett, *Royal Society of Literature: Reports for 1979–80 and 1980–81* (London: Royal Society of Literature, 1981), p. 45.

physique, a physique which he took pride in maintaining well into his sixties.

Bunny and Duncan established an unvarying routine in which they left for work at 7.30, returning at 12.00 for lunch, finishing work at 5.00. Constance, who visited Charleston in late October, observed that Bunny 'looks a perfect picture of a young farmer – in his velveteen coat & his gaiter & his mild sunburnt face'. In contrast she thought Duncan looked very white.[10] At Charleston Bunny established a vegetable garden in which he worked all day on Sundays. Perhaps this gave him the idea to write a gardening manual, based on Alfred Gressent's *Le Potager Moderne*. 'Do you think', he asked Edward, 'a publisher would take the sort of little book I propose because I could turn it out very quickly.'[11] Bunny thought a condensed version of Gressent would provide the English market with a book for the domestic gardener, and that it would help people to produce twice as much food.

After the mangel harvest, Bunny and Duncan were immediately set to threshing, equally tiring and repetitive work. As Bunny told Constance, 'I throw a sheaf every second with my prong off the stack to a man who cuts string & pitches it to a man who lets it into the mouth of the machine. Another man on the stack throws the sheaves to me. So we go hour after hour. The wind blows the thick spray from the steam engine over us, the dust grimes our faces & things clog up our eyes.'[12] Having expected to learn farming, Bunny was surprised to be allocated the most unskilled manual work, including dung-carting in

---

[10] CG/EG, Charleston, 'Friday' [postmark 26 October 1916] [Xerox, R. Garnett: location of original letter unknown].

[11] DG/EG, Charleston, Firle, Sussex, [1916] [HRRC].

[12] DG/CG, Charleston [December 1916] [HRRC].

weather so cold that icicles hung from the horses' whiskers.

He managed to escape occasionally for a weekend in London or at The Cearne. In February 1917 when Frankie returned briefly from France, he and Bunny were so delighted to see each other that they talked non-stop from five in the afternoon until two in the morning. Bunny had a new admirer, the Bloomsbury mathematician Harry Norton, who seems to have fallen for Bunny just as James and Lytton had, and in his eagerness for Bunny's affection, followed the same pattern of rebuffed pursuit. 'There are a thousand questions', he wrote to Bunny, 'one would like to know the answer to – when you're coming – How long you'll be here – whether you'll be alone – whether you'll be nice to me.' 'Shall I dare to make love to you?'[13]

Working steadily at Gressent, Bunny wished he had time to write the novel constantly at the back of his mind. Lytton's comment that Laurence Sterne had written nothing until he was forty-five was hardly reassuring. But the relentless nature of farm work was beginning to take its toll. For Duncan, the effects were largely physical: he lost weight and felt run-down. Bunny, on the other hand, suffered emotionally, particularly as he felt trapped by the enforced nature of their work, and by being confined with Duncan at Charleston. It was the usual problem: if he and Duncan were going to get along, Bunny required the stimulation of diversions and other love affairs. And so, on a rare foray to London in September 1917, Bunny lost no time in wooing Alix Sargant-Florence, a young woman he had met briefly at the Caroline Club in February 1915. He decided, at that first meeting, that Alix was 'one of the women for whom I could feel

---

[13] HTJ Norton/DG, 46 Gordon Square, 25 March 1917 [Northwestern].

raging passion'.[14] The fact that Alix was in love with James Strachey was only a minor inconvenience, as James appeared beyond her reach, himself in love with Noel Olivier.

Alix was striking: nearly six feet tall and stick-thin, she had what Frances Partridge described as a 'Red Indian profile', together with bobbed thick dark hair and 'level grey eyes'.[15] She also possessed a first-rate brain, was highly inquisitive and loved an argument. Like Bunny, she had received little in the way of formal education, until she attended Bedales, hardly the most formal of schools. Like Bunny, she had travelled to Russia. Alix had studied art at the Slade, but disliking this experience, read modern languages at Newnham College, Cambridge, completing her studies in 1914. She was Bunny's exact contemporary, and unusual, even among his circle of independent women, in eschewing any degree of dependency on men.

In his autobiography Bunny described their relationship as 'half friendship, half love-affair'.[16] On his side, at least, it was more: he completely fell for Alix. She was initially put off from having a physical relationship with him, for he took her to Pond Place, where the squalor of his room so disgusted her that she refused to go there again. When entertaining his lovers in London, Bunny was forced to choose between the squalid room at Pond Place and Duncan's flea-infested studio in Fitzroy Street, where on one occasion Bunny killed thirty-six bugs. Perhaps for this reason, Alix preferred Bunny to join her at her mother's country house, Lord's Wood, near Marlow, in Buckinghamshire.

---

[14] DG, Journal, Tuesday [16 February 1915] [Northwestern].

[15] Frances Partridge, *Memories* (London: Victor Gollancz, 1981; Robin Clark paperback edition, 1982) p. 79.

[16] DG, *Flowers*, p. 42.

In response to Alix's first such invitation, Bunny drafted an emotional letter, attempting to explain his feelings for Duncan, and where she would fit into the scheme of things. Mostly it reveals Bunny's confused state of mind. It reads:

> Duncan is very much in love with me, & if I don't say I am in love with him it is not because I feel less for him than he does for me. I love him & am absolutely dependent on his love. I have never been so happy in my life as in his society. It is the thing of the first importance – the air I breathe – But in spite of that I am starved don't laugh at me – it's ridiculous I know. I am starved partly by the war, as everybody is – & partly because none of the things I secondarily want are present.
>
> I want something else [...]. I have hunted for it of course – but there are not many people on the cards to supply it – or anxious to. Another man couldn't – & most women are absolutely impossible [...]. But of course none of the things I've said are really what prepossess me in your favour. You do that partly [by] your looks, partly because I can tell you the truth, chiefly I think because you are the reverse of what is called feminine.[17]

Did Bunny mean he was attracted by Alix's androgynous appearance? Or did he mean that he appreciated her forthright intellectualism? Bunny and Alix's love affair, if it could be so called, fell quickly into a pattern where she would arrange to meet Bunny and then change her mind. The chief problem was James, for she would drop everything in order to be with him.

[17] DG/Alix Strachey, part letter [October 1917] [not sent] [Northwestern].

Alix liked Bunny as a lover but wanted little more; however, her periodic hesitations and retreats fuelled Bunny's ardour, so that when they were together he was inclined to be too intense, whereas she wanted a light-hearted love affair, free from expectations. She told Bunny she wanted something 'cheerful, <u>cheerful</u>, <u>cheerful</u> – & perhaps mildly exciting – & not in the least absorbing – &, if anything, a joke; but nice'.[18] In December 1917 she invited Bunny to Tidmarsh Mill, the home of Lytton Strachey and Carrington. It was not the warmest invitation, as Alix was clearly at a loose end with James otherwise engaged and was absolutely blunt about this fact. Bunny joined her there, a few days before Christmas, but, as he commented wryly in his journal, this was after she had 'thrown me over twice and changed back at the last minute'.[19]

Now passionately in love with Alix, Bunny was ready to jump when she summoned him. This level of uncertainty was terrible for Duncan, who needed time to prepare himself emotionally for Bunny's absences, and was anyway paralysed with jealousy. Believing Bunny was keeping things from him, Duncan took to prying into Bunny's letters, and even prised open a locked drawer in which they were kept. Alix, in turn, embellished her letters to Bunny with remarks designed to taunt Duncan, which only intensified his jealousy.

While Bunny believed his relationship with Alix enhanced his love for Duncan, Duncan could only perceive Alix as a rival. His periodic outbursts and prolonged bouts of jealousy tested Bunny's patience to such an extent that on one occasion he lost

18 AS-F/DG, 60 Frith Street, 'Thursday' [October 1917] [Northwestern].
19 DG, Journal, Saturday 22 December [1917] unpublished MS [Northwestern].

control and hit Duncan. And so their relationship adopted a pattern where Duncan's jealous outbursts were followed by contrition and remorse and Bunny's absences with Alix resulted in tender reconciliations. But these periods of calm could not be sustained. In late December they embarked on an even more elaborate *pas de deux* when almost simultaneously the two men began to confide in separate journals, confidences nevertheless designed to be secretly read by each other. Read together, these journals not only reveal their relationship from both points of view, but also form, as they were designed to, a silent dialogue between the two men, where emotions were batted back and forth like a ball across a table. But Bunny was also scratching away in another journal, one which he kept secret from Duncan.[20]

In January 1918 Bunny recorded (in the more public of his two diaries) that Duncan 'seemed to make demands on my strength. He had a definite attitude of expectation, he would thrust forward the whole time his relation to me. I wanted to have nothing expected of me.'[21] The situation was becoming intolerable. Now, whenever Bunny planned to see Alix, Duncan became hysterical, on one occasion threatening suicide. While Bunny felt restless and tired and could see no way out, Duncan could not find a way through his jealousy. Vanessa wrote to Maynard, telling him 'there have been such storms within for the last month or two', adding, 'I don't think one can go on indefinitely with such constantly recurring crises'.[22] Bunny also turned to Maynard, whom he knew understood Duncan better than

---

[20] This journal is recorded henceforward as 'DG, Journal (1917–18)'.

[21] DG, Journal, Tuesday 15 January [1918] unpublished MS [Northwestern].

[22] VB/JMK, Charleston, 8 February [1918] [KCC], in Marler, ed., *Letters of Vanessa Bell*, p. 210.

most. He had tried to talk to Vanessa, but thought that 'women don't understand & can't understand the relation between two men'.[23] The situation existed partly because Duncan could not understand the relation between a man and a woman.

It was probably at this time that Bunny vented his frustration in a poem entitled 'Trouble':

What is the matter with this house
Where my poor heart would live at ease and sleep?
The spider weaves at peace, the silent mouse
Almost forgets his fears to play bo-peep
Behind the kitchen chairs. We are not thus,
We eat nor sleep, nor scarcely even live.
What is the matter with this house – or us?
What is there wanting? What offering must I give?[24]

Bunny began to think the only solution was to leave Charleston and go to Russia with the Quakers. Duncan, who could not countenance being abandoned, became increasingly unhinged, one morning springing upon Bunny and spitting at him. Bunny felt he had to leave in order to diffuse the situation, and because he could see that Vanessa was also adversely affected by the prevailing atmosphere. As he concluded in the final verse of 'Trouble':

What is the matter? If we so ill together
Within its walls can live, let us walk out
And find in the hoarfrost and rough weather
A fireside for our hearts, – the wind a clout

---

[23] DG, Journal (1917–18), Saturday [?26 January 1918] [Northwestern].
[24] DG, 'Trouble', MS [Northwestern].

Warmer than the cloak of love we tatter
And better than this house, where what's the matter?[25]

Bunny discussed the question of Russia with Robert Tatlock, an old friend from his period in France who had worked with the Quakers in Russia and was now in London. Returning to Charleston later than anticipated, Bunny found Duncan frantic, demanding to know who Bunny had slept with. They fought savagely, Bunny knocking down a shelf in the process. Afterwards they both began to cry, and 'feeling indescribably happy' 'lay locked in each others arms'.[26] 'After living with me for three years' [sic] Bunny reflected, 'Duncan hasn't yet discovered that [...] I am perfectly happy with him, if I am sometimes allowed to have the distraction of an affair with someone else'.[27] But scenes of this nature grew more frequent: lamps were over-turned, slippers flung through doors and boots tossed into the hallway. Bunny and Duncan both recorded ghastly days in their diaries. Bunny recognised this had much to do with the strain of working on the farm, and whenever he could, retreated into watching his bees. Duncan could sometimes see the absurdity of the situation: 'Alix in love with James & the self chosen wife of Bunny. Bunny living with me & a furious womaniser.'[28] Duncan did not, however, record that there was another ingredient in this curious mix: not only was Vanessa in love with him, but they had been having sex in the hope of conceiving a child. Bunny knew about this. In May 1915 Vanessa had confided the matter to

---

[25] DG, 'Trouble', MS [Northwestern].
[26] DG, Journal, 4 February [1918] [Northwestern].
[27] DG, Journal (1917–18), Sunday [?10 February] [1918] [Northwestern].
[28] Duncan Grant, Diary, 19 February [1918] [HG].

him, and was glad she had done so, because, as she told him afterwards

> you were so extraordinarily nice & I saw how generous & magnanimous a nature you have – & those are the most important qualities & the ones I care for most – You are not just pleased that people you like should be happy as most people are. You really mind when they're not & delight in it when they are. I think that's the most loveable quality any one can have.[29]

Bunny oscillated between hoping the situation with Duncan would improve and thinking he had better go to Russia. One evening, when Barbara Hiles was staying at Charleston, Bunny went to wish her goodnight. She gave him a friendly kiss, and he returned to the room he shared with Duncan, to find him in a jealous fury. 'Why', Bunny asked, had Duncan 'become accustomed to treat me like this when he would be ashamed to behave so to Nessa'?[30] The crises were escalating. When Bunny received a telegram from Tatlock summoning him to London, Duncan became extremely upset, believing Bunny would go to Russia. It transpired that Tatlock had recommended Bunny for work in *London* for the Friends' *Russian* Mission. However, Duncan accused Bunny of wanting to abandon him to the farm and again threatened suicide. Unable to take any more, Bunny collapsed in tears. He was physically and emotionally exhausted and felt that he and Duncan were 'like devils chained together by

---

[29] VB/DG, Eleanor Farm (Tonk's Studio) 18 May 1915 [HG].
[30] DG, Journal (1917–18), Friday [1918] [Northwestern].

their tails', that he was enslaved to it all.[31]

When Bunny felt that the world was 'absolutely at its blackest, deadliest most hellish pitch', he learned that Edward had found a publisher for his abridgement of Gressent.[32] Then Duncan was granted leave by the Central Tribunal to work half-days on the farm, giving him time to paint. Just as things seemed to be looking up, Alix informed Bunny that she was not remotely in love with him. Confronting Alix in London, Bunny found her steely and unfriendly. When she told Bunny that she felt 'absolute indifference' to him, his wounded pride turned rapidly to anger. In a scene which he described vividly in his private journal, he caught Alix by the neck and threw her to the ground. After telling him not to be so stupid, she politely invited him to tea. As always, Bunny's anger turned to remorse, and feeling ashamed, he rushed away. He would never again let his anger with a woman turn physical. He might wound verbally and was always dextrous in argument, but he would never lash out like this. Consumed with regret, Bunny returned to Charleston, to be comforted by Duncan and to learn that Vanessa was expecting a baby. 'Thinking about that', Bunny wrote in his journal, 'has been the one outlet for a pure & good emotion I have had.'[33]

---

[31] DG/JMK, Charleston, 2 March [?1918] [KCC].

[32] DG, Journal (1918) Monday [1918] [Northwestern].

[33] DG, Journal (1918) Thursday [1918] [Northwestern].

Chapter Ten

'Never try to write, but above all never have anything to do with publishing or the book trade.' (Edward Garnett's advice to his son)[1]

When he received a letter enquiring whether he would be available to work with the Friends in Russia, Bunny felt mixed emotions. He wanted to go but worried about leaving Duncan working for Hecks. Bunny's dilemma was, however, short lived, as 'Mr Secretary Balfour thought it undesirable that Mr Garnett should go to Russia at present & suggested that his name be omitted from the list'. Harry Norton thought the Garnetts' well-known terrorist sympathies influenced Balfour's decision, telling Bunny: 'you or your mother have been too friendly with the Bolshies'.[2]

In October 1918 Bunny wrote to Constance, 'Relief – oh blessed

---

[1] Quoted in David Garnett, *Never Be a Bookseller* (New York Alfred A. Knopf, 1929; Denby Dale: Fleece Press 1995) [unpaginated].

[2] H.T.J. Norton/DG, Friends' War Victims' Relief Committee, 104 Ethelburga House, 91 Bishopsgate EC2, 6 September 1918 [Northwestern].

relief. They have almost stopped fighting & I can't help believing that one will be able to live happily again occupied with decent things & not, as seemed probable a few weeks ago always be fighting with one's fellows for things that are conceded everywhere but in wars & nightmares.' This statement could equally have applied to Bunny's domestic situation, although in recent months the atmosphere had improved at Charleston, Bunny and Duncan united in caring for Vanessa's wellbeing and keeping matters as tranquil as possible. On the back of a letter to Edward, Bunny scribbled possible names for the baby, including Bulgaria, Havana, Lucretia, Linolia, Titania, Cornelia, Perdita, Leda, Angelica and Lesbia.[3] Evidently he did not contemplate the birth of a boy.

Meanwhile, Bunny was enthused by the success of Lytton Strachey's biographical essays *Eminent Victorians*, which had become an overnight sensation. 'It is amusing', he commented, 'to have a real booming success among our circle'.[4] He was enraged, however, when he read Edward Marsh's Memoir of Rupert Brooke, published as an introduction to Brooke's *Collected Poems*. Bunny disliked the way Marsh white-washed his subject, absenting Brooke's homosexual friends (notably James Strachey and Duncan Grant) and most of the women with whom Brooke had love affairs. Bunny hated what he considered to be false hero-worship, the way Brooke had been turned into a hero and martyr.

On 11 November 1918 when the Armistice was announced, Bunny and Duncan took the first train to London, where they found the streets crammed with revellers. At Montague Shearman's Adelphi flat, they joined in the celebrations with a

---

[3] DG/EG, Charleston, 30 June [1918] [Northwestern].
[4] DG/CG, Charleston, 27 October [1918] [HRRC].

multitude of friends including Maynard Keynes, Diaghilev, Lytton Strachey, Clive Bell, Roger Fry, Ottoline Morrell, Lydia Lopokova and D.H. and Frieda Lawrence. The war over, Bunny considered what he might do. 'I am distinctly in favour', he announced, 'of living in London and in such a way as to have a good deal of freedom & independence.'[5] Influenced by Vanessa and Duncan, Bunny proposed to become a picture dealer. It did not occur to him that he had neither experience of the commercial world nor any particular expertise in art, having only worked in the science laboratory and on the farm. His parents thought this proposal most unwise and that he would be reduced to 'forcibly feeding one's friends with pictures'.[6]

Nevertheless, Bunny pursued the idea. He wondered whether he should have a business partner and concluded that Frankie Birrell, who had worked at the V&A, was the obvious candidate. Frankie – who had no business experience and was hopeless with figures – was delighted with the idea. In a letter studded with emotion, he told Bunny that his main pleasure in life had been the few occasions when the two men had been together since working in France in 1915. He worried, however, about what would happen if they invested everything in the same venture and if his unrequited love for Bunny became intolerable to either of them. 'I am putting this down on paper now at a distance', Frankie wrote from France, 'because when I am with you, I know I should be falling too much in love with you to be able to put it clearly.'[7]

For the time being, Bunny's concerns turned to the impending

[5] DG/CG, Charleston [c. 14 November 1918] [HRRC].
[6] DG/D. Grant, The Cearne [?October] [1918] [HG].
[7] FB/DG, 53 rue de Rivoli, Paris, 21 December [1918] [Northwestern].

birth of Vanessa's baby. He and Duncan gave Vanessa their butter rations and Bunny was a reassuring presence chopping wood for the fires and providing vegetables from the garden. On Christmas Eve he went to fetch the doctor and at 2 o'clock on Christmas Day morning a baby girl was born. 'It is a queer little creature', he observed, 'very lovely and full of independent life.' 'It is a curious emotional experience', Bunny reflected, 'waiting for someone else's child to be born.'[8] Bunny wrote to Lytton Strachey, telling him Vanessa had given birth to a girl. 'My dearest cowboy', he wrote,

> Vanessa was safely delivered of a daughter at two o'clock this morning. [...]. It is extremely beautiful & not in the least what one is led to expect – that is to say not a wizened old man from Mr. Yeats, or a sort of skinned rabbit & boiled lobster – it is simply a very small very lovely naked human, with signs of great will power and intelligence [...]. Its beauty is the most remarkable thing about it. I think of marrying it: when she is twenty I shall be 46 – will it be scandalous?[9]

Although the last sentence does seem scandalous, it was a piece of light-hearted whimsy which Lytton (who confessed to being 'slightly rubbed the wrong way by simple domesticity, babies, & rattles') would have enjoyed.[10] It was a means of conveying an important piece of 'family' news without recourse to the usual details of baby's weight and duration of labour. Bunny's

[8] DG/CG, Charleston, Christmas Day [1918] [HRRC].

[9] DG/GLS, Charleston, Christmas Day [1918] [BL].

[10] GLS/DG, Ham Spray House, Hungerford, 20 September 1925 [Princeton].

outrageous proposal corresponds exactly in tone to his other letters to his 'dearest cowboy'. 'Will it be scandalous?' is gossipy and risqué, a verbal raised eyebrow which Lytton would have relished. It was a piece of Strachey-ese similar in tone to his earlier letter to James Strachey, proposing orgies. Above all it is a *gay* comment, a piece of badinage from one gay man to another, reminiscent of the homosexual poet Brian Howard's alleged remark when confronted with Bryan Guinness's baby son: 'My dear, it is so *modern* looking.'[11]

It was rapidly evident however, that baby Angelica was not thriving and was losing, rather than gaining, weight. Bunny telephoned Noel Olivier, a qualified doctor, who, unable to get away, sent Dr Marie Moralt. It transpired that the local doctor had recommended the baby be fed with orange juice and had prescribed dilute carbolic. Bunny busied himself cycling backwards and forwards to the Lewes chemist, and under a new regime Angelica began to flourish. Bunny stayed on until the end of January 1919, but London and independence beckoned. He took a job at Probsthain's Bookshop on Great Russell Street where he hoped to gain commercial experience.

Bunny persisted with the notion of becoming a picture dealer despite lingering doubts and parental opposition. He would rely on the advice of Vanessa, Duncan and Roger Fry, who would recommend up-and-coming artists. He would also have a monopoly of selling Duncan's work. Bunny assured his mother: 'Vanessa is extremely level headed and quite disinterested [...]. If she thought this scheme were likely to fail & involve me in

---

[11] Quoted in D.J. Taylor, *Bright Young People: The Rise and Fall of a Generation 1918–1940* (London: Chatto & Windus, 2007) p. 114.

continual horrors she would not encourage me in it.'[12] With no capital of his own, Bunny tried to raise funds from his friends. On Armistice night, Harry Norton agreed to help, but in the cold light of January changed his mind. He thought the whole endeavour too risky and that Bunny was not a 'very suitable person to run it'.[13] He also believed the venture could only succeed if Bunny went into partnership with an experienced dealer, apparently disqualifying Frankie. Furthermore, Percy Moore Turner, the owner of the Independent Gallery in London where Duncan exhibited, was not pleased at the prospect of one of his artists being poached. Confronted with such obstacles Bunny decided it would be more pragmatic to run a bookshop.

'What I don't want to do', he informed Constance, 'is to embark hastily on something which however good in itself will completely sidetrack my life for several years'. Characteristically, Bunny did not want to be confined to one quarter, but needed to be able to scurry off in other directions at will. He thought a bookshop would at least enable him to retain some vestigial freedom, although, as he told Connie, 'I don't think it will be a roaring success ever!'[14]

A new love was on the horizon and Bunny was ready to be distracted. In the middle of January when he spent the weekend with his parents and Nellie at The Cearne, they received a visit from Rayne Garnett, the twenty-year-old daughter of Edward's brother Robert. Bunny had not seen her since she was a young child. Rayne, who worked as a gardener for the Duchess of

[12] DG/CG, Charleston [1919] [HRRC].

[13] H.T.J. Norton/DG, Merton House, Queen's Road, Cambridge [1919] [Northwestern].

[14] DG/CG [c. March] [1919] [HRRC].

Marlborough at Crowhurst in East Sussex, arrived clad in her gardener's garb of corduroy coat, breeches and gaiters. Disconcertingly, she confined her conversation almost exclusively to matters of pruning. Initially Bunny found both her directness & her facts rather off-putting, but nevertheless he sat up to talk with her when the others had gone to bed, and in consequence lay awake all night believing he had fallen in love. He found Rayne beautiful, similar in appearance to Rosalind Thornycroft, although more comely of figure, rather like one of Renoir's portraits of women. Still seeking plurality in his relationships, Bunny believed Rayne could offer everything he wanted and that he would find in her 'a sister, a lover, and so on'.[15] Courtship did not proceed smoothly. Bunny adopted a man of the world attitude, lecturing his cousin on the merits of both promiscuity and contraception. Although Rayne eventually capitulated and they became lovers, this was against stern parental opposition. Her father forbade her to visit Pond Place, fearing she would be tainted by the fact of Edward's and Nellie's cohabitation and by Bunny's contamination too.

Bookshop plans were hampered by Frankie's absence in France concluding his work for the Quakers. Bunny was so hard up that Maynard had taken pity upon him, buying him a smart suit, so that at least he might look the part of a businessman. Carrington also came to Bunny's sartorial rescue, sending him a parcel of clothes which had belonged to her brother Teddy, who had died in the war.

Bunny felt his life had reached a watershed, with the doors of Charleston closing and an uncertain future stretching ahead. He noticed that Duncan's feelings had changed. Although Bunny

---

[15] DG, Diary [1919] [mid-January 1919] [HG].

continued to receive letters and invitations from him, and on occasion they had sex, the warmth they once shared had dimmed. As Bunny reflected: 'Duncan is kindness itself & I think is rather worried about me & afraid I may be unhappy.'[16] Yet Bunny still clung to Charleston, spending weekends there and tending his bees. He foolishly orchestrated a situation in which he manoeuvred Rayne into the position of gardener-in-residence at Charleston, as if endeavouring to unite these two strands of his life, to bring his girlfriend into the extended Charleston family. Vanessa and Duncan were not Rayne's natural allies. Vanessa disparagingly described her as 'like a wooden figure out of Noah's Ark or an over-sized doll who has been on a farm'.[17] Duncan was disarmed by Rayne's eagerness to talk about Bunny, finding her openness embarrassing and misplaced. But, expressing a fear which Bunny found it hard to suppress, Duncan predicted that Bunny might 'get rather bored with her society when she becomes more & more dependent on yours'.[18]

With the bookshop on hold, Bunny resolved the only way to independence was to write, and to do so with an eye to popular success: 'With a thousand pounds in the bank one can do what one likes.'[19] He still saw something of Betty May and it was she who gave him an idea for the subject of a book, a 'sevenpenny shocker', which, he informed Edward, 'has no merit, form, style, or anything else', but which Bunny had dashed off in sixteen days. 'It's not simply for the servants' hall', he explained, 'but for

[16] DG, Diary [1919] 2 April [1919] [HG].

[17] VB/JMK, 9 March [1919] [KCC], quoted in Frances Spalding, *Duncan Grant* (London: Chatto & Windus, 1997), p. 216.

[18] D. Grant/DG, Charleston 'Thursday' [pmk 24 April 1919] [HG].

[19] DG, Diary [1919] Wednesday 9 April [1919] [HG].

the young who are ready to accept anything which they think is life.' 'Of course', he added, 'I will spare the name of Garnett the infamy of being on the title page.' Coming from a family where servants' halls were non-existent, it is ironic that Bunny's views about class were still somewhat shaped by this kind of stratification. But his was largely an intellectual snobbery defined in terms of taste and the kinds of books people read, rather than their social background.

Bunny called his seven-penny shocker "Dope-Darling". The story is about Roy, a medical student who is in love with his childhood friend, Beatrice, a qualified doctor. Roy has his eyes opened when he encounters a young night-club singer, Claire, who tells him things 'that no girl Roy had ever met would have said'.[20] Claire is a drug-addict who bears a striking resemblance to Betty May, with a nod to Lillian Shelley. Roy abandons Beatrice and marries Claire, mistakenly believing he can cure her of her addiction. She remains unstable and attempts suicide.

The story is cinematic in its use of melodrama, a verbal narrative resembling the flickering black and white silent films in the picture-houses of the time. Moreover it can also be read, alongside Sax Romer's novel *Dope* and D.W. Griffith's film *Broken Blossoms* (both 1919), against a background of a prevailing preoccupation with the ready availability of drugs, in which fears about the 'fairer sex' being seduced into a sub-culture of drugs were the focus of sensationalist newspaper headlines.

Much of this anxiety was fuelled by concerns about the growing independence of women and the blurring of boundaries between the young working women who smoked cigarettes

---

[20] Leda Burke [pseudonym, David Garnett], *Dope-Darling: A Story of Cocaine* (London: T. Werner Laurie Ltd [c. 1919]), p. 25.

and drank in bars and the *demi monde* of singers, actresses and prostitutes who smoked cigarettes and *worked* in bars. Bunny did not approach his subject from a moralistic or paternalistic viewpoint, but in satirising media headlines, he highlighted the plight of real women like Betty May who came up from the countryside to an unfamiliar urban world where they could easily be exploited by unscrupulous men. Bunny's *Dope-Darling*, however sensational, is closer in intention to Arthur Ransome's *Bohemia in London* (1907), where Ransome comments that artists' models (like Betty May) could provide 'rich material for novelists': 'Some have stories that read like penny novelettes.'[21]

Edward took the manuscript to the publisher T. Werner Laurie, who commented that he doubted it would be a bestseller, but offered to pay the author £15 on account of a 1½d per copy royalty, and to risk publishing it. By late July 1919 the proofs had been set up and the covers printed. Unfortunately the covers had to be printed a second time with the name 'Leda Burke' substituted for that of David Garnett. The advance publicity announced that *Dope-Darling* 'is a page torn from real life, by someone who has watched a similar tragedy from the inside'.[22] *The Times*, however, declared that the story 'revolts the reader without convincing him',[23] and the Irish Independent observed that although there was 'a romance interwoven with the more sordid side of the story' 'it is not a particularly elevating one'.[24]

---

[21] Arthur Ransome, *Bohemia in London* (Oxford: Oxford University Press, 1984), p. 74.
[22] T. Werner Laurie Ltd, 30 New Bridge Street, London, publication notice [1919] [HRRC].
[23] 2 October 1919.
[24] 6 October 1919.

Bunny's first published novel was timely: he had been sacked by Probsthains. He had not much enjoyed working there, but it had provided valuable experience. Bunny's abridgement of Gressent, *The Kitchen Garden and its Management* had also finally been published. He had condensed an enormous text into a pocket-sized book only slightly larger than a seed packet.[25] A *proto* 'Dig for Victory', the little book encouraged the British public to cultivate globe artichokes among other comparative exotica.

Bunny was beginning to find Rayne dull. 'She certainly seems to me a very nice creature', he persuaded himself in his diary, 'but though I am always glad to see her I can imagine greater excitement: it is the sort of pleasure one would get if one had a nice daughter'.[26] For all Bunny's relief at being involved with a straightforward young woman, she could not live up to Duncan. According to Rayne, writing many years later, Bunny let her down gently. She recognised, in retrospect, that she was 'too young and innocent, too ignorant and above all, too unintellectual and undeveloped to hold his affection permanently'.[27] But they remained friends and enjoyed one another's company over the years.

In May 1919 Bunny found his foothold at Charleston firmly undermined. He was used to coming and going, but one weekend he turned up to find he was not welcome. The house was full of

[25] *The Kitchen Garden and its Management: Abridged and Adapted from the Standard French Work of Professor Gressent with Additions by David Garnett* (London: Selwyn & Blount [1919]).

[26] DG, Diary [1919] 19 May [1919] [HG].

[27] Rayne Garnett Nickalls, extract from unpublished memoir 'The Time is Past & Gone' [Caroline White].

guests, and to make matters worse Bunny discovered the painter Edward Wolfe in Duncan's bed. The muddle arose because Duncan had sent Bunny a telegram to The Cearne, stating that the house would be full, but inviting him over once the guests had gone. Instead of forwarding the telegram, Constance sent Bunny a cryptic message which he misinterpreted as an invitation for the weekend. The chilly welcome and the presence of Wolfe combined to wound Bunny's pride and make him feel cuckolded. In tears, he told Duncan he never wanted to see him or come to Charleston again.

That night he slept in the paddock and then spent the weekend walking the Downs. On Monday, after Vanessa and her guests departed, Bunny enjoyed a happy day with Duncan and sat for his portrait. In his diary, Bunny recorded a 'confession', in which he admitted: 'I am an awful character', 'always attracted by something or other [...]. When he has something he wants he throws it away to run after something else.' 'If I were a decent character', he reflected, 'I should now be doing Science & married to Ruth.'[28] It is true that Bunny usually assumed the grass to be greener elsewhere, although he persuaded himself at this time that 'The thing which makes me happy is working hard, & being with someone who loves me & whom I love'.[29]

By July, Bunny had set about the business of obtaining a bookshop in earnest. The main problem was lack of capital, but Bunny hoped Frankie's father might be prevailed upon. Augustine Birrell was no fool and he asked Maynard Keynes whether he thought Bunny and Frankie had any business ability. Knowing they hadn't, Maynard conceived a plan. He thought Birrell

---

[28] DG, Diary [1919] Sunday night [1919] [HG].
[29] DG, Diary [1919] Sunday night [1919] [HG].

might be convinced if the venture included a third partner, one with extensive business experience. And so he called upon C.K. Ogden, who in 1916 had founded the highly successful *Cambridge Magazine*, and was looking for bookshop premises in London which would extend his business profile. In return, Ogden would allow the shop's proprietors free advertising in the magazine, but the shop would trade under the name 'Cambridge Magazine'. Frankie, still in France, was aghast at the prospective involvement of Ogden, whom he disliked intensely. The only option, as far as Bunny and Frankie were concerned, was to manoeuvre Maynard into changing his mind seemingly of his own accord, and for Maynard to consequently advise Birrell that the Cambridge Magazine proposal was not viable. 'Take any steps you can', Frankie wrote to Bunny from France, 'to put a *fait accompli* forward. But for God's sake avoid committing us to anything.'[30]

Bunny identified Ogden's tendency to make increasingly grandiose demands on his own terms, and decided to exploit this, by appearing to be a complete idiot and leading Ogden on step by step. The first measure was for Bunny to 'forget' to turn up for his initial meeting with Ogden. The second was to write to Maynard, after a meeting had finally taken place, seeming to approve of Ogden, while damning him with faint praise. To this end, Bunny wrote to Maynard: 'The advantage of association with Ogden is in free advertisement, but while we are of benefit to him in this way I think it is rather doubtful how much value his advertisement of us would be. He spoke as if he was anxious to form other connections of the same sort with London

---

[30] F. Birrell/DG, Mission Anglo-Américaine, 53 Rue de Rivoli, Paris [pmk 29 August 1919] [Northwestern].

booksellers as well as with us. That would destroy his value to us.'[31] To Constance Bunny wrote jokingly: 'I am developing into rather a sharp business man – I imagine in the strong silent American style.'[32]

Bunny's campaign worked: as he anticipated, Ogden's demands became so ridiculous as to be untenable. On 14 September Maynard wrote to Ogden informing him that he, Bunny and Frankie jointly 'came to the conclusion that in the circumstances it would be no good at present trying to pursue further the project'. 'Birrell & Garnett', he added, 'will therefore go ahead, I expect independently.'[33] As Ogden went on to abandon the Cambridge Magazine for a career as a psychologist, it was probably as well. Duncan commented to Bunny: 'It will be splendid if you become a real writer won't it with a book shop to fall back on.'[34] The situation worked out well in respect of Augustine Birrell's contribution too, for he put in £1,000. Although Bunny estimated they would need £2000 a year for two years, the start-up capital amounted to Birrell senior's £1,000 together with £200 from Constance and £100 from Edward.

Frankie remained in France, leaving Bunny to find suitable premises, but it proved impossible to find a shop at an affordable rent. Bunny therefore took a large ground floor front room at 19 Taviton Street, off Gordon Square. The building was in the hands of Margaret Bulley, a friend of Frankie's, and she let rooms to friends who lived there on a communal basis. Birrell & Garnett

---

[31] DG/JMK, 19 Pond Place [15 August 1919] [KCC].

[32] DG/CG, 19 Pond Place [?September] [1919] [HRRC].

[33] JMK/DG, 'copy of letter I've sent Ogden', Charleston, 14 September 1919 [Northwestern].

[34] D. Grant/DG, part letter [postmark 16 September 1919] [HG].

first opened its doors in late 1919 or early 1920. Although the shop was in a reasonably good location within Bloomsbury, it was not in the best position to attract the casual passer-by, and would have benefited from a closer proximity to other bookshops like Mudie and Probsthain. Frances Partridge, who later worked as the shop's assistant, recalled that the clientele was 'limited almost entirely to friends, and friends of friends, and were for the most part denizens of Bloomsbury, both physically and spiritually'.[35] Other similarly bookish clients included Joseph Conrad, who submitted one of the first orders, the artist John Singer Sargent and the poet Walter de la Mare. E.M. Forster was one of their best customers, responsible for two large orders: one from the state of Hyderabad for educational books, and the other to equip Palestine with terrestrial globes. Birrell & Garnett triumphed, too, when they were able to supply Bertrand Russell with all the books for his expedition to China in 1920, from existing stock.

In selecting their stock, Messrs Birrell and Garnett favoured eighteenth-century French and English literature, everything published by Leonard and Virginia Woolf's Hogarth Press and anything written by their friends. Frankie was particularly knowledgeable about the latest French literature, and of course Bunny promoted Russian literature, in his mother's translations. Their stock was bolstered by sets from their respective fathers' libraries, and in one coup they discovered that first editions of Henry James were still in print, issued a catalogue, and were deluged with orders from America. In many respects it was hard work. Bunny attended auctions of second-hand books, travelling backwards and forward to country sales. Catalogues had to be drawn up and issued, orders packaged, parcels sent. For all their

---

[35] Partridge, *Memories*, p. 75.

inexperience, Birrell & Garnett gradually established a reputation as serious booksellers. *The Bookman* commented that:

> It is a business which deals for the most part in old books, but the firm does not disdain new books of distinguished literary quality, and its catalogues are already such as to make one read them with respect [...]. One can tell the caliber of the partners by the quality of the notes which accompany the titles of the books which figure in their lists.[36]

As Augustine Birrell feared, neither Bunny nor Frankie were natural businessmen. Frankie found it embarrassing to sell books for profit. According to Bunny, he would exclaim, '"I cheated him quite successfully," after selling a second-hand book much below its real value but for more than we had paid for it'.[37] Early on, when Bunny sold a copy of Shelley's *Revolt of Islam* for £4, the customer returned it, pointing out that it had been inscribed by the author and offering to sell it back at the purchase price. Bunny was too proud to accept, but he learnt a lesson. He sometimes found himself doing the lion's share of work. Frankie would disappear to Paris, ostensibly on a book-buying expedition, but also to meet a lover who lived there. But Frankie's charm and affability contributed much to the unique character of Birrell & Garnett. Bunny generously attributed the shop's popularity to him:

> He had a quick sympathy and eager enthusiasm and was always able to help any customer in difficulties. But, most

---

[36] *The Bookman* (New York: George H. Doran Company) [undated magazine clipping, probably 1923].
[37] DG, *Flowers*, p. 204.

150

important of all, he charmed almost everyone who came into the shop so that they wanted to come again. What did it matter that his fingers made paw marks on the books? Or that he would do up his fly-buttons in the middle of a conversation about Gide, or scratch himself very thoroughly in intimate places of his anatomy, standing on one leg to do so more freely [...]. It was Frankie's personality which enabled us to keep the shop going and pay ourselves a pittance of three pounds a week each.[38]

Frances Partridge found Frankie a less benign presence, 'standing in the centre of the room like a fierce Aberdeen terrier, with an abrupt bark of "Yes? What d'you want?"' She added that 'manners were not his forte [...]. The result was that any casual customer attracted by the window display was quickly frightened away.'[39] Bunny, on the other hand, was sometimes too shy to serve a customer, his natural reserve in the face of strangers causing him to scurry behind the book shelves, or to force his nose more firmly between the pages of a book. Both partners spent as much time as possible reading the stock, Frankie casually flicking his cigarette ash here and there and prizing open uncut pages with a clumsy thumb. What they enjoyed most was 'always meeting interesting people' and the continuous 'good talk'.[40] It became quite a meeting place in Bloomsbury, a hub where friends could meet, flop down on a sofa and discuss the latest literary sensation; as Frances Partridge commented, it was 'a centre for friendliness and conversation'.[41]

---

[38] DG, *Flowers*, p. 204.

[39] Partridge, *Memories*, p. 75.

[40] DG, *Never Be a Bookseller*.

[41] Partridge, *Memories*, p. 75.

Part 3

RAY

Chapter Eleven

'The bride [...] was a more than ordinarily beautiful and agreeable woman [...]. In manner she was reserved almost to shyness, but perfectly self-possessed, and perfectly well-bred.'[1]

A respectable businessman by day, in the evenings Bunny still frequented London's Bohemia. Lytton Strachey commented that Bunny looked peaky – that he had been 'sitting up too late o'nights'.[2] He spent one night wandering the streets with Betty May, followed by a policeman. She remained as lovely and enigmatic as ever, although Bunny detected a new darkness around her eyes. A few weeks later he was surprised to be introduced to her husband, a man who had apparently reformed her and turned her into a housewife. 'For some reason', Bunny told Lytton, 'it squeezed my heart with pity far more to see her sober & settled than it had done when she had been lying about drugged & drunk.'[3]

---

[1] David Garnett, *Lady into Fox* (London: Chatto & Windus, 1922), p. 4.
[2] GLS/DG, Tidmarsh, 26 May 1920 [Princeton].
[3] DG/GLS, Birrell & Garnett [11 June 1920] [BL].

By May 1920 the shop was doing relatively well and Bunny was living above it, having taken one of the rooms. The household comprised Margaret Bulley, Bunny's Quaker friend Robert Tatlock (now editor of *The Burlington Magazine*), the novelist Ethel Sedgwick and an artist Cecily Hey (like Carrington, known by her surname). Residents had individual rooms and shared a sitting room. The establishment was presided over by a housekeeper, Mrs Speechley, who lived in the basement with the latest in a line of ailing husbands.

It was at this time that Bunny became better acquainted with Theadora Fordham, the daughter of former neighbours of the Garnetts at both Hampstead and Limpsfield. He had last seen Thea in 1914, when aged seventeen, she had surprised him at The Cearne by bestowing upon him 'two vehement child's kisses'.[4] Now twenty-three, she was, according to Bunny, 'a wild creature; at moments fierce, at others confiding'.[5] She was a home student at Oxford, where she played lacrosse for the university. But she wasn't a jolly-hockey-sticks sort of girl. Rather, she was sensitive, troubled and undecided about which direction life might take. She was also kindly and intelligent: someone said of her 'a crust shared with Thea would have a flavour'.[6] In the vacations, Thea lived with her parents in a Georgian house on Well Walk, Hampstead. She invited Bunny to visit her there, 'because the view from my bedroom is marvellous'.[7] But like Alix Sargant-Florence, Thea blew hot and cold, frequently muddling dates, missing assignations

---

[4] DG, Diary notes, April 1914 [unpublished MS] [Northwestern].

[5] DG, *Echo*, p. 261.

[6] Quoted by Mrs Julia Rhys, telephone conversation with the author, February 2010.

[7] T. Fordham/DG, 40 Well Walk, 11 July 1920 [HG].

or changing arrangements. 'My dear', she began a letter in April 1920, 'I really want to write you a long letter & tell you about every thing I feel about us – but I seem to be in such a completely undecided state of mind that what I may say tonight will probably be quite different to what I might say tomorrow.' Partly she worried that Bunny, now twenty-eight and five years her senior, was too much a man of the world for someone of her relatively sheltered upbringing. 'Remember', she wrote to him, 'you are talking to a child & that your world is quite new to her.'[8]

Thea was not the only person occupying Bunny's thoughts. A young artist, Rachel Alice Marshall, had moved into Taviton Street, and he could not help but enjoy her humour and sense of fun. Moreover she was a joy to tease. Known as 'Ray', she was oddly beautiful, olive-skinned, with high cheekbones, wide-set eyes, a mobile mouth and bobbed brown hair. Her body was lithe, with muscular, shapely legs conditioned by the long country hikes she enjoyed. Bunny thought her a 'woodland creature'[9]. She was the girl with whom he had danced a decade earlier at Crosby Hall. Bunny was delighted when Ray invited him for a weekend walk on the Downs near Chichester, along with Tatlock and Hey. On his return, he decided he was in love with her, recording in his diary in September 1920: 'Rachel has come to attract me more and more.' The attraction was so compelling that Bunny found himself uncharacteristically drawn into 'domestication', 'guilty of all sorts of horrors – cocoa [...] outings of the household to theatres etc', which he considered unnatural 'to an individualist like myself'.[10]

---

8   T. Fordham/DG, 40 Well Walk NW3, 22 April [1920] [HG].
9   DG, *Flowers*, p. 234.
10 DG, Diary 1920–21, 27 September [1920] [Northwestern].

Ray was the product of upper middle class parents who valued education, science and creativity, tempered by vigorous outdoor pursuits. Her father, William Cecil Marshall, was a successful architect, runner-up in the first Wimbledon lawn-tennis championship and an amateur figure-skating champion. Ray's mother, Margaret (known by her initials as 'Mam') was a woman's suffragist and talented musician. Ray had an older brother and sister, Horace and Judy, and, in descending order, a younger brother Tom,[11] and two sisters, Eleanor and Frances.[12] The Marshalls lived in Bloomsbury, at the corner of Bedford Square and had a country house, 'Tweenways', near Hindhead, designed in the Arts-and-Crafts style by Ray's father.

Ray was shy. As a child she would leave the room rather than answer a well-meaning question from a family friend, and some found her shyness disconcerting. But Francis Meynell, an inveterate thrower of parties, perceptively observed that 'when she came in her own face she was silent and apart; but if it was a fancy dress affair she wore a mask, and was then the gayest, the most approachable and approaching of women.'[13]

Bunny was attracted to Ray for several reasons beyond the obvious: that she was sexy. First, she was an artist, and had already achieved considerable success as an illustrator of several published books including *A Ride on a Rocking Horse* (1917), a simple nursery tale which she wrote as well as illustrated. Bunny admired artists and through Duncan and Vanessa had come to view the world with an artist's eye. He and Ray also shared a love of the outdoors and of long walks and fresh air. Like Bunny, she

[11] T.H. Marshall, the distinguished social scientist.
[12] Later Frances Partridge.
[13] Francis Meynell, *My Lives* (London: The Bodley Head, 1971), pp. 188–9.

had visited Russia, where she travelled at the age of twenty-two in 1913, unable to speak a word of Russian. There was another similarity between Bunny and Ray: although Bunny was gregarious among friends, with strangers he could be shy. One customer found him retreating behind his desk 'like some innocent wild animal that has never seen man before but who knows by the promptings of instinct that man is something to be mistrusted'.[14]

In September 1920 Bunny wrote to thank Lytton for a happy weekend, adding, 'Miss Marshall has [...] said nothing. She is more silent than anyone I ever met – but her eyes are eloquent. She has been looking at me all day long & I suppose I have been looking at her too [...] then when our heads get too close she turns her head aside.'[15] On the occasion when Ray touched Bunny's hand as they passed on the stairs, he felt the full force of an electric current. He had experienced the first intimation of the deeply sensual nature of this apparently shy and silent woman. When Ray suddenly announced she could pursue the relationship no longer Bunny broke down in tears, declaring: 'I am in love with you. I don't know what to do [...]. I felt so happy yesterday & so too on the stairs, but now I am upset.'[16] In this confused frame of mind, he travelled to The Cearne where Thea was staying, following the death of her mother.

Thea was having a doubly hard time: not only did she have to contend with grief over her mother's death, but she felt it incumbent upon herself to hold the family together. In term-time,

---

[14] Sylvia Townsend Warner, 'Theodore Powys and Some Friends at East Chaldon, 1922–1927: A Narrative and Some Letters', *The Powys Review*, Number 5, Vol. III, Summer 1979.

[15] DG/GLS, Birrell & Garnett [21 September 1920] [BL].

[16] DG/RAG [1920], [Northwestern].

Thea lived in Oxford, but in the vacations felt she had to be in London to make a home for her father and two brothers. She felt torn, telling Bunny that she lived at home 'because I love them there & I know they need me – so I say, "I must live their life if I really want to do my bit well, as long as I am here". And the things I alone love are consequently made to suffer & wait until I am free. I am trying to live two ways at once.'[17]

When Thea went to The Cearne she expected to find only the reassuring presence of Constance. Bunny knew Thea would be there that weekend, and told himself to avoid 'entanglements'. But when he arrived, Thea's glance of 'radiant happiness' was all the encouragement he needed. He soon forgot his resolutions, gladly accepting her invitations to bed on both nights. Thea told Bunny she was in love with him. 'I don't know if she is', he mused, 'but anyhow I feel as if I had done some good in my life, as I have cheered her up & made her happy.'[18] Early in the morning, hearing Constance's gasp of surprise on seeing his empty bedroom, Bunny rushed up to the attic, from whence he nonchalantly emerged pretending he had been collecting apples. (In his autobiography he emerges from the attic clutching a copy of Caesar's *Gallic Wars*.) Afterwards, Thea wrote telling Bunny what a comfort he had been to her.

Back at Taviton Street, Ray had changed her mind about Bunny and they were again on good terms. He knew he was in love with her, but wondered how long this could continue without sex. For the time being, however, he had an arrangement with Thea who decided 'to have a perfectly settled sort of relation with me – that of seeing me once a fortnight or once a month &

[17] T. Fordham/DG, 40 Well Walk, NW3, 22 April [1920] [HG].
[18] DG, Diary 1920–21, 27 September [1920] [Northwestern].

of going to bed with me after having dinner & a bottle of wine'. For Bunny, with his need for diversion and variety, this might have been ideal but he had had enough of chasing rainbows and wanted 'someone who loves me & whom I love'. When Ray invited him to Tweenways to meet her family, he accepted, but not before warning himself to 'take care not to marry her before I am absolutely certain'.[19]

Bunny rehearsed his feelings in a letter to Ray – feelings so convoluted that they appear contradictory. 'There are some people', he wrote, 'whom the more one sees & lives with the more precious they become [...]. Others one loves and when one has been with them for some time one feels that they are not for oneself.' 'How can I tell', he asked, 'which you are?' He added: 'I shall never be indifferent to whether I hurt you & shall never hurt you on purpose though I shall by being myself, but I cannot help that.'[20] He knew he was an unlikely candidate for exclusivity, but had the comforting certainty that if he strayed, it would all be down to his genes. It was a handy evolutionary get-out clause.

Both Bunny and Ray were aware of the importance of that weekend. Would it mark a turning point, in which their love for each other strengthened, or would it have the opposite effect? According to Bunny's diary, they had a long walk together followed by a picnic on a damp hillside. But there, frustratingly, the entry ends. On the next page, Bunny is back at Taviton Street and in the arms not of Ray, but Thea.

This was very much the pattern of Bunny's life in the last months of 1920. One evening he would be with Thea, another

---

19 DG, Diary 1920–21, 27 October [1920] [Northwestern].
20 DG/RAG, 19 Taviton Street WC1 [late October 1920] [Northwestern].

with Ray. Sometimes he saw Betty May, who told him her latest husband had left, that she had been married twice previously and had no money. Bunny gave her £5, borrowed from the shop till. He continued to see his Bloomsbury friends, spending a late night with Lytton at Taviton Street, and an even later one with Duncan at Gordon Square. Meanwhile Ray returned to Tweenways where her father was dying. She wrote to Bunny, telling him she wished he was with her: 'Different as we are I think there are a lot of things we might enjoy together if the barriers were broken down. There is no use in being afraid of me now.' 'If you're going to hurt me', she added, 'you're going to hurt me – as you would say.'[21] Although he confided his feelings for Ray to Lytton Strachey, Bunny largely kept her apart from his Bloomsbury friends. When he and Frankie threw a party at the bookshop attended by most of Bloomsbury, Carrington could only report vaguely to Lytton that they were joined by 'a young lady of Bunny's from the floor above'.[22]

By February 1921 Bunny's relationship with Ray had become sexual and Ray informed Bunny she wanted to have a child by him. Bunny told Constance: 'I get on with Ray better than I have with any woman for some time, and as she is in love with me & I with her we are very happy.' 'I daresay', he said, 'we shall get married though the less that is talked up the better.' Mindful of Bloomsbury's antipathy to marriage in general, and to marrying outside the fold in particular, he hoped the matter could be hushed. He informed Constance that he was 'quite sure' marriage would make him 'happy for a time', and that in any case 'it is

---

[21] RAG/DG [pmk 23 December 1920] [Northwestern].
[22] Carrington/GLS, 41 Gordon Square [3 January 1921] in DG, ed., *Carrington*, p. 172.

obviously worth it. If we get tired of each other we can drift apart & it will still have been an excellent thing, particularly if we had a child.'[23] His attitude to marriage was hardly one of 'till death do us part'.

Nevertheless, on 31 March 1921 Bunny and Ray were married at the St Pancras Register Office, with Tatlock and Hey as witnesses. Given Bunny's expressed ambivalence to marriage and that he felt destined to hurt Ray, why did he marry? There is no doubt he loved Ray, but on his terms and in his way. He loved her deep sensitivity to her surroundings and enjoyed her outbursts of high spirits. In contrast to Thea, who was emotionally fragile and often exhausted, Bunny admired Ray for her stamina and strength, telling Constance 'she is physically sound, & never ill'. He also valued her talent as an artist and that she disdained to 'change the plates or dust the mantelpiece every day'.[24] A more pragmatic reason for their marriage might be inferred from a poem which Bunny wrote for Ray in celebration of their spring wedding. It concludes with the lines:

These shiny bursting buds, drenched with showers
And unexpected love for those forgotten flowers
All this is spring
And this the cause & the occasion of our marriage
Men cannot celebrate it. It may be sacred
Like loneliness men destroy it,
Like flowers crush it with their boots
But birds announce it, and lambing ewes

---

[23] DG/CG, Birrell & Garnett [1921] [HRRC].
[24] DG/CG, Birrell & Garnett [1921] [HRRC].

The stirring in the hive,

   All things newborn, reborn, young, alive,

Make marriage music, bring us wedding gifts.[25]

Notwithstanding the pessimism at the heart of this verse, it celebrates the fecundity of spring, promising another kind of birth.
Ray told Bunny she wanted a child by him, and he had intimated
to Constance that marriage would be a good thing 'particularly if
we had a child'. Even a pronounced 'individualist' like Bunny
knew of the enormous stigma attached to children born outside
marriage and to unmarried mothers. Bunny had also lived at
Charleston at the time of Vanessa's pregnancy and knew the
great joy which a baby can bring. It seems very likely that Ray
was pregnant when they married on 31 March as she was visibly
pregnant by early July. Perhaps pregnancy expedited marriage,
but they were already committed to the idea of having children.
Even Lytton had heard that Bunny and Ray intended to 'have a
very large family'.[26] Ray was thirty in 1921, and for a woman of
her generation this was a relatively advanced age to be embarking on a first pregnancy. Less than a month into the marriage,
closing the stable door after the horse had bolted, Bunny informed
Duncan he was 'thinking of beginning a family at any moment'.[27]

Bunny thought Edward the only person who approved of the
marriage, 'and realised almost from the first that I had made a
wise choice and been very lucky'. Constance was less easily won
over: Bunny believed she would have preferred him to marry

---

[25] Unpublished MS [Northwestern].

[26] GLS/James Strachey, 51 Gordon Square, 14 April 1921 in Paul Levy, ed.,
The Letters of Lytton Strachey (London: Viking, 2005), p. 484.

[27] D. Grant/DG, 46 Gordon Square [pmk 22 April 1921] [HG].

someone she already knew, perhaps Thea.[28] Although Constance soon became fond of Ray, Bunny's Bloomsbury friends were aghast at the marriage, which, according to Lytton 'raised a universal howl of execration' in Bloomsbury.[29] Frankie Birrell was 'distinctly cut up about it', and Carrington thought Bunny was losing his eyesight 'as well as his wits'.[30]

Duncan was furious. He wrote reproaching Bunny for not consulting his friends and for his selfishness in failing to take into account how they would feel. 'It is a ridiculous argument', Duncan stated,

> that there is no difference between a liaison & a legal marriage. A liaison is a relation between 2 individuals with no contracts & no reality in the eyes of the world. A legal marriage is at once a reality in the eyes of the world of the most odious sort [...]. Also it apparently entails living together which makes it very difficult for your friends to forget that when they want to see you or ask you out there is somebody else who considers herself with superior claims left alone.[31]

Duncan still felt entitled to 'claims' upon Bunny, but he also worried about the extent to which his relationship with Bunny was known to Ray. He told Bunny, 'my happiness depends on

[28] DG, *Flowers*, pp. 233–4.
[29] GLS/James Strachey, 51 Gordon Square, 14 April 1921 in Levy, ed., *Letters of Lytton Strachey*, p. 484.
[30] Carrington/Alix Strachey, The Mill House, Tidmarsh, 15 April 1921, in DG, ed., *Carrington*, p. 174.
[31] Copy by D. Garnett of letter from D. Grant to DG [original returned to D. Grant], 'Private', 46 Gordon square, 17 April 1921 [HG].

something you can give me. But it must be alive & not dead.'[32] Duncan managed to contain his anger sufficiently to paint Ray's portrait as a wedding present, although he commented dismissively that Ray 'sits like a cream cheese on a plate'.[33]

It would be some time before Bunny and Ray had a permanent home in which to display Duncan's portrait. The newly-weds moved from Taviton Street to Wells Street, just off Goodge Street, where they took two small rooms overlooking a cemetery. But Ray spent little time there, embarking on a protracted period in the countryside for the sake of her health and that of her unborn baby, as influenza remained rife after the epidemic of 1918. And so Ray adopted a nomadic existence, travelling between relatives and joined by Bunny at weekends. In some ways this suited them both. It obviously appealed to Bunny given his need for variety and diversion. As for Ray, as Bunny explained, 'Ray was a woodland creature. She wanted the protection and shelter that woods gave, and among the beeches and the pines I saw her as I never could see her in London.'[34]

Ray spent most of July with her sister Judy and brother-in-law Dick Rendel who were staying at Warbarrow Bay, near Lulworth Cove, in Dorset. There Ray, now visibly pregnant, felt self-conscious bathing before the young men on the beach. Bunny worried she might slip on the rocks or catch a chill, and warned her to avoid sailing at all costs. Ray revelled in her pregnancy, excited every time she felt the baby move, perceiving something 'so alive' within her. Bunny rehearsed names for the baby on the back of an envelope,

---

[32] D. Grant/DG, 'Copy of covering letter, 46 Gordon Square, Thursday 17 April' [1921] [HG].

[33] DG, *Flowers*, p. 233.

[34] DG, *Flowers*, p. 234.

scribbling: 'Richard Duncan Sable Garnett is fixed.'[35]

Bunny was busy in the shop, but he and Duncan often spent evenings together at the cinema or ballet. Bunny was also sitting to Duncan for his portrait and posing as a sailor for one of Duncan's *Bankside* paintings. Despite his marriage, Bunny couldn't let go of Duncan, still feeling he loved him 'more than anyone in the world'.[36] Ray's absence, therefore, gave Bunny the opportunity to enjoy the best of two possible worlds.

Exiled in the country, Ray lived for Bunny's letters and for his irregular weekend visits. Her return to London depended on her mother providing a comfortable base, but having sold Tweenways, Mam was still house-hunting. In October she eventually took possession of number 27 Brunswick Square, in the heart of Bloomsbury. Even so, it would be some time before the house was ready as various improvements were required. Mam proposed to run it on communal lines, with bed-sitting rooms for her unmarried daughters Frances and Eleanor; Bunny and Ray's quarters would comprise a large ground-floor sitting room and a bedroom on the second floor.

As the birth approached, Ray became fearful. She experienced 'distinctly swelling movements' one afternoon, which she felt sure were 'the last dying movements' of her unborn child. 'But', she reassured Bunny, 'I have done nothing violent & feel very well'.[37] As the days passed, she became progressively alarmed, for the baby's movements seemed to diminish. In October, Bunny received a frantic letter from her:

---

[35] Envelope, RAG/DG [pmk 25 July, 1921] [Northwestern].

[36] DG, Diary [1920–21], Sunday 19 December [1920] [Northwestern].

[37] RAG/DG, Glebe Cottage, Goring-on-Thames, Tues 13th [September, 1921] [Northwestern].

I have to see another doctor. Dr Rooke thinks its all wrong – that the baby is dead. She is not sure – & anyway would want a second opinion. She has sent me to Dr Fairburn, 40 Wimpole St – 5.30. If it is so, I shall have to go into a nursing home almost at once – they do something to bring on the labour – When I recover everything is as before. If you can do come to Wimpole St [...]. I long to see you.[38]

Bunny accompanied Ray to the consultant, who informed them that they might have to wait as long as a fortnight before knowing for certain whether the baby was dead. To compound matters, Bunny had vacated their rooms at Wells Street that very morning. As Brunswick Square was not ready, Duncan had lent Bunny his studio and Ray was to have gone to stay with Constance at The Cearne. They went instead to Pond Place where they stayed overnight. The next morning, still homeless, and with no anticipation of a happy event, Ray entered the nursing home, Number One Nottingham Place. 'She is suffering from shock a good deal', Bunny informed Edward.[39]

Bunny was also in shock. Having dashed off a letter to Constance, apprising her of the bare bones of the situation, that evening he sent her a more optimistic letter. Ray had experienced pains during the night and Bunny dared to hope this might signify the child was alive. 'It is a great blessing', Bunny wrote, 'that when people are tired they can't feel, & that when they are in physical pain they feel only that'; as ever protective of Constance, he added: 'you needn't think I am suffering [...]. It

---

[38] RAG/DG [October 1921] [Northwestern].

[39] DG/EG, Birrell & Garnett, 'Friday' [October, 1921] [Northwestern].

has been a great shock to Ray, but it will soon be over I suppose.'[40]

Bunny's hopes were unfounded. The child had been dead for about two weeks.[41] The cause of the stillbirth is not recorded. Modern antenatal care was in its infancy and foetal monitoring minimal. Ray did not seem to have been affected by placental abruption, the most frequent cause of stillbirth, as she did not experience the symptoms of searing pain or internal bleeding. Neither did she develop pre-eclampsia or eclampsia. For one third of stillbirths, then as now, there was no identifiable cause. In the 1920s there was no bereavement counselling, no funeral for stillborns, nothing to mark the passage from life to death. It was not something people discussed.

Ray remained in the nursing home for two weeks. Bunny visited every afternoon, reading to her from *Robinson Crusoe*. He still felt numb: 'I can't go into the question of <u>feelings</u>', he told Constance, 'except to say that I think the war took my feelings out of me [...]. I can't feel anything acutely for more than four or five days. Ray I'm afraid can.'[42] With the move to Brunswick Square still delayed, Bunny rented rooms at Caroline Place. There he installed the Marshalls' old nursemaid, Nan Croucher, to care for Ray on her return. But when Bunny did finally move into Brunswick Square, he did so alone. Ray was on the move again, recuperating with Judy and Dick Rendel.

---

[40] DG/CG, [October, 1921] [HRRC].

[41] When not induced, stillbirths usually begin spontaneously two weeks after the death of the foetus; if, as seems likely, Ray had gone into spontaneous labour, she may have been spared some of the more gruesome and gruelling aspects of stillborn deliveries practised at that time. These included surgically breaking the bones of the dead baby *in utero*, prior to extraction.

[42] DG/CG, Birrell & Garnett [October, 1921] [HRRC].

With Ray away, Bunny turned his attention to the shop, which had cash-flow problems, partly because the proprietors were inclined to offer customers extensive and informal periods of credit. In November 1921 Siegfried Sassoon alone owed £75: an immense sum. Lytton thought the shop 'a queer business', commenting 'somehow it subsists, though how one hardly knows, considering the extreme dreaminess of the shopmen'.[43] Bunny and Frankie had anyway become rather bored with the business. They considered selling the stock to Bumpus, the booksellers of Oxford Street, and working as employees there. This idea was abandoned in favour of taking on a third partner who would bring fresh capital. In early 1922 they were joined by Ralph Wright, whom they had met when he worked at the Central Library for Students. Bunny described Wright as 'a rather short man, whose head of glossy black hair, brushed straight back' resembled 'a seal's head, emerging from the water'.[44] He was sympathetic, sensitive and warm, and particularly well-versed in French and English literature, which endeared him to the two original part-ners. But his chief qualifications were a love of reading and flair for conversation, both prerequisites at Birrell & Garnett.

Bunny missed Ray, telling her how unhappy he felt in her absence. She missed him too: 'just when I'm in the mood for you[,] you lovely man, you bending bough, you star'. 'I may not want you on Saturday', she added, 'Then it'll be kiss me my love – God be wi' you & I must be going in the morning'.[45] Bunny still saw something of Thea. In November she wrote inviting

[43] GLS/James Strachey, 51 Gordon Square, 14 April 1921, in Levy, ed., *Letters of Lytton Strachey*, p. 484.

[44] DG, *Flowers*, p. 235.

[45] RAG/DG [November, 1921] [Northwestern].

him 'to eat somewhere first & then we will see', carefully direct-ing the letter to the bookshop and not to Brunswick Square.[46] But by early 1922 Ray felt completely well, and was, at last, living with Bunny there. With a permanent base, Bunny could revive the Caroline Club, and once again enjoy convivial play readings. Ray's sister, Frances Marshall, the new assistant at Birrell & Garnett, was roped in too, but Ray would not take part, prefer-ring to listen from the side-lines. It was not long, however, before her perambulations resumed: in April she learned she was preg-nant. Once again Ray departed for the country, where in July she returned to Judy and Dick Rendel. Experiencing déjà vu, she told Bunny, 'This place reminds me of this time last year'.[47]

[46] T. Fordham/DG, 'Monday' [pmk November 1921] [HG].
[47] RAG/DG, Glebe Cottage, Goring [July, 1922] [Northwestern].

Chapter Twelve

'Perhaps the saving grace of man is to be an adjunct to a work of art.'[1]

Bunny was researching foxes, reading about their habits, visiting the zoo and sites where there were dens. This interest arose because Ray had inspired him to write a story. They had been staying at The Cearne, where one day Bunny took Ray to the High Chart where he was convinced there were fox cubs. Finding there were none, Bunny turned to Ray, commenting "There's no hope of seeing a fox – unless you were suddenly to turn into one". He teasingly told her 'how like she was to a wild animal, and how easily my intense love for her would overcome the trifling difficulties that would arise if she actually were transformed into one'.[2] Bunny turned these whimsical musings into a synopsis for a book, which he entitled 'The Metamorphosis of Mrs Tebrick'. He would write the text, but Ray's illustrations would be integral.

Ray looked forward to Bunny's weekends with her in the

---

[1] DG/Trystan Edwards, The Cearne [?late 1918] [Northwestern].
[2] DG, *Flowers*, pp. 243–4.

country, but in the summer of 1922 he often kept away, explaining that the shop and his novel claimed his time. Ray chided him for his 'talk of being busy' and for being 'cruel'; 'You make me angry talking such nonsense to your own wife'.[3] But Bunny's time was also taken up with three new friendships, each destined to be highly significant.

In June, Mina Kirstein, an American intellectual and blue-stocking appeared in the bookshop. She had bobbed dark hair, beauty and brains. It did not take long for Bunny and Mina to fall in love, although Mina later declared, 'Our relationship from his point of view had certain limitations and remained uncomfortably platonic in spite of both our efforts to overcome my scruples'.[4] Mina believed in the sanctity of marriage, or at least in saving herself for the moment.

A month or so later, Bunny made friends with the young sculptor Stephen 'Tommy' Tomlin, who had come into the bookshop looking for books on art. Bunny was attracted by his charm and the 'delightful intimate smile' which 'played about his mouth'.[5] According to Frances Partridge, Tommy was not conventionally good-looking, but 'short and strongly-built, with the profile of a Roman emperor on a coin, fair hair brushed back from a high forehead, a pale face and intelligent grey eyes.' She added that he 'dented the hearts or minds, or both, of most people who met him'.[6] At twenty-one, Tommy was nine years younger than Bunny. He had left Oxford prematurely partly as he had lost interest in

---

[3] RAG/DG [pmk 8 September 1922] [Northwestern].

[4] Mina Curtiss, *Other People's Letters* (London: Macmillan, 1978), p. 15.

[5] David Garnett, *The Familiar Faces* (London: Chatto & Windus, 1962), p. 1.

[6] Frances Partridge, ed., *Julia: A Portrait of Julia Strachey by Herself and Frances Partridge* (London: Victor Gollancz, 1983; Penguin Books, 1984), pp. 106–7.

studying law, but mainly as a result of a breakdown following the drowning of his close friend, Michael Llewelyn-Davies, one of J.M. Barrie's 'Lost Boys'. Tommy then took up his vocation as a sculptor, training under Frank Dobson. He lived, at least part of the time, in the village of Chaldon Herring, otherwise known as East Chaldon, in Dorset. Here he befriended the writer T.F. Powys, and through him, came to know another writer, Sylvia Townsend Warner. It was she who Tommy sent to Birrell & Garnett in August, and who was to become the third of Bunny's trio of new friends.

Sylvia arrived at the bookshop clutching Powys's manuscript, *Hester Dominy*, which Tommy thought Bunny might help to get published. There Sylvia encountered 'an extremely young-looking man whose hair was long and thick and untidy and whose suit was so blue that I felt he might blow up his horn at any moment'.[7] Retreating behind a bookshelf, Bunny observed 'an alarming lady with a clear and minatory voice, dark, dripping with tassels [...] with jingling earrings, swinging fox-tails, black silk acorn hanging to umbrella, black tasselled gloves'. She addressed him 'in sentences like scissors'.[8] Their friendship, which always remained platonic, was consolidated when Bunny accompanied Sylvia to the Blackwater marshes in Essex, a landscape which she loved. She was touched when Bunny pulled an acorn from his pocket and planted it in a field. Bunny adored Sylvia's humour and admired her writing, and they embarked upon a friendship lasting more than fifty years. Unusually, both Sylvia and Mina addressed him as 'David'.

---

[7] Richard Garnett, ed., *Sylvia & David: The Townsend Warner/Garnett Letters* (London: Sinclair-Stevenson, 1994), p. 2.

[8] DG/STW, The Nonesuch Press, 16 Great James Street, London WC1 [c. 24 November 1927] in RG, ed., *Sylvia and David*, p. 35.

Tommy invited Bunny to East Chaldon, which Bunny described as 'bewitched', 'with the moonlight slanting down between the high and mighty sycamores, the thatched cottages like a covey of sleeping partridges huddled together in a hollow of the downs'.[9] From there he wrote to Ray, now staying with Connie at The Cearne, to tell her how charming Tommy was and that 'We have been leading an idle life – talking till 2 am about Jesus & Blake & so on'. 'The principal excitement', he added, 'is Powys'. 'He is an amusing man of fifty[10] or so with piercing blue eyes, an ecclesiastical mouth & a very humorous smile.'[11]

Tommy dented Bunny's heart, writing to him after his return to London: 'There are lots of soul stirring things I want to say to you […]. I am glad you liked being here. If you enjoyed it half as much as I enjoyed – you know the formula […] – but I mean it. I like you […] Love Tommy.'[12] Although there is no direct evidence of an affair between Bunny and Tommy, it seems highly probable. In a letter to Ray, written in 1928, Bunny referred to the ease with which he could make friends and fall in love, adding: 'You were not jealous of Tommy.'[13] Tommy was bisexual, and as Julia Strachey, who later married him, noted: 'One thing was paramount: Tommy's daemon insisted that not only with their souls but definitely with their *bodies* everyone must him worship.'[14]

---

[9] D. Garnett, 'Theo Powys', in *The Borzoi 1925* (New York: Alfred A. Knopf, 1925), p. 89.

[10] Powys was forty-seven.

[11] DG/RAG, East Chaldon, Dorset, 'Monday' [c, August 1922] [Northwestern].

[12] S, Tomlin/DG, Chaldon Herring, 10 October [1922] [Northwestern].

[13] DG/RAG, Hilton Hall [1928] [Northwestern].

[14] Partridge, ed., *Julia*, p. 129.

Bunny became one of Tommy's main patrons, commissioning seven sculptures, including a stone bust of himself.[15] Tommy featured prominently in Bunny's autobiography, where Bunny sometimes wrote cryptically so that the casual reader might infer one meaning, and those *in the know*, could interpret another. Quoting the following lines from Blake, Bunny compared Tommy to the angel in the verse, a comparison which could be read as alluding to Tommy's bisexuality:

I asked a thief to steal me a peach,
He turned up his eyes.
I asked a lithe lady to lay her down,
Holy and meek she cries.
There came an angel who without one word said,
Had a peach from the tree
And still as a maid, enjoyed the lady.[16]

In the autumn of 1922, Birrell & Garnett moved to larger premises on Gerrard Street, in the heart of Soho and in what is today Chinatown. 'I don't know how they can possibly survive such a thing', Lytton exclaimed. 'They seem to me [...] to live in a complete mist. A twelve years lease!'[17] In the 1920s Soho was at the centre of London's Bohemia, the location of restaurants serving 'foreign' food, of nightclubs, coffee houses and brothels. Moreover the location was hardly the centre of

---

[15] Now in the garden at Charleston.

[16] DG, *Familiar Faces*, p. 2; typically Bunny misquoted the last two lines of the poem and missed out intervening lines.

[17] GLS/Carrington, Oriental Club, Hanover Square, 1 March 1922, in Levy, ed., *Letters of Lytton Strachey*, p. 511.

London's book trade. The Taviton Street premises at least had the advantage of being within Bloomsbury in the neighbourhood of many customers. It was not that Gerrard Street was any great distance from Bloomsbury, more that London districts have distinct identities which can change abruptly at the turn of a corner.

Meanwhile, Bunny had completed his story and sent it to the publishers Chatto & Windus, reminding them that they had published Ray's *A Ride on a Rocking Horse*. He emphasised that his novel was not a children's book, despite the brevity of the text and inclusion of illustrations. Chatto & Windus considered it too short, requesting an additional story to go with it. But by the end of July, they decided to publish the story alone. Bunny had changed the rather clumsy original title to the more elegant and precisely accurate *Lady into Fox*. Whereas he might have been expected to dedicate his novel to Ray, it is dedicated to Duncan.

Lady into Fox was published in autumn 1922. It was unusual: an illustrated novel, written for adult readership. Initially it was marketed on the back of Ray's success as a published illustrator, the dust jacket announcing: 'A rare and sympathetic interpretation is provided by twelve woodcuts, the work of Mrs Garnett, formerly Miss Rachel Marshall, and well known as the illustrator of *A Ride on a Rocking Horse*.' The story concerns Richard Tebrick, whose loving and devoted wife, Sylvia, turns into a fox. Initially she stays at home with her husband, dressed in her Edwardian clothes, but gradually the metamorphosis becomes more complete and she acquires the instincts and behaviour of a vixen. Mr Tebrick realises he must let her follow her instincts, releasing her into the wild, where she meets and mates with a dog fox, producing cubs (one of whom, in honour of Vanessa's and Duncan's daughter, is named

'Angelica'). Mr Tebrick visits her and the cubs, aware that he cannot protect her any more. Eventually she is pursued by hounds during a fox hunt and comes to grief.

Lady into Fox was a literary sensation, achieving both critical and popular acclaim. Gerald Gould, in the *Saturday Review* stated it contained 'not one false note'. Unlike some critics, who speculated about potential symbolism or moral undertones, Gould proclaimed, perceptively: 'To the truly intellectual, the husband of a lady who has turned into a fox is the husband of a lady who has turned into a fox [...]. A work of art is, anyway, its own meaning. And "Lady into Fox" is certainly a work of art.'[18] *The Times Literary Supplement* (*TLS*) declared the book 'a real morsel of art', in which Bunny's words 'spread an eighteenth century aroma, an atmosphere where all is sensible and lucid'.[19] The reviewer in the *Sketch* pondered 'What does it all mean? *Is* there a meaning?' concluding wrongly that the story was an allegory in which 'all women are potential vixens'.[20] Later Bunny explained that 'the style employed and the attitude of the author to the reader, were adopted in order to make this inherently impossible story appear credible'. He admired Defoe and adopted 'his methods of inducing credulity in the reader. The slight archaism in the style was deliberately chosen because it helped to keep the author and the reader at arms-length.'[21] It was only after the book was published that Bunny realised it was a metaphor for what he believed to be the absurdity of fidelity in marriage.

---

[18] 27 January 1923.

[19] 2 February 1923.

[20] 4 April 1923.

[21] DG, 'Author's Note to the Present Edition', 20 May 1965 [Northwestern] [contribution to the 1966 Norton edition, ed. Vincent Starett].

'My fame increases every day', Bunny wrote to Mina Kirstein in January 1923.[22] The success of *Lady into Fox* had made him popular in many quarters. Jonathan Cape wanted to publish Bunny's next book, and T. Werner Laurie hoped to re-issue *Dope-Darling* under the Garnett name. Both offers were cordially declined. His new found fame caused Bunny to receive a deluge of letters. Carrington liked the book so much she thought Bunny must have written it especially for her. Bunny received warm praise from Joseph Conrad, H.G. Wells, Virginia Woolf and E.M. Forster. The novelist George Moore pronounced it a 'masterpiece'. In Farnborough at the RAF School of Photography, the book had been borrowed by 'room after room' and was handed round 'from bed to bed', or so T.E. Lawrence reported to Edward.[23]

Soon Bunny had something else to celebrate. On 8 January 1923, at Brunswick Square, and in the big bed in which Ray had been born, she gave birth to a healthy baby son. Two hours later, Ray laid 'serenely' in bed, the baby beside her, 'apparently', Bunny told Constance, 'as well as I ever saw her in my life'. After all Ray's apprehension, and her terrible foreboding that history would repeat itself, she and Bunny had a baby boy, in all respects 'perfect & complete'.[24]

During the birth, Bunny sat on the stairs, anxiously reading *Tristram Shandy*. Immediately afterwards, he rushed in to see Ray and their baby, whom he weighed and helped to bathe. In appearance, he considered the baby to have 'Ray's eyes', but otherwise to be 'a terrible little Garnett', the upper lip & nose reminding him of Edward. 'You can't imagine', he enthused to

---

[22] DG/Mina Curtiss, 30 Gerrard Street, 26 January 1923 [Berg].
[23] T.E. Lawrence/EG, 7 December 1922 [Bodleian].
[24] DG/CG, 27 Brunswick Square [8 January 1923] [HRRC].

Constance, 'how satisfactory this business is, I have never been so pleased with anything as this creature.'[25] According to Sylvia, Bunny looked at the baby suckling at the breast and pondered, 'it is rather difficult to make out whether he will prefer Keats or Shelley'.[26] Bunny wrote to Mina, asking: 'Did I tell you that my wife presented me with a most delightful boy [...]? He is a very lovely creature with a perfect complexion and I think a rather philosophic disposition. Both he and Ray are in excellent health. I should like you to meet her some day.'[27] This was news to Mina: during six months of ardent friendship, she had no idea Bunny was married, let alone a father-to-be.

Duncan bought Ray an enormous bouquet of roses, and the next day Bunny had lunch with him and Vanessa, Lydia Lopokova and Maynard Keynes, sharing his happiness with his old friends. As for the baby's name: Bruin was a strong possibility. However, Bunny and Ray settled on Richard, after a succession of Garnetts, followed by 'Duncan' and 'Carey', a name almost identical to that which Bunny had chosen, a year and a half before, in anticipation of his first-born. Thus Bunny again commemorated his love for Duncan; but if he hoped this would cement a bond between his friend and his son, or draw Duncan into a closer relationship with Ray, he was wrong. Three decades later, Duncan gave Richard and his wife, Jane, a handsome wedding gift. Otherwise, Duncan maintained little more than a distant interest in Bunny's family, continuing to see his

[25] DG/CG, 27 Brunswick Square [8 January 1923] and 9 January 1923 [HRRC].

[26] STW/Paul Nordoff, 8 May 1946 [but re 1923], in William Maxwell, ed., *Letters: Sylvia Townsend Warner* (London: Chatto & Windus, 1982), p. 93.

[27] DG/Mina Curtiss, 17 January 1923 [Berg].

friend on his own terms, mostly away from the domestic arena.

Two weeks after Richard's birth, Bunny confessed to Mina that he was rather tired. This was not a result of sleepless nights with a new baby, but because he had been seeing friend after friend and attending numerous parties. Bunny's pocket diary in the early months of 1923 was studded with engagements and he seemed to see Tommy and Mina on an almost daily basis, as well as dining or breakfasting with Duncan regularly. He was still involved with Thea Fordham with whom in late January he had a tryst at Leith Hill, near Dorking in Surrey, where Edward kept an old-fashioned wooden barrel-shaped caravan. Meanwhile, Bunny wrote to Mina, 'I love you very very much. I am very very fond of you & shall be so <u>always</u> & I feel very much happier from knowing you.'[28]

Bunny celebrated his thirty-first birthday, on 9 March 1923, by hosting a party in Duncan's studio behind No. 8 Fitzroy Street. Duncan was present, together with most of Bunny's Bloomsbury friends. Frances Marshall came, as did Tommy, and Mina Kirstein, bringing her friend Henrietta Bingham, the wealthy daughter of an American newspaper proprietor. Mina and Henrietta contributed an enormous cake decorated with a reproduction of one of Ray's woodcuts from *Lady into Fox*. Entertainment was provided by Henrietta, who sang African-American spirituals in her husky Southern voice and by the ballerina Lydia Lopokova, reprising her Covent Garden solo of earlier in the evening. Ray was there too, on one of the rare occasions when she mixed with Bloomsbury *en masse*.

It was around this time that the publisher and book designer Francis Meynell wandered into the bookshop, enquiring whether there was space available for a small publishing venture. As the

---

[28] DG/Mina Curtiss, [c. April] [1923] [Berg].

basement was vacant, Meynell decided to take it. A few days later Bunny was alone in the shop when someone came in from the landlord's office insisting that Mr Meynell sign the rental agreement immediately, otherwise it would be let to someone else. Masquerading as Meynell's business partner, Bunny duly signed the agreement. In fact Meynell already had a business partner, his girlfriend, Vera Mendel, who provided the £300 working capital to fund the venture. But recognising that Bunny would be an asset, Francis and Vera invited him to become the third partner in the Nonesuch Press. Now publisher as well as novelist and bookseller, Bunny could claim to be involved in every aspect of book production.

Francis Meynell was a year older than Bunny, already well established in the world of printing and publishing, having founded the Pelican Press in 1916. He was a socialist and like Bunny, a former conscientious objector. The two men had much in common, not least literary mothers, as Francis's mother was the poet Alice Meynell. According to Bunny, Vera was 'lean, very beautiful, and insolently sure of her outstanding intelligence'. As Bunny got to know her, he was disturbed by her open disdain for those she loved, and noticed that her affectionate treatment of him was sometimes mingled with a 'tinge of contempt'.[29] She and Francis had chosen the title 'Nonesuch Press' because they liked a device in a tapestry in Nonesuch Palace, which they thought would make a strong visual image for the venture, and they commissioned the illustrator Stephen Gooden to translate it into a colophon for their business. The Nonesuch ethos was simple: they wanted to produce beautiful books, in limited editions, for people who wanted to read them, rather than simply to own them. They were also interested in bringing back into

---

[29] DG, *Familiar Faces*, p. 19.

print books which had literary or intrinsic artistic merit. They were thus largely responsible for the resurgence of interest in Restoration literature and drama, and with Geoffrey Keynes – surgeon, scholar and bibliophile – as one of their main editors, they reignited interest in the poet William Blake.

The three partners did not want to produce books which were unduly expensive. On the contrary, by out-sourcing their printing, rather than becoming laboriously involved in typesetting, they could produce exquisite limited editions at relatively affordable prices. As Francis explained: 'Our stock-in-trade has been the theory that mechanical means could be made to serve fine ends; that the machine in printing was a controllable tool. Therefore we set out to be mobilisers of other people's resources; to be designers, specifiers; rather than manufacturers; architects of books rather than builders.'[30]

From the outset, Birrell & Garnett and the Nonesuch Press had a symbiotic relationship. The bookshop provided a convivial atmosphere and its stock of second hand and rare books furnished a library-like repository for the Nonesuch editors. Both scholars in their own right, Bunny's bookshop partners also contributed to Nonesuch publications: Frankie as a translator of Plato's *Symposium* (1924), and Ralph as translator of Lamartine's *Fraziella* (1929). Bunny, who led a rather frenetic existence as a partner in two separate ventures within the same small building, 'was readily available to *all* his partners, both upstairs and down in the cellar'.[31] The three

---

[30] Francis Meynell, 'The Personal Element' in A.J.A. Symons, Desmond Flower and Francis Meynell, *The Nonesuch Century* (London: The Nonesuch Press, 1936), p. 43.

[31] John Dreyfus, *A History of the Nonesuch Press* (London: The Nonesuch Press, 1981), p. 21.

publishing partners got on well, partly because they all enjoyed what they were doing: Francis Meynell designing books, Vera organising everything, and Bunny exercising his literary judgement and writing the prospectuses. None of them particularly relished the more mundane administrative tasks, but it was typical of the *joie de vivre* they brought to the enterprise that they would circumvent boredom by throwing 'invoice bees' in which they invited their friends to write invoices between drinks. In May 1923 the first three books were published, including John Donne's *Love Poems*, which sold out within the year. In most years they produced between eight and twelve books, and throughout the 1920s the business was very successful and much respected within its sector.

That summer of 1923, Bunny attended the Derby Day races with Mina, Henrietta and Tommy, where they were joined by an American attorney, Christopher L. Ward, for whom Bunny inscribed a copy of *Lady into Fox*. The following year, Ward sent Bunny his latest book, *Gentleman into Goose*. This affectionate parody was published by T. Werner Laurie, who perhaps enjoyed a gentle retaliation for Bunny's refusal to allow him to republish *Dope-Darling*. (Some twelve years later the National Fur Company embarked on an advertising campaign under the banner 'Lady into Mink', which rather missed the point of the original, proclaiming 'our little mink will find a fit monument in the fair figure of his possessor, and for such glory he might well be content to die'.[32]) Meanwhile, *Lady into Fox* was published in the US by Alfred A. Knopf, and was being translated into French by Jane Bussy, Lytton Strachey's half-French niece. She found the translation problematic: how to convey the archaic Defoe-inspired tone? How to

---

[32] National Fur Company Lady into Mink [publicity brochure] (London: National Fur Company [c. 1935]).

184

communicate the concept of fox hunting to the French, who didn't hunt foxes? And thus, how to render words like 'blooding' and 'smeared'? The task of finding a French publisher for this translation was in the hands of the poet Brian Rhys, a friend of Thea Fordham's, who was then working for J.M. Dent et fils in Paris.

In early July, Bunny wrote to Constance, 'Here is a <u>secret</u>. Please do not tell <u>a single soul</u>.'[33] He was to be awarded the Hawthornden Prize of £100 for *Lady into Fox*. On 11 July Bunny attended the award ceremony. According to the *Evening Standard*, 'There was a diaphanous assembly in the dimness of the Aeolian Hall yesterday afternoon to see Mr G.K. Chesterton hand the Hawthornden prize to Mr David Garnett, the boyish-looking author of "Lady into Fox" '.[34] The prize was (and still is) awarded annually to an English writer for the 'best work of imaginative fiction'. The panel does not invite submissions and in some years no awards have been made. Other writers who received the prize in the 1920s included Sean O'Casey, Vita Sackville-West, Henry Williamson and Siegfried Sassoon, while recent winners have included William Fiennes and Hilary Mantel.

Bunny was exceptionally busy. Not only was he running the bookshop, but he was engrossed in the Nonesuch, writing occasional pieces for Vogue, contributing a story to Robert Graves's *The Winter Owl*, reviewing for the *Nation* and revising his latest novel, *A Man in the Zoo*. He had also started to write a 'London Literary Letter' for the *Louisville Courier-Journal*, a newspaper owned by Henrietta Bingham's millionaire father, Robert Worth 'Judge' Bingham, in which Bunny shamelessly plugged his friends' books and Nonesuch publications. In a few short months

---

[33] DG/CG, Birrell & Garnett, 30 Gerrard Street, 3 July 1923 [HRRC].
[34] 12 July 1923.

he had become a father, a literary sensation and a publisher. Now he was a journalist, too. Consequently he felt swamped and irritable, firing off a grumpy letter to Mina: 'Really how foolish it is the way you write to me with incessant complaints about my behaviour [...]. I should have thought it might occur to you [...] that I am busy.' 'I am not', he added pompously, 'an idle young man dancing attendance on women'.[35] But he was dancing attendance on one particular young woman: Henrietta Bingham. Bunny commemorated their affair by commissioning Henrietta's other lover – Tommy – to sculpt her head.

Nearly thirty years later, when Mina re-read her early correspondence with Bunny, she concluded: 'What a bore I must have been, always wanting reassurance, always wanting to be told the exact amount of love you felt for me.' 'But then', she added, insightfully, 'I decided that you were pretty silly to have expected me – inexperienced, un-sophisticated, bookish, romantic young idiot that I was [...] to know how to behave in a love-affair with a married man.'[36] In August 1923, Bunny tried to rid himself of this particular complication, informing Mina that 'the two people for whom I care most in the world are Duncan and Ray. You also know that I love you very much, but not as much as I love them.' 'I can't help hurting you', he added, echoing his earlier comment to Ray.[37]

There was one other person whom Bunny loved unconditionally, and whom he felt never made undue demands: Thea. Their relationship continued much as it had, with assignations in the countryside or occasional dinners followed by sex. But in the summer of 1923 Thea went to Paris, and when she returned she

---

[35] DG/Mina Curtiss, Birrell & Garnett, [pmk 16 August 1923] [Berg].
[36] M. Curtiss/DG, Ashfield, 2 October 1949 [Northwestern].
[37] DG/Mina Curtiss [?c. August] [1923] [Berg].

186

wrote Bunny a typically cryptic letter: 'Once a red rose in my heart, blossomed & blossomed for so long it would have died – but before it died a white one flowered by it & they both flower together.'[38] The red rose was Bunny; the white rose Brian Rhys, the poet who endeavoured to find Bunny a French publisher. Concerned that Brian would usurp him in Thea's affections, Bunny had scribbled a desultory note on one of her letters: 'TF had been seeing Brian Rhys in Paris.'[39] That October Thea wrote to Bunny telling him she didn't want to see him for a while. She explained: 'I do feel something particular towards you', but added that those feelings did not 'fit with my love for Brian.'[40]

While Thea vanished from Bunny's life, so did Mina and Henrietta, who returned to America. Although Bunny missed his American friends, there was compensation. Henrietta had left Bunny in charge not only of her car, but of her chauffeur, ostensibly on the condition that Bunny would sell the vehicle for her. Leaving Ray and Richard with Mam, Bunny enjoyed several excursions with friends including Duncan, Maynard Keynes and Lydia Lopokova. He spent a weekend motoring with Harold Hobson, and another walking with a new friend, Alec Penrose, whom he had met when Penrose tutored Mina's younger brothers in London that summer. Bunny described Alec as an 'elegant, charming and wholly delightful dilettante', and as 'a passionate character', but 'full of fear'.[41] Although his brother Roland was

---

[38] T. Fordham/DG, Grove House, Mobberley, Cheshire, 'Monday' [pmk 1 October 1923] [HG].

[39] On envelope, T. Fordham/DG, 166 Boulevard du Montparnasse, Paris XIV, 18 July [1923] [HG].

[40] T. Fordham/DG, 40 Well Walk, 'Monday' [pmk 22 October 1923] [HG].

[41] DG, *Familiar Faces*, p. 44.

a well-known artist and British 'Surrealist', Alec eschewed modern art, in favour of the preservation of a traditional 'English' aesthetic. Now Alec joined Duncan, Frankie and Tommy as one of Bunny's coterie of intimate male friends.

'I do have the devil's own luck don't I?' Bunny wrote to Mina in October.[42] He had just received another literary award: the James Tait Black Memorial Prize, amounting to £144. Based at the University of Edinburgh, the prize had been established in 1919 and has been likened to the Booker Prize.[43] Two prizes were awarded annually, one for the best work of fiction, the other for the best biography. That year Percy Lubbock won the biography prize for *Earlham*. D.H. Lawrence, E.M. Forster and Walter de la Mare were among others who won the fiction prize in the 1920s, while A.S. Byatt, Ian McEwan and Jonathan Franzen are more recent winners. Bunny was particularly glad to be in the company of Lytton Strachey, who won the biography prize the previous year.

While Bunny gallivanted about with his friends, Ray was less mobile, feeling trapped at The Cearne with baby Richard. She wrote complaining to Bunny that it was hard looking after a baby with no help and in 'another person's house', which 'doubles the trouble'.[44] She informed him she would be going to East Chaldon the following week, for Ray had met Theo Powys and his wife Violet on one of their rare sorties to London. Meanwhile, Bunny discussed the possibility of moving to East Chaldon with Tommy, but decided against the idea. Ray had not been party to this discussion.

[42] DG/Mina Curtiss, Birrell & Garnett, [pmk 5 October 1923] [Berg].
[43] Eliot Weinberger, 'Who Made it New?, *The New York Review of Books*, 23 June 2011.
[44] RAG/DG, The Cearne, Edenbridge, 'Thurs' [1923] [Northwestern].

Chapter Thirteen

'I never much enjoy writing itself but the wonderful thing is to go about living in two worlds: a real double life.'[1]

In January 1924 Bunny and Ray took a holiday, travelling in Spain where their destination was remote Yegen in Grenada, where they were guests of Gerald Brenan. It was a timely vacation, for Ray's nomadic existence had contributed to a growing sense of disloca-tion from Bunny. With nothing to distract them, except donkeys and magnificent scenery, they could focus entirely on each other. The break was such a positive experience that they planned to rent Gerald's house later in the year when he returned to England.

Meanwhile, Edward had read the manuscript of *A Man in the Zoo*, which he returned to Bunny with several pages of comments. Bunny admired his father's critical acumen and had praised his book, *Friday Nights*, published the previous year, telling Edward, 'No one in the world has your gifts […] you never miss the small-est individual flavour'.[2] Edward was renowned for his incisive

---

[1] DG/Mina Curtiss, Hilton, 23 June 1955 [Berg].
[2] DG/EG, [The Cearne], 'Sunday' [22 May 1922] [Northwestern].

thoroughness with authors, but Bunny hadn't bargained for quite how thorough his father would be in dissecting his own work. Edward wrote page after page, underlining points, rewriting dialogue, indicating areas where he thought narrative tension or tone might be improved. 'In "L into F" he wrote, 'it was the <u>emotional integrity</u> of the man's mood that enabled one to stand the close detailed texture of the style [...]. Here, I think, you should try to introduce little (quiet) shafts of satire at various points – & thus relieve the rather <u>wearing</u> monotony of the love narrative.'[3]

Bunny knew Edward was a hard taskmaster, but Bunny wasn't one of his authors, and he gave his father his manuscripts to read as a mark of respect as much as for critical analysis. This created a tension in their relationship. Hitherto Bunny had been very much his own person, forging a career, or careers, without recourse to parental advice. But now he was working in the very field in which his father's critical faculties were so finely honed. Bunny needed to strike a balance between following his own creative instincts and appearing to respect, rather than reject, his father's counsel.

A Man in the Zoo did not have quite the critical success of *Lady into Fox*, although it sold extremely well. The signed, limited subscribers' edition was oversubscribed, and the ordinary edition was re-printed three times in the first couple of months. Once again the book was enhanced by Ray's exquisite woodcuts, although again Bunny failed to dedicate it to her, dedicating it instead to Henrietta Bingham and Mina Kirstein. Reviewers mainly perceived the book as a fantasy engaging with

---

[3] EG/DG, 19 Pond Place, Chelsea, 'Friday 1' [February 1924] [Northwestern].

metamorphosis in the style of *Lady into Fox*. Instead it was a more philosophical and scientific enquiry into the nature of man as a species and whether a hierarchy of species exists with man at the apex. There is also a dig at what was to become Bunny's *bête noire*: organised religion. And so the plot spins on an argument, during a visit to London Zoo, between a young Scotsman, John Cromartie, and his girlfriend, Josephine Lacket, on the nature of love. Cromartie believes that Josephine's Christian ethos in loving all men is incompatible with fully loving one man. He storms off and volunteers himself as an exhibit in the ape house, on the premise that the species *Homo sapiens* is missing from the zoo.

The story works on the principle that animals are social beings which should not live in solitary confinement. Moreover, in a zoo where there is no privacy, love cannot flourish, as it is an essentially private emotion. Cromartie is badly mauled by a neighbouring orang-utan and is taken to hospital. When he recovers he discovers the ape house has become a man house, the orang-utan replaced by an African-American man. When Cromartie informs the zoo authorities that he and Josephine want to marry and live together in his cage, the authorities insist he is released. Hand in hand, he and Josephine disappear into Regent's Park. 'Nobody looked at them, nobody noticed them. The crowd was chiefly composed of couples like themselves.'[4]

The *Evening Standard*'s critic thought that Bunny had established for himself a genre in which he told 'a preposterous story in a perfectly convincing fashion';[5] the *Scotsman* concurred, stating that Mr Garnett had created his own 'stylistic convention' in which he led the reader willingly to enter into the 'suspension of

---

[4]   David Garnett, *A Man in the Zoo* (London: Chatto & Windus, 1924), p. 93.
[5]   24 April 1924.

disbelief'.[6] Leonard Woolf, in the *Nation* commended Bunny for moving beyond the '*tour de force*' of his first novel, to produce a second in which his own voice could be discerned.[7] In the *New Statesman*, Raymond Mortimer, henceforward Bunny's most loyal reviewer, predicted that Mr Garnett 'will take his place in the textbooks of the future as one of the fixed stars of twentieth-century English literature'.[8] The reviews were generally positive, but, as often with second novels, anxious about which direction Bunny would take in his next book.

The Northern Whig, published in Belfast, announced that the success of Mr Garnett's first two novels 'will break up one of the most interesting partnerships in London'. Mr Garnett would be leaving Birrell & Garnett, to devote more time to writing, and 'His present plan is for Mrs Garnett and himself to take a house in Spain'.[9] Bunny was able to leave the shop to focus on writing because Chatto & Windus, under the benevolent guidance of Charles Prentice, offered guaranteed terms for Bunny's next three books. Bunny was also fortunate in finding a purchaser for his share of the business, which was bought by Graham Pollard, a twenty-one-year-old undergraduate at Oxford who would become one of the most respected bibliographers in the business. The shop, which never made much money, was eventually sold to Quaritch in 1939.

Bunny's plan to move with Ray to Spain had to be abandoned because Ray was pregnant. She informed Bunny that if she was to have another child, they would need to have a proper home

---

6 24 April 1924.

7 Undated press cutting [?May] [1924].

8 26 April 1924.

9 Undated press cutting [?May] [1924].

where they could live together as a family. 'You must', Bunny agreed, 'have a settled home in England, in the country & you must have it at once'. He also promised that he would not 'have love affairs with women without talking to you about it at the time & I will try not to have any at all if I can help it'. 'I don't know', he added, 'how not to hurt you […]. I want your love, & depend on your love. There is nothing else in my life that I value at all – but I am a selfish pig.'[10] Whilst Bunny behaved like a selfish pig in London, Ray made a base of sorts at East Chaldon, where Bunny visited her and Richard at weekends, bringing with him a succession of friends including Tommy's brother, Garrow Tomlin.

In September 1924 Bunny wrote to Sylvia Townsend Warner: 'Such excitements, my dear, have been happening to me. It's not a person, but a – no, not an animal – but a house that I have fallen in love with this time. And I feel as I did when I was twenty, that it was irretrievable, irrevocable – that if I cannot live in that house I shall never live in another.'[11] The property had been advertised in *Country Life* and Bunny had wasted no time in viewing it. He had fallen in love with Hilton Hall, a handsome, mellow, weathered red-brick, three-storey, seventeenth-century house in a small village some dozen miles from Cambridge. 'There is a staircase of oak', he told Sylvia, 'carved beams, a wide hall, splendid dining-room and drawing-room. Six bedrooms. A bath, hot and cold water, two wcs, a convenient kitchen with a good range.' It was well-appointed outside too, with two acres of orchard, a tennis court and a seventeenth-century square dove house, itself large enough to accommodate

---

[10] DG/RAG, Nonesuch Press [April 1924] [Northwestern].
[11] DG/STW [September 1924], in RG, ed., *Sylvia and David*, pp. 8–9.

a human, rather than avian family.

Bunny was desperate to buy the house; Ray, who had seen and admired it, was more cautious, partly because she worried that Bunny would 'fall out of love with it'. He wrote to Ray, now at The Cearne, demanding that she made up her mind regarding the purchase. 'What an absurdity', she replied, 'here we are only 26 miles apart settling such an important thing as whether I shall spend ½ my capital on a house by a note from you demanding yes or no by return.'[12] The asking price was £2,000 (c. £60,000 today). Ray's offer of £1,600 was accepted.

Bunny couldn't get used to the idea of a house of his own, because he had always lived in other people's houses. In anticipation of their finally living together under their own roof, Bunny wrote to Ray, telling her he loved her. 'I love you most tenderly and I want to be with you and for us to understand & love each other [...]. You will never find anyone you love as much as me; I shall never find anyone I love as much as you. Why', he added, 'do we poison one another?'[13] The 'poison', as Bunny called it, arose from their differing attitudes to marriage. Bunny expected Ray to understand that she was the most important woman in his life, but that he needed the diversion of other love affairs. Ray wanted constancy.

As they possessed next to no furniture, Bunny purchased items from local sale rooms, but even so acknowledged that some rooms would need to remain empty, as he was broke. But he relished the quiet and tranquillity of Hilton, with 'Only the tap tap of the smith's hammer ringing on the anvil almost whenever

---

[12] RAG/DG, The Cearne, Friday [September 1924] [Northwestern].
[13] DG/RAG, 'Friday' [October 1924] [Northwestern].

one listens for it'.[14] Vanessa and Duncan viewed the house, Tommy helped Bunny move in, and Edward came to visit, declaring that he was 'simply delighted with Hilton House. It has a rare personality & charm.'[15]

Hilton seemed an odd choice of location, far from Sussex or Kent with their proximity to London, Constance and Charleston. But Bunny remained conscious of his parents' position as 'outsiders' and wanted to live in a village where he and his family could participate in village life. Moreover, the bleak, flat fenland area surrounding Hilton had the kind of challenging appeal which Bunny always loved. He preferred countryside which did not relinquish its charms too easily, where beauty was offered slowly if you were prepared to seek it. Hilton was close to Cambridge, where Bunny had many friends and Ray had a brother, Horace, and near enough to London to travel there quickly and easily. It was also far enough from London for Bunny to feel that he could, if need be, maintain city life and country life in entirely separate compartments.

Bunny did not exaggerate when he told Sylvia he had fallen in love with a house; his love for Hilton Hall would endure, and he soon came to love it the way he loved The Cearne. Like his parents, he was not a believer in luxury, and although the house gradually acquired more furniture, it remained cold, draughty and Spartan. Gerald Brenan informed Carrington that he admired the house, 'but rather shuddered at its discomfort'.[16] Bunny and Ray were generous and hospitable hosts providing delicious meals and plenty of wine, but they never seemed to

---

[14] DG/CG, Hilton [October 1924] [HRRC].
[15] EG/DG, 19 Pond Place, 11 November 1924 [Northwestern].
[16] G. Brenan/Carrington, Tuesday night, 29 December 1926 [TGA].

remedy the chill which issued from the stone floors and penetrated every corner. According to Frances Partridge, 'The vast beamed fireplaces in the drawing-room and dining-room gave out virtually no heat at all from their log fires in winter, even at close range. That was the snag – Hilton was the coldest house I have ever spent a night in.'[17] Over the years Hilton was embellished with many beautiful things including paintings by Duncan and Vanessa. Tommy's sculpted head of Henrietta Bingham was soon joined by those of Duncan, Lytton Strachey, Julia Strachey and Virginia Woolf, a gallery of friends who gazed silently upon the residents of Hilton Hall.

Early in 1925 Ray wrote from Hilton to Sylvia Townsend Warner, reporting that:

> Bunny is roaming round now looking & imagining what this place will be like in 20 years time. He has planted all the little apples in the orchard, the cherries & the peaches & the quince. We have planted a nut hedge [...] & apples on espaliers by the lawn – a walnut! & today a tiny Mulberry not 4 ft high but with a Mulberry curve in its stalk. We considered carefully which way it would curve to look best in 100 years time from the drawing room window.[18]

The garden was the recipient of all the love and attention which Bunny could lavish upon it. Having 'fallen in love with working on the land' at Wissett, Bunny's love affair continued at Hilton.

---

[17] Frances Partridge, *Everything to Lose: Diaries 1945–1960* (London: Victor Gollancz, 1985; Phoenix paperback edition 1997), p. 197.

[18] RAG/STW, Hilton [c. January 1925] [Berg].

He planted the fruit and vegetables he wanted to eat – globe artichokes, *haricots verts*, aubergines and courgettes – vegetables which he had earlier promoted in his version of Gressent. He and Ray liked the kinds of dishes which Elizabeth David would champion twenty-five years later – largely French and Mediterranean. Bunny enjoyed not only the fruits of his labour, but also physical engagement with the earth. He loved to be outdoors and relished feeling his strength as he dug, raked and hoed the soil. He approached his garden scientifically, understanding the importance of compost and manure, of soil, light, water and air. But it was also a place where he could be part of the changing seasons, observing the natural world around him. Very soon he and Ray acquired chickens and ducks, and of course Bunny lost little time in making Hilton a home for bees. Now dividing his working life between the Nonesuch Press and writing, the garden provided an outlet for his physical energy.

The Nonesuch Press had moved from its crepuscular basement on Gerrard Street to more spacious premises. Profits had been sufficient to allow Vera to purchase a substantial and graceful property, a former eighteenth century coffee house at 16 Great James Street, around the corner from Great Ormond Street, bordering Bloomsbury. The main office was on the ground floor, where Bunny also had a small office. Francis and Vera (now married) had adjoining offices on the first floor. A 'war widow', Mrs Stephens, was taken on as secretary, and two young women worked in the office as well. Bunny usually came in for a couple of days a week, conveniently spending the night in one of the spare bedrooms above the offices, returning to Hilton the evening of the second day. But he took Nonesuch work home, reading manuscripts, deciding which authors to bring back into print, corresponding with editors and working on the prospectuses through which he and his partners marketed their books.

That first autumn at Hilton, Bunny was working on a new novel, *The Sailor's Return*. Edward had read the book, in draft, but Bunny felt his father had neither grasped what he was trying to achieve, nor understood the importance of the tone in which the book was written. 'The effect at present', Edward reported, 'is a bit too much as though it had been run into a mould.'[19] Bunny found it difficult to contradict Edward, venturing that his story was 'better than you think', adding, lamely, 'who knows you may like it better when you see it next'.[20] But Bunny did not wish to be deflected from his artistic purpose; he wanted his story to remain cast in the narrative form of his own devising. And so he took the manuscript along to Ebury Street in London's Belgravia, to the home of the writer George Moore, who had earlier pronounced *Lady into Fox* a masterpiece.

Bunny had met Moore in 1924 when Moore approached the Nonesuch Press with a proposal to compile and edit an anthology of verse, in which he would propound his theories regarding the essence of *Pure Poetry*, the anthology's title. Initially Francis and Vera opposed the idea, but Bunny thought Moore's name would enhance the Nonesuch list. Francis, however, disliked Moore on personal grounds, and eventually only conceded to the publication on condition that Bunny would be responsible for all dealings with the author. Then in his seventies, Moore was formal in bearing, a gentleman of the nineteenth century who fastidiously observed social niceties and adhered to established routines. Attuned to such archaisms, Bunny was able to respond

---

[19] EG/DG, 19 Pond Place, 14 February 1925 [Northwestern].
[20] DG/EG, Hilton Hall [pmk 18 February 1925] [Northwestern].

with due *politesse*, always addressing Moore as 'Mr Moore' and careful to flatter this egotistical individual. Thus the two men established a cordial and formal friendship built upon the subject of books.

Perhaps Bunny turned to Moore specifically because he knew Edward didn't rate Moore's work. In contrast, Constance considered *The Mummer's Wife* and *Esther Waters* 'among the greatest realistic novels in English', although she thought his work overall inconsistent, and liked to quote her father-in-law's dictum that Moore was 'a bit of a goose and a bit of a genius'.[21] It was odd that Bunny had not been put off by Moore's procrastination over his poetry book. Moore revised repeatedly, neither satisfied with what he had written nor the poems he had selected. Even when the book was being printed, he submitted additional paragraphs then changed his mind.

Bunny should have delivered his complete manuscript to Prentice in January 1925. Although he had finished the book, he wasn't happy with the result. He had already re-written it once, but still felt it was 'a question of grouting the rubble in the piers'. Unfortunately Knopf had anticipated announcing the novel in his Spring List, and Bunny worried that he would be annoyed about the delay. He also worried that one of his main characters might be of dubious acceptability to his American publisher: 'I have broken it to him', Bunny informed Prentice, 'that Tulip is a negress'.[22]

Hopeful that Moore might be able to help grout the rubble in his manuscript, in early March 1925 Bunny dined with him at Ebury Street. This set the pattern for subsequent meals, in which

---

[21] DG, *Familiar Faces*, p. 73.
[22] DG/Charles Prentice, Hilton, 29 January [1925] [Reading].

the menu invariably consisted of whiting (a fish Bunny detested) followed by miniscule mutton cutlets and potato, and then fruit tart; all washed down with a single diminutive glass of sauternes. If Bunny disliked Edward's minute dissections of his text, it is hard to understand how he endured those of George Moore. It was as though in turning his back on his father's critical judgement, Bunny jumped from the frying pan into the fire. For Moore not only pedantically questioned individual words, but constantly changed his mind about the words he questioned. He disliked the novel's 'dismal' ending, and even when the English edition was in print, tried to persuade Bunny to alter it for the French translation. All this continued until Bunny finished writing the book towards the end of May. Between times, he dutifully journeyed back and forth to Ebury Street, suffering the whiting and the procrastination, the criticisms only slightly sweetened by the sauternes.

Moore's involvement alarmed Edward. 'I hope to goodness', he declared, 'you will not catch his <u>manner</u>', adding dismissively, 'This is all very well for his writing & for people who like it. But if you caught his manner it would be a reflection of something reflected.'[23] Thenceforward it was Edward who read Bunny's manuscripts, for having experienced the mentoring of Moore, Bunny felt comparatively at ease under his father's affectionate scrutiny and more confident in his own powers of judgement. Even so, Bunny dedicated the book to Moore, perhaps as an act of deference rather than gratitude.

The Sailor's Return was an unusually brave book for its time, as its subject was inter-racial marriage and the prejudice which ensued. The plot is simple: set in the nineteenth century, it

---

[23] EG/DG, 19 Pond Place, Chelsea, The Cearne, 'Whit Monday' 1925 [this is misdated; it was Easter Monday] [Northwestern].

revolves around an English sailor, William Targett, who finds himself marooned in Africa, where he falls in love with a young African princess, Tulip. He marries her, they have a son, Sambo, and when the child is three years old, Targett brings his family to England. They settle in Dorset in a village called Maiden Newbarrow, closely based on East Chaldon, where Targett becomes publican of the local inn, The Sailor's Return.[24] Tulip's dowry, in the form of gold and jewels, allows Targett to rent the inn and buy fine clothes for his wife.

From the outset, Tulip and Sambo meet with hostility, not only from the locals, but also from Targett's sister, Lucy. Various efforts are made to hound Tulip and Sambo from Maiden Newbarrow, but these are thwarted by Targett's loving protection. Eventually he is set upon by a local carrier and his henchman, and dies from his wounds. The 'dismal' ending, to which Moore referred, finds Tulip fleeing to Southampton in an effort to obtain a passage to Africa for herself and Sambo; only Sambo can be taken aboard; Tulip returns to Maiden Newbarrow, where she becomes skivvy to the new publican. Ironically, she is now accepted in the village, for she has become invisible, and wearing rags rather than fine clothes, no longer presents a threat by muddying the waters of race and class. In the eyes of this fictional community, she finally occupies her rightful position as a serf or slave. As for Sambo, there is no resolution: the reader remains ignorant of his fate.

By means of Bunny's now customary simple, direct and lucid prose, he distanced himself from his text, like a scientist looking

---

[24] The Sailor's Return is the name of the inn at East Chaldon, which still exists. Bunny often stayed there on his visits to Tommy, T.F. Powys and Sylvia Townsend Warner, who also moved there.

through a microscope to reveal the complexity of the specimen beneath. At the same time, he consciously approached the craft of fiction 'as a painter & not as a writer should work'.[25] He always acknowledged that those years with Duncan and Vanessa in the First World War had a formative effect on his writing. 'All writers', he said, 'have a great deal to learn from painters, for painting is a purer art than story-telling.'[26] By this he meant that he liked to see the story unfold visually before him. 'It takes time for the images to solidify', he wrote later, adding, 'I may not say whether a donkey on the beach is light grey or chocolate but I have to know it myself'.[27]

If Edward worried that Bunny was confining himself to a formula, he need not have done. Although the directness and immediacy of the prose remained, conferring a style which was becoming identifiably that of David Garnett, the subject matter was a complete departure from his two previous works of serious fiction. As Bunny told Lytton Strachey, it was 'a big canvas, drawn entirely from the imagination'.[28] Moreover, although some reviewers perplexingly failed to identify any moral core to the story (perhaps a sign of the times), the theme reflected Bunny's belief in the personal rights of freedom and free will. He didn't underline any particular message, expecting his readers to make up their own minds, but the message is not hard to discern, and chimes with Bloomsbury's emphasis on the priorities of personal relationships. In choosing Tulip, Targett exercised

---

[25] DG/GLS, Hilton Hall, 20 May 1925 [BL].

[26] *The London Artists' Association, Recent Paintings by Duncan Grant with a foreword by David Garnett* (London: The Cooling Galleries) [1931].

[27] DG/AVG, Charry, 24 July 1974 [KCC].

[28] DG/GLS, Hilton Hall, 20 May 1925 [BL].

his right to make his own choices in love irrespective of the mores of a wider society. *The Sailor's Return* underlines this dichotomy between private and public morality. Bunny believed that whereas individual morality could be employed in relation to oneself and to the outside world, 'The community has no morals, it only has power which it uses with greater or less expediency & intelligence or stupidity'.[29]

Reviews were largely very favourable and universal in praising Bunny's prose, 'the exquisiteness with which the story is told', 'that simple, exact English of his';[30] 'death and violence seem a mere ripple of prose. Perhaps it is the short simple words he uses.'[31] Some praised the honesty and 'truthfulness' of the story: 'Mr Garnett [...] does not shirk the truth of things, and the reader who has followed the poignant story from beginning to end will be forced to admit that it must have happened so, though he will also reflect mournfully on man's inhumanity to man.'[32] The *Daily Telegraph* declared: 'the action moves inevitably forward at an even pace to its sad end, with nothing arbitrary or unnatural to enhance the tragedy, only the inevitable pressure of circumstances and the malice of the ignorant'.[33]

There were a few dissenting voices. R. Ellis Roberts in *Weekly Westminster* shared George Moore's concerns about the 'miserable ending', feeling Bunny should have allowed Tulip and Sambo to leave – or to die – together, 'as simple and savage people can

---

29 DG, 'Morals', unpublished MS [Northwestern].
30 Sylvia Lynd, *Daily News*, 17 September 1925.
31 *Liverpool Post*, 17 September 1925.
32 *The Scotsman*, 24 September 1925.
33 29 September 1925.

die'.[34] The *Daily News* disliked 'the black heathen's' attitude to
Christian customs, and felt it lacked imagination to allow 'the
heathen' to show herself 'less cruel than the Christians'.[35] The
TLS review began by asking, 'Exactly what Mr Garnett's intention may be in writing this tale of a sailor who married a negress
and settled down in a Dorsetshire village', concluding 'we have
no means of knowing'.[36] This, however, inspired a riposte from
Bunny's friend, the doyen of literary critics, Desmond MacCarthy,
writing as 'Affable Hawk' in the *New Statesman*. He devoted several
pages to the review, demolishing the *TLS* review word by word.
MacCarthy affirmed that 'It is a sad enough story, but it does not
damp one's spirits', pronouncing it 'a work of art'.[37]

While Bunny was in the thick of writing and re-writing, he
and Ray were excited about the imminent birth of their baby –
or babies – the local doctor was certain that Ray was carrying
twins. On Easter Sunday, 12 April, a fine boy was born at 8.45
in the morning. Bunny was delighted with the timing, because he
had to fetch the doctor away from church. There was only one
infant, but he weighed a hefty 9lb 6oz. According to Bunny, the
baby had Garnett hands, which he thought miniature examples
of those of Edward and Dr Richard Garnett. Bunny and Ray
named their second son William Tomlin Kasper. Tommy was
thrilled to be commemorated thus. 'My dear', he wrote to Bunny,
'I do wish your new baby the greatest luck in the world, & if his
good fortune in happening on his parents be an augury for the
future, he should do well enough [...]. I think of you both (as I

---

[34] 19 September 1925.
[35] *Daily News*, 17 September 1925.
[36] 17 September 1925.
[37] 3 October 1925.

always do) & of your family & your establishment & your work with a great deal of love & admiration.'[38]

Bunny's establishment came alive at weekends, when he and Ray filled the house with friends and family. Cambridge had long been an outpost of Bloomsbury (or was Bloomsbury an outpost of Cambridge?) so Hilton was ideally positioned to welcome those of the Bloomsbury–Cambridge axis, and their friends and friends of friends. One letter from Bunny to Constance, written in June 1925, gives a flavour of Hilton's hectic social whirl:

> Garrow Tomlin has been with us since the Friday before Whitsun [...]. We have also had two friends of Ray's camping here, visits from Cambridge [Ray's brother Tom Marshall and his wife Nadine], & on Friday last the Partridges [Carrington and Ralph Partridge]. On Saturday Lytton came to tea [...]. In the evening we went to the play [in Cambridge], followed by a dreary party. Next day [John] Hayward, Frances Marshall, Lettice Baker and someone else came out for tea & dinner [...]. Tomorrow Rayne [Bunny's cousin] & John Nickalls & Christopher are coming to tea [...]. On [...] Saturday Francis Meynell brings down a cricket eleven – Francis & Vera stay the weekend.[39]

This was the first of several Hilton Village versus Publishers cricket matches, for which Bunny and Ray would prepare an enormous cold lunch and cricket tea. In the evening there would

---

[38] S. Tomlin/DG, Widcombe, Hillside Road, [pmk 16 April 1925] [Northwestern].

[39] DG/CG, Hilton, 5 June 1925 [HRRC].

be dinner, the publishers' team seated around the long dining table in Hilton Hall.

Bunny and Ray were conveniently placed to offer hospitality to a changing cast of Cambridge undergraduates, bright young men and women who had caught the eye of a Harry Norton or Maynard Keynes. One such was John Hayward. He was a remarkable man. Not only was he more than competent to edit the Nonesuch Press *Collected Works of Rochester* while still a twenty-year-old undergraduate, but he did not let the matter of his progressing muscular dystrophy interfere with living life to the full. Bunny thought him 'exceptionally courageous', 'gay, affectionate and very witty'.[40] He was a considerable literary scholar, an assiduous collector of books, and in the 1930s his London flat buzzed with the conversation of writers and intellectuals. Hayward was a flamboyant character, a dandy, but not a fop who, according to Bunny, had the air of a seventeenth century dramatist about him. When Bunny wrote praising Hayward's Introduction to *Rochester*, the young editor replied that it was 'the kindliest letter I have ever had'.[41] Like many others to come, Hayward was always grateful to Bunny for this early support of his literary career.

---

[40] DG, *Familiar Faces*, p. 48.
[41] JDH/DG, King's College, Cambridge, 24 January [?1926] [Northwestern].

Chapter Fourteen

'My life now is divided into two parts. Nonesuch & Hilton.
Two or three days a week I go to town [...]. Then I am a
business man, well dressed, & a devil for work. I go to parties
etc. Here I look after my bees, potter in the garden, fiddle
away at a big book I have in my head & entertain weekend
visitors.'[1]

In the summer of 1925 Bunny began another book, a re-working
for an adult audience of the tale of Puss in Boots. In order to
concentrate on writing, he decided to accompany Alec Penrose
to France, where they would spend a month at Cassis, on the
Provencal coast. In mid-July, Ray, Richard and baby William
were dispatched to Judy and Dick Rendel in Kent, while Bunny
and Alec left for France.

Alec's wife Bertha and young daughter Sheila were already
installed at Cassis, together with Alec's brother Roland Penrose
and his beautiful girlfriend, the poet Valentine Andreé Boué. In

---

[1] DG/M Curtiss, Nonesuch Press, 16 James Street [but from Hilton], 30
May 1927 [Berg].

the circumstances, it was difficult for Bunny to focus on writing, and he was easily seduced by conversation and the delights of swimming in a warm sea. He wandered about wearing only trousers and a singlet, his arms bare and brown; swam every day, sailed in Roland's boat, and consumed delicious meals, drinking a bottle of wine at each of them. He attended fêtes and festivals, danced with lovely girls, and enjoyed something of a celebrity status with people joking about foxes turning into women.

All this he relayed to Ray in letter after letter. 'I love & treasure the thought of you every moment of the day', he wrote, 'You don't know how much I bless the day that sent you to me, for my own sake & my children'.[2] In his desire to share his happiness with Ray, he did not stop to consider how she felt, languishing in England with a small child and baby in tow. She was exhausted, but staying with relatives was not the kind of holiday she needed. Neither did she need to be told by her husband that he was having a fine time in close proximity to a glamorous beauty. He could not keep his eyes off Andreé, telling Ray she 'interests me very much. I want to make real friends with her.' 'I am not', he added disingenuously, 'the least in love with her or excited by her though she is beautiful beyond anything one is used to. She is the most beautiful creature I know.'[3]

Ray's anger manifested in silence: she punished Bunny by refusing to write. Why should she write happy responses to Bunny's descriptions of a woman with whom he seemed besotted? Bunny's protestations of love for Ray, often expressed in the context of her role as the mother of his children, might well have made her feel like a brood mare. But instead of understanding

---

[2] DG/RAG, Clos du Plan, Cassis [July 1925] [Northwestern].
[3] DG/RAG, [Cassis] part letter [August 1925] [Northwestern].

the cause of her silence, Bunny began to pen increasingly petu-
lant letters in which he questioned Ray's love. 'You are a cold
hearted unimaginative thing', he scolded, '& you have hurt me
by your misery of silence'.[4] Ray finally capitulated because she
needed to know about Bunny's plans to return home. 'My nerves
are raw', she wrote, '& I am very tired. This means nothing to
you as I've said it often before but my God I am tired & it seems
a pity to be too tired to be happy now that Richard & William
are small & adorable & want me all the time. When they are
older I expect they will be as unkind as you are & give me the
heartache same as you do.'[5]

Bunny and Andreé did not have an affair, but his inability to
dissimulate and self-indulgent assumption that Ray would want
vicariously to share his every experience, damaged his marriage.
He could never understand that the characteristic Bloomsbury
way of articulating, analysing, sharing, scrutinising and being
open about personal relationships was not appropriate for Ray.
She wanted to be happy, she wanted Bunny to love her, and she
hoped he loved her exclusively; but she did not want to know
about any other claims on his affections, real or imagined.

Ray also wanted to be taken into account; it was ironic that at
the very time when she, above all people, deserved a holiday,
Bunny should abandon her and go on vacation himself. It was
another example of that selfishness manifest since his childhood,
whereby he rarely did anything he didn't want to do and
conversely usually achieved what he wanted. The vacation was
also an example of his need for compartments, his urge to
prevent the domestic sphere from merging with his wider social

---

[4] DG/RAG, Clos du [Plan], Cassis, [August 1925] [Northwestern].
[5] RAG/DG [August 1925] [Northwestern].

circles. While he welcomed friends to socialise with his wife at Hilton, he rarely transported Ray into the external life he shared with them.

As Bunny told Lytton, 'France was delightful. For a month I recaptured my twentieth year.'[6] That was exactly what Bunny wanted: he wanted his family and all the happiness it brought him but also to be able to access a different world, in which he could return to a carefree youthful existence. In one of his earliest letters to Ray he told her, his tongue only slightly in his cheek, that what he wanted in life was 'Freedom', 'Unbounded Admiration', 'Universal success with women' and 'Eternal Youth'.[7] These were neither realistic long-term choices nor the most appropriate to a happy marriage, but they did reflect his boundless enthusiasm for living life to the full. Bunny lived very much in the day (though he liked to have something appealing on the horizon) and he liked to be in love because every new love affair provided a fresh affirmation that life had not become stagnant or moribund, but could offer new experiences and be eternally renewed.

That autumn, Bunny heard from his American publisher that 'Puss' had been turned down. He knew the decision was fair, conceding it 'a meaningless story badly done'.[8] But this was a blow: the first time he had suffered a rejection of his work. To compound matters, he felt directionless: even as Bunny worried about putting food in his children's mouths, he could not settle to work. Instead he whiled away his time remodelling the garden or playing badminton, joined in both enterprises by Tommy's

6 DG/GLS, Hilton, 'Monday' [?August] [1925] [BL].
7 DG/RAG, Birrell & Garnett [c. 1920] [Northwestern].
8 DG/Charles Prentice, Hilton, 3 September 1925 [Reading].

brother, Garrow Tomlin, who was spending more and more time at Hilton. Edward advised Bunny that the only way forward was 'to seclude yourself & go on day after day at it <u>more or less all day</u>'.[9] But his advice fell on deaf ears: Bunny allowed himself to be endlessly distracted, attending numerous parties, including one where he saw Picasso talking to the film star Douglas Fairbanks.

There were parties and parties: those of Bloomsbury tended to be more intellectual, with 'good talk' a priority. But there was dancing too, Lydia accompanying Maynard dancing the 'Keynes-Keynes' or everyone pushing back the furniture and dancing to gramophone records. Fancy-dress parties were favoured, Bunny and Geoffrey Keynes on one occasion encased in the rear and front of a dappled horse, like a pantomime pony. Light-hearted plays were performed on topical themes, usually with one member of Bloomsbury impersonating another. At one party, hosted by Bunny, Tommy came dressed as a fortune-teller, remaining unrecognised by his friends as he read their palms in an insalubriously shady alcove (the toilet in Duncan's studio). Bunny later acknowledged that the main aim was 'to get the young woman whose eyes answered one's own downstairs in an empty room among the hats and coats'.[10] It was as though he had not progressed beyond youth.

As if Bunny did not have sufficient opportunity to socialise, he and Tommy established a dining club, for the purpose of good conversation among select friends. They called it the Cranium Club, after Thomas Love Peacock's Mr Cranium, the brainy

---

[9] EG/DG, Portland House, St Davids, Pembrokeshire, 9 September 1925 [Northwestern].

[10] DG, *Familiar Faces*, p. 67.

character with the enormous domed head, in *Headlong Hall*. The club met monthly, initially at the Verdi Restaurant on Wardour Street, later at the Reform Club. New members had to be proposed by two existing members, and then not be blackballed, which guaranteed nepotistic exclusivity. The list of members reveals just how much Bunny's influence prevailed. In 1929, four years after the club's formation, members included Frankie Birrell, Bunny's brother-in-law Tom Marshall, Garrow Tomlin, Gerald Brenan, Duncan Grant, Raymond Mortimer, Alec Penrose, Leonard Woolf, E.M. Forster, Charles Prentice, Lytton Strachey, James Strachey, Adrian Stephen, Maynard Keynes and Ralph Wright. It was all highly informal, but as Bunny's son Richard commented (having become a member in 1950) 'We were a distinguished lot.' 'It was an occasion to talk on equal terms with Stephen Spender or Isaiah Berlin or hear Christopher Strachey talking about computers when they had barely been invented.'[11] The club was very private, with no publicity. There were no papers or presentations, it was simply an occasion for people to meet, dine and converse. It is also interesting, looking at that list of members, to note that Bunny was probably the only person on it who had not attended public school. But he had now indubitably joined the literary and artistic elite and was no longer an 'outsider'.

Shortly after Christmas 1925 Bunny wrote to Edward, declaring, 'I have at last got my feet on solid rock'. He had conceived a novel, 'all of which stands clear in my mind like a lovely scene in the early morning: the elms with rooks cawing, the fields still soaked with dew, the first sounds of men moving about … all in early summer.' 'My difficulty now', he added, 'is only to find the

---

[11] Richard Garnett email to author, 14 June 2010.

right words … to mix my paints & lay them on with clear strokes.'[12] But as the months passed, Bunny struggled with the novel, *Go She Must!* In June 1926 he wrote despairingly to Prentice: 'I hate my heroine & do nothing […]. Most of the book is filthily badly written. I don't even know the heroine's name.'[13] A few weeks later, he handed Prentice the manuscript, seeking his opinion on one particular episode in which Bunny had 'introduced a scene of copulation'.[14]

This cannot have been good news for Prentice, as at this time, publishers and even printers could be prosecuted for anything the official censor deemed obscene. But Bunny abhorred censorship and continually nudged at the censor's margin. In *Lady into Fox* he had mocked the idea of fidelity in marriage but escaped the censor by means of ingenious metaphor: making the heroine metamorphose into an animal and commit adultery with a dog fox. The reader was being asked to consider whether animals could be adulterers. It was, as Bunny said, a *reductio ad absurdum* of the idea of fidelity in marriage.

In *Go She Must!* the central character, Anne Dunnock, is the daughter of a rector in the fenland village of Dry Coulter (Hilton). She feels friendless and unfulfilled until she meets an artist, Richard Sotheby, to whom she is drawn as he promises freedom in the form of Paris. Anne follows Richard to Paris, where he lives with two friends, Gerald Grandison and Gerald's mistress, Ginette. Anne assumes Richard is in love with Ginette; in fact he is in love with Gerald. Given the censor's watchful eye, Bunny could not be overt about Gerald's bisexuality and

---

[12] DG/EG, Hilton Hall, [1926] [Northwestern].

[13] DG/C Prentice, 'Thursday' [C&W stamp 21 June 1926] [Reading].

[14] DG/C Prentice, Hilton, 10 July [1926] [Reading].

213

Richard's homosexuality, but it is implicit as Gerald explains to Anne, ' "there has been a great deal between Richard and me" ', adding, ' "You see, Richard was very fond of me; he cares about nobody else" '.[15] This particular sentence caused Bunny much concern. He wrote to Prentice explaining that he felt it essential to the book, although recognising that it was one of his narrative's 'chief improprieties'.[16]

Gerald falls in love with Anne, abandoning both Richard and Ginette for her. The Richard–Gerald–Ginette trio echoes that of Bunny, Duncan and Vanessa, and there is one scene in particular which is a direct *homage* to Duncan Grant, for it replicates that first night he and Bunny spent together, when Bunny slept in Duncan's bed in his studio and Duncan lay on the floor. In the novel, Anne occupies Bunny's position on the bed and Gerald lies on the floor. 'For a long while Anne went on stroking his hair, and when at last they fell asleep he was still grasping her hand in both of his and holding it to his lips.'[17]

Go She Must! embraces several themes to which Bunny returned, including his belief in the fluidity of sexuality, that it is the person to whom one is attracted, not their gender: ' "Why on earth will you persist in regarding Ginette as a woman?" ' Gerald demands, ' "Ginette is Ginette, just as I am Gerald and you are Richard" '.[18] Bunny's dislike of organised religion filters through the figure of Anne's father, the increasingly deranged Reverend Dunnock, whom Bunny places outside normal society, which he represents as the natural world of ploughmen and village life.

[15] David Garnett, *Go She Must!* (London: Chatto & Windus, 1927), pp. 221–2.
[16] DG/C Prentice, Hilton, 1 August [1926] [Reading].
[17] DG, *Go She Must!*, p. 229.
[18] DG, *Go She Must!*, p. 183.

The vicar refuses to give the ploughmen a donation on 'Plough Monday'[19] because he can't understand any tradition beyond that of the ritual of church. However, he experiences an epiphany after his wife's death, when he tells himself that she has gone to Heaven and is surprised 'that the words with which he comforted others held no consolation for him'.[20] The Reverend Dunnock's religiosity recedes as he becomes increasingly like his namesake, the diminutive brown-and-grey bird which creeps nervously in the margins of gardens. He feeds the birds, and eventually removes all the windows in the vicarage so they can fly freely in and out. As his home becomes theirs, he merges with them, and they perch upon him as if he were St Francis of Assisi. The vicar thus finds redemption in the natural world, and calling his birds 'angels' turns from Christianity to pantheism. It is another metamorphosis.

Bunny dedicated *Go She Must!* to Stephen Tomlin: it would not have been the kindest of titles to dedicate to Ray. The scene of copulation to which Bunny referred seems to have been excised, presumably replaced with the more chaste bed and floor sleeping arrangements. But the covert references to homosexuality and the overt depiction of an independent young and single woman would have had far greater potency for readers in the 1920s than they do today. Moreover, such themes were extremely 'modern', part of a general movement among British authors to attain the same principles of free expression that could be found in France. It was no accident that the book's heroine acquired both personal and sexual freedom in Paris.

Although the novel was generally well received, some of those

---

[19] The first Monday after Epiphany; an East Anglian tradition.
[20] DG, *Go She Must!*, p. 66.

closest to Bunny expressed reservations, largely because they detected the taint of George Moore. Sylvia Townsend Warner felt there were 'little early Moore inflections, which muffle your outline',[21] and Edward confessed to feeling prejudiced against the book because of Bunny's 'absorption of the George Moore method of telling a story'.[22] Bunny's penchant for Moore's novels was well known among his friends, who tolerated it up to a point. One evening at the Cranium, Gerald Brenan fled after hearing too much of Bunny 'invoking the merits of George Moore whom I detest'.[23]

As a novelist, journalist and publisher, Bunny was a major player in the London literary scene of the 1920s. He was also beginning to exercise influence over other writers' careers. His work for the Nonesuch Press introduced new editors and authors to the world of books, not least John Hayward and Geoffrey Keynes, both of whom went on to have distinguished literary careers. But Bunny was also in a position to make recommendations to other publishers. In Chatto & Windus, and especially in Charles Prentice, Bunny found a publisher who was not only willing to consider new talent, but had an innate facility to discern it. After the First World War, Chatto & Windus had one of the strongest stables of new authors in Britain. Bunny had already persuaded Prentice to publish T.F. Powys, and now he did the same with Sylvia Townsend Warner's *Lolly Willowes*, which, he informed Prentice, would be a 'sure-fire success'.[24]

---

[21] STW/DG, 121 Inverness Terrace, 9 November 1927, in RG, *Sylvia and David*, p. 33.

[22] EG/DG, 19 Pond Place, 30 September 1926 [Northwestern].

[23] G. Brenan/Carrington, Monday 3 May 1926 [TGA].

[24] DG/C. Prentice [C&W stamp 6 February 1926] [Reading].

Bunny's renown was such that the newspapers celebrated both Theo Powys and Sylvia as the 'discoveries' of Mr David Garnett. He was so well known that he appeared on the wireless in the series Walks through London, where celebrated writers described the district they knew best. Bunny's subject was Bloomsbury, and according to the *Radio Times*, 'Mr David Garnett [...] holds the franchise of the district'.[25]

In the autumn of 1926, Bunny sent a parcel of books to a young woman called Mollie Everitt, in London for two months, from South Africa. She was Vera Meynell's younger sister, married to a man named Clem who remained in Johannesburg. Mollie suffered from blinding headaches, and, like Thea, wasn't particularly happy or fulfilled. She was a keen horsewoman, and Bunny put her, as Cynthia Mengs, in his next book, *No Love*, where he described her as 'very beautiful, with broad cheek-bones, a delicate, straight nose, a pucker in her forehead, and a tired, drooping mouth'.[26] Bunny took her to the theatre and to the ballet. They became lovers, Duncan lending them his studio for their assignations. On 20 November Mollie returned to South Africa, leaving Bunny distraught. He felt he should have stopped her from going as he was certain she was only returning to unhappiness. On the day of her departure Bunny wrote a brief memoir of their last days together, describing her extreme sadness at leaving. At the bottom of the page, in pencil, and in Bunny's later hand, he scribbled, 'I saw Molly's death announced in *The Times* in 1943'.[27] She was killed in a steeplechase. In his autobiography, still disguising her as 'Cynthia Mengs', he reflected that Mollie

---

[25] *Radio Times*, 3 December 1926.

[26] David Garnett, *No Love* (London: Chatto & Windus, 1929), p. 129.

[27] DG, 'Molly Everitt', 20 November 1926 [unpublished MS, Northwestern].

'had been trying to break her neck for years'.[28]

At Christmas, Bunny and Ray were joined by Garrow Tomlin and they all decamped to Alec and Bertha Penrose's house in the neighbouring village, Fenstanton. Lionel Penrose was there, and Gerald Brenan too, who pronounced that 'Bunny was at his best', enlivening all their 'very gay parties'.[29] Bunny loved Christmas, feeling it epitomised all that was best about domesticity and family. He loved the food, the traditions, the holly, the carol singers and the wonderful gifts Edward invariably bestowed on them all. Contrary to appearances, Bunny was miserable that Christmas. Although he and Mollie had known each other for only a short time, he could not stop thinking about her, attempting several drafts of a letter begging her to return, proposing to leave Ray and the children. The letters remained unsent.

Work at the Nonesuch Press became more demanding when in 1927 Vera left for six months to edit *Vogue*. Unbeknown to Bunny, changes were also afoot in his writing life. Alfred Knopf wrote to Harold Raymond, Prentice's colleague at Chatto & Windus, in February 1927, pleased that *Go She Must!* had sold well in America, but questioning whether his publishing arrangement with Bunny should continue. He felt the three-year contract had not been particularly satisfactory as Bunny had produced relatively few books. Bunny had been extremely fortunate in the agreement which provided the financial security which enabled him to write his last three books. Had he been able to deliver his novels more rapidly the arrangement might have been more to his publishers' advantage, and they might have allowed it to continue. The agreement, therefore, was not renewed and as a

---

[28] DG, *Familiar Faces*, p. 72.
[29] G. Brenan/Carrington, Tuesday night, 29 December 1926 [TGA].

result, like many writers, Bunny would need to turn his hand to other ways of earning a living. His salary from the Nonesuch, while useful, was insufficient to provide for Bunny's family and lifestyle. It was, anyway, unusual for authors to support themselves from their novels alone. Many turned to journalism, like Aldous Huxley's fictional poet in *Those Barren Leaves* (1925), who earns his living as editor of the 'Rabbit Fanciers' Gazette'.

One unusual journalistic opportunity arose in the spring of 1927, when Lydia Lopokova turned to Bunny for help in writing twelve articles about Russian cookery for the *Evening News*. They decided to collaborate, dividing the fee of seven guineas per article between them. Lopokova's biographer, Judith Mackrell, described the resulting articles as 'the best prose she had ever written – hurtlingly ungrammatical, brilliantly biased and delivering an exuberant snub to anyone in Cambridge and Bloomsbury who had ever made her feel like a babbling, badly behaved intruder'.[30] Bunny always enjoyed Lydia's English usage: when he asked her what she missed most in London he was tickled when she replied, '"A very low taste Bunny, sunflower seeds"'.[31] He adored her idiom and would have much enjoyed polishing it until it sparkled in print.

That summer, Ray and Bunny went with the children to a cottage at Salcombe Regis, near Sidmouth in Devon. Bunny wrote to his parents, telling them about the children and the sea, and also that Ray was soon to have an operation. She required stitches, which should have been put in when William was born in 1925. Bunny left Salcombe before the end of the holiday, as

---

[30] Judith Mackrell, *Bloomsbury Ballerina: Lydia Lopokova, Imperial Dancer and Mrs John Maynard Keynes* (London: Weidenfeld & Nicolson, 2008), p. 292.
[31] DG/CG [Spring 1927] [HRRC].

work commitments called him away, but Ray and the children stayed on. The ensuing correspondence between Bunny and Ray charted a crisis in their marriage. For once the cause was not Bunny's infidelity, although this was a contributing factor. The crisis had arisen because Ray was having an affair.

Ray's pocket diaries for 1926 and 1927 are not confessional journals, but records of appointments. Many pages are empty, but some are littered with the single letter 'G'.

The initial stood for Garrow Tomlin. Bunny had known Garrow since 1923, when the two men rapidly became close friends. Garrow was a frequent visitor at Hilton, where Bunny described him as 'always full of boyish enthusiasms'.[32] He was twenty-five, training for the Bar, Francis Meynell's chief male friend and also, of course, Tommy's brother. In appearance the two siblings could not have been more different: unlike the diminutive Tommy, Garrow was tall, long legged, fair haired and muscular, quite similar in appearance to Bunny. Like Bunny, he enjoyed outdoor pursuits, especially bathing, walking and camping. Like Bunny he was also extremely attractive to women, and enjoyed attracting as many of them as possible. Unlike Bunny, he did not believe in marriage. He warned one lover, Alix Kilroy,[33] that he was polygamous, and that if she became dependent on him he would be horrible to her. Looking back at their relationship, she observed 'it is clear that he had no intention of entering into any single-partner relationship. He probably intended from the first to get me into bed; according to his code, it was a pleasant and natural part of friendship, and not for one

---

[32] DG, *Familiar Faces*, p. 118.

[33] Alix Meynell after her marriage to Francis Meynell.

partner only.'[34] Bunny and Garrow may have shared the same code, but Bunny certainly did not want to share his wife.

Shortly after leaving Salcombe, Bunny received a letter from Ray, casually informing him that Garrow was taking a week's holiday and proposed to join her there. Bunny issued an ultimatum: 'Understand', he wrote, 'for this is definitive: If you live with Garrow whether in the same bed or the same house, you never live again with me.' Bunny tersely suggested that she telegram Garrow to put him off, 'otherwise I shall understand all is over'.[35] Ray tore the letter into fourteen pieces.

Meanwhile, Bunny took the matter into his own hands. First he wrote to Garrow, stating that 'it would save a great deal of pain for all parties' if he did not join Ray. 'It is idle to pretend', he added, 'to being reasonable when one is not'.[36] He didn't send the letter and instead arranged to meet Garrow that evening at his London flat. There Bunny informed him that if he were to join Ray at Salcombe, it would radically alter the Garnetts' marriage. Bunny wrote to Ray afterwards telling her: 'when I think of you, of Richard, of William, of everything my happiness is built on, then I am in despair, am dead'.[37] Ray replied: 'you know that I have lived in torture for months because of my feelings about you – & my unhappiness didn't seem to hinder you at all. I've been in despair so often.' The problem was that Bunny and Ray loved and needed one another, but their

[34] Alix Meynell, *Public Servant, Private Woman: An Autobiography* (London: Victor Gollancz, 1988), p. 105.

[35] DG/RAG, 5 Clifton Place, [July 1927] [HG].

[36] DG/G Tomlin, Nonesuch Press, Friday 22 August 1927 [misdated; should be Friday 22 July] [HG].

[37] DG/RAG, The Nonesuch Press, Friday [22 July 1927] [HG].

expectations were completely different. Ray knew Bunny would go off with someone else again, whenever he chose to do so. 'What a hypocrite you have been', she added, asking: 'Darling Bunny do have sense – do you love me or not.'[38]

The problem was Bunny's double-standards, his assertion that 'I cannot be other than I am', while insisting that Ray remained at home, holding the babies and waiting for him to return at weekends.[39] Although he always maintained that jealousy was a redundant and unnecessary emotion, he was not immune to it. But it angered Ray that Bunny could be jealous while all the time he insisted that she should not. Bunny may have been particularly jealous because this was not Ray's first affair. In a letter to Ray of 22 July, Bunny referred to 'this second affair'[40] and in a later letter on the subject of fidelity, he asserted 'I was jealous of Theo'.[41] Was Theo Powys Ray's lover? Did she have an affair with him, perhaps when she stayed with him at East Chaldon in February 1926, at which time she referred to him as 'a darling'? Or was he instead a kindly father figure to Ray?

After the holiday, Ray went into the nursing home, as planned. From Hilton, Bunny wrote her a letter full of muddled emotions: love, anger, remorse for his own behaviour, confusion. His rational self wanted to permit her to 'Do what you like, love whom you like. Be yourself as I am myself.' But, he admitted, 'I can never pretend to offer you equality'. 'I shall never forget this, or forgive it, I shall never feel again for you the certainty & happiness that the

---

[38] RAG/DG, 'Monday' [pmk 26 July 1927] [HG].

[39] DG/RAG, The Nonesuch Press, 'Friday' [22 July 1927] [HG].

[40] DG/RAG, The Nonesuch Press, Friday [22 July 1927] [HG].

[41] DG/RAG, Hilton, [1928] [Northwestern].

swallow feels: the air will not let it fall & bruise its poor feathers.'[42]

Ray had barely recuperated when Bunny took off again for France, this time with Duncan, en route to Cassis, where Vanessa had taken a house.[43] From France he wrote exuberantly to Ray, in a shaky hand, as if under the influence of alcohol: 'Darling', 'I want you I want your company as a friend, as a lover, I want you […]. I long to see you, to run my eye over you: to hug you in my arms […]. I am starved of everything I hold dearest being away from you.'[44] Absence, or absinthe, had clearly made his heart grow fonder.

---

[42] DG/RAG, Friday 12 August [1927] [Northwestern].

[43] DG/RAG [Cassis] [October 1927] [Northwestern].

[44] DG/RAG, Tarascon, Hotel des Empereurs, 'Friday' [October 1927] [Northwestern].

Chapter Fifteen

'In all marriages there are disagreements, in which one of
the parties has to give way to the other.'[1]

In the spring of 1928, Bunny was working on a new novel, *No
Love*, and contributing an introduction for the latest Nonesuch
volume, a selection of Joseph Conrad's *Letters* which Edward was
editing. Bunny was in the unusual position of commenting on his
father's writing, although this he did tentatively. 'One or two
sentences', he advised, 'need thinking over.' 'Please don't', he
added, 'be incensed by this criticism.'[2] Bunny found Edward's
selection heart-warming. 'I love you', he wrote to his father, 'I
think of you very often; especially lately I have been all through
the Conrad letters in revise proof twice & they help me to recreate you as you were at different ages.'[3]

Although Ray's affair with Garrow Tomlin had angered
Bunny, it did not affect the friendship between the two men. It

---

1   David Garnett, *No Love* (London: Chatto & Windus, 1929), p. 17.
2   DG/EG, Nonesuch Press, 6 March 1928 [HRRC].
3   DG/EG, Hilton, Easter Monday [9 April 1928] [HRRC].

seemed perfectly natural for Bunny to spend a weekend away with Tommy and Garrow and the latter's visits to Hilton continued much as before. But at Easter, when Frances Marshall and Ralph Partridge were staying at Hilton, Frances noticed that Ray had over-powdered her face and that her eyes were red. Conversation turned to whether some people were essentially tragic while others were comic. Ray said, 'I feel I'm a very tragic character, though I'm not unhappy. I feel like [...] some [...] mutilated thing.'[4]

In June Ray set off at short notice, taking Richard and William with her to La Bergère, Vanessa's house at Cassis. Duncan had only recently written to Bunny, presciently as it happened, telling him that the house was available for rent during the summer. Shortly after Ray's departure, Bunny wrote to her from Hilton, saying he was all right and progressing with *No Love*. 'I think it unlikely', he added, 'that I shall see Norah this month'.[5] Norah was Norah McGuinness, a thirty-six-year-old artist, married to the poet Geoffrey Phibbs (also known as Geoffrey Taylor). Bunny had met her earlier in the year when she brought some drawings to the Nonesuch office hoping to find work as an illustrator. She was beautiful, with large dark grey eyes, bobbed wavy brown hair, serious cheekbones and a generous smile. According to a paper Bunny wrote many years later for the Memoir Club, he had become sexually obsessed with Norah. It was this obsession which caused Ray to flee to France.

'Darling Ray', Bunny wrote, 'you ask me to write to you & tell you what I am feeling quite honestly.' He told her he was unhappy without her, that he wanted her badly 'in every way'; missed her,

4   Quoted in Partridge, *Memories*, pp. 148–9.
5   DG/RAG, Hilton, 'Sunday' [June 1928] [Northwestern].

could not bear to be separate from her. And then with his usual misplaced candour, he undid any good he might have done, stating that he felt 'wretched' about Norah.

> I don't love her as I love you – how could I when she is almost a stranger to me – but I like her very much, I am quite charmed by her. She is headover heels in love with me, and what's to be done. It is a hopeless business [...]. All human emotions are wrong; mine particularly. I am in love with you, depend upon you, but I cannot bear not seeing her, & want her to amuse me. I often wish I were an eunuch: it would simplify things: too much I dare say for my happiness.[6]

Ray responded in the way she knew would hurt most: with silence. Bunny wrote remonstrating with her for her lack of communication. 'You might reflect', he chided, 'that I'm extremely lonely & continually tormenting myself.'[7] He had in fact been enjoying a sociable time with the Meynells at their new house in Essex. Garrow was a fellow guest, and they spent their time basking naked and wrestling in the sun. Bunny informed Ray that he had easily thrown his adversary. 'Just now', he crowed, 'I am in rather splendid condition.'[8]

In Ray's absence Bunny had time to reflect, again acknowledging his hypocritical treatment of her. 'Honesty is the only way: & if I'm honest I say that I need you desperately, that I cannot share you with anyone. And then I have not the character

[6] DG/RAG, Hilton, Thursday 14 June 1928 [Northwestern].
[7] DG/RAG, Hilton, 'Friday' [1928] [Northwestern].
[8] DG/RAG, Hilton, 'Saturday' [June/July 1928] [Northwestern].

or the desire even to be faithful myself.'[9] 'You say', Ray countered, 'you must love others & I must not – & you don't know what I object to. I suppose really I feel very much the same as you. I am too unhappy living with you when you are longing always for someone else. I'm miserable because I can't satisfy you in any way.' 'Sometimes', she remarked pointedly, 'people can forget other longings when they love one another & trust one another.' 'Of course', she added, 'I love you & want your fidelity. I think of you as the one solid thing in life.' But Ray knew this was an illusion, for at the back of her mind she feared that 'bye & by [sic] you will find someone free to go with you & you with them & you will be gone'.[10]

Bunny justified his double-standards in evolutionary terms: 'For you to be jealous of my loves is as if you were jealous of my reading books & bursting into tears over their pages. For me to [be] jealous of you is selfish but the wisdom of preservation.'[11] It did not seem to occur to him that such wisdom might not have been a uniquely masculine attribute. Ray's response was appropriately sarcastic: 'What it is to be a man.'[12]

With Ray out of reach, Bunny characteristically came to find her more appealing than ever. 'Every now & then', he said, 'I take out your photograph from my pocket-book & gaze at your bottom & your lovely legs, & the reflection of your face & your breasts.'[13] 'Soon', he told her, 'we shall be together again, and a pair of happy lovers I think, as we have so often been in the past.'

---

[9] DG/RAG, Nonesuch Press, Monday 18 June [1928] [Northwestern].

[10] RAG/DG, [Cassis] [June 1928] [Northwestern].

[11] DG/RAG, Hilton, Monday 25 [June] [1928] [Northwestern].

[12] RAG/DG, 2 July 1928 [Northwestern].

[13] DG/RAG, Hilton, 'Saturday' [late June/early July 1928] [Northwestern].

Bunny proposed joining her at Cassis, announcing he would arrive on 12 July. She told him not to come, but when William became ill with diarrhoea, changed her mind, feeling the return journey would be easier with another adult pair of hands. 'I expect', Ray remarked caustically, 'we shall hate one another when we meet as much as we do now.'[14] Bunny spent ten days at Cassis before returning with Ray and the children to England. There is no record of the nature of their reunion, but less than a month later, Ray was in East Chaldon, staying with Theo and Violet Powys.

In early September Ray wrote to Edward, asking if she could come and see him. 'I am very unhappy', she explained, 'and should like to talk to you because I think you'd be sympathetic to both Bunny & me.'[15] Edward was very fond of Ray and felt much sympathy for her. Even though he was a great tease, he always teased Ray in a kindly way, as evinced by a poem which Ray sent him, ostensibly from Richard:

Has anybody seen my grandada
A saucy man is he
If you find my grandada
Tease him as he Teases me.[16]

Ray found it an enormous relief to confide in Edward. He was not disloyal to Bunny, on the contrary he tried to reassure Ray about the strength of his son's love, but he provided a sympathetic ear at a time when she was most in need of one. For Bunny

---

[14] RAG/DG [Cassis] 7 July 1928 [Northwestern].
[15] RAG/EG, [Hilton], 'Thursday' [pmk 6 September 1928] [Northwestern].
[16] RAG/EG, [?11] January 1928 [Northwestern].

had taken rooms in Hampstead where he was living with Norah McGuinness.

Bunny had visited Norah in Ireland in early September, and while there, he met her husband Geoffrey Phibbs, who had written to Bunny suggesting they meet. Ironically, the situation may have been convenient for Phibbs, as he had come under the spell of the poet Laura Riding, Robert Graves's mistress, with whom he had recently started to live in Hammersmith in a ménage *à quatre* with Graves and his wife Nancy Nicholson.

At twenty-eight, Phibbs was charming and rather shy. Bunny could not help but like him.

Ray threatened to leave Bunny but she was not in a position to do so. She was financially dependent upon him, and even though she continued to work as an illustrator, such work was sporadic and had to accommodate the children. Moreover, in an unequal society, divorcées were stigmatised. Adultery remained the only acceptable grounds for divorce and although Bunny had committed adultery, it was a messy business proving it. Ray would not have wished to cite his lovers, and Bunny would not have enjoyed spending a night in a hotel with a paid prostitute in order to be 'caught in the act'.

When she needed to get away, Ray left the children at Hilton with Mrs Thorpe, who helped in the house. In London she stayed in Bunny's basement flat, at 37 Gordon Square, two cramped rooms rented from Vanessa, who lived above. Despite their proximity, the two women had little contact, Vanessa reporting to Bunny: 'your mysterious wife haunts the basement & I sometimes see her flitting like a bat round the square.'[17] On one occasion, Bunny saw Ray pass on the Tube and he thought she saw him, too.

---

[17] VB/DG, 37 Gordon Square, 11 November [1928] [HG].

Bunny continued to insist that he loved Ray passionately while protesting that he could not 'escape the blind folly of loving Norah'.[18] 'My love for Norah', he informed Ray, 'does not conflict any more with my love for you than my love for Tommy conflicts with my love for Lytton, or Duncan.'[19] Ray responded with silence. It was the only weapon she had and she deployed it well. Within a month of moving in with Norah, Bunny was yearning for Ray. He returned to Hilton on 13 November and, by early December, Ray was again basking in his uxorious warmth.

The cost of financing a Hampstead flat, Bloomsbury basement and Hilton Hall had left Bunny very short. He could not draw upon his Nonesuch salary as they had cash-flow problems. In December he turned to Prentice for an advance on *No Love*. Prentice agreed, but wary of both the censor and Bunny's tendency to stretch the boundaries of literary propriety, Prentice wanted assurances that Bunny was not writing another *Well of Loneliness* (Radclyffe Hall's recently banned 'lesbian' novel). Bunny reassured Prentice that the book was 'entirely heterosexual', although it contained 'a good deal of love – including adultery'.[20] That year Sir Archibald Bodkin, the Director of Public Prosecutions, had banned James Joyce's *Ulysses* on grounds of alleged gross indecency. The Nonesuch Press responded by issuing a prospectus entitled *Bodkin Permitting*.

In November Bunny wrote a fan letter to another author, Dorothy Edwards, whose short stories, *Rhapsody* (1927), he

[18] DG/RAG [1928] [Northwestern].
[19] DG/RAG, Hilton [1928] [Northwestern].
[20] DG/C .Prentice, Hilton, 15 December [1928] [Reading].

admired. 'Who and what are you?' he asked her.[21] She replied, 'As to who & what I am. I think if this is a mystery it is that I am Welsh.'[22] The two writers arranged to meet in January 1929, when Dorothy would pay one of her infrequent visits to London. She told him that he would recognise her, because she would be wearing a grey cloak 'and a slightly provincial air'.[23]

Dorothy Edwards was twenty-six and living with her widowed mother near Cardiff. Her outlook on life had been heavily influenced by her father, an ardent socialist and Independent Labour Party leader. Although Dorothy had a degree in Greek and Philosophy, literature was her first love, and she supplemented her mother's meagre pension by writing stories for magazines. When Dorothy met Bunny, as arranged, at the Nonesuch Press, he encountered a dumpy, short, buxom, fresh-complexioned, blue-eyed young woman, 'eager, ardent, embarrassed, shy'. He could not bring himself to kiss her, perhaps because of the complication of her 'almost horizontal protruding teeth', but he gave her lunch in his basement, where they sat talking in the half light. He liked her so much that he decided to ask her to become his adopted sister. He explained that he had made this request because he was anxious not to jeopardise their friendship with a love affair. He believed that if they adopted each other it would solidify their relationship without the complication of sex. This explanation was disingenuous, for Bunny did not find Dorothy remotely attractive, comparing her to 'a young Jersey heifer – a sweet and clean and good creature, but from a sexual point of

[21] DG/D. Edwards, Hilton, 22 November [1928] [Reading].
[22] D. Edwards/DG, 9 Pen y dre, Rh[?uw]bina, Cardiff, 27 November [1928] [Northwestern].
[23] D. Edwards/DG, West Kensington [pmk 9 January 1929] [Northwestern].

view non-existent'.[24] Dorothy accepted his offer with enthusiasm, although Ray remained sceptical.

Shortly after meeting Dorothy, Bunny met Colonel T.E. Lawrence for the first time. The two men had been corresponding for over a year, although they had never met, despite Lawrence's friendship with Edward. Bunny first wrote to Lawrence to thank him for his indirect gift of the limited subscribers' edition of *Seven Pillars of Wisdom*. Lawrence had hesitated about publishing the book, and eventually opted to produce this lavish limited edition at his own expense, to be sold at thirty guineas. He gave a copy to Edward, who had already subscribed, so Lawrence suggested that Edward give the second copy to Bunny. Bunny's letter was characteristically forthright; he was not going to be in awe of Lawrence, or at least, he was not going to let it appear as though he was. In his first letter (of 5 November 1927) his deferential gratitude was nicely balanced by a reprimand about the subscribers' edition: 'I should like to say first that I think it was a terrible mistake to publish it in this limited form, and that I think you ought to publish it in a cheap and accessible edition [...]. Great books exist for everyone to read: they are not part or property of the author: still less are they the property of a hundred and ten rich men.'[25]

Lawrence had copied his manuscript of *The Mint*, a revealing record of his life among his fellow air force men, into a small bound volume which he gave to Edward, informing him that he was burning the original manuscript. Bunny read it, afterwards telling Lawrence how grateful he was for being allowed to do so.

---

[24] DG, *Familiar Faces*, p. 94.
[25] DG/TEL, Hilton, Guy Fawkes Day [5 November] 1927 [Bodleian].

The Mint affected him profoundly, bringing back the horror of institutional life he had experienced at school, 'this instinct or emotion of a weasel in a steel trap'. Bunny thought it beautifully written, and told Lawrence, 'Words are your medium, words, not deeds, and not thoughts. <u>Words</u>.'[26]

When Bunny and Lawrence did meet, it was in February 1929, at the Nonesuch Press office. They wandered over to Bunny's basement in Gordon Square, where instead of sitting comfortably in the bed-sitting-room, they perched in the kitchen-cum-bathroom, Bunny on the table by the gas cooker, and Lawrence on the side of the bath. There they talked for almost two hours. Lawrence had recently translated *The Odyssey*, so Bunny asked him which name he would use on the title page. Lawrence replied that he thought of calling it 'Chapman's Homer', alluding to his father's name, Thomas Robert Chapman. Bunny didn't understand the joke at the time, but later thought it proof that Lawrence was not bothered about his illegitimacy. (It may have been a double joke, alluding to George Chapman whose translation of *The Odyssey* was published in *The Whole Works of Homer* in 1616.) Bunny rashly asserted his belief in Samuel Butler's theory that *The Odyssey* had been written by a woman. Lawrence later gave Bunny a copy of his book, which bore no translator's name, but carried Lawrence's inscription:

T.E.S.[27]

Who is responsible (under Homer) for all but the appearance of this

---

[26] DG/TEL, Hilton, 20 May [1928] in A.W. Lawrence, ed., *Letters to T.E. Lawrence* (London: Jonathan Cape, 1962), pp. 83–4.

[27] Lawrence was 'Aircraftman Shaw' at this time.

Book most regretfully obtrudes it into the Presence of D.G. WHO
KNOWS BETTER. 25.XI.32 Plymouth

Bunny admitted that the rebuke always made him feel 'hot under
the collar'.[28]

Lawrence paid several visits to Hilton and one weekend, when
both Dorothy Edwards and the novelist H.E. Bates were staying,
Lawrence unexpectedly roared up on his motorbike. Bunny
introduced him to his guests as 'Aircraftman Shaw'. When
Lawrence began a discussion on Greek poetry, Dorothy was
visibly irritated and more or less turned her back on him. After
he had left, Ray asked Dorothy what she thought of Shaw, and
Dorothy replied that she thought him 'very ordinary'. According
to Bunny, 'she seemed to resent a common aircraftman joining
in as an equal in a conversation about the Greeks'.[29]

Bunny was under no illusions about either Dorothy or
Lawrence. He loved Dorothy for her independence of thought
as much as her writing and he loved her despite her egotism and
inclination to look down on people whom she considered intellectually inferior. Bunny believed that Lawrence compensated
for his alleged lack of sexual drive and disinclination to have
children through another stronger urge, the urge to 'understand
his fellows', manifested in 'an immediate and sympathetic
response when they needed help'.[30] Bunny stated that he never
considered himself an intimate friend of Lawrence's. 'It seemed
more as though I was one of those with whom he wished to keep

---

[28] DG, *Familiar Faces*, p. 103.

[29] DG, *Familiar Faces*, p. 90.

[30] DG, *Familiar Faces*, pp. 110–11.

in touch, or of whom for some reason he approved.'[31]

That month, Bunny handed Prentice the completed manuscript of *No Love*. He sent a copy to Edward, to whom he confided that he thought the writing thin and that although it was the longest book he had written, it was a mere synopsis. Unfortunately Prentice's fears regarding censorship were realised when the printers, R. & R. Clark, wanted passages to be excised on grounds of propriety. They wrote to Bunny assuring him that they were not querying his writing, 'but in these days when the authorities are exercising their powers so strictly we must, in our own interest, take care that our firm is not brought under their ban'.[32] The passages to which they objected included: 'Benedict and Leah swam together in the estuary and lay naked beside each other in the sun.'

Prentice asked Bunny if he would re-write the offending passages, but Bunny refused, telling him either to find alternative printers or to print the pages with blanks, inserting an 'Author's Advertisement' which Bunny would pen, explaining to his readers why the blanks existed. This was an untenable course of action, to which Prentice would never have agreed. But Bunny was extremely angry, particularly as he did not consider it was the printers' role to censor his writing. He was so angry that he wrote to Edward, Duncan, Vanessa, Maynard and Lytton, canvassing their advice and support. Lytton thought Bunny's advertising plan ingenious, although he pointed out that the printers were hardly likely to agree to print an advertisement against themselves. Maynard considered the printers' behaviour 'outrageous', asking Bunny to send him the 'most dangerous' passages and suggesting they might 'invoke Arnold Bennett',

---

[31] DG, *Familiar Faces*, p. 15.
[32] Quoted in DG/GLS, Wednesday 27 February 1929 [BL].

who 'would probably be very decent about it and carries much influence in the Commercial World'.[33]

Bunny was relieved when the printers backed down and *No Love* was eventually printed. He made one minor concession, changing the word 'bugger' to 'b-', in the sentence 'Here's a toast: To Love and Freedom, and b- the Navy'.[34] Now able to proceed, Bunny needed an illustration for the title page. He briefly considered asking Duncan, or John Banting, another artist friend, but decided in favour of Ray. Her illustration, however, had to be put on hold as in early March 1929 she discovered small lumps in one of her breasts.

Bunny took her to his old friend Geoffrey Keynes, now assistant surgeon at St Bartholomew's Hospital. A pioneering general surgeon with a particular interest in breast cancer, he advocated conservative treatment in preference to radical surgery, especially in younger women in whom the cancer was not advanced. He had found that radium treatment, in which hollow needles containing radium chloride were inserted around the tumour, could have dramatically beneficial results. Moreover the treatment was less invasive than radical surgery, and at a time before antibiotics, it was also safer. It was, however, very expensive, in 1928 costing £1,500 (c. £50,000 today) per patient per course of treatment, and as there was no National Health Service the patient had to foot the bill.

Radium treatment was relatively new. Bart's had introduced it as recently as 1924 and in the intervening four years only forty-two patients were treated by this means. When Geoffrey advised against operating on Ray, she and Bunny accepted his guidance.

---

[33] JMK/DG, King's College, Cambridge, 4 March 1929 [Northwestern].
[34] DG, *No Love*, p. 190.

Radium treatment was not only less invasive than mastectomy, but also, in removing cancer cells from surrounding tissue, more effective at that time than "lumpectomy". However the treatment was gruelling. The patient's skin was first punctured with a scalpel around the site of the tumour. Then platinum needles were inserted, each measuring nearly five centimetres; typically thirty-five needles would be employed. It took three people to insert each.[35] All this was achieved with only gas and oxygen for anaesthesia. Finally, the protruding needles were covered with gauze and a layer of wool. Ray remained in this uncomfortable state for seven days. When Bunny took her back to Hilton, she felt it 'was like waking from a nightmare'.[36]

They endured several anxious weeks before Geoffrey could determine the effectiveness of the treatment. As Bunny informed his mother, the waiting was 'disturbing & often agonising, & so is ignorance'.[37] But at the end of March Ray was able to write to Edward with positive news. Geoffrey said the lumps were diminishing satisfactorily and would disappear altogether in time. Ray felt 'very pleased and light headed', for she had not 'really believed in the cure', but now didn't 'quite believe in the disease'.[38] On 26 April she travelled to East Chaldon to recuperate with Theo and Violet Powys.

That same day, Bunny found himself embroiled in a bizarre coda to his affair with Norah McGuinness. On Norah's recommendation Geoffrey Phibbs unexpectedly turned up at Hilton.

---

[35] G. Keynes, 'Radium Treatment of Primary Carcinoma of the Breast', *The Lancet*, 21 July 1928.

[36] RAG/EG, 13 March 1929 [Northwestern].

[37] DG/CG, Hilton, 13 March 1929 [HRRC].

[38] RAG/EG, [pmk 1 April 1929] [Northwestern].

Despite an apparent reconciliation with Norah, Phibbs had been drawn again into Laura Riding's *ménage*. Assuming she had lost him for good, Norah fled to Paris. But Phibbs wanted shot of the whole nightmare and turned to Bunny as a giver of good advice. Two telegrams arrived at Hilton, one from Nancy Nicholoson, the other from Robert Graves, written in the hand of Mr Hardy, the Hilton postmaster, 'C/O Garnett', but addressed to Phibbs. Both demanded Phibbs's immediate return.[39] Robert Graves also telephoned Bunny, threatening to kill Phibbs.

While Bunny and Phibbs were having supper, Graves arrived unexpectedly and in an agitated state. Laura Riding had sent Graves to retrieve Phibbs, as he had some slight acquaintance with Bunny, presumably from 1923 when Bunny contributed a story to Graves's publication, *The Winter Owl*. Phibbs was persuaded to return with Graves and there Bunny assumed the matter would end. However, the next day Phibbs was back again at Hilton, in a much shaken condition. Phibbs had refused to move back to Hammersmith and so Laura Riding drank *Lysol* and jumped from a window, according to Phibbs killing herself in the process. In this last respect he was mistaken, Riding had a broken pelvis and crushed vertebrae from which she made a complete recovery. All Bunny could do was to take Phibbs's mind off it all with a tour of Cambridge colleges.

No Love was published in the spring of 1929. It was well received, *The Times* rhapsodising over 'the beautiful precision of some of the scenes, the unobtrusive, detached humour which is peculiar to Mr Garnett'.[40] H.E. Bates thought it Bunny's best

[39] N. Nicholson/Geoffrey Phibbs, 26 April 1929 [Northwestern]; R. Graves/ DG, 26 April 1929 [Northwestern].

[40] 23 April 1929.

book to date, and one in which he had finally found his own voice. Not only had Bunny found his voice, but he articulated it in his own tone, rather than one that looked back to the eighteenth century or towards George Moore. Perhaps he achieved this because the novel was autobiographical, shaped by memories of his youth. It contains some of Bunny's most beautiful writing about the natural world, as if the hedgerows and meadows of his boyhood had been translated exactly onto the page.

The story concerns two families inhabiting a tidal island near Bosham in Kent. The Lydiates consist of Roger, a farmer, his wife Alice and Benedict, their son. Roger is based on Edward, with a touch of the adult Bunny; Alice is reminiscent of both Connie and Ray but not directly based upon either; Benedict is Bunny as a young man. The second family, the Kelties, comprises Eustace, an admiral, his wife who is not graced with a first name, and Simon, their son.

The Lydiates live in genteel poverty in a crumbling farmhouse, Tinder Hall, an amalgam of Hilton Hall and The Cearne. The Kelties live in a brand new Tudor-bethan extravaganza, 'The Jumblies', complete with billiard room. Although the ghastly name nods at the Marshalls' country house, 'Tweenways', this house was based upon the much derided 'Pendicle', the home of Bunny's childhood playmates, Michael and Nicholas Pease. Thus Bunny polarised the old and new, nature versus development and art against consumerism.

The novel follows the lives of the two sons, as they come together and diverge from young childhood to early middle age. It touches less on incidents in the lives of Bunny (Benedict) and Edward (Roger) but draws heavily on their characters, beliefs and the environments in which they lived. Benedict and Simon, for instance, bathe, sail and sleep outdoors like the Neo-Pagans;

Roger has a wicker day-bed on the porch of Tinder Hall, where he spends his evenings drinking red wine, just as Edward did at The Cearne. Bunny acknowledged that the character of Simon was loosely based on Alec Penrose, for like Alec, Simon was prone to nightmares and fears. 'He had such warmth', Bunny later wrote of Alec, 'such charm & such a deep love of beautiful things – and was so twisted around inside.'[41]

Bunny later considered *No Love* one of his best books, commenting: 'The fusion of memories of boyhood and of observations made in manhood is complete and unity is preserved while there hangs about the whole story the indefinable melancholy and hopelessness of life.'[42] In this he was accurate. Unity is partly achieved because the book is set in the years and time-frame of Bunny's own life to-date. His protagonist, Benedict, is therefore all the more plausible because through him Bunny recreated his own experiences of growing up. The book is suffused with the melancholy of hindsight, as the narrator views youth with the nostalgia of one who knows that happiness is elusive. This elusiveness is most poignantly realised in the character of Cynthia Mengs, the Jewish girl from South Africa who enters a disastrous, cold marriage with Simon. She falls in love with Benedict and they snatch five perfect days together in London. She leaves Simon, not for Benedict, but to live with another man. Cynthia was closely based on Mollie Everitt, also Jewish, also living in South Africa, whom Bunny replicated down to the way she wrote her letters and furrowed her brow.

In this, the most personal of Bunny's novels, where he presents such an affectionate portrait of his father (to whom the book

---

[41] DG/Mina Curtiss, 31 August 1950 [Berg].
[42] DG, *Familiar Faces*, p. 81.

is dedicated), Bunny was also able to introduce a tribute to Geoffrey Keynes in gratitude for his care for Ray. In early middle age, where the story ends, the Benedict–Bunny figure has become a scientist. When Benedict meets Simon again, after many years, he tells him: 'I'm supposed to be doing cancer research. They really are going to cure it now, you know, with radium needles.'[43] This was the only optimistic note at the end of a book in which no one achieves enduring happiness, where there is 'No Love'. It was also an expression of hope in relation to Ray.

---

[43] DG, *No Love*, pp. 258–9.

Chapter Sixteen

'Oh joy, oh blessed world! They were in the sky, riding on
the air, and all the groping dirtiness of earth forgotten.'[1]

Although he regularly saw Duncan and Vanessa in London,
Bunny had not been to Charleston for five years. When he eventually returned in August 1929, Bunny walked with Duncan on
the Downs, read Julian Bell's poems, and was amused by the
infectious giggles of ten-year-old Angelica. Afterwards, Bunny
received a warm letter from Duncan, saying how pleasant they
all found it to see him 'back in your old haunts'. 'I do not',
Duncan added, 'mention my own feelings.' He signed the letter
'love from your devoted Duncan'.[2]

Bunny and Ray seemed to have regained something of their
former happiness. In the autumn Ray wrote Bunny an affectionate but ambivalent letter, telling him she wanted to 'love someone
so badly – it is like madness.' 'At this moment', she said, 'I feel it

[1] David Garnett, *The Grasshoppers Come* (London: Chatto & Windus, 1931;
     Pelham Library 1941), p. 100.
[2] D. Grant/DG, Charleston, 25 August 1929 [HG].

is you that I am in love with & must cherish & praise & abandon myself to – & hold by the ear & kiss in the neck & grudge nothing to.' But she worried that the reality of him might instead make her 'feel mad with irritation' because 'you won't let me alone to feel a little free'.[3] Ray had the capacity to put a brave face on their marriage, to try to see it from the most flattering angle, but the inequality of their relationship was a perennial problem. Bunny could spread his wings, but at Hilton Ray's remained clipped.

One evening in October when Bunny and Ray were strolling past the Conington Flying Ground near Cambridge, they stopped to watch a plane above. Having enquired whether it was possible to go up in one, they were each given a five minute flight. Initially Bunny worried that he would die of fear, but, as he told T.E. Lawrence 'there is nothing so exciting in the world: the rushing hedge and soaring up', 'I am now wanting to go up every day, wanting to fly myself, wanting to have a machine of my own'.[4] Bunny could hardly contemplate such extravagance. Not only was he still unable to draw any salary from the Nonesuch Press, but as a result of the Slump his investments had fallen. Maynard Keynes, an astute investor, had suffered losses on his own investments and on those made on behalf of others, including Bunny. In October 1929 the Wall Street Crash presaged even leaner times.

There was, however, cause for cautious optimism. In early November Bunny received an enquiry from the film company 'British Talking Pictures', about the film rights to *The Sailor's Return*. The company wanted to make what would be one of the

<hr>

[3] RAG/DG, [pmk 9 October] [Northwestern].
[4] DG/TEL, Hilton, 25 October 1929 [Bodleian].

earliest British talkies. Britain was slightly behind the United States in this respect: the first all-talking American film, *Lights of New York*, was released in July 1928. But the first European drama-talkie, Alfred Hitchcock's *Blackmail*, was not premièred until June 1929. *The Sailor's Return*, therefore, would be in the vanguard.

Bunny was whisked away to Wembley in the Rolls-Royce sent to collect him. There he met representatives of the company, including Sergei Nolbandov, a Russian film editor, and Berthold Viertel, the Austrian screen writer and director. He was promised untold riches: £1,000–£2,000 for the film rights and an additional thirty pounds a week as an advisor during filming. But there was one detail that had to be settled: the question of Tulip, the novel's African heroine. Mr Woodhouse, a young American whose manner, according to Bunny, 'suggested that he had been boiled on Sunday, carved on Monday and served up cold on Tuesday' went over and over the same ground, objecting to the colour of Tulip's skin.[5] The issue seemed irresolvable and Bunny recognised, correctly as it happened, that the film was unlikely to be made.

For Christmas 1929, Duncan sent Bunny *foie gras* from Fortnum & Mason and invited him, Ray and the children to Angelica's eleventh birthday party in London. He confided a new love affair to Bunny, inviting him to Charleston to meet his lover, George Bergen. 'I had rather you did not tell anyone', he said.[6] Bunny continued to go to the cinema and dine with Duncan, but their relationship had changed subtly, Bunny now assuming the role of confidante and advisor. In January 1930 Bunny spent a

---

5   DG/RAG, Nonesuch Press, 'Tuesday' [November 1929] [Northwestern].
6   D. Grant/DG, Charleston [pmk 3 February 1930] [HG].

weekend with Duncan and George, sitting to them both for his portrait. George was twenty-seven, a handsome American Russian-Jewish artist. Bunny warmed to him, and enjoyed his visit enormously, the three men dancing to gramophone records. Duncan was besotted with George, and the younger man had the power to raise or dampen his spirits at will. Throughout their turbulent relationship, Bunny was a constant support, providing an understanding ear and affectionate friendship. 'Darling Bunny', Duncan wrote, 'It does me the greatest good in the world to see you from time to time.'[7] 'You are the only person', he said, 'I can talk freely to about my feelings.'[8]

Julian Bell, now a Cambridge undergraduate, ran with the beagles and was glad of a hot bath at Hilton afterwards. Bunny was very fond of Julian, enjoying his uproarious humour and incessant urge to rehearse anecdotes about family and friends. Sometimes Julian came to Hilton with Vanessa and Angelica, and on one occasion he brought the Woolfs over for tea. Virginia played with Richard and William, pursuing them into the bushes on her hands and knees, growling that she was a 'she-wolf'. Bunny was impressed by Julian's poems, and it was on his recommendation that Chatto & Windus published *Winter Movement*, Julian Bell's first volume of poetry, that year.

In early June Bunny received devastating news: Thea Fordham had committed suicide. She had carefully positioned herself on a railway line to ensure a tidy death. Her brother Michael had the distressing task of identifying her body, of sadly surveying 'the beauty of her severed legs'.[9] Bunny was consumed by grief.

---

[7] D. Grant/DG, 8 Fitzroy Street, 'Friday' [pmk 5 April 1930] [HG].

[8] D. Grant/DG, Grosvenor House, Twickenham, 1 August 1930 [HG].

[9] M. Fordham/RG, Beaconsfield, 6 September 1989 [RG].

'I loved her & understood her', he told Edward. 'I feel as though part of myself had been killed.' Bunny knew that Thea had been unhappy the previous year; she wouldn't see any of her old friends. He blamed her husband, Brian Rhys, but acknowledged that Thea had 'a complicated life & character'.[10]

In July the magazine *Everyman* featured the first of a series of articles revealing the working methods of leading English writers.[11] Bunny was the subject, photographed in his room at Hilton, seated at his paper-strewn desk, with books floor-to-ceiling on the shelves behind. Asked whether his characters were taken from life, he said they were not, curious given his recent portrayals of Edward and Alec in *No Love*. He explained that his books were conceived as a whole, each a product of a few ideas which played off each other and then combined into the complete story. He confessed that good weather was distracting, the allure of the garden too strong to resist.

The weather must have been fine that summer, for Bunny could not concentrate on his new book, *Castle Bigod*. His financial problems persisted, causing him to request another advance from Prentice. 'It is a gloomy request', he admitted, for it 'always makes me think the book won't get finished or won't sell.'[12] Bunny's lack of funds was partly caused by his absorption in a new and expensive pastime. Since that first exhilarating brief flight in 1929, Bunny had been consumed with a passion for flying and had been taking flying lessons for the best part of a year, latterly at Marshalls' Flying School, Cambridge. Throughout his training Bunny recorded his experiences in a diary, later

[10] DG/EG, Nonesuch Press [early June 1930] [HRRC].
[11] Louise Morgan, 'How I Write', *Everyman*, 10 July 1930.
[12] DG/C Prentice, Nonesuch, 15 August 1930 [Reading].

published as *A Rabbit in the Air* (1932). His first flight above the clouds affected him profoundly: 'The scene was wonderful', 'a plain of white where nothing stirred, where no living creature would ever set his foot, because it was really Heaven.'[13] On 22 July 1930 Bunny made his first solo flight.

Bunny was among a small and elite group of amateur aviators. Flying was replete with glamour and adventure, as epitomised by Charles Lindberg, who had achieved the first solo non-stop crossing of the Atlantic in 1927. Although Bunny's readers might have wondered why he styled himself a rabbit (in sport it refers to a duffer or beginner) *A Rabbit in the Air* furnished a vicarious means of achieving what for most was unachievable. As *The Times* review stated: '40 years ago the experience which Mr Garnett records existed only in the imagination.'[14]

Flying had diverted Bunny's energies from London and for the time being at least, this absorbing pastime had taken the place of a mistress. But his and Ray's happiness was dented again, when Ray discovered she was pregnant. Against all their instincts, Bunny and Ray agreed to follow Geoffrey Keynes's advice, and in September 1930 Ray had an abortion. Geoffrey was concerned that hormonal changes during pregnancy might cause Ray's cancer to return. Although abortion was then illegal, it was permitted if deemed necessary to save life. The surgeon cost fifty guineas, an unwanted additional expense in straitened times. But Bunny cared less for the expense than for 'the miserable waste of emotions & ten days of Ray's life at least'.[15]

---

[13] David Garnett, *A Rabbit in the Air* (London: Chatto & Windus, 1932; Pelham Library edition, 1941), p. 179.

[14] 26 April 1932.

[15] DG/CG, Nonesuch [c. 18 September 1930] [HRRC].

In December Bunny sent Prentice the completed manuscript of his latest book. It was not *Castle Bigod* but a novella which Bunny called variously 'Man & Locust', 'Wings over Asia', 'Storm of Locusts' and 'Living Rain', eventually settling upon the more lyrical *The Grasshoppers Come*, even though the insects in the book were locusts. On Boxing Day Bunny wrote again to Prentice, thanking him for his generous terms, including an advance on royalties from the book. Prentice was always the most open-handed publisher where Bunny was concerned.

The Grasshoppers Come is quite unlike anything Bunny had previously written. He always endeavoured to try a new genre, to find a new form and not to repeat any potentially winning formula. He acknowledged that his first two novels had been works of fantasy, but it irritated him that he continued to be seen as a fabulist. If Bunny was influenced by other authors, it was the lyrical descriptions of W.H. Hudson and Edward Thomas which he admired, together with the straightforward narrative style of those eighteenth century authors he favoured, particularly Richardson, Sterne and Defoe.

The Grasshoppers Come is a powerful psychological novel, exploring the inner life of a working-class airman, marooned in the Gobi Desert. The story begins with Mrs Beanlands, a rich widow, and her gold-digger lover, Wilmot Shap, embarking on an attempt to break the world record for a long-distance flight. The journey is to be taken in a custom-built monoplane, and the plane is to be flown by Jimmy Wreaks, a heavily scarred one-eyed man with a broken nose. Wreaks is one of Bunny's most convincing characters, a man aware that his social position distances him from his employers, and that his appearance distances him from mankind in general.

The first part of the book describes the endless voyage; like Wreaks's passengers floating above the clouds, the reader is lulled into a false sense of tranquillity. But the plane crashes; Wreaks is wounded, and is temporarily unable to walk; meanwhile Mrs Beanlands and Shap set off in search of civilisation. Wreaks is left to fend for himself in a barren, rock-strewn, dry-river valley. After several days, during which he dispassionately calculates the remaining length of his life, salvation appears in the shape of a swarm of locusts, some of which Wreaks cooks and eats. But nature, the bountiful provider, is also the mighty enemy. The locusts return in such torrential quantities that Wreaks almost drowns in them. Attempting to thwart this new enemy, he turns on the plane's propellers. His satisfaction at the demise of the insects soon turns to despair, when the petrol in the fuselage ignites, and the plane, Wreaks's only form of shelter, is consumed by flames. A Chinese scientist and aeronaut has been following the swarms, and seeing the burning wreck, rescues Wreaks. Typically, Bunny does not end on an optimistic note, but with a disquisition on the life-cycle of the locust, a creature which occupies a particular evolutionary niche.

The book was very well received. In the *Observer* Gerald Gould referred to 'That queer, special, illuminating vision' of Garnett's 'which he turns with the calm assurance of genius on to our mere times and places'.[16] *The Times* stated: 'A journey through the air has never been described with such perfection; to read it is as real as an adventure.'[17] The *TLS* concluded 'No writing of to-day has quite the incandescent clearness of Mr Garnett's; it has its own special quality of precision [...] and yet it can give warmth and colour to its subject.'[18] Many of Bunny's friends

---

[16] 31 May 1931.
[17] 29 May 1931.
[18] 28 May 1931.

wrote in praise of the book. T.E. Lawrence declared that it 'has pleased me quite beyond what I had thought possible. It is the first account of real flying by a real writer who can really fly.'[19]

After a gap of many months, in January 1931 Bunny resumed contact with Dorothy Edwards, just at the moment when she felt so low that she couldn't 'see light anywhere'. 'You give me', she wrote, 'as nothing else has succeeded in giving me, some kind of feeling that there is a significance in this [her writing], and perhaps even a remote possibility of happiness.'[20] They met in London, and Bunny took her to the cinema to see Charlie Chaplin's *City Lights*. John Hayward, who had dedicated his latest volume, *The Letters of Saint Evremond*, to Bunny, told him, 'You have an extraordinary capacity for making me happy; ever since I remember meeting you for the first time [...] you have exercised it'.[21]

Bunny realised that if he was going to make Ray happy he would need to devote time exclusively to her. They had both loved Yorkshire since 1927, when they drove to Wharfedale to see the total eclipse of the sun. He later described that first encounter with the Yorkshire Dales as a 'Revelation', which was to furnish 'The chief happiness in Ray & my life.'[22] In the intervening years they spent several happy holidays walking for miles in Yorkshire, far from anywhere with only each other, the wind, rain and sheep for company. If they became lost during a long trudge in bitter sleet and snow, that was part of the fun. Bunny fell in love with the landscape, and Ray told Constance that it was a 'great joy to

[19] TEL/DG, Plymouth, 10 June 1931, TS transcription [Bodleian].

[20] D. Edwards/DG, 9 Pen y dre, Rh[?uw]bina, Cardiff, 19 January [1931] [Northwestern].

[21] JDH/DG, 125 Queen's Gate, [pmk 6 November 1930] [Northwestern].

[22] DG, Draft Autobiography, Vol. 1, Synopsis [unpublished MS, HRRC].

me to walk again in the kind of country I loved as a child & to scramble beside the same kind of clear stream rushing over a stony bed with lovely bare trees on the bank'.[23] These holidays were the glue which bound Bunny and Ray together, which enabled them to recapture the essence of their love and served as a beacon for future renewal during times apart.

In London, Bunny was overwhelmed with Nonesuch work. Following the Wall Street Crash sales had fallen sharply and Bunny still drew no salary from the business. The Meynells now had a young son, Benedict, and with the Nonesuch in dire financial straits Francis had to take a job elsewhere to support his family. It was left to Bunny to take on the lion's share of work. In September 1931 Leslie Hotson, one of the authors with whom Bunny had been working particularly closely, wrote to thank him for his support. 'Just now', he wrote, 'I feel that if the book has any success it will be thanks to you. You have done more to maintain my enthusiasm and faith than I would have believed possible.'[24] The book in question was *Shakespeare Versus Shallow*, which the Nonesuch Press published that year. They had also published Hotson's first book, *The Death of Christopher Marlowe* in 1925. It was this which established his career and reputation as an assiduous but sometimes controversial literary detective.

Castle Bigod was temporarily shelved, unfinished, as Bunny had feared. He confessed to Constance that he was hoping to write a biography of Pocahontas, the seventeenth-century Native American princess. His desk at Hilton was already covered with volumes of research material. His main concern, however, was just

---

[23] RAG/CG [April 1930] [Northwestern].

[24] Leslie Hotson/DG, On board the Cunard RMS "Carinthia", 'Saturday' [pmk 5 September 1931] [Northwestern].

how to render the psychology of a Native American young woman. After months tied to the Nonesuch desk, he decided the only way to proceed would be to take a sabbatical. Duncan knew of a house to-let in France, in the town of Génainville, Val d'Oise. In November 1931, Bunny and Ray drove there, taking the children.

Bunny first fell in love with France when taken by Constance to Montpellier as a child. He felt absolutely at home there. Every day he bought ingredients for the picnic lunch, things which were hard to find in England: croissants, chicory, paté, sausage and inexpensive wine. After one such picnic and a powerful bottle of red, to his horror Bunny discovered that he had lost the manuscripts and typescripts of both *Pocahontas* and *Castle Bigod*. He was driving in an era when a car's trunk was not what we know today as the 'boot', but a free-standing container strapped onto a luggage-carrying platform. During their picnic, Bunny had un-strapped the trunk in order to extract a letter and had omitted to secure it back in place. It was only when they had travelled some distance that Richard noticed it was missing. They returned to their picnic site, where a bystander reported that the trunk had been picked up by a car which appeared to be trying to catch up with Bunny. Bunny stopped at various Mayoral offices and also left details at the local police station, together with a promise of a financial reward if the trunk and its contents were handed in. By then he feared his sabbatical to write *Pocahontas* was redundant. The next day he learned the trunk had been found, but his delight soon turned to horror when he opened the lid to find both manuscripts missing. It was only then that he remembered that he had repacked them and placed them, wrapped in his dirty shirts, under the driving seat, where they remained all along.

Bunny returned briefly to England to deliver a lecture in Leicester on 12 December. That same day he received a note from Garrow, inviting him to dinner. The dinner never took place, as on the 13th Garrow died in a flying accident. His machine spun, apparently out of control and crashed. Only two weeks before he had written to Bunny, announcing he had obtained his flying licence. He thanked Bunny for setting the example, explaining he had always wanted to fly, but didn't think he would have started had it not been for Bunny's initiative. Heartbroken, Bunny blamed himself for Garrow's death.

Garrow's funeral took place on 17 December in the village of Ash in Kent. Bunny was accompanied by Francis and Vera Meynell and two of Garrow's girlfriends, Alix Kilroy (later Dame Alix Meynell) and Barbara Mackenzie-Smith. Afterwards Alix wrote to say how much she had appreciated his sympathy, and asked him to let her know if he found out anything about the circumstances of the accident. Bunny felt so responsible that he wrote to Garrow's pilot instructor, asking what he knew. The instructor replied that in his opinion Garrow had tried to spin his plane on a day when the cloud was too low for such a feat. Bunny's haunting remorse was only assuaged by a letter from Garrow's mother, written a month to the day after his death. She wanted to reassure Bunny that she did not begrudge one hour of the pleasure her son obtained from flying. She felt Garrow wasn't 'cut out for a life spent in sleepy chambers' and asked Bunny not to be sad for him. 'I feel', she said, 'he has escaped from so much that he would have had to face had he lived.'[25] Ray could not quite take in the fact of Garrow's death. 'I can't yet believe', she wrote to Edward, 'that he won't turn up at Hilton when we get home.'[26]

[25] Marion Tomlin/DG, 5 Clifton Place, Sussex Square W2, 13 January 1932 [Northwestern].
[26] RAG/EG, 19 December [1931] [Northwestern].

Chapter Seventeen

'It is going on living with the ghosts & memories which is so horribly painful.'[1]

In London, before returning to France, Bunny bumped into thirteen-year-old Angelica Bell. She was very forthcoming, making eyes at him, which caused him to playfully run away, much to her delight. Bunny had hoped to see Duncan but they missed each other at the Nonesuch Press. Duncan had gone down to Hungerford, to visit Lytton Strachey who was ill at Ham Spray.

Back in France, Bunny could not resist the call of Sommeilles. He had not been there since 1915 and was curious to know whether the huts had survived and if any of his old friends remained. When they arrived Bunny found he had 'walked straight into a familiar piece of land between unfamiliar buildings'. Some huts had survived, now employed as sheds. Georges Leglais appeared, and Bunny reflected that he admired him 'as much as one can admire a human being who combines honest &

---

[1] DG/M Curtiss, Hilton, 27 April 1932 [Berg].

complete courage of every sort'.[2] The visit was extremely moving.

Bunny, Ray and the children returned home at the end of January though *Pocahontas* remained unfinished. In France, Bunny had received encouraging news about Lytton's slowly improving health, so it came as a shock to learn that he had died from stomach cancer on 21 January. Bunny's lingering sadness at the death of two close friends was soon compounded by a nightmarish series of events, 'the sequence of horror', as Bunny called it, which unfolded during the following weeks.[3] The first of these concerned an artist whom Bunny had befriended in the autumn of 1930. Small, thin and blue-eyed, Frank Weitzel was then twenty-five, a New Zealander of German parentage, who had recently moved to London. He had taken his drawings to the Nonesuch Press, hoping for work. Bunny did not much care for the drawings, but he admired Weitzel's sculptures and commissioned two heads, one of Ray and the other of Richard. Through Bunny's benevolent friendship Weitzel met many influential artists, leading to exhibitions with Epstein and the brothers Paul and John Nash.

While Bunny was in France Weitzel lived at Hilton Hall, afterwards lodging in the village, where he used the carpenter-cum-undertaker's workshop as a studio. One evening, Bunny was summoned to Frank's lodgings, where he found him in agony and unable to open his mouth. Bunny called the doctor, who recognised that Frank had lockjaw and was suffering from tetanus. As Bunny told Edward, it was 'a terrible thing to see'.[4] He carried him to the car, and drove him straight to hospital, but within

---

[2] DG/JDH, Das Goldenes Scaf, Edenkoben, 23 January 1932 [KCC].

[3] DG/C Prentice, Hilton, 'Wednesday' [C&W stamp 31 March 1932] [Reading].

[4] DG/EG, Nonesuch Press, 'Tuesday' [March 1932] [Northwestern].

twenty-four hours Frank was dead. Bunny arranged his burial and notified his sister, in Australia.

On the day Frank died, Ray had a consultation with Geoffrey Keynes. She had discovered another lump on a different part of her breast. Geoffrey proposed to use the radium needles again, and told Bunny there was every hope that the treatment would be successful. This time he generously waived his fee, Bunny paying only for the nursing home and anaesthetist. The children were sent to The Cearne while Ray endured another gruelling round of radium, afterwards recuperating at her sister Judy's home, at Rye in Sussex. From there she wrote to Bunny, 'Oh if only this is a success – Darling Bunny I love you, please go on loving me.'[5] Preoccupied with her recovery, Ray forgot that she was writing to Bunny on his fortieth birthday.

Two days later, on 11 March, Bunny was in London, staying in the room he now rented in Frances Marshall's and Ralph Partridge's flat on Great James Street. The telephone rang; it was the Ham Spray gardener, who told them Carrington had shot herself, was gravely wounded but still alive. Ralph called Carrington's local doctor, and then Bunny drove them to Ham Spray at breakneck speed. They found Carrington in her bedroom lying on the floor in a pool of blood. She had not been able to face life without Lytton. Carrington died, and afterwards Bunny looked at her 'when the nurses had turned her into a tidy corpse'. He thought she looked a 'hard, proud woman'.[6]

Bunny suddenly felt careworn. 1932 seemed aeons away from those carefree years of the 1920s. Looking back, Bunny called it 'that strange paradisial decade'. 'During it', he wrote to Francis

[5] RAG/DG, Rye, Sussex, 9 March 1932 [Northwestern].
[6] DG/M. Curtiss, Hilton, 27 April 1932 [Berg].

Meynell, 'all that we did was good – including the work that we did together … Fortified with the illusion that love and not hate would rule the world in future, we did our best to make up for the losses of the war.'[7] The 1920s had indeed been a gilded decade for Bunny, bringing him fame, critical appreciation, respect among his peers and a degree of financial security. But in 1932 he could take none of these for granted. For the first time he found writing difficult; he appeared to have chosen a subject which could not be constrained by his rigorous economy of words; the Nonesuch Press had become more a liability than an adventure in publishing; Bunny no longer had any guaranteed income; Ray's illness cast a shadow of uncertainty over his family; his friends seemed to be dying around him. At this stage in his life paradise seemed irrevocably lost. When, in March, Richard broke his arm, Geoffrey Keynes commented: 'Your disasters come in droves, my poor Bunny.'[8]

Richard was nine years old and it was time for Bunny to consider his education. Bunny was a devoted father. He was the kind of father who delighted in activities with his sons, ringing birds, teaching the boys to fish, boating, swimming, building things, skating on the Fens. The previous year he had given Richard a printing press for his eighth birthday, instilling in him a lifelong love of printing, typography and design. 'We are going to print books', Bunny informed Constance, predicting, accurately as it happened, that Richard 'will be the world's champion proof corrector when he's older'.[9]

Towards the end of Ray's convalescence, Bunny had driven

---

[7] Quoted in Dreyfus, *A History of the Nonesuch Press*, p. 18.
[8] G. Keynes/DG, 11 Arkwright Road, Hampstead, 29 March 1932 [Northwestern].
[9] DG/CG, Hilton, 18 January 1931 [HRRC].

her to view several prospective schools. They settled on Beacon Hill School, which had been founded in 1927 by Bertrand Russell and his wife Dora. It was located on the South Downs, near Petersfield, an area familiar to Bunny from his youthful visits to Edward Thomas at Steep and to Noel Olivier at Bedales. Like Bedales, it was progressive, though comparatively small. Beacon Hill was a fee-paying school, run on extremely liberal lines. No pupil was expected to attend lessons, although most did. This education did Richard, and later William, no harm. They came from a highly informal, un-regimented family background in which they were valued as interesting individuals in their own right, and where they addressed their parents as 'Ray' and 'Bunny'. Bunny sent Richard there because he assumed he would be taught mathematics by Bertie Russell. But by the time Richard was a pupil, Russell had lost interest in both the school and his wife. It was therefore left to Dora to run the school, and it was her influence, rather than her husband's, which prevailed. The school was co-educational, and the prospectus promised 'complete frankness on anatomical and physiological facts of sex, marriage, parenthood and bodily functions'.[10] All these factors converged on Richard's first day at school: breastfeeding her baby, Dora Russell handed her new pupil a mug of breast milk.

Ray was convinced the latest course of treatment had done no good. At a follow-up consultation at the end of May, she was surprised when Geoffrey Keynes told her that the lump had gone. Meanwhile Bunny struggled with *Pocahontas*. He still felt there was much to do and worried about getting the chronology

---

[10] Quoted in Deborah Gorham, 'Dora and Bertrand Russell and Beacon Hill School', *Russell: the Journal of Bertrand Russell Studies*, Vol. 25, Issue 1, Article 4 (2005), p. 41.

wrong. 'It is the most peculiar book I have ever tried to write', he told Constance. 'Everything in it is as true as possible.'[11] For the sake of veracity, Bunny visited Heacham in Norfolk, to see a mulberry tree Pocahontas was said to have planted there, and he even grew tobacco seedlings on a radiator. Bunny consulted maps of Virginia sent over from America, and eventually began to feel more satisfied. His American publisher, however, thought the whole thing would be improved if Bunny came to America, visited Virginia, and saw 'the Virginia creeper growing'.[12]

Bunny could not possibly afford such a trip, but an old friend came to the rescue. Mina Kirstein had married Henry Tomlinson Curtiss in 1926, but after only one happy year together, he died. Mina was now what Bunny called a rich widow, but she had always been fiercely independent, and for some years had been Professor of English at Smith College, Massachusetts. She lived at Chapelbrook, Ashfield, Massachusetts and had an apartment in New York City. Mina offered to pay Bunny's passage and all expenses and to accompany him, along with her brother Lincoln Kirstein, on a tour of Native American sites in Virginia. Bunny was not certain the trip would help, but, as he told Constance, 'it will be better to have gone than for the visit to be relegated to the grand list of might have beens'.[13]

Bunny embarked in early July. He spent much of the voyage sea-sick, but approaching New York, was impressed by the skyscrapers, which he thought looked like 'religious relics of a strange Stonehenge pyramid civilization'.[14] He wrote to Ray

[11] DG/CG, Hilton, Thursday 2 June [1932] [HRRC].

[12] DG/STW, Hilton [19 June 1932], in RG, ed., *Sylvia and David*, p. 50.

[13] DG/CG, Hilton, 'Thursday evening' [23 June 1932] [HRRC].

[14] DG/RAG, 'Thursday' [Northwestern].

from New York, describing the city as 'a jumble of slum & magnificence & everywhere these vast brick shafts rise'.[15] In New York, Bunny was entertained by Mina and her brother Lincoln, now twenty-five. Bunny had not seen him since he was a schoolboy tutored in London by Alec Penrose. Lincoln was a talented, handsome bisexual Harvard graduate; he would go on to found the New York City Ballet, which he directed for more than forty years. He had, as Bunny described, 'the authority and the very rare charm which comes from complete intellectual detachment'.[16] Bunny enjoyed meeting his hosts' circle of friends, which included Dorothy Parker and the poet Archibald McLeish.

After what seemed an all too-short time in New York, Bunny, Mina and Lincoln began their tour. They were joined by Taylor Harden, a journalist from Virginia who was passionate about fox hunting and had a talent for obtaining moonshine whiskey in this prohibition era. They set off in two cars, Taylor and Bunny in one, Mina and Lincoln in the other. Their expedition covered an enormous amount of ground. They were based for some time at Williamsburg, from where they explored Jamestown Island and saw the ruins of Pocahontas's father's house. The reality was rather different to Bunny's imagined descriptions of the terrain. He deleted quantities of text, despair turning to happiness as the narrative became grounded in the solidity of place.

Mina considered the whole tour fantastic, although she noted that Bunny omitted 'certain ironic aspects' of it in his autobiography. 'Suffice it to say', she commented, 'our historical interests were discrepant.' According to Mina, Bunny was not interested

---

[15] DG/RAG, The Shelton, New York, Wednesday 13 July 1932 [Northwestern].

[16] DG, *Familiar Faces*, p. 134.

in any events post-1617, the year of Pocahontas's death, nor was he able to feign a polite interest in his guides' knowledge of American history. 'It soon became obvious that as Lincoln's and my interest in Pocahontas dwindled rather sharply it would be wiser for the four of us not to change driving partners each day as we had planned.' This left Bunny paired with Taylor Harden, who took him on a tour of various hospitable relatives, all of whom plied them with 'white mule'. Bunny arrived at Mina's hotel room one evening, 'in spirits as high as the emanating aroma of whiskey'. ' "Now, my dear", he said, "you may tell me about this Mr Jefferson of yours" '.[17]

From Chapelbrook, Bunny mentioned casually, in a letter to Ray, that a very attractive woman, Priscilla Fairchild, was with them. Priscilla worked for Time Magazine, was intelligent, witty and beautiful, with level grey eyes. Bunny fell for her when they climbed Pony Mountain, the steep rock behind Mina's house. Bunny gave her the nickname 'Puss' and as he told Mina, her 'claws dug very deep into me'.[18] Before returning to England, Bunny spent a few days in New York at Mina's Manhattan apartment, from where he wrote to Ray, telling her how much he liked Priscilla, adding 'Darling I love you with all my heart & soul'.[19]

Bunny returned to England on 22 August. He felt rejuvenated. Pocahontas was finished and Prentice read it with approval. There was another light on the horizon, one which might add lustre to Bunny's coffers. Ellis Roberts was vacating his position as literary editor of the *New Statesman and Nation*. Harold Nicolson,

---

[17] Curtiss, *Other People's Letters*, p. 17.
[18] DG/M Curtiss, Hilton, 13 October [1958] [Berg].
[19] DG/RAG, Four-Sixty-One East Fifty Seventh Street, 23 July [1932] [Northwestern].

the diplomatist who wrote for the *Evening Standard*, was interested in the position, and so, too was Bunny. Maynard Keynes, who had been closely identified with the *Nation* before its 1931 merger with the *New Statesman* and remained on the company's board, promised Bunny that he would have a word with the editor, Kingsley Martin. As Bunny later said, 'No man (not even his brother Geoffrey) had ever been kinder or more generous to me than Maynard Keynes'.[20]

Bunny was unsure whether journalism was his *métier*. He told Constance that he had 'done something stupid' in applying for the job. 'If I don't get it – well & good' was hardly enthusiastic.[21] He worried it would be a waste of life, but conceded that a regular salary would be useful. Initially Bunny was guaranteed the 'Books in General' page, there being some delay deciding about the literary editorship as a whole. But on 11 November Kingsley Martin informed Bunny that he had been appointed literary editor, in the first instance for six months. The appointment would begin on 1 January 1933 at a salary of £500 per annum.

Soon after learning he had obtained the post, Bunny received a letter from Harriet Roberts, Ellis Roberts's wife, inviting him to dine so that she might warn him about his new job. 'I don't mean', she added mysteriously, 'that we could tell you the whole truth about Kingsley Martin's character.'[22] Bunny wrote again to Connie, reporting that he had got the job and felt gloomy in consequence, anxious that he would be incapable of doing it justice.

Bunny was also worried about his American publisher, Brewer &

---

[20] DG, *Familiar Faces*, p. 149.

[21] DG/CG [c. 16 September 1932] [HRRC].

[22] H. Roberts/DG, 11 New Square, Lincoln's Inn, 'Monday' [late November 1932] [Northwestern].

Warren, which was in financial difficulties. This was a blow given that *Pocahontas* was due to be published in Britain in January 1933 and in America shortly afterwards. Brewer & Warren had also promised a sizeable advance, and Bunny feared that a new publisher might be less generous. He was therefore relieved to learn, after several anxious weeks, that Harcourt Brace would take him on exactly the same terms. Bunny's prospects had improved dramatically. Not only was he soon to embark on a new job with a regular salary, but the Book Society had chosen *Pocahontas* as their January book, guaranteeing increased sales and publicity. Bunny also received a fillip from his old friend Bertie Farjeon, who declared that Bunny wrote 'better English than anybody now alive', adding, 'I have never mentioned this trifling fact to you, but should like to do so now'.[23]

On 30 December *The Times* announced that 'Mr David Garnett has been appointed literary editor of the *New Statesman and Nation* as from the New Year'. He intended to review under the pseudonym 'Mercury Patten' in homage to an ancestor on his mother's side.[24] There was to be another major change in Bunny's life: Ray insisted that they live in London together. She did not want to risk his finding another woman with whom he would spend the better part of the week; neither did she want to remain lonely at Hilton. And so they arranged to rent a flat at 3 Endsleigh Street, adjacent to Taviton Street, around the corner from Gordon Square. Bunny and Ray were returning to Bloomsbury and would be living only a stone's throw from the house where they had fallen in love.

---

23 H. Farjeon/DG, Camden Cottage, Round Hill SE26, 29 November 1932 [Northwestern].

24 A Jacobean herald and calligrapher.

Chapter Eighteen

'Journalism I am absolutely unfitted for.'[1]

Pocahontas was published in Britain in January 1933. Bunny's pleasure at the relatively large print run was tempered by nerves about the book's reception. It was quite unlike anything he had written, but then as he told Constance, 'I don't repeat myself'.[2] He need not have worried: *Pocahontas* was widely and well reviewed on both sides of the Atlantic. In the *New Statesman*, Ellis Roberts magnanimously praised his successor's 'fine imaginative piece of historic fiction' and the 'exquisite detail and noble intention' with which he portrayed 'a young woman who slowly moves away from her customary world of savagery; yet moves away from it with an acute remembrance of the fine things of her tribal life'. The *New York Herald Tribune* singled out Bunny's 'almost perfect prose', declaring it 'an exquisite book'. Unable to resist an old chestnut, *Week End Review* limply captioned its

---

[1] DG/CG, [1919] [HRRC].
[2] DG/CG, The Nonesuch Press, 16 Great James Street, [December 1932/ January 1933] [HRRC].

column 'Lady into Wife', but concluded that Bunny had written his historical novel 'just about as well as it could be done'.

The book revolves around the legend of Pocahontas,[3] the daughter of Powhatan, a Native American chief in the Tidewater area of Eastern Virginia. It takes place in the early years of the seventeenth century, when John Smith and other English colonists settled there. Bunny charts Pocahontas growing up in her own culture, while observing the alien culture of the English colonists around her. As a young woman, she is captured and held hostage by the English. Her father allegedly fails to deliver part of the ransom, so Pocahontas, who by now has learnt to speak English, is baptised a Christian and chooses to remain with her captors. She meets and marries an Englishman, John Rolfe, with whom she lives on his tobacco plantation for two years. They have a son and then Rolfe takes Pocahontas to England where she encounters and is encountered by a very different world. A year later, she becomes ill and dies on the point of returning to Virginia.

Bunny emphasised the rigorous nature of his research and the difficult task of 'calling my characters from their graves'. 'Such a reconstruction', he explained, 'in my hands at all events, is inevitably a work of fiction [...]. My ambition has been two-fold: to draw an accurate historical picture and to make it a work of art.'[4] Bunny's version of the life of Pocahontas is part biography, part fiction. It is not his best book because it was difficult to adhere to facts and to chronological events while creating a work

---

[3] There is some debate regarding whether this was her given name, a nickname or the name used in front of the English.

[4] David Garnett, *Pocahontas or the Nonparell of Virginia* (London: Chatto & Windus, 1933), p. vii.

of imagination. The book is overburdened with the technical detail he employed to convey an authentic sense of a particular Native American culture, and its cast of characters is often two-dimensional. But he does achieve something very characteristic with his heroine: he makes her sensual. T.E. Lawrence told Bunny that he admired the book's 'build, mastery and vigour', but added, accurately, 'I found little of yourself in it'.[5] Bunny dedicated the book to Frances Partridge, who had helped with the research.

Pocahontas was an odd subject for Bunny to choose. Although the Pocahontas story is a potent myth, in printed form it had largely gone into abeyance by the time Bunny wrote the book. Most of the books written about her were published in the eighteenth or nineteenth centuries, or later in the twentieth century, particularly around the time of the eponymous Disney film of 1995. Nowhere did Bunny articulate his reasons for this choice of subject, but as a boy he had loved James Fenimore Cooper's *Leatherstocking Tales*, so thoughtfully given him by Joseph Conrad. While *The Last of the Mohicans* (1826) is the most famous of the series, all the books centre on the figure of Natty Bumppo, a white boy who grows up among Native Americans and absorbs and acquires their ways. It was a potent image for a solitary boy with a highly developed imagination, running wild in the Kent countryside. Moreover Bunny appreciated other cultures and learnt young to question ideologies of British empire and supremacy.

With *Pocahontas* off his hands Bunny had to consider his role as a journalist. He was dreading his editorial debut, but scribbling

---

[5] TEL/DG, 13 Birmingham Street, Southampton, 3 November 1933, TS transcription [Bodleian].

down initial ideas he decided to get rid of what he considered the rather gloomy 'English high horse contributions' by using more American writers. He listed the names of potential contributors, a list reflecting his strong Bloomsbury allegiances and his recent American tour: Julian Bell, Dorothy Parker, Archie McLeish, Lincoln Kirstein, Gerald Brenan, Virginia Woolf, E.M. Forster and Julia Strachey. Ever the loyal friend he also included Ralph Wright, Sylvia Townsend Warner and Dorothy Edwards.[6]

On 7 January, Bunny's first 'Books in General' page was published above the name 'Mercury Patten'. He soon dispensed with the pseudonym, realising it debarred any personal authority in writing about authors he knew. Kingsley Martin hoped that Bunny would inject new vigour to the arts-section of the paper, which had hitherto been a poor relation to the lively political front half. Bunny certainly succeeded in this respect, transforming the back section and elevating it to a level it had not previously attained. The preceding four literary editors, even the brilliant critic, Desmond MacCarthy, maintained a stasis: 'they were not originators, they all worked within a certain convention, a set of rules'.[7] Bunny enjoyed giving young writers a foot on the ladder, whether as authors or reviewers, although he chastised Julian Bell for making sweeping generalisations: 'I think it is untrue and unjust to accuse bad poets of being fakers', he said, pointing out that 'These poets [...] are writing from the fullness of their hearts'.[8]

---

[6] D. Garnett, 'Literary Side of the *Nation* and *New Statesman*', unpublished MS [Northwestern].

[7] Edward Hyams, *The New Statesman: The History of the First Fifty Years 1913–1963* (London: Longmans, 1963), p. 156.

[8] DG/J. Bell, *New Statesman and Nation*, 11 April 1933 [Sussex].

Bunny was himself a relatively kind critic. If he had to review a badly written book, he would always find something if not to praise, then at least to encourage as a source for potential improvement (though he found it difficult to be kind in his review of Jessie Conrad's demeaning memoir of her husband). Bunny's columns reveal his extensive reading and wide knowledge. As his son Richard commented, 'His journalism was, like his after-dinner conversation, unhurried'.[9] Although he had his favourite types of book, especially those on country matters, he could write a scholarly article on almost any subject. He delighted in dictionaries of every kind, and was not averse to checking their accuracy, on one occasion berating a French–English dictionary for not adequately acknowledging the distinctions between '*les scaroles et les endives*'.[10] As a reviewer, he was loyal to his friends – Virginia Woolf, H.E. Bates, H.G. Wells, E.M. Forster, Leslie Hotson, D.H. Lawrence, T.E. Lawrence and Geoffrey Keynes – were all reviewed more than once. But Bunny did not, by any means, prioritise his own coterie of writers, nor did he refrain from teasing, if it suited. He used Arthur Ransome's *Coot Club* as a vehicle for a double-tease, questioning the higher morality of Ransome's children, and asking whether in his next book one of them could steal the novelist Hugh Walpole's clothes while he bathed in Derwentwater.

He reviewed all sorts of writers and all types of book and could not resist the occasional foray into something highly technical, including a volume on aviation which (joking at his own expense) he declared 'all the more exciting for being a record of

---

[9] Richard Garnett, 'Seven Wasted Years? David Garnett's *New Statesman* Reviews, unpublished TS [c. 2007] [RG].

[10] 'Books in General', *NS&N*, 17 March 1934.

facts provided with pages of tabulated statistics'.[11] While this particular book may not have been to every reader's taste, it was this sheer variety which made Bunny's page so exciting. He was never predictable in his choice of books. Bunny's innovation was to weave a brilliantly crafted and discursive essay around the book or books he had chosen. Sometimes he would launch straight into the review, at others the book in question seemed no more than a hook on which to hang a scholarly disquisition or discursive cogitation. Occasionally there were no books at all, but a lively reverie on an apparently trivial subject.

In mid-January 1933 Bunny and Ray moved into the Endsleigh Street flat. Richard had returned to school and William would attend a local school. They had also invited Dorothy Edwards to lodge rent free in the attic, in the hope that away from her mother, she would be able to write. Now resident in London for five or more days each week, Bunny threw himself into the clubbable existence he had hitherto enjoyed on a more limited scale. He had licence to do so, as the convivial lunch was an important aspect of his role as literary editor. Although he and Ray sometimes dined with friends or family, Bunny was always on the go, and he often spent both day and evening away from Endsleigh Street. He could join Edward and his cronies for lunch at the Commercio; go to the theatre or cinema with Duncan; dine with Edward and Nellie at Pond Place; nip down to The Cearne to see Constance or pop over to Ham Spray for a weekend with newlyweds Frances and Ralph Partridge who had made it their home. Ray was sometimes included (although unlike Bunny, she was not a witness at her sister Frances's marriage on 2 March) but the largely masculine world of journalism was Bunny's exclusive territory.

---

[11] 'Books in General', *NS&N*, 12 May 1934.

As a distinguished literary figure, Bunny needed a portrait photograph for publicity purposes. On 3 April he made an appointment with Barbara Ker-Seymer, a talented, professional photographer who had a studio above Asprey's, the jewellers on Bond Street. The resulting photograph reveals a highly-groomed version of Bunny, in a good three-piece suit, handkerchief in breast pocket, hair marshalled into place, a cigar drooping loosely between his fingers. This was the London Bunny, professional, clubbable, celebrated. Another contemporary photograph, shows Bunny at Hilton, in shirt-sleeves and braces, hair wavy and tousled, skin bronzed, muscles flexed digging out a swimming pool. This was the country Bunny, the man who could not resist the lure of the outdoors, who enjoyed strenuous physical exercise and liked to feel the wind in his hair and the sun on his skin. Would he be able to relinquish this version of himself? Would he tire of London living? Would he need the diversion of a regular change of terrain? Would he be able to forgo the opportunity to escape from one world to another? It was not only journalism which unnerved him, but the prospect of the changes in lifestyle which a full-time London job entailed.

One evening at Pond Place, Bunny and Edward were joined by Sean O'Faolain, the publisher's reader Rupert Hart-Davis and publisher Jamie (Hamish) Hamilton. The conversation was generally about literature, but Bunny and Jamie, 'quietly Philistine in a corner', discovered a mutual interest in flying.[12] A German Klemm aeroplane was on the market and Bunny and Jamie decided to buy it. In May 1933 it was duly purchased for £180 (c £6,650 today). They believed it to be second-hand, but

---

[12] Hamish Hamilton, 'Pocahontas (the aeroplane)', unpublished MS, n.d. [Northwestern].

eventually discovered they were the latest in a long series of owners.

Jamie was taken aback on first sight of the plane, as he was accustomed to something more solid looking. Instead he was confronted with 'a brown low-winged monoplane, apparently made entirely of wood, with enormous wings, a naked engine sticking out in front, ridiculously small propeller and wheels, and a dash-board covered with German words'.[13] He thought it resembled a broody hen, and could not believe it was safe. They named it 'Pocahontas'. Bunny told Constance about his 'mad purchase', reassuring her that it was safe because it was slow.

Jamie was impressed when Bunny made his first cross-country flight, landing in a field near Hilton Hall. The journey was only fifteen miles along a main road, but Jamie declared it worthy of Bleriot. On one flight Bunny heard the terrible sound of the engine cutting out and, though he landed safely, his legs shook badly afterwards. This experience did not deter him from flying over to visit friends for lunch, where he found eager audiences at both ends of the journey.

In August he flew to Ham Spray, completing the hundred mile trip from Cambridge in one-and-a-quarter hours. There he swam in the pool, had lunch with Frances and Ralph and stayed for tea, before flying to Tilton, near Charleston, the home of Maynard Keynes and Lydia Lopokova. As he passed over the farms where he had laboured during the war, he melodramatically reflected that the outcast of 1917 was now 'floating over them in his own aeroplane'.[14] Swooping down to land, Bunny caused Roger Fry, driving along with Duncan beside him, to

---

[13] Ibid.

[14] DG, Flying Diaries, 5 August 1933 [Northwestern].

crash into a gatepost. Fourteen-year-old Angelica Bell rushed towards Bunny, throwing her arms around him, enthusiastically kissing him on the lips. Bunny looked every part the dashing aviator in sheepskin bomber-jacket, leather flying gauntlets, a close-fitting leather helmet and aviation goggles. He occasionally took Ray up, but flying was largely a solitary activity, albeit for social ends. It was another means of keeping Ray and family separate from Bloomsbury.

In the months since his portrait photograph in April, Bunny and Barbara-Ker-Seymer's acquaintanceship had taken a significant turn. So much so, that in September Bunny declared love. Barbara, or 'Bar' as she was known, came from a wealthy family, although her father had gambled away his fortune. She had studied at both the Chelsea College of Art and the Slade, and at this stage in her career was a pioneering avant-garde photographer. Bar was attractive, short-haired with a rather boyish flat-chested figure, and renowned for her sharp-tongue. 'Though she was in some ways diffident and lacking in self-confidence, no-one would have guessed it from her offhand manner.'[15] That summer of 1933 she was involved in a love affair with Goronwy Rees, at the time a leader writer with the *Manchester Guardian*. She also enjoyed a short love affair with Ralph Partridge that year.

Bunny was happy to take things casually and was anyway preoccupied with concern for Frankie Birrell, who had been operated on to remove a brain tumour. Bunny also worried about the Nonesuch Press, as by July 1933 it was in debt to the bank. In November, Francis Meynell negotiated a merger with Desmond Harmsworth Ltd, a private press. Unfortunately this

---

[15] Jane Stevenson, *Edward Burra: Twentieth-Century Eye* (London: Jonathan Cape, 2007), p. 51.

led to the dismissal of Mrs Stephens, and it was Bunny, disgusted at her treatment, who obtained her a position as secretary to Maynard Keynes, though he regretted the waste of her knowledge and experience in publishing. Thereafter Bunny continued to attend board meetings, but his role in the business was much reduced.

Meanwhile at Endsleigh Street, Bunny and Ray were finding Dorothy Edwards a strain. Dorothy had always been poor, and although Bunny and Ray were not rich, they could afford wine and decent food. Gradually Dorothy came to resent them, feeling they represented the bourgeoisie, able to enjoy luxuries. Bunny began to be irritated by her frenzied typing, and found her proximity almost intolerable, 'disliking quite irrationally the traces which she left of her presence, particularly in the bathroom'.[16] Finding it difficult to write, Dorothy turned her resentment onto her hosts. As the summer progressed she was more often resentful than friendly. In October, desperate to escape, Bunny and Ray decided to go north. Dorothy then wrote to Bunny, apologising for being disagreeable. 'You came to my rescue', she said, 'when I was feeling as though I was looking over the edge of the world.'[17]

To his surprise, Bunny enjoyed his work at the *New Statesman*. He always liked embarking on new schemes and his guaranteed salary was a bonus. But eleven months into the job, Bunny made a silly error. On 11 November he published a short piece of work by a fourteen-year-old girl. It began 'Dinner was ready', and resulted in a deluge of indignant Letters to The Editor. 'The

---

[16] DG, *Familiar Faces*, p. 96.
[17] D. Edwards/DG, 9 Pen y dre, Rhiwbina, Cardiff, 13 October [1933] [Northwestern].

paragraph headed "A Dinner" is an impudent piece of plagiarism', wrote (Mrs) Margaret Chapman[18]; 'Is it not strange that Miss Jacqueline Stiven and Mrs Virginia Woolf should have sat down to a dinner identical in composition', asked another piqued reader.[19] Henry G. Strauss of Chelsea demanded 'Why is the extract from Virginia Woolf's "A Room of One's Own" [...] signed "Jacqueline Stiven (aetat 14)"?'[20]

Bunny had well and truly shot himself in the foot. Of all writers, he should have recognised Virginia's Woolf's work, particularly as only a few weeks previously he had written in eloquent and fulsome praise of *Flush*, a review which contained an affectionate tribute to Virginia's friendship with Lytton Strachey. It ended with Bunny quoting the final lines, where the spaniel dies. Recognising the similarity of Virginia's death-scene to Lytton's rendition of Queen Victoria's death, Bunny concluded that Flush was: 'The first animal to become an Eminent Victorian.'[21]

Virginia wrote to thank him for his generous review, adding 'what a good critic you are'.[22] She was less impressed when she discovered his blunder although she wasn't particularly bothered. Bunny rushed round to Tavistock Square to apologise and in the *New Statesman* referred to making 'a proper fool of myself', explaining that the passage had been sent to him 'in good faith

[18] 12 November 1933 [Northwestern].

[19] Enid K. Swire/The Editor, *NS&N*, 11 November 1933 [Northwestern].

[20] 11 November 1933 [Northwestern].

[21] 'Books in General', *NS&N*, 7 October 1933.

[22] V. Woolf/DG, 52 Tavistock Square, 'Sunday' [8 October 1933], in Nigel Nicolson and Joanne Trautmann, eds, *The Sickle Side of the Moon: The Letters of Virginia Woolf 1932–1935* (London: Hogarth Press, 1979), pp. 231–2.

by a lady who mistook a piece of school dictation for an original composition'. In mitigation he said that although he was disappointed not to have discovered a young Jane Austen he nevertheless consoled himself with the reflection that he spotted Virginia Woolf's literary merit. He suggested that some other 'fiendish little girl' might want to try to catch him out with a passage from *Lady into Fox*, 'But it is so easy to have me on toast that it is hardly worth the trouble'.[23]

Having returned to Hilton for Christmas 1933, it was there in January that Bunny received the news that Dorothy Edwards had been hit by a train and killed. She had gone to Wales in December, telling Bunny and Ray that she was leaving the London flat and would not return. Bunny thought she seemed strained and she was evidently struggling with her writing. The inquest announced the usual verdict of "Suicide during temporary insanity". Dorothy left a note stating: 'I am killing myself because I have never sincerely loved any human being all my life. I have accepted kindness and friendship, and even love, without gratitude and given nothing in return.'[24] These sentiments chillingly echoed those she had expressed to Bunny on at least two occasions.

Although shocked to learn of Dorothy's suicide, Bunny thought it somehow characteristic. Strangely, he and Ray had been discussing her only the day before, when Bunny told Ray he feared Dorothy was mad. Somehow the Press heard of Bunny's friendship with Dorothy, and a Sunday Express reporter drove as far as nearby St Ives on the way to see Bunny, but had the presence of mind to telephone before turning up on the

[23] DG, 'Books in General', *NS&N*, 18 November 1933.
[24] *Cardiff Times*, 13 January 1934.

doorstep. "I'm sorry to butt in on your privacy" he started, only to receive Bunny's terse: "You won't".[25] Bunny consoled himself that in one of their last conversations he had told Dorothy how much he believed in her genius as a writer.

Later that January he had such a horrible row with Ray that he felt compelled to note it in his pocket diary. Despite their living together in London, and despite their weekends at Hilton, they had drifted apart. Bunny still kept his friends to himself. Although they entertained at Hilton, Ray was not satisfied with these crumbs from the table. In London she was lonely. This was largely because Bunny now had a semi-regular mid-week engagement to spend the evening, and inevitably part of the night, with Barbara Ker-Seymer, at her flat on the King's Road.

---

[25] DG/B. Ker-Seymer, *NS&N*, 15 January 1934 [TGA].

Chapter Nineteen

'The extremes among animals who over-specialise, like the sabre-toothed tiger, tend to die out while the present still holds a place for that gentlemanly compromise, the domestic cat, which can lap up its cream or go off and support itself by hunting in the woods wherever it likes.'[1]

With Bar approaching centre stage, Bunny was increasingly tied in with her activities, which often revolved around drinking with her artist friends. In his midweek jaunts with Bar, Bunny found himself swept along by tides of alcohol, and although he was hardly abstemious, he had not previously spent long hours propping up cocktail bars. As over-indulgence increased Bunny's tendency to bad temper, their relationship soon became punctuated by drunken nocturnal rows.

Stephen Tomlin was very much part of this drinking culture, and now separated from Julia Strachey, was back in London. He was manic depressive and turned to alcohol in his black moods. In the past he had been able to dissimulate, to pretend to be the

---

[1] DG, 'Books in General', *NS&N*, 14 April 1934.

life and soul of any party. Julia Strachey had 'puzzled greatly as to how people could be so taken in by what one of the few who comprehended him had described as "the inspired charade of normality" that Tommy managed to assume'.[2] Now his friends began to worry, and for Bunny, those wild times with Tommy in London were tinged with anxiety.

In the spring Bunny flew down to Ipsden in south Oxfordshire, to visit Rosamond Lehmann and her husband Wogan Phillips. Part of the attraction was that Bar was there for the weekend, together with their mutual friend, the artist John Banting. After lunch everyone wanted a ride in the Klemm, and with only one passenger seat Bunny had to take each up individually. He was consequently late leaving, returning to Cambridge in the dark as the plane had no lights. He arrived back terribly late, causing the ground crew grave concern. Ray had gone to meet him at the aerodrome, but had given up waiting and gone home terrified that he had crashed. It was their thirteenth wedding anniversary.

Bunny wrote to tell Bar that he was 'more in love with you than I was a year ago & I was crazy about you then'.[3] He appreciated her independence; she was not looking for a husband, did not seem prone to that devil, jealousy, and was content for Bunny to slot into her life on his terms and at his appointed times. The relationship seemed to suit her as much as it did him, so much so that their mid-week assignations expanded into two or three evenings together. 'Darling', Bunny wrote, 'you were angelic on Thursday & on Wednesday & on Tuesday. I love you a lot.'[4]

---

[2] Partridge, ed., *Julia*, p. 126.

[3] DG/BK-S, *NS&N*, 1 April 1934 [TGA].

[4] DG/BK-S, *NS&N* [pmk 27 April] [1934] [TGA].

In early May 1934 Bunny took Ray and his father to stay in a cottage in Yorkshire. The plan was that Ray and Edward would leave together after about ten days and Bunny would stay on. Bunny's side-plan was that Bar would join him after they had left. In the event, Bunny found himself caught between the pincers of both Ray's and Bar's anger. He had offended Bar at their last meeting. Having gone to bed with her, he left late in the evening, but instead of returning to Endsleigh Street, he went on to a party at Tommy's prior invitation. Bar thought Bunny had been secretive about the party and that he preferred to spend the night carousing with Tommy rather than lingering with her. It had not occurred to Bunny that Bar would believe he had deceived her, and he assured her that his actions had saved him 'from the impossible feeling of going into Ray's presence, surcharged with emotion which I could not, & cannot hide & cannot refer to'. He explained that normally he would construct a temporal divide between Bar and Ray by walking 'round & round Gordon Square after dashing back in a taxi […] trying to make myself think of something else & not you'.[5]

Ray was annoyed because she was sick of Bunny coming back to Endsleigh Street at all hours of the night, where he would find her awake and silent. She was also worried about her health. She had been reassured after another recent scare, but such recurrent alarms took their toll. In consequence throughout her time in Yorkshire, Ray was on edge, and Bunny wondered whether it had been a good idea to take Edward with them. It meant they did not have that salve of being completely alone together, that opportunity to re-connect. Some months later Ray wrote to Edward to say she felt sorry she had been in Swaledale with him

---

[5] DG/BK-S [c. 17 May 1934] [TGA].

and Bunny. 'I was extremely unhappy then & ought not to have come & I am afraid you thought me sulky.'[6]

When Bunny invited T.E. Lawrence to Hilton for a flight in Pocahontas, Lawrence suggested that instead Bunny should fly down to Southampton for a trip in an air-sea rescue boat, which Lawrence was then testing. On 10 June Bunny arrived at Lawrence's lodgings. Initially he feared the visit had been a mistake, observing 'something celibate, clerical almost, and pedantic' about Lawrence. When Lawrence proceeded to talk about Southampton's medieval fortifications, Bunny felt that he might have been a scoutmaster. But as soon as they climbed into the seaplane the 'scoutmaster vanished and there was a red-faced weatherbeaten tough mechanic in his place'.[7] As they cruised out through Southampton Water, Lawrence realised something was wrong with an engine and, instructing Bunny to take the helm, proceeded to rip open a floor board, and stand on his head to investigate the bilges. According to Bunny, 'it was then that I first fully realised how wise he had been to enlist in the ranks of the RAF. He had done a great deal for it, but it had done a great deal for him by giving him the ease and intimacy which comes from doing work with other men.' Lawrence's death following a motor-cycle accident eleven months later, in May 1935, prompted an entire 'Books' page, in which Bunny began his appreciation by describing his day with Lawrence on Southampton Water. It was Lawrence the writer whom Bunny wrote about, declaring his death 'a tragedy for English literature'.[8]

Tied to the *New Statesman*, Bunny feared he was losing his

---

[6] RAG/EG [pmk 7 October 1934] [Northwestern].

[7] DG, *Familiar Faces*, p. 108.

[8] DG, 'Books in General', *NS&N*, 1 June 1935.

identity as a novelist, or at least that he was losing sight of it. Initially he had enjoyed his job and the status it conferred, but he was not a natural administrator and the unvarying day-to-day, week-by-week routine seemed relentless and became dull. In June he received a letter from Prentice setting out terms for another three-year book deal, with a fixed annual salary of £300 ahead of royalties like a joined-up advance, similar to that he had enjoyed in the early 1920s. It was a generous offer. Presumably Bunny was testing the water for an alternative income to his *New Statesman* salary.

On 16 July the Endsleigh Street experiment ended. It had lasted just over a year and a half, and from Ray's point of view had not been a success. She had endeavoured to take control in insisting they live together in London. It was supposed to have kept Bunny close, but even in London his will to live life on his terms prevailed: he had cloistered Ray through his own absence with another woman. With no London base, Bunny opted to lodge with Bar. This was not ideal for either of them. She had never been exclusive, and at this time was involved with both Stephen Tomlin and Rosamond Lehmann's husband, Wogan Phillips. Bunny had discovered Bar with Wogan, and the worse for alcohol, let rip his temper. A few days later he wrote to her: 'I have thought a good deal about you & me', 'the last week seems so horrible that I can't bear it or face a repetition'.[9] And then, magnanimously reasonable, he suggested that Bar and Wogan should go away together. Both reactions were typical. Bunny always claimed to be immune from jealousy, but he was only immune at a distance where he could consider his reactions dispassionately.

---

9 DG/BK-S, c/o Bernard Penrose, Lamb's Creek House, Old Kea, Truro, 'Tuesday' [pmk 28 August 1934] [TGA].

When Bar blamed Bunny for keeping her in London all summer waiting for him, he retorted that he disliked her hurt, sacrificial and scolding tone. He was beginning to feel claustrophobic, that Bar was making too many demands, expecting him to offer more than he could give. 'I feel sure', Bunny said, 'that my staying with [you] every week as a habit is a mistake: it puts us both in a false position & spoils both love & friendship. It's a sort of make believe marriage with the bad features of marriage rather than the good.'[10]

'My relations with Barbara', he explained to Ray, 'which grew out of her falling in love with me & offering me gaiety & light heart – are now false.' To what extent he felt the need to review his relationship with Bar in the light of her other love affairs is uncertain, but it was typical of Bunny to turn to Ray just at the moment of retrenchment. 'I beg you', he wrote, 'to bear with me; to remember how much I do love you & not to drive me away when we might come together.' Once more he asked Ray to be patient, to accept his love. He told her, just as so often before, that he would not hurt her if he could help it.

Bunny believed the strength of his love for Ray should enable her to remain fixed at the centre of his universe, to withstand his taking off to explore satellites in the knowledge that he would return. He always did return, but Ray could only endure so much. Since Bunny had moved in with Norah, and latterly with Bar, Ray's reserves of trust were seriously depleted. If he was capable of leaving for short spells, would he, one day, leave permanently? Ray had, anyway, heard it all before. 'I suppose', she said to Bunny, 'we will go on together as before only with less respect for one another – a little less love & a good deal less trust.'

---

[10] DG/BK-S, Hilton, 'Wednesday night' [TGA].

She put up a brave but resigned defence, telling Bunny that the last year had crushed her, that his indifference was terrible to her. 'I've never defended myself for being jealous. But I will say this now. Almost anyone would be in my place.' Ray saw through him, because she was familiar with the pattern: 'A short time ago you said you wanted her [Barbara] always for half your life [...]. It seems to me that you wanted a dream & there's no hope of making the best of what's real.'[11]

'You know', Bunny replied, 'however much I have wounded you & been cruel to you, that I do love you more than anyone in the world. You know that though your dumbness exasperates me, that I love you permanently. I do love you & beg you to live with me now & to give me a little while to leave Barbara without hurting her too much.' 'I am', he added, 'a bloody messer up of my own & other lives.' In the depths of this letter, surrounded by a thicket of words of love, Bunny inserted his usual terms and conditions: 'I don't think I could ever be faithful to you for very long. I can't bear to feel bound.'[12]

In early November Bunny went to see Frankie who had been ill for some time. His head was badly swollen and when Bunny saw him, he remained asleep. On 2 December Raymond Mortimer wrote with bad news. After another exploratory operation it seemed certain Frankie had another brain tumour. 'Yesterday', Raymond said, 'there was barely anything left of the Francis we know. He is not afraid of death, but he is afraid of watching himself grow steadily worse.'[13] Bunny planned to visit

---

[11] RAG/DG, [?9] September 1934 [Northwestern].

[12] DG/RAG, *NS&N*, 'Monday' [1934] [Northwestern].

[13] Raymond Mortimer/DG, 6 Gordon Place, 2 December 1934 [Northwestern].

Frankie again, but a few days before the proposed visit, he received a letter from Maynard telling him that Frankie had only a couple of days to live. Maynard advised against visiting, as Frankie had been unconscious for over a week. 'Dear Bunny', Maynard ended his letter, 'I know how devoted you were to him, and he to you.'[14] Touchingly, Bunny placed this letter in his 1914–15 journal, where Frankie graced so many of the pages. Frankie died on 2 January 1935. 'All his life', Bunny wrote, 'he had sought next to nothing for himself, done all he could to help others and to be kind.'[15]

For Bunny, Frankie was fixed in those carefree days of early adulthood when the two young men thought they could achieve anything. They had been bound together at the Caroline Club, in France among the Quakers and in their bookshop. Despite the imbalance of their love, they had been and remained devoted friends. Frankie's death seemed the end of an era. Bunny was nearly forty-three; he no longer felt that the future outweighed the past and he began to see himself as middle-aged. Although otherwise physically fit, he had recently suffered recurrent bouts of sciatica. Twelve-year-old Richard had improvised a verse: 'Aching back, / Knees crack, /With rheumatism & the gout / The old people can't go out.'[16] Bunny assumed he was the subject. His shock of hair remained as thick as ever, but now it began to turn white.

Disgruntled with his personal life, Bunny was dissatisfied with the *New Statesman*. He felt unable to write, and craved the space in which to begin a new book. He discussed the situation with

---

[14] JMK/DG, Six Gordon Place, 30 December 1934 [Northwestern].
[15] DG, *Familiar Faces*, p. 155.
[16] DG/F. Partridge, Hilton, 10 April 1935 [KCC].

Maynard. Always generous where Bunny was concerned, Maynard agreed to support his request for three months' leave. Consequently, at the end of December 1935 Bunny was temporarily free, his friend Raymond Mortimer taking over his work. Nevertheless, Bunny felt gloomy and irritable, unable to do anything. As Ray told Edward, 'When he wants to write & can't it is like a great weight crushing us all'.[17]

Bunny did not feel entirely comfortable as a literary critic because he considered criticism inferior to imaginative writing. When William Golding, an aspiring young writer, approached Bunny for guidance about a literary career, he was told that reviewing was not a good job.[18] In this respect, Bunny did himself few favours where Kingsley Martin was concerned, particularly when he paraded his negative views on the 'Books in General' page with such generalisations as: 'It is for those deficient in aesthetic sense that the critics really write'[19] and 'The literary critic, in my opinion, is a not very valuable parasite'.[20]

The main problem was that Bunny and Kingsley Martin had never hit it off. Despite mutual friends, Bunny avoided him socially, even though in 1934 Martin had moved into a flat above the Nonesuch offices. Bunny recognised that Martin thought him arrogant, while, in turn, Bunny told Constance that the political tone of the *New Statesman* 'is one which I *execrate*: the superior nose out of joint air'.[21] Martin's antipathy to Bunny

---

[17] RAG/EG, Hilton [pmk 12 February 1935] [Northwestern].

[18] John Carey, *William Golding: The Man Who Wrote* Lord of the Flies: *A Life* (London: Faber and Faber, 2009), p. 69.

[19] 'Books in General', *NS&N*, 22 March 1934.

[20] 'Books in General', *NS&N*, 7 August 1937.

[21] DG/CG, 30 November 1923 [HRHC], quoted in RG, *Constance*, p. 341.

may also have had something to do with Maynard supporting Bunny as the candidate for the literary editorship while Martin wanted Raymond Mortimer for the post. He may also have disliked what he thought to be Bunny's mercenary attitude towards the job. Martin considered his writers should be proud to write for the *New Statesman* and that financial recompense should not be their motivation.

Despite this mutual antipathy, Bunny was surprised when in March 1935 he received a letter from Raymond Mortimer stating that Martin wanted Mortimer to remain in post as literary editor. Caught in a difficult position, Raymond diplomatically informed Bunny that he had told Martin he assumed Bunny would want to return to the *New Statesman*, particularly for financial reasons. 'Naturally', he added. 'I don't want to snatch a job from you.' Throwing Bunny a line, Mortimer mentioned that he could continue his 'Books' page, and 'it might suit you not to have any editorial work, if you get well enough paid for the other. And my impression is that he [Martin] would go a long way to meet you in this respect.'[22]

Bunny felt he should receive compensation for having his salary cut at two weeks' notice, and wrote to Maynard seeking his support. As Mortimer surmised, Martin did go to some length to meet Bunny (with the impetus of Maynard and the Board behind him), and he agreed to pay Bunny £400 a year to continue the 'Books' page, with an initial additional £100 to compensate for loss of salary. Bunny came out of it all rather well: he had a guaranteed income and more leisure to write. He was sanguine about working under Mortimer, believing, rightly

---

[22] Raymond Mortimer/DG, Six Gordon Place, 'Sunday' [March 1935] [Northwestern].

as it turned out, that there would be no friction between them.

Having spent the best part of two years based largely in London, Bunny found himself again restructuring his life, returning to the pattern of his Nonesuch years, going backwards and forwards between Hilton and London. He had also given up flying. Jamie Hamilton had crashed Pocahontas three times, and although he remained unscathed, the plane required expensive repairs and he and Bunny decided to sell it. Bunny never flew an aeroplane again. Having vacated the literary editor's desk and given up flying, it only remained for Bunny to extricate himself from Bar. 'The trouble is', he informed her, 'though we love one another, I can't give enough.' He told Bar how happy she had made him, but that 'the framework of my life is set. I have a wife & sons whom I must support & spend a lot of my time with & consider; I also have a feeling of duty about writing'. 'Darling', he ended, 'perhaps we must part.'[23]

As if to underline his dedication to his family and return to village life, Bunny threw himself into preparations for King George V's Silver Jubilee. Richard and William sported fancy dresses as the Lion and the Unicorn, and Ray created a magnificent tubular flag in the form of a red fish with silver spots and blue fins, which flew from an immense bamboo pole in the garden. In the afternoon children's sports were followed by a bonfire and Bunny was moved by the sight of the whole village holding hands & dancing around it. That summer he finished building a swimming pool at Hilton, a modest plunge pool into which various small children contrived to fall fully clothed, and in which William learnt to swim.

Despite the advantageous arrangements with the *New Statesman*

---

[23] DG/BK-S, Hilton, Tuesday 2 April 1935 [TGA].

and Chatto & Windus, Bunny was broke. It was partly a legacy of renting Endsleigh Street, but mainly a result of paying for Pocahontas's repairs. When Bunny received two enquiries about filming his books on the same day, he allowed himself to hope that the situation might be resolved. W.B. Lipscomb, the script writer for the film *Clive of India*, was interested in dramatising *A Man in the Zoo*, and the actress Elsa Lanchester (whom Bunny had known for a couple of years) wanted to buy the film rights to *Pocahontas*. Given his previous experience of the film industry, he recognised, rightly, that the offers were pipe dreams. Ironically, at this time a group of friends were making a home movie of *The Sailor's Return*. Produced by Cecil Beaton and John Sutro, and filmed at Ashcombe, Beaton's house, it starred Beaton as Targett, Lady Caroline Paget as a rather pale Tulip and John Betjeman as the clergyman. It was never intended for commercial release, Bunny never made a penny from it, and it was abandoned without sound track.

That summer of 1935 Bunny was writing an account of his experience with the Quakers in France, for inclusion in Julian Bell's forthcoming anthology *We Did Not Fight*, a collection of memoirs by conscientious objectors. Bunny produced a fine and moving tribute to the resilience and determination of the French, but he felt it would have been better written by Frankie, who had spent so much longer in France than he had. Although Bunny could look back and clearly explain his reasons for being a conscientious objector, looking forward he began to feel very differently. In the early 1930s he remained anti-war, and as recently as March 1934 had referred to the futility of war in his 'Books' column. To some extent he may have still been toeing Kingsley Martin's 'no-more-war' line. But like many other former conchies, Bunny's views began to change in the light of developments in Europe.

By the mid-1930s many in Britain believed war inevitable.

Bunny's page of 18 July 1936 certainly opened in uncompromising style. 'Hell is all around us' he began, comparing Dante's 'apocalyptic vision' with Mussolini's treatment of the Ethiopians.[24] That Christmas, instead of his customary joyful rumination upon tradition, Bunny began his page with an explosively ironical 'Peace on earth! Goodwill among men!' asking whether there would be 'a clean patch of sand, on which no blood has dribbled, in which we can bury our ostrich heads over Christmas'.[25] Bunny's awareness of Hitler's actions had taken a practical turn as early as 1934, when he and Ray provided a temporary home at Endsleigh Street for a German girl 'turned out of her country because of a Jewish grandmother'.[26]

Despite general speculation regarding the prospect of war, in 1935 life went on, and Bunny hadn't quite achieved a clean break from Bar. He still saw her, though more rarely, and they managed 'to make each other happy & miserable by turns'.[27] Bunny tried to focus on Ray and his family, but he couldn't resist an invitation, in September, to Charleston for Angelica's birthday party. She was nearly seventeen, and as her birthday fell on Christmas day, allowed to celebrate it at any time of the year she chose. When Bunny, Duncan and Vanessa dined with Maynard and Lydia at Tilton, that weekend, they were joined by T.S. Eliot and the Woolfs. Vanessa commented that Bunny and Tom Eliot 'made a very good couple, one slow in the American and the other in the English style – and both keeping us in roars of laughter'.[28]

---

[24] DG, 'Books in General', *NS&N*, 18 July 1936.

[25] DG, 'Books in General', *NS&N*, 26 December 1936.

[26] DG/BK-S, *NS&N*, 17 March 1934 [TGA].

[27] DG/BK-S, Hilton, 'Thursday' [pmk 12 July 1935] [TGA].

[28] Quoted in Spalding, *Vanessa Bell*, p. 274.

But at Hilton, that autumn Bunny identified what was, for him, an unusual malaise: he was bored. 'Ray, my mother, even the children, this place, my work, the time of year, my friends & my lack of friends, money, my own character – all bore me.'[29] London was no longer the centre of his working life, and although he still had his column, it did not provide the clubbable diversions of the literary editorship. Bunny now had to discipline himself to write, but writing was always more appealing woven into a tapestry of other, more colourful, activities.

[29] DG/BK-S, Hilton, [?late September 1935] [TGA].

Chapter Twenty

'Tomorrow will fall again
But he whom we carry to the grave
Will never more return.'[1]

Beany-Eye was published in October 1935. The story is narrated
by a nine-year-old boy; his father and mother are the central
characters, together with the eponymous 'Beany-eye', referred to
by his given-name, Joe. It is a heroic tale in which the hero is the
father, a figure palpably based on Edward Garnett. The mother,
a translator of Russian classics, is obviously Constance, and the
boy narrator Bunny. The house at the centre of the tale is The
Cearne, and Beany-eye/Joe is based upon Bill Hedgecock, a
labourer who had at one time been employed by Edward.

On 6 February 1901 Olive Garnett recorded in her diary:
'Edward came to dinner and gave us a long account in the style
of "Lord Jim" of his exciting adventures with poor Bill who went
mad at The Cearne and had to be taken to the infirmary as a

---

[1] Chinese burial song, quoted in DG, *Familiar Faces*, p. 178.

criminal lunatic.'[2] It was this episode which formed the nucleus of Bunny's novel. *Beany-Eye* is an utterly convincing account of an outcast in an uncomprehending society, a helpless soul whose life spirals out of control.

Joe is homeless. Unable to rein in his temper he is regarded with suspicion and imprisoned. On his release, the father takes pity on him, and allows him to live in his barn, employing him as a casual labourer. Resolving that Joe would best be served if he could be set up as a hawker, the father puts up stock, a donkey and dray. But Joe does not understand this act of kindness or the independence expected of him. He destroys his working stock, defaces his benefactor's property, and becomes paranoid and progressively unhinged. In a highly filmic scene worthy of both Alfred Hitchcock and Stanley Kubrick, Joe lays siege to the family, endeavouring to hack his way into their house with an axe. With great courage and immeasurable patience, the father finally manages to entice Joe away. Joe is placed in an asylum, where under sympathetic treatment he eventually becomes stable enough to leave. The father takes him to Liverpool, paying for his passage to a new life in Canada.

'Why', Bunny asked, 'are there so few madmen in literature?'[3] He set himself the challenge of rendering the inner life of someone who becomes insane, portraying both the confusion of the condition as experienced by Joe, and the fear of those witnessing his breakdown. It is a highly sympathetic portrayal of vulnerability, in which Bunny conveys the inherent dignity of Joe's suffering. When he assembles an armoury of knives, scythes and other weapons, and places them in a semi-circle with the

---

[2] Quoted in RG, *Constance*, p. 189.
[3] DG, *Beany-Eye*, p. 92.

blades outwards, it was 'proof that Joe had been mad for some time, for he could hardly believe that a sane man had been making preparations for going insane'.[4] Bunny posited the question about where precisely the line could be drawn between sanity and madness. He knew, from his friendships with Thea, Dorothy and Tommy that mental illness was not easily categorised and not always visible.

Beany-Eye sold steadily: an exciting tale wrapped in some of Bunny's most perfect prose. His narrative of madness and fear is thrown into sharp relief by lyrical descriptions of the countryside, where hazel-wands are twisted into withy bonds and life is ordered by the slowly shifting seasons. Bunny inscribed Edward's copy of the book 'with love and gratitude'. Olive later considered it 'a finer tribute to Edward's courage and humanity than any of his more formal obituaries'.[5]

Early in 1936 Edward was offered a more public form of tribute: the University of Manchester wished to award him an honorary degree. Constance feared he would reject it, especially given his earlier response to her own Civil List pension. Bunny urged Edward to accept, explaining that in honouring him, all the writers he had championed and encouraged would also be honoured. Edward was adamant that he did not want the degree. He wrote to decline it explaining that he would feel burdened by it, that he considered himself an 'outsider, a solitary person unacademic in essence'.[6] This almost caused a breach between Edward and Bunny. They exchanged numerous letters on the subject and Edward, the literary lion, finally pulled rank on his

---

[4] DG, *Beany-Eye*, p. 57.

[5] RG, *Constance*, p. 190.

[6] Transcription enclosed in EG/DG, 31 January 1936 [Northwestern].

cub, aiming a devastating swipe by accusing Bunny of being an insider. 'By your Lady into Fox', he said, 'you jumped right into a large circle of literary friends'. 'I prefer to be plain Edward Garnett, & why you should not understand this & not let me remain freely & simply myself discloses a rift in spirit between us.'[7] In many respects Bunny and Edward were alike: both fiercely proud, both quick to anger. But Bunny loved his father so much that he apologised though he still believed Edward was wrong.

Bunny and Ray had taken on the lease of a tiny cottage in Swaledale. They could get away together easily now, for Richard and William were weekly boarders at the Beltane School in Wimbledon, another progressive school. The Yorkshire cottage was known variously as Butts Intake and Duke Mary's, the latter after a former inhabitant, Mary, the daughter of Marmaduke Metcalfe. A tough and hardy shepherdess, she had, according to legend, given birth to one of her children out on the moor. The remote cottage was approached by a green track branching from a steep lane. It had no electricity, sanitation or running water, but commanded a magnificent view up Swaledale to Gunnerside and the hills beyond.

Bunny had come tantalisingly close to signing a deal with Charles Laughton for the film rights to *Pocahontas*. Laughton was attracted to the role of John Smith, as he had been the previous year to that of Captain Bligh in *Mutiny on the Bounty*. Bunny had known Laughton and his wife Elsa Lanchester for a couple of years, dining with them or attending star-studded parties at their house in Gordon Square. On one occasion he dined with them at Boulestin's together with the movie mogul Sam Goldwyn and his wife Frances

---

[7] EG/DG, 19 Pond Place, 31 January 1936 [Northwestern].

Howard. Goldwyn was well known as the perpetrator of such 'Goldwynisms' as 'I want to go where the hand of man has never set foot'. Bunny thought him 'crassly ignorant even of ordinary words', and found Mrs Goldwyn 'cold as outer space'. "Is it <u>unborn</u> lamb they are serving us?" she demanded to know.[8] Afterwards they went on to see some short plays by Noël Coward, and then to the Embassy Club, where Goldwyn filled them with champagne.

It was presumably through Laughton that Bunny met the producer and director Alexander Korda. By now Bunny knew not to count chickens where film rights were concerned, but in March 1936 he had an interview with Korda which resulted in a commission to write a synopsis or treatment for which he would receive £300 (c. £11,100 today). The subject was that perennial white elephant, 'Castle Bigod'. If the treatment was acceptable Korda would notify Bunny within three weeks of submission, and pay him a further £1,700 (c. £62,900) for the motion picture rights. Bunny felt rather daunted and tried not to think about the huge sums dangled before him. On 14 March, a touch syco-phantically, he devoted his 'Books' page to a glowing review of Korda's film *Things to Come*.

Like many others, Bunny was preoccupied with the growing certainty of a major European war. It was now a matter of when, not if. Writing to Julian Bell in March 1936, he said he would probably join the auxiliary air force and 'prepare to burn or be burned'.[9] His resolve to enlist in this war was as profound as his conscientious objection to the previous one. 'I am no longer a Conchy', he told Julian, 'for I think we are back in the dark ages and that ethics depend on the time in which one is living. Pacifism

---

8   DG/Julian Bell, Hilton, 18 March [1936] [KCC].
9   DG/J. Bell, Hilton, 18 March [1936] [KCC].

seems so foreign to the present environment as the Cats Home would have been in the time of Nero.'[10]

In the spring of 1936 Bunny embarked on a friendship which would prove rewarding and frustrating by turns. It all began when he took delivery of a 30lb salmon. It was the biggest, at the time, that the writer T.H. White had ever caught, and it arrived by train at St Ives, near Hilton. The accompanying note explained he had sent it because Bunny was responsible for 'the biggest success I have ever made'.[11] Tim White's magnanimity came with a caveat: Bunny was instructed to remove the guts, stuff the cavity with nettles and salt, surround the fish with more nettles, wrap it in greaseproof paper and to dispatch the tail end to a friend of Tim's at Stowe. This set the pattern for a friendship which on Tim's side often had strings attached.

The success to which Tim referred was caused by Bunny's review, three years previously, of his novel *They Winter Abroad*, written under the pseudonym James Ashton. In January 1936 Bunny received a letter from Tim, asking him to review his latest book, *England Have My Bones*. Bunny's review concluded that the book was delightful. 'Its subject is all the things that he has liked doing; a love of Nature and the instinct for action expressed in one kind of sport after another: salmon-fishing, hunting, shooting, learning to fly, playing darts in pubs, and taming snakes. He writes of them so well, with such appetite, that one shares the thrill of the thing done.'[12] Of course it was the thrill of the thing done which Bunny also enjoyed and which attracted him to Tim.

---

[10] DG/J. Bell, Hilton [c. late October] [1936] [Sussex].

[11] THW/DG, Dalmally Hotel, Dalmally, Argyll, 29 April 1936, in David Garnett, ed., *The White/Garnett Letters* (London: Jonathan Cape, 1968), p. 14.

[12] DG, 'Books in General', *NS&N*, 7 March 1936.

A shared love of the outdoors and especially fishing formed the focus of their friendship. By April it was on a firm footing and Tim had stayed at Hilton.

Bunny was taken first with 'the size of the man', but then noticed 'the brilliant blue, rather bloodshot, unhappy eyes, and the patient voice which usually sounded as though he were very carefully explaining something to a child and which would then split with the sudden realisation of an absurdity, or a shared joke'.[13] But Tim was a loner, preferring the companionship of his Irish Setter Brownie and pair of peregrine falcons to that of humankind. Over the years Bunny extended many kindnesses to him, but their relationship was always happiest conducted through correspondence. Their friendship was based on a good-humoured extended game of one-upmanship, each trying to trump the other with superior knowledge of obscure subjects. On matters Irish, folkloric and heraldic Tim was inclined to wield the upper hand.

It was while fishing in Scotland in June, with his cousin, Dicky Garnett, that Bunny discovered he had unwittingly involved Mina in a situation which caused her grave embarrassment. She had asked Bunny to help obtain an English publisher for her latest book, so he approached Chatto & Windus. They turned it down following a scathing reader's report, but unfortunately, inadvertently included the report inside Mina's returned manu-script. Bunny felt responsible for exposing her to this humiliating situation. He obtained an apology from Harold Raymond but it had put him in a difficult position. Mina had, after all, been so generous to Bunny; he would have liked to have been able to reciprocate.

---

[13] DG, ed., *White/Garnett Letters*, pp. 11–12.

As both a literary critic and writer Bunny was in a position of some influence. If he failed to get Mina's book published, he did succeed in negotiating a rapid publishing deal with Chatto & Windus for his old friend H.G. Wells's *The Croquet Player*. He also read some stories which Julian Bell had sent him from China. They had been written by Ling Su-Hua, the woman with whom he was in love, and Julian hoped Bunny might be able to help get them published. At Julian's request, Bunny forwarded them to Vanessa, incidentally mentioning that someone had written to him to say he had seen Duncan in the company of a lovely model. 'The only face I could fit to the description was Angelica's', Bunny commented, asking Vanessa to 'Give Angelica my warmest love'.[14]

That summer Ray was worried again about her health. She had been experiencing pain in her breast and went to see Geoffrey Keynes. He wrote reassuring Bunny that he was sure there was no recurrence of the disease, but nevertheless recommended removing some breast tissue. According to Geoffrey, the double-dose of radium treatment had caused Ray's breast to become fibrosed, and he confessed that he had seldom seen so much contraction of the skin and muscle. Ray wished she had been told before that the breast tissue would harden. 'I think now', she wrote to Bunny, 'it would be a relief to know what he expects to happen.' 'I hate the business', she added, 'I'd rather it was some other part of me.'[15] With Richard and William at school, Bunny was able to stay at Pond Place and to visit Ray in the nursing home.

Unfortunately Geoffrey Keynes was forced to revise his earlier

---

[14] DG/VB, Butts Intake, 'Saturday' [May 1936] [HG].
[15] RAG/DG, [?June] [1936] [Northwestern].

opinion. Ray's breast did contain active growth and he performed a mastectomy. Nevertheless Geoffrey told Bunny that there did not seem any reason for despondency. 'She has gone on so long now without sign of dissemination that probably all will be well.'[16] As Ray had to remain in the nursing home longer than anticipated, Bunny returned to Hilton for the boys' summer holiday. From there he wrote: 'Darling Ray', 'I love you, darling, progressively', 'I seem to love you more & more as time goes on'. His letter ended, 'I love you, & you know how Richard & William do & I've so many kisses to give you'. Bunny tried terribly hard to reassure Ray that he still wanted her, that despite her operation she remained desirable. He sent her 'a hundred kisses & caresses' and signed his letter, 'Your lover Bunny'.

Ray returned to Hilton at the end of August. She had spent a month in the nursing home, and now had to be taken into Cambridge every day to see a doctor. By the end of September she was well enough to go to Butts Intake. Bunny bought her a Leica camera, something she had wanted for some time. He knew that if anything could raise her spirits, Yorkshire would.

Neither he nor Ray had anticipated that the summer would be so fraught. During all this distraction Bunny found that Korda had not kept to the terms of his contract. Bunny had delivered the treatment, but Korda did not get round to reading it within the stipulated time. In fact it was months later, on 28 September that Korda eventually wrote to tell Bunny he thought 'Castle Bigod' required further work, but would make a good film. Bunny arranged to see Korda in early October. In the meantime he remained in a state of fizz, hoping the film would go ahead as

---

[16] G. Keynes/DG, 11 ˙ Arkwright Road, Hampstead, 9 July 1936 [Northwestern].

299

the money would be useful, particularly given Ray's nursing home fees. But Bunny's meeting with Korda left him none the wiser: Korda could not make up his mind.

Bunny had begun to see more of Duncan and Vanessa. After such a stressful summer, he felt the need to retreat into that old established quasi family of his youth. As he told Julian Bell, 'I see a fair amount of your family who are the people I am happiest with'. At almost eighteen, Angelica was growing up and Bunny wrote her an avuncular letter, inviting her to have dinner with him and then to go on to the cinema or theatre. They dined on oysters and saw a film.

That December Bunny was concerned for Stephen Tomlin, who had been admitted to hospital in Bournemouth, suffering from septicaemia following the extraction of a tooth. Bunny worried about him throughout Christmas, anxious for the daily telephone report on his condition. When Tommy died on 5 January 1937, Bunny was heartbroken. In his obituary in *The Times*, he described Tommy as 'universally loved', someone 'with whom most ordinary people frankly fell in love, irrespective of age or sex'.[17]

Six weeks later, while on a fishing expedition in Wales with Tim White, Bunny received a telegram from Ray stating that Edward had died suddenly of a cerebral haemorrhage at Pond Place. Nellie had been with him. Bunny immediately left for The Cearne where he broke the news to Constance. Edward's death, on 19 February, came at a time when Bunny felt particularly low, having learned that Korda had decided against 'Castle Bigod'. Moreover, Bunny hadn't really recovered from Tommy's premature death. Edward was sixty-nine; Bunny recognised it was a

---

[17] DG, 'The Hon. Stephen Tomlin', obituary, *The Times*, 6 January 1937.

good way to go, but felt the loss deeply. He had at least seen Edward, four days before his death, just before leaving for Wales.

Bunny spent the following days backwards and forwards between The Cearne and Pond Place. He registered Edward's death, dealt with undertakers, and began the depressing process of clearing Edward's flat and distributing or disposing of his belongings. As he said to John Hayward, 'The odd thing about a death is just when there's nothing whatever to be done, one has to start doing things at once'.[18] Edward's body was cremated at Golders Green. Neither Constance nor Nellie attended the funeral, but Bunny took Nellie out to lunch and spent the night afterwards at The Cearne.

Bunny received dozens of letters of sympathy. Alec Penrose poignantly recollected how companionable and youthful Edward had been. Noel Olivier told Bunny that she had always felt Edward 'a kind of parent of mine too'.[19] Edward left Constance and Bunny his books having already given Richard and William the manuscript of T.E. Lawrence's *The Mint* and the Oxford *Seven Pillars of Wisdom*. Nellie, who remained close to Constance and Bunny, moved into a small flat in north London, and devoted her time to teaching crafts to the women in Holloway Gaol. Constance retained her redoubtable independence. Bunny told Vanessa that his seventy-six-year-old mother was 'frail & feeble, but an incorrigible character – hasn't really seen a doctor & has a horror lest I should force her to do so'.[20] Bunny knew that her greatest fear was not illness, but that she would have to give up living alone at The Cearne.

---

[18] DG/JDH, Hilton, 25 February 1937 [KCC].
[19] Noel Richards/DG, Nunnington Farm, West Wittering, Sunday 21 February 1937 [Northwestern].
[20] DG/VB, The Cearne, [September 1937] [HG].

Edward's death left a large gap in Bunny's life. There were no more lunches at the Commercio, no convivial evenings at Pond Place, no letters to be written to Edward or letters to be received from him. With his father's death, part of the fabric of Bunny's life crumbled away. As the years passed he still found himself thinking 'I wish I could talk to Edward about that'.[21]

In April Bunny's three year contract with Chatto & Windus came to an end. Charles Prentice had left the firm in 1934, so Bunny now dealt with Harold Raymond or Ian Parsons. Raymond wrote to tell Bunny that his unearned balance was £760, 'but there is still Castle Bigod plus a book of short stories due under the contract, and these two should, with any luck, square the balance'.[22] Bunny still had not delivered 'Castle Bigod' and he struggled with it into the autumn. 'I don't know', he told Ian Parsons, 'whether, short of a miracle, Castle Bigod will ever be written'.[23] Both Raymond and Parsons were good editors, largely sympathetic towards Bunny. But Prentice had been so much more. He had been both a loyal friend and vital to Bunny's sense of worth as a writer, for he had a particular talent for injecting optimism in his authors and always responded with encouragement even to Bunny's most gloomy missives about a current book. Prentice's kindly and gentle support had formed the perfect counterpoint to Edward's more forthright criticism. With Prentice gone and Edward dead, Bunny had lost the two people whose opinions he most respected.

At this time Bunny turned to his friends, Francis Meynell,

---

[21] RG/SK telephone conversation.

[22] Harold Raymond/DG, Chatto & Windus, 1 April 1937 [Reading].

[23] DG/Ian Parsons, Brunthill, Walls, Shetland, 7 September [1937] [Reading].

John Hayward, Geoffrey Keynes and especially Duncan and Vanessa. In April he accompanied Duncan to see eighteen-year-old Angelica on the stage, for she now attended drama school in London. At Charleston, Bunny had a long talk with Maynard, who overwhelmed him with his kindness, offering to pay the boys' school fees, an offer which Bunny could not afford to decline. Julian Bell was back in England, preparing to join an ambulance unit in Spain. Bunny tried to persuade him to forgo the Spanish Civil War in order to prepare for what he believed to be inevitable war with Germany, but Julian left for Spain on 8 June. Bunny wrote shortly afterwards to Vanessa, trying to reassure her that she should not worry. Vanessa replied that Bunny was 'one of the few people who understand what one feels & talks to me sensibly'.[24]

Six weeks later Julian's ambulance was hit by a shell on the Madrid front. Julian was dead. Bunny thought his death inevitable, the outcome of a 'temperamental love of danger and absence of caution'.[25] When Vanessa had gained sufficient strength to think ahead, she asked Bunny to write a memoir of Julian, for inclusion in a proposed anthology of his essays and letters. 'I think', she said, 'you are the only person I could stand doing it.'[26] Bunny accepted the task, but worried lest the combined grief of recent months should make whatever he wrote ring false. 'I want to see you very much', he wrote, adding that he would 'love to be at Charleston': 'I belong to you in some way.'[27]

---

[24] VB/DG, 8 Fitzroy Street, 11 June [1937] [HG].

[25] DG, *Familiar Faces*, p. 166.

[26] VB/DG, Charleston, 25 August [1937] [HG].

[27] DG/VB, Brunthill, Walls, Shetland, 30 August 1937 [HG].

Bunny received a letter from Angelica, addressed to 'Dearest, Darling Bunny', sending him fourteen kisses, and then 'some more hugs & XXXXXXXX'.[28] Bunny replied asking whether Angelica would give him a real hug rather than a paper one when they saw each other. Vanessa had noticed Angelica's secrecy where Bunny was concerned. Usually she would let Vanessa read any letters she received, but she squirreled Bunny's away. Vanessa told Bunny that Angelica was writing him 'a love letter of the most passionate description'. 'I only hope' she teased, 'you remember you're a married man.'[29]

[28] AVG/DG, Charleston [4 September 1937] [KCC].
[29] VB/DG, Charleston, 17 September [1937] [HG].

Chapter Twenty-One

'The only thing which matters is to live according to one's own nature & to refuse absolutely to be what one is not.'[1]

In April 1937 Bunny was asked to edit the letters of T.E. Lawrence. This would provide vital income, if not on the scale he dreamed of earning from films. It would involve painstaking work and as Bunny was to discover, would draw upon all his resources of charm and diplomacy. The *Letters* were commissioned by the Trustees of Lawrence's estate, headed by his younger brother, Arnold (A.W.) Lawrence. Some work had already been done by E.M. Forster, who originally accepted the commission, but illness and fear of libel made him decide to withdraw. The *Letters* were to be published by Jonathan Cape, for whom Bunny now also worked as a reader, in this respect having stepped into Edward's shoes.

Unusually, all matters concerning the letters had to go through the Trustees' solicitor, rather than the publisher. But Cape reassured Bunny that they would shoulder all the risk regarding any

---

[1] DG/AVG, Hilton [1938] [KCC].

action for libel. Such reassurance came with strings: Cape would have the final word about what was included in the book. The Trustees' lawyer would also have jurisdiction on the matter. Bunny was thus subject to two sets of scrutiny on his work. He would not be paid an advance, instead receiving £50 for expenses, together with one-third of net income from sales.

Many of the letters had already been collected by the Lawrence Trustees. After Lawrence's death, A.W. published a request asking those who had kept his brother's letters to allow the Trustees to make copies. Some sent originals; others sent transcripts, reluctant to lend such precious items. But there were still a number of letters whose owners would not relinquish them in any shape or form. Charlotte Shaw, George Bernard Shaw's wife, was chief among this fiercely protective few.

Forster had started to put the letters into subject order, but Bunny decided they would only work chronologically, and that way he could add explanatory footnotes and write introductions to each section, outlining the historical context and background events. In total he included nearly 600 letters to 146 correspondents. As Bunny made clear in the Preface, 'My dilemma has been to avoid repetition, which becomes wearisome, without mutilating too many letters – which becomes exasperating'. To this end he stated that he had 'omitted many passages where Lawrence simply was repeating what he had already written elsewhere'.[2] This was not strictly true, and certainly where Lawrence's letters to Bunny were concerned, Bunny cut what he considered sensitive passages. Thus in a letter referring to the Graves/Riding/Phibbs imbroglio Bunny circled passages,

---

[2]   David Garnett, ed., *The Letters of T.E. Lawrence* (London: Jonathan Cape, 1938), p. 31.

against which he inserted the word 'omit'. In the published *Letters*, Bunny excised the whole affair, even though it had occasioned colourful correspondence between him and Lawrence. No doubt Bunny wanted to protect those involved and wished to avoid libel; doubtless he chose to cast a protective veil over his own participation in an embarrassing event. In so doing, that arch opponent of the censor had become the censor himself.

Bunny worked closely with A.W. Lawrence, who proved invaluable in providing introductions to sergeants major and other people outside Bunny's milieu. Fortunately Bunny and A.W. got on well and became firm friends. An early duty was to meet with Lawrence's mother, 'a fierce old white-haired creature' 'who knows her son was a saint'.[3] Bunny was rather nervous at the prospect, but disconcertingly found himself spending the interview thinking back to Christmas 1914, when Lytton Strachey had read from his naughty story 'Ermyntrude and Esmerelda'. For Mrs Lawrence lived at Lytton's former residence, The Lackett.

Bunny was soon immersed in Lawrence material. He told Maynard that he thought 'T.E.', as he called him, would have been a 'fine subject for a Pirandello play: the character moulded differently to suit the needs of all his friends & even, as a hero, the world at large'.[4] Bunny discovered far more about T.E. than he could conceivably have done during his life. But he could not help feeling sorry for Lawrence, believing that as he 'did not strive to satisfy the sexual appetite', he missed out on 'love and desire and all the range of tenderness between them [...], the ecstasies and contentments of physical intimacy' and 'the sharp

---

[3] DG/JMK, Hilton, Friday 16 July 1937 [KCC].
[4] DG/JMK, Hilton, Friday 16 July 1937 [KCC].

joys and alarms of parenthood'.[5] Of course, the absence of such appetites and emotions was inconceivable to Bunny, for they were central not only to his happiness, but to his identity.

Bunny found himself spending most of his time in London. It was a convenient base from which to interview many of the Lawrence correspondents, and for his work as a reader for Cape, which involved weekly luncheon meetings. He was also now an occasional reader for Chatto and still wrote his 'Books' page for the *New Statesman*. Bunny no longer lodged with Bar, instead taking up H.G. Wells's offer of his mews flat at Hanover Terrace, known as 'Mr Mumford's room' after a former incumbent. This became Bunny's London base, though he also stayed with various friends. One night at Geoffrey Keynes's, just before midnight the telephone rang, calling Geoffrey to Bart's to perform an appendectomy. Geoffrey took Bunny along, introducing him as Dr Garnett. Bunny scrubbed in, donned surgical robes and entered the theatre. Ever the scientist, he found the whole thing fascinating. Having only dissected dead animals, he was intrigued by the business of operating on living flesh.

When in September 1937 Bunny snatched a weekend at Charleston, he found two roses in a vase in his room. He assumed Angelica had left them there, and writing to thank her, introduced a cautionary note: 'We shall meet in Nessa's studio & she will say we are flirting outrageously which I hope isn't true, as whatever you do, I simply show my feelings which are too strong for me to hide [...] but I'm afraid that's as far as it will go.'[6] While Bunny wrote Angelica chatty avuncular letters, which most often ended by his sending her a 'warm hug', he could not mistake the

5   DG, *Familiar Faces*, p. 110.
6   DG/AVG, Charleston, 'Monday night' [30 September 1937] [KCC].

increasingly demonstrative tone of her letters to him, nor could he ignore her exuberantly affectionate behaviour in his presence. A few years before, when Angelica was fifteen or sixteen, she had curled up on Bunny's lap, carelessly circling his neck with her arm and resting her cheek against his. Vanessa had looked on with amusement, but Bunny realised that Angelica was growing up, and had started to view him in a less childish light.

Angelica asked Bunny to take her to London Zoo, 'I love it & would especially with you. Or let's go to the seaside or ask me to come and spend a day at St Ives.'[7] Instead, Bunny invited her to dine with him in London. She turned him down, as she had accepted Virginia Woolf's invitation to the opera, and felt she could not refuse her aunt; 'as I'm not so frightened of you', she replied to Bunny, 'can I dare ask you if another day would do[?]'[8] Judging by Bunny's pocket diary, it would seem they did not have their dinner, but instead Angelica went, with Duncan, to Hilton for the weekend of 11 and 12 December. Richard and William were at home. On the Sunday Bunny, Richard, William, Duncan and Angelica walked to a nearby village. The next day Bunny took Angelica and the boys to Cambridge to catch an early train to London, where Richard and William returned to school. What Ray did that weekend, or what she thought, is unrecorded.

Bunny and Angelica were partly drawn together through shared grief. They had both suffered major bereavement in recent months. Bunny had lost his father and Tommy; Angelica had lost her adored brother; Julian had also been an important part of Bunny's life for more than twenty years. From Angelica's point of view, she had known Bunny since earliest childhood: he

---

[7] AVG/DG, 3 Rue Bonaparte [Paris], 2 October 1937 [KCC].
[8] AVG/DG, 8 Fitzroy Street, 5 November [1937] [KCC].

was familiar, trusted, part of the fabric of her family. She did not need to make the same effort as she would with someone new or her own age: the repertoire of jokes, teasing, mutual friends and shared history was already in place. Of course, Bunny could have tried more actively to discourage Angelica. He might have toned down his expressions of affection; he might have invited Duncan to Hilton alone; he might have stopped treating Angelica like the sophisticated young woman she wanted to be.

But Bunny was flattered; he worried about aging: surely Angelica's evident attraction to him was proof that he remained desirable? Moreover, Angelica was extremely beautiful. With her well-defined regular features, generous cupid-bow mouth, large grey eyes shaped like those of a classical sculpture and perfect amalgamation of Vanessa's and Duncan's best features, she was irresistible. It wasn't only Angelica's looks which appealed. She was intelligent, although her intelligence was formed more by the Bloomsbury love of good talk and intellectual discussion, than any more formal schooling. At school she had been allowed to drop subjects which failed to interest her, so her education was largely restricted to art, English literature, music and French in which she was already well versed.

Bunny did not set out to find himself a young girl. He was not a lascivious or predatory older man, but Angelica's youthful exuberance was appealing. Youth promised health and vigour, the very attributes which were diminished in Ray. For the last two years Bunny's relationship with Ray had been compromised by the uncertainties of her health. She could no longer perform some physical activities, like rowing, as the radium treatment had weakened the muscles in her right arm, and her pectoral muscles had also weakened following her mastectomy. But it was not only the physical effects of her cancer which were corrosive:

the psychological aspects of the disease, the ever present fear of its return, remained unspoken between Bunny and Ray. As he later wrote in his autobiography: 'all the time the fear was there in both of us and just as the diseased cells crept slowly back and multiplied after being checked by radiation or carved out by the knife, so fear grew in her and terrified her'.[9]

Angelica was like a fresh canvas: there was no history of deceit, no unhealed wounds and no recriminations. It was the freshness of her untroubled life which appealed, a freshness which momentarily seemed to blow all his cares away. Although their relationship had been conducted largely by correspondence, in February 1938 Bunny suggested to Angelica that 'we might get in the habit of meeting when we're in London'.[10]

Bunny asked Duncan how he would feel if he (Bunny) 'became too fond of Angelica'. Duncan reflected that

> Nessa & I had often remarked about A's affection for Bunny & we had even joked to A about her frequent letters from Bunny, I took the whole matter as rather a joke & it was not until Nessa asked me if I thought there was anything serious in A's feelings (& remarked how she refused to read Bunny's letter when it arrived till after breakfast which she thought indicative of a certain excitement & anticipation) that I began to consider the whole thing seriously.[11]

---

[9] DG, *Familiar Faces*, p. 116.

[10] DG/AVG, Hilton [February 1938] [KCC].

[11] Duncan Grant, Diary, Tuesday 18 April [misdated; the 18th was actually a Monday and the diary entry refers to events which had occurred some days previously], 1938 [HG].

While Duncan pondered whether it might be better if Angelica fell in love with someone her own age, Vanessa seemed more sanguine. In typical Bloomsbury fashion she was content to keep everything circulating within the Bloomsbury family, remarking to Duncan 'that in any case A must fall in love with someone very soon & that perhaps Bunny was not a bad person to start on.' A few days later Vanessa had evidently thought more upon the matter, because in an unusually Victorian manner she told Duncan to ask Bunny about 'his intentions'. And so Duncan trumped Bunny's question with another: 'By the way what are your intentions regarding my daughter?' He used the word 'intentions' wryly, amused by its old-fashioned tone.

Bunny countered prickly by demanding what Duncan had meant by using the word 'intentions'. Annoyed by Bunny's 'excessively emotional condition', Duncan became angry. In turn, Bunny accused him of behaving like a Victorian father which made Duncan more enraged. Duncan reflected that the episode had given rise to 'all sorts of unnecessary emotions', asking himself, in his diary, whether he was jealous, but failing to mention of whom. They had fallen into that same pattern of behaviour which had proved so destructive at Charleston during the Great War. Duncan worried about the 'uncontrolled self ignorance of B when he falls in love'.[12] It was a difficult situation: for Duncan knew Bunny all too well in the very way he feared Angelica might come to know him, too.

Bunny immediately wrote to Vanessa, telling her about his talk with Duncan. 'My love for Angelica', he explained, 'is made up of every sort of love; it is mixed up with my love of you & Duncan & the past; but it is extremely strong & sincere & I think

---

[12] Ibid.

unselfish as far as love can be unselfish.' But he made clear that he had scruples and that he and Angelica were not lovers: 'If she were five years older, or had had a love affair, we should almost certainly have been lovers long ago', he said, adding 'I shan't try to seduce Angelica.' He told Vanessa that she and Duncan needed to recognise that Angelica was no longer a child and deserved to be treated as an adult.[13] A few days later Bunny wrote again to Vanessa, to clarify what he had said about being 'unselfish': 'What I meant was I should never hurt her if I could help it & that I accept the fact that I shall be hurt myself.'[14] This was the first time he considered that he might be the recipient as well as the perpetrator of pain. Bunny then appealed to the Bloomsbury insularity to which Vanessa was prone, reasoning with her that he at least was a safe bet, for Angelica might otherwise fall in love 'with someone who feels ill at ease with all of you & profoundly hates & despises all the things you care about'.[15]

Vanessa wrote Bunny a surprisingly placatory letter in which she stated: 'I must tell you that I really feel only so glad when I see how happy & alive she is with you. I agree with you in thinking you can have an intimate relationship which will be happy for you both – & even if there are risks involved when aren't there? […] I want her happiness more than almost anything & I'm simply very grateful to you for giving her so much.'[16] Vanessa thus gave Bunny her blessing over Angelica, just as she had given him her blessing over Duncan many years before.

Nevertheless, the question of the age difference between

---

[13] DG/VB, Hilton, [pmk 16 April] [1938] [HG].

[14] DG/VB, Hilton, Thursday 21 April [1938] [HG].

[15] DG/VB, Hilton [1938] [HG].

[16] VB/DG, 8 Fitzroy Street, 20 April [1938] [HG].

Bunny and Angelica was less straightforward than he made out. As usual when embarking on an important love affair, Bunny put his feelings into verse, but this time the verse contained a sense of disquiet, a nagging ambivalence, and in the use of the word 'trouble', a disturbing echo of the poem he had written at Charleston many years before:

> First love comes but once & love is blind
> Or else my name could never have been written
> If she had eyes she must have seen my hair
> Is white, my body fat, my chin double [...]
> And marks of weariness, & fear of death, & trouble
> Seam all over my guilty face [...][17]

Bunny's hair was indeed white, but still thick; he wasn't fat; his chin remained single and at forty-six he wasn't particularly old. However, his relationship with Angelica had a curious effect upon him. On the one hand he felt refreshed and rejuvenated by her youth and vitality. On the other he realised that the age gap was not going to close. Its very existence reminded him of his age and he began to be preoccupied by fears of aging and mortality.

The Lawrence *Letters* were not progressing as smoothly as Bunny hoped. Charlotte Shaw and Lawrence had exchanged six hundred letters, but she would not contemplate their inclusion in the book. Her reluctance stemmed from the fact that she was both a singularly determined and fiercely private woman. Lawrence was something of a surrogate son to her and she confided in him, confessing her private opinions on

---

[17] Inserted in DG/AVG, Hilton, Friday 22 April 1938 [KCC].

subjects including marriage. Although devoted to GBS, Charlotte Shaw was always ill at ease with his public profile and hated the idea of being in the spotlight herself. Unaware of the deeply personal nature of her correspondence with Lawrence, Bunny went to see Mrs Shaw in August, hoping he could change her mind. Realising she was immovable, Bunny tried another tack, informing her that he had lost his heart to her. Such charm was wasted. She relinquished only ten letters, and these were to her husband.

Bunny and Vanessa had entered into a regular correspondence. It began with mutual concerns about Duncan's feelings and continued with Vanessa seeking Bunny's advice about her own relationship with Angelica. 'My dear', Vanessa wrote to him, 'you know that if my loving you & needing you is any good there I am – we are intimate I think, you & I'.[18] In between times, Bunny had taken Angelica to Mr Mumford's room. 'I wish' he wrote to her afterwards, 'I hadn't made love to you, but you are so adorable & wound your arms round me & your hair comes down & I can't help it'.[19] Angelica replied that she loved him very much, but did not want to be his lover. For all her flirting, she found the reality of a grown-up love affair more difficult to contend with. Bunny told her not to worry: 'If I can't be one thing – a lover – I must be another: – a[n] old friend of the family you are to talk to: & are pleased to see.'[20]

Angelica had lost interest in acting and decided instead to be a painter. Her relationship with Vanessa had also become problematic. Vanessa confided to Bunny that she was very upset by

---

[18] VB/DG, Charleston, August [1938] [HG].

[19] DG/AVG, Hilton, Wednesday 24 August 1938 [KCC].

[20] DG/AVG, Hilton, [August 1938] [KCC].

this, and worried lest her grief over Julian was the cause. 'Bunny dear', Vanessa wrote, 'I wonder if you can make things easier at all?'[21] The previous year Vanessa had revealed to Angelica that her father was Duncan, not Clive. Now Vanessa wondered whether this had any bearing on Angelica's icy distance. Vanessa's confessional manner was strikingly similar to the way she had behaved over Bunny's affair with Duncan. In ostensibly offering her daughter to Bunny, Vanessa was in fact attempting to hold onto Angelica. Bunny was right to think that Vanessa could not accept Angelica's growing up. Vanessa had recently lost one child and did not want to lose another, but her over-protectiveness caused Angelica to flee. Angelica did not dare go far: she could only escape into familiar arms, arms moreover which had long encircled her family.

In September 1938 Bunny worked hard completing the Lawrence *Letters*. With Vanessa, Duncan, Quentin and Angelica on holiday in France, he stayed in Vanessa's Fitzroy Street studio, working round the clock correcting proofs. The consequences of the Munich Crisis were evident on the streets outside. As Bunny told Vanessa, 'London is full of dugouts. Some of the Tubes were converted into shelters for Whitehall [...]. The hospitals were emptied. Billets were found for ½ million London school-children in the country. Everyone was given a gas mask.'[22] These were uncertain times.

Bunny eventually finished the book in late October. 'I am saturated', he wrote to Vanessa, '& drugged with the thousand details of the life of the most abnormal person I have ever had

---

[21] VB/DG, Charleston, 25 August [1938] [HG].
[22] DG/VB, Hilton, 5 October [1938] [HG].

anything to do with.'[23] Bunny's work passed unscathed through the hands of both Jonathan Cape and the Lawrence Trustees. On 10 November, just ahead of publication, the first in a series of three articles containing a selection of the letters appeared in *The Times*. Twelve days later, when the *Letters* was published, *The Times* declared that Bunny 'was the ideal editor for the purpose. He is quite unobtrusive, but no editorial direction could be more concise, more helpful, more illuminating than his.'[24] The *Letters* sold extremely well: Cape could not keep up with the demand.

From Hilton, during Christmas, Bunny wrote to tell Angelica that she left him 'beaming fatuously because you are <u>obviously</u> fond of me'.[25] Angelica replied that her feelings were in turmoil, she could think only of him, that she loved him 'too much but not enough' and wanted him to 'believe I love you really – which I don't'.[26] Bunny responded with delight: 'It is clear that you don't love me much – and that at the same time you love me a good deal.'[27] A few days later Angelica wrote, 'The words I love you might escape me but if they do you must pretend you haven't heard them for I still won't admit on any grounds that I do'.[28] With Hilton full of friends and Christmas cheer, Bunny carried in logs, cut the cake, carved the meat and talked to his guests, all the while thinking about his secret life with Angelica in London.

[23] DG/VB, 'Saturday' night', 29 October [1938] [HG].

[24] 22 November 1938.

[25] DG/AVG, Hilton, [?23] [December 1938] [KCC].

[26] AVG/DG [28 December 1938] [KCC].

[27] DG/AVG, Hilton, 'Thursday' [29 December 1938] [KCC].

[28] AVG/DG, 8 Fitzroy Street, [12 January 1939] [KCC].

Chapter Twenty-Two

'Your freedom may involve acute misery & anguish to the
person you love [...]. So what are you to do? Surrender
your freedom – which means poisoning yourself slowly. Or
lie, or break up a relationship which may be the most important in your lives?'[1]

In January 1939 Bunny became conscious of a subtle change in
Vanessa's attitude. She seemed more hostile, tending to side
with Duncan, inclined to hover over Angelica like a watchful
mother hen. Bunny's love affair was, anyway, hampered by the
want of a room where he and Angelica could be alone. Neither
Mr Mumford's nor Angelica's bedroom at Fitzroy Street were
ideal, both lacking privacy. In consequence, Bunny and
Angelica looked forward to snatching a weekend alone together
at Charleston. When Vanessa and Duncan announced they
had changed their plans and would join them, it seemed like
sabotage. 'How can such a frail fleeting love affair as this between
age & youth last more than a moment or two?' Bunny pondered

---

[1] DG, Notebook, n.d. [Northwestern].

in his journal. 'If we were free & let alone, it could take its course [...]. But if we are dogged & watched we shall go mad.'[2]

How could Bunny imagine they could be free? He had Ray to consider and his children. Whether or not he and Angelica cared to think about them, they were an unassailable fact. For the moment Bunny and Angelica preferred to maintain the illusion that life consisted only of each other. Within their bubble of happiness, Bunny gave Angelica all his attention, telling her she was beautiful, worshipping her. She found his charm and sophistication irresistible. He took her to restaurants, fed her oysters and lobster and gave her an antique ring. She wore the kilt he had given her, piled up her hair the way he liked, told Bunny she was sure of her love for him. Melodramatically, Bunny pronounced this the 'last love of my life', adding 'owing to Angelica's youth, it is like first love in many, very many ways'. He felt 'half the time a boy; less than half an elderly man'.[3] Angelica's youth was an elixir which made him youthful too.

With that Bloomsbury propulsion towards honesty, Bunny informed Ray that he was in love with Angelica and that Angelica seemed to reciprocate his feelings. Ray retorted that there must be something wrong with Angelica, accusing him of cruelty. He felt compassion for Ray but could not keep away from Angelica. It was not simply a matter of what he called 'passionate love', but a growing depth of feeling. 'Isn't it queer', he reflected, 'that at 46, I should experience greater intimacy, feel more absolute devotion than ever before?'[4]

Bunny asked Vanessa outright whether he was in her good

---

[2] DG, Journal, Wednesday [18 January 1939] [HG].

[3] DG, Journal, Monday [23 January 1939] [HG].

[4] DG, Journal, 'Thursday' [sic: Tuesday] 7 February [1939] [HG].

books, and was not surprised when she confirmed what he suspected: she had turned to Duncan's point of view. Vanessa feared Bunny would make Angelica unhappy because as a married man, he could only spend part of his life with her. She spoke from experience: it was this part-time situation which she had endured throughout her relationship with Duncan; his absences with lovers, the knowledge that he was not wholly hers. Bunny could not admit to Vanessa what he privately knew: that Ray might die, that he might be able to dedicate himself to Angelica, after all.

Bunny had always enjoyed enormous energy, but now the demands of a complicated personal life had him charging in all directions. On a single day in February 1939 he spent the morning at Hilton, afterwards driving to London where he lunched with Angelica in her room and they spent the afternoon in bed. He then drove on to Wimbledon to collect the boys from school and delivered them to Hilton. Everyone remained in their appropriate compartments, Bunny transferring between environments with the ease of a chameleon changing colour.

When Ray discovered a small lump below her collar bone, Bunny knew what it was. It was the first sign of disseminated cancer. On 1 March 1939 he took her to see Geoffrey Keynes, who recommended a five-week course of x-ray treatment. Bunny told Constance that Geoffrey was on the whole reassuring. But he shielded the truth from Constance just as he did from Ray. Ray's x-ray treatment was delivered externally and she did not need to stay in hospital. In theory Ray was unable to stay with Bunny in London because he resided between Mr Mumford's and an unappealing hotel room. In practice she could not stay with him because his nights were reserved for Angelica. Ray thus stayed with her mother. She and Bunny were again in the same city, and while it might have been expected that he would live there with her, that he might accompany her to her exhausting treatment, that he might comfort her afterwards, he lived only for Angelica. It was a cruel repetition of his behaviour over Norah and Bar.

Bunny stretched his midweeks in London to four or five days, dining with Angelica almost every evening, sometimes lunching with her too. Their nights were spent clandestinely together, decorum dictating a parting in the early hours, when Bunny would leave Angelica's room or deliver her back from Mr Mumford's. As this was not ideal, Bunny took a room at number 15 Charlotte Street, a stone's throw from Angelica's room at Vanessa's Fitzroy Street studio. He bought second-hand furniture from the Caledonian Market and Angelica gave him an antique patchwork quilt for the bed. Now they would be able to make love without fear of the key rattling in their door, without anxiety that Duncan or Vanessa were hovering nearby. During the day they could pretend they lived together in this makeshift home. But reality intervened in the early hours, when Angelica returned to Fitzroy Street, to maintain the charade of being in her bed when Vanessa knocked to wake her in the morning.

Bunny delighted in his 'secret room', where he and Angelica spent as much time as possible, wrapped in each other's arms, cocooned together, hidden from the world. He wrote Angelica a poem celebrating the coming of summer. It was strikingly similar to the verse he had given Ray in 1921.

You are the forward popprin pear
That blossomed while the trees were bare
Dusting with gold the bee's rough head
That sipped of nectar. The petals fell

A bridal shower in the breeze;
The fruit set safe; and now, howe'er it freeze,
'Twill grow and ripen well.[5]

Just as in Bunny's references to bursting buds and lambing ewes in his poem for the pregnant Ray, Bunny's imagery of pollination and ripening fruit unmistakably alluded to fecundity. When Bunny's contraception failed, he found himself unable to refrain from nurturing a hope that Angelica was pregnant, though he recognised the havoc this would cause. Fortunately for everyone, his hopes were unfounded.

It was 1939: Bunny's German translator, Herbert Herlitschka and his wife Marlys had fled Austria and sought refuge in London where Herlitschka hoped to find work. Just when Hilton Hall needed to be at its most calm and restful for Ray, Bunny offered the Herlitschkas his home as 'an asylum'.[6] They arrived on 24 March, Bunny's gesture saving them from the fate of many so-called 'enemy aliens', who were rounded up and interned. Anti-Semitism remained rife in many quarters in Britain at this time, easily disguised as suspicion of German spies. It was characteristic of Bunny to help a Jewish colleague, even though he barely knew him.

In early April the conclusion of Ray's treatment coincided with a letter from Constance to Bunny, which unusually contained the merest suggestion of censure. 'I expect', she said, 'you won't want or need to be in London except just for the day on Wednesdays & now that the boys are home & Ray's treatment over you'll want to be back at Hilton as soon as you can.'[7] Was

---

5   DG, 'To Angelica', 30 April 1939 [unpublished MS], [KCC].
6   DG, Journal, Tuesday 7 March 1939 [HG].
7   CG/DG, The Cearne, 28 March 1939 [HRRC].

Constance aware of Bunny's affair with Angelica? As ever with his mother, Bunny could not easily dissimulate. One evening his compulsion to share his happiness was so profound that he showed her a photograph of Angelica. Although Constance was the last person to judge, she was fond of Ray. She had always proceeded with Bunny on the basis of the subtlest of interventions. This time it did not work. A few months later, when Bunny took Angelica to tea with his mother at The Cearne, Angelica felt a little shy, wondering whether she would be welcome. As she later recalled, 'I needn't have worried', as Constance 'had long ago decided that Bunny's love affairs had nothing to do with her, and were in any case peripheral to her passionate need for him'.[8]

Bunny lost little time in telling Ray that he had taken a London room. Of course she knew why. It was, according to Bunny, 'a painful talk but not unfriendly and did not leave any new bitterness with either of us'.[9] Ray had no energy for bitterness: her treatment had left her drained and ill. Bunny hoped that her spirits, at least, would be lifted by a stay at Butts Intake. They found everything in the house covered with mould; the wind raged; it rained. Even so, Bunny felt there was 'something which makes up for everything – the shape of the ground – the way the stone haybarns rise out of the green grass – the gills tearing down in cascades of brown water'.[10] He could not help living in the moment, enjoying the beauty of his surroundings, exhilarating in bracing walks with the boys, proudly observing their increasing strength and independence. Ray felt too ill to take the exercise she always enjoyed.

---

[8]   AVG, 'Connie', 1986, unpublished TS [Northwestern].
[9]   DG, Journal, Tuesday 4 April [1939] [HG].
[10] DG/AVG, 'Monday' [17 April 1939] [KCC].

Back at Hilton, the fact of Bunny's London room sank in. Ray cried because she believed it meant Bunny would leave her. How could she compete for his affection with a healthy twenty-year-old? At a time when she had a right to stability, Ray could do nothing to contain her husband. Her distress moved Bunny but the moment he was away from her 'the physical happiness of being in love & being loved' overwhelmed him.[11] The situation was all the more difficult because neither could acknowledge to one another the nature of her illness. Ray suspected that her cancer had returned; Bunny was certain it had, but in order to protect each other the subject was skirted around, the name of the illness unspoken.

When Bunny left for London, Ray could not conceal her distress, for his Charlotte Street room symbolised life apart from her, and with the Herlitschkas in residence at Hilton, she felt dispossessed. Bunny had issued an open-ended invitation to them, assuming Herbert would soon find employment as an interpreter or translator. Bunny ferried him backwards and forwards to interviews in London, to no avail. He found it stressful maintaining a constant polite sympathy for his guests, even though he felt compassion for their predicament. He escaped to work in his room, or to dig the garden and plant potatoes in readiness for war.

On 15 May the Ballet Rambert production of *Lady into Fox* opened at the Mercury Theatre, London. Choreographed by Andrée Howard, Sally Gilmour had the lead role. Bunny took Angelica to the opening night, though Ray had been the inspiration for the book. Later that month, with Quentin as chaperone, Bunny and Angelica travelled to France. Unsurprisingly, the

---

[11] DG/AVG, Hilton, Thursday 27 April 1939 [KCC].

holiday gave rise to what Bunny described as a day of reckoning with Vanessa and Duncan. In taking Angelica away, Bunny felt 'as though I were suddenly transformed into Robert Browning & that Fitzroy were Wimpole Street'.[12] Although Angelica retorted that such an idea was 'an insult to Bloomsburyan tradition', in this corner of Bloomsbury, at least, Bunny appeared to be absconding with the very fruit of Vanessa's and Duncan's union.[13] For Vanessa this was like his taking Duncan from her all over again. In Duncan's eyes, it was a more than painful reminder of Bunny's penchant for women during their love affair: it was Bunny's ultimate heterosexual conquest.

Bunny wrote to Ray, reassuring her that he was bound to her and loved and needed her. But then he announced he wanted to divide his time between her and Angelica. Ray had been in this position before. Then, following a pattern to which they had both become accustomed, Ray resorted to silence. Bunny chastised her: 'You detect coldness or falsity in me & then become dumb – & your inability or refusal to speak drives me to an irritation & cruelty I should not otherwise show.' 'I wish', Bunny concluded, 'we could arrange our lives with as little mess as my father & mother & Nelly.'[14]

Bunny could not understand Ray's feelings precisely because he doggedly assumed the triangular relationship between his parents and Nellie Heath furnished a civilised template that could be easily emulated. He did not stop to consider whether or not this triangle had been entirely successful, or whether Nellie and his parents had simply appeared happy in front of him. It

[12] DG/AVG, Hilton, 'Wednesday evening', 17 May 1939 [KCC].

[13] AVG/DG, 8 Fitzroy Street, 'Thursday' [18 May 1939] [KCC].

[14] DG/RAG, Hotellerie Chavant, Uzerche [May 1939] [HG].

suited him to believe his parents' marriage the epitome of enlightened bliss. He had been attracted to Bloomsbury because it emphasised similar freedoms. Ray's sister, Frances Partridge, had negotiated a love affair with Carrington's husband to whom she was now married, although it was common knowledge that Ralph Partridge was not faithful. But Ray was not of Bloomsbury. Partly Bunny kept her out; partly she did not share the same values.

Ray wasn't going to accept Bunny's statement regarding his parents' marriage. Whereas Constance did not want Edward as a lover after Bunny's birth, Ray needed physical love. She asked Bunny if he expected her to settle into a position like Constance's, adding, 'I have wanted people as lovers & have gone on loving you. I cannot settle down to a life like your mothers with you as a frequent visitor[.] I would rather never see you again than that.'[15]

Bunny's French interlude was anyway less idyllic than he pretended. Angelica felt ill much of the time, with headaches and intermittent fever. She spent several days in bed and even in France they maintained the fiction of separate rooms. In Bunny's pocket diary, he recorded that he had told Angelica 'about Duncan & myself which she did not know'.[16] He did not otherwise record her response to this momentous news.

In Bunny's absence, Ray wrote to Tim White, who was shocked to receive a dark letter in which she stated that she was 'dieing / dying / dyeing'. But it was with Angelica's health that Bunny was preoccupied. Soon after their return from France, Angelica developed a pain in her side. Bunny took her to see a

---

[15] RAG/DG, 5 June 1939 [Northwestern].
[16] DG, Pocket Diary, Friday 2 June 1939 [Northwestern].

doctor who advised admission to a nursing home, where she was diagnosed with a kidney infection. Angelica did not want Vanessa or Duncan to worry, asking Bunny to keep it from them, but he told Duncan. Of course Vanessa could not be kept out of the picture, but still fragile from Julian's death, she was distraught.

Visiting Angelica, Bunny experienced an unsettling sense of dèja vu for she occupied the same room in the very nursing home where Ray had given birth to their still-born child. Vanessa invited Bunny to dinner to discuss the situation, although he soon discovered that 'the friendly spirit of collaboration in a crisis had gone'. Vanessa wanted to know whether Angelica was pregnant, and demanded that in the event of a pregnancy, she should be informed in order to arrange a termination. Bunny was outraged, recording melodramatically in his journal: 'When Vanessa demanded a promise that I should help her destroy my unborn child, without pausing to inquire what Angelica wanted […] my blood absolutely froze.'[17] Only a few days before, Angelica had said she wanted to have his child, but they agreed the timing was wrong. Although Bunny was not against abortion *per se*, it was something he found hard to countenance in relation to his own potential offspring, partly as a result of the experience of having a stillborn child. He and Ray had both struggled when she had to have an abortion for the sake of her health. Although Angelica was not pregnant, Bunny knew in his own mind that had she been, he would have fought for the baby to be born.

Vanessa was furious with Bunny for taking matters into his own hands. Bunny was angry with Vanessa for treating Angelica like a child. He felt his loyalty was now to Angelica, he could no longer 'run with the hare and hunt with the hounds'. Vanessa

---

[17] DG, Journal, Thursday [22 June] [HG].

tried to insist on taking Angelica home, the doctor advised other-wise. Angelica felt powerless confronted with her mother's steely determination. She wrote to Bunny from the nursing home, telling him that 'In spite of all the things that have happened lately to show that our love is not going to have an easy time of it, I feel very happy. I love you more than I've ever loved you before.' 'If we both love each other', she reasoned, 'and under-stand what the other feels, it doesn't matter what happens, we can deal with anything.'[18]

While Angelica recuperated at Charleston, Bunny contem-plated his role in what seemed like an incontrovertible war. He told Mina Curtiss that he could not face another war as a mere spectator, believing he would go crazy 'if I were not taking some part in what I care more intensely about than anything'.[19] In August 1939 he offered his services to the Air Ministry. His inter-view at Whitehall went well enough, but everything remained rather vague. Soon afterwards, Ray and the boys left for a camping holiday in Ireland with Noel Olivier and her family. They would later join Bunny and Tim White in Mayo, but in the meantime, Bunny took Angelica to Yorkshire, where he had the good grace not to stay at Butts Intake.

Afterwards, Bunny rendezvoused with Tim White at Stowe, from where they set off to Ireland in a car crammed full of the dead rabbits and pigeons required to feed Tim's two peregrine falcons, which occupied a perch placed across the rear seats. Bunny crouched uncomfortably in the front trying to avoid their vicious pecks, Tim's setter Brownie in his lap. The holiday at

---

[18] AVG/DG, [between 30 June and 2 July 1939] [KCC].
[19] DG/Mina Curtiss & Lincoln Kirstein, The Cearne, 20 September 1939 [Berg].

Mayo was not successful: Bunny worried about Ray, who was far from well, and about the prospect of war. Tim could see that Ray was trying to hide the extent of her illness from her sons, and, he thought, from Bunny. He found her stoicism remarkable, commenting, 'I have never met a greater woman than Ray'.[20]

Bunny did not stay long. On 3 September, when Britain declared war on Germany, he received a telegram from the Air Ministry asking him to report straight away. Leaving Ray and the boys with Tim in Ireland, he returned to London. A few days later he received a letter from Richard: Ray had been seized with convulsions and fainted. It had taken her a long while to come round, and Richard sat talking to her for half an hour while she remained dazed. Somehow she managed to drive back from Ireland to deliver the boys to school.

Everything was uncertain. Bunny was unsure what role he would play in the Air Ministry, having turned down the post of Assistant Private Secretary to Sir Samuel Hoare, Lord Privy Seal, on the basis that Hoare was 'a fuss-pot & very correct'.[21] At Hilton the Herlitschkas had taken in six refugee children, two teachers and a spaniel. Ray and Noel Olivier were thinking of renting a cottage for the duration at Melksham, Wiltshire, to be close to the boys' school, which had relocated there from Wimbledon. Angelica, beside herself with worry that she would not be able to see Bunny, urged him to reconsider enlisting. Bunny's main concern, however, was sixteen-year-old Richard, who hoped, in time, to go up to King's College, Cambridge. Worried that his son would be conscripted at eighteen, Bunny

---

[20] DG, ed., *White/Garnett Letters*, pp. 54–5.
[21] DG/CG, Hilton [but from Charleston], Thursday 14 September 1939 [HRRC].

turned to Maynard Keynes for advice, and was reassured that undergraduates remained exempt until the age of twenty-one.

Bunny was commissioned on 20 September. 'I am afraid', he told Mina Curtiss and Lincoln Kirstein, 'it only means very humdrum office work. Really I find it hard to imagine myself in a uniform & feel some trepidation at what I have done: like a boy going to a new school.'[22] Having passed his medical exam, Flight-Lieutenant Garnett was soon installed in Room 84/111 of the Air Ministry, King Charles Street, Whitehall. Curiously, the non-conformist Bunny immediately took to his uniform (drawing a rather fetching doodle of his uniformed self). Eddy Sackville-West thought Bunny looked 'terrific in uniform'.[23] Frances Partridge noted, 'There was a side to Bunny that entered enthusiastically into what he was doing, down to the details of dressing up for the part'.[24]

Bunny wrote to Constance saying that his work was interesting but he was still vague as to his exact job. In the meantime he immersed himself in absorbing as much information as possible, 'simply soaking, like a dry sponge, in water, in the facts & background of this war'.[25] If Bunny did not know much about his new job, he knew it was hush-hush. Like many writers and journalists, Bunny was shunted into intelligence work in the Second

---

[22] DG/DG, Mina Curtiss and Lincoln Kirstein, The Cearne, 20 September 1939 [Berg].

[23] John Banting/DG, 33 Roehampton Lane, SW15, 1 January 1940 [Northwestern].

[24] Frances Partridge, *Everything to Lose: Diaries 1945–1960* (London: Victor Gollancz, 1985; Phoenix paperback edition, 1997), p. 118.

[25] DG/CG, Room 84/111, Air Ministry, 'Thursday night' [September 1939] [HRRC].

World War. He would be working under Air Commodore Percy Groves, the Deputy Director of Intelligence in the Air Ministry, in AI.4, a new section of Air Intelligence. Groves had known T.E. Lawrence, so there was already a point of connection between the two men, and they immediately took to one another. Bunny could not have asked for a kinder or more sympathetic superior. Anyway, he found it all very exciting. As he told Angelica, 'my secret vice is a passion for doing new things'.[26] Not such a secret vice perhaps, but it was another opportunity to be reborn.

---

[26] DG/AVG, Whitehall, 'Friday afternoon' [September 1939] [KCC].

Chapter Twenty-Three

'You can have two emotions at the same time. One makes the other even more acute.'[1]

Bunny was engaged in writing a weekly news sheet, circulated to RAF stations to boost morale. He knew that the British RAF strength was considerably inferior to that of Germany, information he had ascertained from Air Commodore Groves. Nevertheless, it was Bunny's job to maintain the fiction of British superiority and to suppress his instinct to tell the truth.

Fully occupied with war work, Bunny had to stop writing his 'Books' page. This he did willingly, feeling he had wasted his best years in journalism. Nevertheless, the *New Statesman* contains some of his finest writing. The essay format suited him, and his columns are delightful, reflecting his humour, intelligence, scholarship and wide-ranging interests. Reviewing Virginia Woolf's *Flush: A Biography* (1933) he began: 'Looking at the curlews vanishing on strong wings over the moorland, there can have

---

[1] David Garnett, *Aspects of Love* (London: Chatto & Windus, 1955; Penguin 1984), p. 125.

been few men so unimaginative as not to envy them their freedom.'[2] It is a typical David Garnett opening, one which appears to bear little relation to the subject, until a few lines in Bunny links the curlew's freedom with that of the author of *Flush* in choosing her subject. Another opening:

The snow has come down and there is more to follow in those leaden clouds to the north, but I shall seize the moments of sunshine, put on my coat and muffler, take my stick and step out bravely, for I must see a little life and breathe a little air; I cannot live with books all the time. There is air certainly, arctic air, but there is not much life on the whitened roads. The doctor has visited the village and the treads of his tyres are freshly marked, but everyone else seems to have spent the morning hurrying indoors, and even if I caught sight of a child hurrying along in Wellington boots with a milk-can in his hand I should not have added much to my stock of knowledge.[3]

This eventually arrives at a review of Pirandello, but not before a lengthy perambulation around the subjects of family stories and those of village life. As his son Richard commented, Bunny's 'Books' pages 'give a richer impression of the interests of his civilised and well-filled mind than can be found elsewhere, even in his three volumes of autobiography'.[4] Bunny's *New Statesman* articles are highly personal, reflecting not only his interests and scholarship, but also where he was or what he had been doing

---

[2] DG, 'Books in General', *NS&N*, 7 October 1933.
[3] DG, 'Books in General, *NS&N*, 25 February 1933.
[4] RG, 'Seven Wasted Years?'

around the time of writing. The curlews in the *Flush* review signify he had been in Yorkshire, the snow in the Pirandello essay that he had been out in Hilton. Writing to Bunny from China in 1936, Julian Bell had commented, 'I keep in touch with you more than most of my friends, thanks to the Statesman and your habit of writing autobiography in it'.[5]

Bunny could not know, in September 1939, that he would spend most of the next six years involved in writing propaganda and that he would have no time to write novels. What he did recognise, with some panic, was that he was ceasing to be a free agent. The boy who detested school and the young man who did not enlist in the Great War was now a middle-aged Air Force man, a tiny cog in the great machinery of war. From the outset, Bunny's working hours were long and his free-time short. With only Sundays off, it was difficult to get to Hilton or to visit Angelica at Charleston.

London had undergone rapid transformation. With the introduction of petrol rationing, it was almost devoid of cars; parks were dug up to make allotments; the Oval cricket ground was turned into a POW camp; shelters were springing up everywhere and statues taken down. Eros had flown Piccadilly Circus, the National Gallery was empty of art and soon the city's sign posts and street names would be removed too. At night London was cloaked in black, lit only by an intermittently benevolent moon.

Bunny kept up a social life of sorts, dining with H.G. Wells, A.W. Lawrence, Geoffrey Keynes, Francis Meynell and his old flame, Barbara Ker-Seymer. But there was one friend whom Bunny missed: Duncan had been a mainstay in his life for

---

[5] J. Bell/DG, National Wu-Han University, Wuchang, China, 23 February [1936] [KCC].

twenty-five years. He was the male friend Bunny loved best. But Duncan could not accept Bunny's relationship with Angelica. Usually extremely polite, Duncan was so angry with Bunny that in November 1939 he cut him dead when they met by chance at Victoria station.

Bunny had not been to Hilton since before the fateful holiday in Ireland and wondered whether he would ever live there again. The Herlitschkas finally departed in early October, Herbert sending Bunny a touchingly grateful letter for all he had done. When Bunny returned on 7 October he did so with some trepidation, feeling desperate in the knowledge that Ray's condition would worsen, and that circumstances dictated that neither he nor the boys could be there to make life more tolerable. He was relieved when Ray's old friend, Cecily Hey, agreed to act as her paid companion.

Bunny turned to Geoffrey Keynes, who advised that although he was certain Ray had secondary growths in her brain, she should not be told she had anything more than fainting fits, but must be stopped from driving. Keynes and the distinguished radiologist, Dr N.S. Finzi colluded in telling her all was well. Ray was in a dreadful position, aware that her doctors were not telling the truth, but as she could not discuss her predicament with them, it was as though her illness was a shameful secret.

With Bunny in London, Ray became progressively fearful, lying awake at night worrying about her fate. She told Bunny, 'The Horror seems to be beginning'.[6] 'One can't go on for ever crawling just out of reach like an injured mouse only to be dragged back by the cat's claw.'[7] Now she began to talk of

---

[6] RAG/DG, 18 October 1939 [Northwestern].

[7] RAG/DG [1939] [Northwestern].

'cancer', although Bunny tried to deflect her from such fears. He sent her an anthology on the subject of 'Courage', but Ray commented to Nellie with some bitterness, 'now I am inclined to lie thinking of cancer on the brain at night I can open my booke [sic] & read how Nurse Cavell died'.[8] There was no question, now, of Ray taking a cottage at Melksham. As the weeks passed Hey was joined by Ray's sisters Judy and Eleanor, the three women taking turns to care for her.

Bunny's weekly news sheet had given way to a daily bulletin. Believing he would write more competent bulletins if he had direct experience of the RAF's work, he decided to witness the work of Coastal Command. In November he was taken by boat from Pembroke Dock to a big Sunderland, a flying boat, in which he and several officers took off at dawn, flying between the Welsh hills into the Western Approaches, where they were under orders to observe a convoy of ships and look out for U-boats. Conditions were particularly rough; the plane kept hitting air pockets and being swept by squalls of rain. Bunny was not alone in being airsick, but it came as something of a surprise. Later that month he flew again with Coastal Command, this time from Leuchars, near St Andrews in Scotland.

Meanwhile, Angelica was largely confined to Charleston. When she managed to snatch a whole week with Bunny at Charlotte Street, he wrote to her afterwards: 'I don't doubt your love darling', 'Your tears are so vivid: the feel & taste of them & I am ashamed you should shed them for me'.[9] Angelica's tears masked a growing confusion regarding her feelings for Bunny. She was not seeing enough of him and could not make up her

---

[8] RAG/EMH [late October 1939] [Northwestern].
[9] DG/AVG, Air Ministry, 'Monday' [November 1939] [KCC].

mind whether or not she remained in love. The cause of Angelica's confusion was a young German man called Eribert, whom she had met at a book stall on the Charing Cross Road and for whom she felt an attraction. They had barely spoken, but nevertheless, encouraged by Duncan, Angelica invited Eribert to her twenty-first birthday party at Charleston. Bunny felt vulnerable, fearing Angelica would prefer the younger man.

After the party, Angelica told Bunny that she was 'immensely relieved when disillusionment came and he turned out to be exactly the wrong sort of person for me, & I could write to you & tell you so'.[10] An odd statement: was Angelica in love with the idea of falling in love? With so many young men disappearing into the Forces, did she feel the need to snatch at the opportunity Eribert appeared to offer? Or was she testing the strength of Bunny's love by causing him jealousy? She succeeded on that count: 'I quite nauseated myself with my own jealousy', he told her, 'an emotion which I loathe.'[11]

At the Air Ministry Bunny took turns as weekend Duty Officer, which involved being on duty round the clock, sleeping in a camp bed in the Director of Intelligence's office. Given Ray's now rapidly failing health, it was particularly hard on them both that Bunny had to work over Christmas, although the house resounded with happiness when Noel Olivier arrived with her husband Arthur Richards and their children. Bunny bought Ray a shooting stick to rest on while walking in the garden and gave her a magnificent patchwork quilt, which she had made into a dressing gown with a sort of farthingale skirt. It kept her warm and gave the impression that she glided about on wheels.

---

[10] AVG/DG, Charleston, Monday 8 January 1940 [KCC].
[11] DG/AVG, Air Ministry, 'Wednesday' [early January 1940] [KCC].

Returning to Hilton for four days' leave on Boxing Day and emerging from a climate of secrecy, Bunny wondered whether Ray's fears would subside if she were told the truth about her condition. 'But', he reasoned, 'one cannot tell a living creature, clinging to life, that there <u>is no hope</u>.' On one occasion, trying to reassure Ray, Bunny had to find a pretext to leave the room, unable to control his voice or disguise his emotion. He found himself automatically ordering seed for the garden, a pointless and unbearable exercise. He worried about Richard and William, about what they saw, how they perceived their mother, whether they knew how ill she was. As Bunny told Constance, 'During the week I have to try to invent lies about our hopeful prospects of the war – that is child's play to lying when I get home.'[12] Ray told him, 'You must lie to me if necessary but lie well'.[13] Preoccupied with Ray, Bunny found it difficult to concentrate on anything. He apologised to Angelica for seeming rather remote, explaining that confronted with Ray's worsening condition, he felt paralysed. 'I often cry', he told her.[14]

In January 1940, when the boiler burst at Hilton, Ray became cold and took to bed. She rapidly weakened. A nurse was brought in and Richard built a bird table outside Ray's window, so she could watch the birds. Bunny could now spend two days a week with Ray, and he exhausted himself staying up with her at night, reading aloud from her favourite detective fiction. Ray did not want to go into hospital and Bunny had no intention of letting this happen. Instead he explained the situation to Groves, who in February granted Bunny compassionate leave.

---

[12] DG/CG, Air Ministry, 14 February 1940 [HRRC].
[13] RAG/DG [Air Ministry stamp 6 February 1940 [Northwestern].
[14] DG/AVG, Air Ministry, 'Saturday' [?19 January 1940] [KCC].

'Life has settled into the curious routine when extreme illness governs the house', Bunny told Constance.[15] Now he, Hey and Judy took turns to sit with Ray throughout the day and to go to her at night. Bunny found it a comfort to be with her, that they could talk together, although he often broke down in tears, and wished there was more he could do to alleviate her suffering. 'If only I could have a heart attack', she told him, 'and not recover.'[16] But with Bunny at Hilton, Ray's fears began to subside. Now there was a tacit understanding between them that she would not get better, but this unspoken acknowledgement brought her more peace. Bunny asked the local doctor to administer morphine and heroin, one for the pain, the other to raise her spirits. Thus made comfortable, Ray was able to bring the family photograph albums up to date, Bunny having hastily taken the most recent films to the chemist to be developed. As Ray declined he observed it was 'like watching a sandcastle being destroyed by the tide'.[17] She was perceptibly thinner and Bunny began to worry about the Easter holidays, believing it would be distressing for the boys to see her in this state, or worse still, if she were to die while they were at home. Ray too had been pondering these questions, and they agreed the boys should stay away.

Bunny had also taken another important decision: he resigned his commission in the RAF. This was partly for political reasons as Groves had left and Bunny thought his new superior might not be as sympathetic and might recall him prematurely. Mainly Bunny wanted to leave because he could no longer stand manufacturing lies, a realisation underlined by the fact that he and

---

[15] DG/CG, Hilton, Tuesday 27 February 1940 [HRRC].
[16] DG/AVG, Hilton, 28 February 1940 [KCC].
[17] DG/CG, Hilton, Tuesday 27 February 1940 [HRRC].

Ray could now speak openly about her health. But there was another reason for his resignation. 'That I want to be with a Jelly Cat & that the Jelly Cat wants me to resign.'[18] 'Jelly Cat' was Bunny's nickname for Angelica.

Bunny felt very close to Ray, relieved that they could talk about the boys' futures. She wished Bunny luck and happiness, saying she hoped Hilton would one day be full of children again. When Bunny mentioned William, Ray 'cried out joyously: "William! There he is! I can see him lifting his head to look at me!" Bunny found the happiness in Ray's voice heart-rending. He felt utterly miserable, knowing she longed to die, knowing death would bring relief to them both, but wishing she had not had 'such damned cruel bad luck'.[19]

On the evening of Easter Sunday, 24 March, Ray died. Bunny had put her beloved cat on the bed beside her. With one hand stroking the cat, and the other clasped in Bunny's, Ray died, 'almost imperceptibly', 'a fortunate & peaceful death'.[20] As Bunny told Richard and William, she 'died so gently that the nurse could not be sure when it was'.[21] Afterwards, Bunny cried out "Thank God. Oh Thank God", reflecting it was an odd response, as he did not believe in God.[22] He and Ray had been married for nineteen years, the shadow of illness gradually darkening the last eleven. Bunny wrote to Duncan, pouring out his grief to his dearest friend. He said he would no longer live at

---

[18] DG/AVG, Hilton, 'Good Friday' [22 March 1940] [KCC].

[19] DG/AVG, Hilton, 'Easter Sunday' [24 March 1940] [KCC].

[20] DG/THW, Hilton [late March 1940], in DG, ed., *White/Garnett Letters*, p. 62.

[21] DG/RG and William Garnett, Hilton, 26 March 1940 [RG].

[22] DG, *Familiar Faces*, p. 218.

Hilton, 'I can't bear it. I can't bear the waste: the silly unnecessary cruelty of Ray's death [...]. Ray made this house: was often unhappy in it, but loved all the things which made it what it is. And now all the flowers are coming out: and I am turning out the jars of mincemeat she made last autumn.'[23]

Among the letters of condolence was one from Morgan Forster in which he clumsily chirruped about his mother and a friend of hers, both in their eighties. Ray's body was cremated and on 29 March Bunny went to Ham Spray, collecting the boys from Hungerford station. Frances Partridge found seventeen-year-old Richard 'self-possessed and talkative', but William, only fifteen, 'sunk and hunched in tangible gloom'. Bunny, she noticed, looked exhausted.[24] Afterwards, Bunny took Richard and William to The Cearne, where they spent several days with Constance. Then Bunny wrote to Vanessa to ask whether he could come to Charleston, bringing his sons. She obviously acquiesced, as he later wrote to thank her for all her kindness and hospitality. Was Bunny easing Angelica into his sons' lives? Did he want them to taste the pleasures of Charleston, the house which for many reasons had played an important role in Bunny's life? Given Duncan's and Vanessa's antipathy towards Bunny, it seems astonishing he should have imposed himself upon them. No doubt the visit was intended to demonstrate the possibility of the evolution of another family unit, one which included both Angelica and his sons.

Returning home towards the end of April, Bunny worried that the boys would feel Ray's absence. He involved them in

---

[23] DG/D. Grant, Hilton, 27 April 1940 [HG].

[24] Diary entry for 29 March 1940 in Frances Partridge, *A Pacifist's War* (London: Hogarth Press, 1978; Robin Clark paperback edition 1983), p. 34.

sorting through her things, using the opportunity to rekindle memories of the past. They both seemed fine, but Bunny noticed that at bed-time, William returned his kiss and hug, which was unusual. Bunny had never seen Hilton more beautiful, the plum and cherry trees in full blossom. He was considering letting the house, the memories of Ray too painful for him to stay. Every now and then he suddenly remembered her, not the 'dying despairing creature' 'but the woman with whom I came here to live & whom I loved most passionately'.[25]

Despite his terrible sadness, Bunny recognised how fortunate he was, because unlike many bereaved, he felt he had a future. 'Thanks to Angelica I can forget my life & the waste almost as though I were walking out of a tragic matinee into the spring sunshine.'[26] He and Angelica planned to stay at Butts Intake when the boys returned to school. Bunny wrote to Vanessa, describing the place, hoping to regain her confidence. But Vanessa and Duncan were both against Angelica's living with Bunny, were perhaps embarrassed by it, for they wanted as few people to know as possible. They also worried that Angelica would end up a skivvy to Bunny's sons. Bunny assured Vanessa that Richard was quite capable of mending his own socks. He counselled Angelica to be gentle with her parents: 'remember they are losing you – and losing you to someone whom everybody would think an ill suited companion, and about whom they have strong feelings of justified resentment'.[27] If it seems odd that Bunny should think their resentment justified, as a parent himself, he could at least see the situation from their vantage point.

---

[25] DG/AVG, Hilton, 'Tuesday evening' [April 1940] [KCC].

[26] DG/D Grant, Hilton, 27 April 1940 [HG].

[27] DG/AG, Butts Intake, 30 April [1940] [KCC].

At Butts Intake, Angelica hid when the postman called; for propriety's sake Bunny informed Mrs Appleton, from whom he purchased milk, that Angelica was his secretary. Initially it was like a honeymoon, but even so, Bunny often experienced a numb feeling of unreality. He kept mentally going over and over his life with Ray, and if he allowed himself to feel happy, his happiness was undermined by the burden of the past, a burden made heavier by his sense of guilt. Bunny responded to emotional shock with what he described as 'photographic sensitiveness to my physical surroundings', and in Yorkshire he was transfixed by the hawthorn blossom, by nesting birds and everything in nature which seemed 'rich, warm, sunlit, peaceful'.[28]

Such beauty and peace contrasted markedly with what Bunny heard on his wireless. On 4 June the evacuation of Dunkirk was reported, accompanied by Churchill's celebrated speech, 'We shall fight on the beaches, we shall fight on the landing grounds'. Bunny was not idle; he was abridging the Lawrence *Letters* for a Book Club edition. But that summer of 1940, as the weeks passed and as England lived under the shadow of expected invasion, he regretted having resigned from the Air Ministry and felt removed from the centre of things.

While Bunny feared Constance would be in the area most likely to be bombed, his mother's concerns were more prosaic. She asked Bunny outright what he intended to do in the school holidays: 'You could hardly have the boys with Angelica & you at Butts, could you?' 'You must give them time', she advised, adding, 'with discretion couldn't you get them gradually used to feeling Angelica a sort of adopted (and very delightful) sister'.[29] At twenty-one, Angelica

---

[28] DG, 'Burst Balloons', unpublished MS [c. 1970] [RG].
[29] CG/DG, The Cearne, 13 June 1940 [HRRC].

was only four years Richard's senior, but given the nature of her relationship with Bunny, Constance's proposal was untenable. Angelica had anyway remarked to Bunny (when he took the boys to Charleston) that she thought from the way Richard looked at them 'he guessed or half guessed what relationship we bear to each other'.[30]

Bunny and Angelica remained in Yorkshire until the end of July, when the boys broke up from school. He decided his sons' holiday should be spent at Hilton, but ignoring his mother's concerns, installed Angelica there. The presence of Noel Olivier and her five children helped deflect attention from Bunny and Angelica and diminished any sense that Angelica was stepping into Ray's shoes. The arrangement worked surprisingly well, Bunny busying himself bottling plums, Angelica painting, Richard in charge of the little ones and William doing the housework.

In contrast, Charleston remained firmly antipathetic to the couple. Bunny decided there was no point going there after one stilted afternoon with Maynard Keynes and Morgan Forster in attendance, when Bunny and Angelica had to pretend there was nothing between them, for Duncan's sake. It was extraordinary that such pretence should be necessary at the heart of Bloomsbury, but even Bloomsbury baulked at the Bunny–Angelica–Duncan helix with its inter-generational tangle. The real problem was that the helix was a visible reminder of another well-kept secret: that Angelica was Duncan's daughter. On one level this was obvious, as Angelica so closely resembled her father. But it wasn't something openly acknowledged or discussed.

In July the Germans began aerial attacks on airfields around

---

[30] AVG/DG, Charleston, 'Thursday' [April 1940] [KCC].

London and on 24 August dropped their first bombs on central London. When Bunny's barrel of plum wine blew a bung in the middle of the night he thought it was a bomb. More worryingly, a bomb rocked The Cearne, leaving Constance anxious. Bunny reassured her that only a direct hit could damage such a solid house, but he bought her a helmet to wear in the garden. On Saturday 7 September 1940 the Blitz began. This heavy and concentrated bombardment of London would continue for months. Bombers flew over by day and night, devastating the docks and destroying warehouses and their contents. In the Bloomsbury district, Vanessa's and Duncan's Fitzroy Street studio was destroyed as was Bunny's room on Charlotte Street, which, fortunately, he had emptied only three weeks previously. In Mecklenburgh Square, Virginia's and Leonard's flat and Hogarth Press premises were destroyed, while in Regent's Park, Adrian and Karin Stephen's house lost its roof to bombs. It had been six months since he left the Air Ministry, and with invasion a real concern, Bunny felt he had been too long away from war work and from London.

Having finally found a tenant for Hilton, in October Bunny and Angelica moved to Lower Claverham Farm at Berwick in Sussex. As Vanessa had complained to Bunny that she could not bear to be separated from her daughter, Lower Claverham was selected for its relative proximity to Charleston. Bunny disliked it from the outset: it was cramped, they had insufficient furniture, and knowing it was a temporary let, Bunny couldn't invest in cultivating a garden. There he and Angelica received several visits from Leonard and Virginia Woolf. They came in March 1941, just a week before Virginia drowned, having weighed down her pockets with stones. Her death was a great blow to Angelica, who returned to Charleston, briefly united with Vanessa and Duncan by grief.

It was with little regret that after eight months Bunny and Angelica vacated Claverham in June 1941, their landlord requiring it at short notice. After some searching (by bicycle as petrol was rationed) they found a thatched bungalow at Alciston, even closer to Charleston. But then Angelica became liable for National Service. She took up an offer from Mrs Curtis, the headmistress at her old school, Longford Grove, to work there as an art mistress. Angelica's departure coincided with Richard's decision to enlist in the RAF marine aircraft section, responsible for flying boats and Air Sea Rescue. Bunny wondered whether he should have discouraged him from enlisting, but recognised that Richard was his own man with his own moral outlook.

Bunny received a commission from the Air Ministry to write a propaganda book, *War in the Air*, intended for American consumption. He told Constance, 'I never realised how terrific our victory in the air had been last summer. Thus my book has a magnificent subject.'[31] Bunny was also asked by the Ministry of Information to write a pamphlet on the campaign in Greece and Crete. This type of propaganda involved placing events in an historical context so close as to be almost immediate. Bunny was disciplined and scrupulous in this work. His method is apparent in advice he gave to the American historian Bruce Campbell Hopper on the subject of writing a history of air warfare: 'Start with the scientific technical advance whatever it may [be]: show how that influences policy by making something new & [a] practical proposition – then tell the story of the actual air warfare as an illustration of carrying out this policy & using the new weapon. In that way the reader will never be allowed to forget

---

[31] DG/CG, Claverham Farm, 26 February 1941 [HRRC].

that the means are changing every few months.'[32]

In September 1941, when Air Commodore Groves invited Bunny to become his private secretary he jumped at the offer, but the job went through so many bureaucratic hoops that it emerged unrecognisable. The following month, however, a suitable post was found. Bunny would be working again under Groves, but as a civilian at the newly established Political Warfare Executive (PWE). 'As you know', he wrote to Angelica, 'I can say nothing about my work. But it is certainly most interesting.'[33] Once again Bunny was to be involved in hush-hush propaganda.

Lodging with Leonard Woolf in his Clifford's Inn flat, Bunny was glad to be in London again. Dining, one day, in a restaurant he saw Duncan at an adjacent table, but his old friend cut him dead. Angelica longed to be with Bunny in London. She dreamed about an ideal life, telling Bunny it would be 'purely domestic – to have a moderate sized family and a house – a large house where we could be really free and live as we liked […]. I should like to have a great many friends and to live in an atmosphere of being alive – I would paint every day.'[34] Bunny responded with a pragmatic proposal. 'I am going now', he wrote in November 1941, 'to do something which may annoy you & which many people would think very unscrupulous. That is to ask you to marry me.'[35]

---

[32] Quoted in DG/RG, The Cearne, 13 June 1943 [RG].

[33] DG/AVG, 159 Clifford's Inn, 13 November 1941[KCC].

[34] AVG/DG [Longford Grove], [16 November 1941] [KCC].

[35] DG/AVG, 159 Clifford's Inn, 18 November 1941 [KCC].

Part Four

Angelica

Chapter Twenty-Four

'The most important work in this war is propaganda [...].
It is a writer's job & as we have truth on our side [we] shall
have a wonderful opportunity.'[1]

Bunny's marriage proposal was made with no great confidence.
He was doubtful about the ethics of marrying a woman twenty-
six years younger than himself and concerned that it would
cause an irreparable breach between Angelica and her parents.
He thought the age difference would curtail their marriage,
doubting they would stay together for longer than a decade.
Such pessimistic considerations were hardly the most romantic
bases for wedlock, but Bunny was acutely aware that it was a
huge step for Angelica, and he did not wish her to take it lightly.

In asking Angelica to marry him, therefore, Bunny laid before
her all the objections he could think of. Time and again he asked
her to carefully consider the situation, to think about the implications of having children, to realise her freedom would thus be
constrained. He told her not to embark on marriage or children

---

[1] DG/THW, Hilton [September 1938], in DG, ed., *White/Garnett Letters*, p. 34.

'unless the desire to do so is your own'. 'I am already old', he explained, '& the risks for you are therefore greater as I am much more likely to get ill & die, or to become unable to adapt myself after the war & so fail to earn a living. Your tastes will also diverge more & more from mine because you will be expanding in every direction, while I shall be contracting or standing still.'[2] Writing to Angelica on 18 November 1941, Bunny declared outright that he would not be hurt or annoyed by a refusal.

Bunny's attitude towards marriage with Angelica was markedly different to that of his marriage with Ray. He informed Ray that he could not be faithful and was likely to hurt her. Now he assumed Angelica would not be faithful and would consequently hurt him. He told her she could trust him 'to behave as you would wish if you fall in love with someone else'.[3] He thought that even if he were to dislike this hypothetical lover, he would be able to behave in a civilised manner. On the positive side, Bunny recognised marriage would make things easier socially, because he and Angelica could acknowledge publicly that they were a couple. Bunny also hoped it might encourage Vanessa and Duncan to accept the relationship. Most importantly, marriage would enable Angelica to avoid war work, as conscription of single women was to be enforced in December 1941. If Angelica remained unmarried, she would have to join one of the women's forces.

Angelica replied: 'The fact that you have asked me to marry you makes me happy & rather proud.'[4] She did not reject Bunny's proposal and on the whole thought the pros outweighed the cons.

---

[2] DG/AVG, Political Intelligence Department of the FO, Centre Block, Bush House, Aldwych, 'Tuesday' [c. late March 1942] [KCC].

[3] DG/AVG, 159 Clifford's Inn, 18 November 1941 [KCC].

[4] AVG/DG, Eyewood, Friday 21 November [1941] [KCC].

She was, anyway, in love with Bunny: he filled a gap in her life which neither her putative father, Clive, nor genetic father, Duncan, was able to fill. When Angelica was asked, in relation to this biography, what attracted her to Bunny, she replied 'he was warm and rather slow – and all that added up to someone to me very attractive because what I needed was a father-figure and that he was exactly'. She also found him 'very well-made, physically'. Referring to a photograph where he is captured from back view, climbing into a first-floor window wearing only a pair of espadrilles, she said: 'you can see exactly how beautiful his body was'.[5]

At the beginning of December Angelica told Bunny, 'I now naturally often think of our getting married, and I think I am drawing nearer and nearer to the assumption that we shall be'.[6] She tried to discuss the matter with Vanessa, but Vanessa could not get beyond concern for Duncan's feelings. The upshot was that Vanessa told Angelica that 'we – this household – can't really share your happiness as we might if you were living with someone who could easily & freely come here with you'.[7]

Bunny endeavoured to get to The Cearne to see Constance once a fortnight. Now eighty, she was physically frail and nearly blind, but still retained her fierce independence and clear mind. Angelica recalled Connie's joy at seeing Bunny, which resembled 'the unbridled pleasure of a puppy on the return of its master'.[8] He remained the centre of her world. One evening when Bunny was at The Cearne, Constance suddenly began speaking gibberish. Bunny helped her to bed and she regained her speech after

5 AVG interviewed by the author, Forcalquier, France, 3 January 2008.
6 AVG/DG, Eywood, Tuesday 2 December 1941 [KCC].
7 VB/AVG, Charleston, 2 December [1941] [KCC].
8 AVG, 'Connie' [Northwestern].

a while, but it was a worrying episode.

Now a civil servant, Bunny needed a uniform appropriate to status. On Savile Row he was fitted for an 'extremely smart & expensive' dark suit, in which, he declared, he looked 'as gloriously respectable as a jackdaw in his spring plumage'.[9] He couldn't resist adding a black hat and umbrella, the latter, according to Frances Partridge, 'the best make, perfectly rolled and taken out in all weathers'.[10] In town he was inclined not only to dress smartly, but with some flair. He liked well-tailored suits and sky blue was a favourite colour.

Through Duncan's connections, Angelica obtained a job working for the Cotton Board based at the National Gallery. Bunny was overjoyed: if they were both working in London they could live together. But there was the problem of where William would go in the school holidays. Bunny wanted to get rid of Alciston and Leonard's flat was too small for them all. For the time being, William would be billeted on Barbara Bagenal, Frances Partridge or Noel Olivier. Angelica could not wait to live with Bunny, telling him 'my heart is beating twice as fast nearly all the time for thinking of coming back and being with you'. 'We must never', she added, 'be separated for so long again.'[11] Leonard generously offered to vacate his flat so that Bunny and Angelica could live there. But Bunny decided to find another and in January 1942 he moved from 159 to 134 Clifford's Inn.

Bunny enjoyed his work at the PWE, but doubted his suitability, the 'penalty of getting a job in which everyone is picked for

---

9   DG/AVG, Political Intelligence Department of the Foreign Office, 2 Fitzmaurice Place, London W1, Tuesday 2 December 1941 [KCC].

10 Partridge, *A Pacifist's War*, p. 124.

11 AVG/DG, Eywood, 'Tuesday' [10 December 1941] [KCC].

brains'.[12] According to the historian Andrew Roberts, the PWE 'recruited some of the most exceptional, unusual and talented people of any of the nine secret organisations of the Second World War'.[13] Established in September 1941, it was largely responsible for coordinating British foreign propaganda and was staffed with writers and journalists who, it was assumed, would be good propagandists because they could write and use their imaginations. Certainly the PWE included some remarkable intellects, Noel Coward, Raymond Mortimer, Freya Stark, E.H. Carr and Richard Crossman among them. But initially it was somewhat chaotic as most recruits were new to propaganda – itself a relatively recent innovation. Recruits were given no formal instruction and were expected to learn on the job.

Moreover, the PWE took some time to find a niche as it had been established by Churchill in the shadow of the Special Operations Executive (SOE), and took over some of the SOE's responsibilities. This caused friction between the two organisations, resulting in time-wasting and point-scoring. While it might have been sensible to merge the two organisations, creating a single department, this did not happen. Instead, according to the historian Charles Cruickshank, 'For the rest of the war the two bodies were forced to live together, suffering all the discomforts of a close union, and enjoying none of the blessings'.[14]

At the outset, the PWE underlings – and there were many of them – were completely unfamiliar with the 'Whitehall machine,

---

[12] DG/AVG, 159 Clifford's Inn, Monday 17 November [1941] [KCC].

[13] Andrew Roberts, Introduction, in David Garnett, *The Secret History of PWE: The Political Warfare Executive 1939–1945* (London: St Ermin's Press, 2002), p. xiii.

[14] Charles Cruickshank, *The Fourth Arm: Psychological Warfare 1938–1945* (London: Davis-Poynter, 1977), pp. 26–27.

which consists of a large number of cogs at the lower levels enmeshing with a progressively smaller number of cogs enjoying greater seniority, experience, innate ability, and remuneration'.[15] As might be anticipated, in an organisation staffed with independent-minded writers, the little cogs often questioned the decisions of the big wheels. Soon after admission, Bunny sensibly proposed that PWE propaganda leaflets should mimic the printing and design current in the countries in which they were to be dropped. This proposal fell on stony ground, but gradually, and under the direction of Robert Bruce Lockhart, the PWE would become a potent force in British propaganda.

The PWE was housed in small and inconvenient quarters on the south side of Berkeley Square. When Bunny and his immediate superior, David Stephens, Secretary to the Executive, were instructed to find other accommodation, Bunny favoured taking over the upper portion of Bush House, above the BBC. Given that the PWE was, in theory, supposed to vet the BBC's foreign-services broadcasts, this seemed a perfectly sensible solution. Both Stephens and Bruce Lockhart supported the move, which took place in early 1942.

Bunny worked extremely hard often until late in the evening, writing propaganda leaflets and items for overseas broadcasts. John Lehmann, the editor of *Penguin New Writing*, bemoaned 'the steady drain of authors of every sort into the war-machine, either into the Armed Forces, or into jobs which allow them little or no time or opportunity for writing'.[16] As George Orwell commented while working for the external services of the BBC:

---

[15] Ibid., pp. 31–2.

[16] Quoted in Robert Hewison, *Under Siege: Literary Life in London 1939–45* (London: Weidenfeld & Nicolson, 1977; Readers Union edition, 1978), p. 55.

'To compose a propaganda pamphlet or a radio feature needs just as much work as to write something you believe in, with the difference that the finished product is worthless.'[17] By 'worthless', he meant of no lasting value to the author.

In January 1942 Frances Partridge observed that her nephew William Garnett 'is at the stage when it's as much as life is worth to let any expression cross his face, and he remains silent and impassive until some gust of amusement creates an explosion from within'.[18] So like his mother in his long silences, William had to adjust to many changes. Not only had he lost Ray and his childhood home, but his great friend and ally, his brother Richard, had gone to the war. Now seventeen, William would soon need to consider which direction to take, a decision made all the tougher by the realisation that the war might continue beyond his eighteenth birthday.

On 7 May Frances and Ralph Partridge were surprised when Bunny telephoned asking if they would come up to London the following day to act as witnesses at his marriage to Angelica. Having hastily purchased presents, they joined William, Bunny and Angelica for lunch at the Ivy before attending the wedding, which took place in the City of London register office, a temporary office, as that in the Guildhall had been destroyed by bombing. Angelica, who looked lovely in a funereal black hat and veil, was twenty-three and Bunny fifty.

There is no evidence that Bunny recalled the flippant remark he made twenty-three years previously about marrying 'it'. Why would he? It was an entirely private remark intended to amuse Lytton

---

[17] George Orwell, 'As I Please', *Tribune*, 13 October 1944, quoted in Hewison, *Under Siege*, p. 56.

[18] Partridge, *A Pacifist's War*, p. 124.

Strachey. As Bunny said of Lytton, 'Everything, including his own deep feelings and beliefs, was the subject of constant jokes and gay exaggerations. To take Lytton *au pied de la lettre* is to misunderstand him entirely.'[19] The same might be said of Bunny in this context.

Maynard Keynes wrote to Bunny, saying he thought he was doing wrong in marrying Angelica. Bunny wondered whether Maynard had been spurred to write the letter by Duncan or Vanessa. He chose not to reply, but later regretted this, as he might have explained that he and Angelica wanted a child. Back at Clifford's Inn after the ceremony, Angelica commented, 'Now perhaps at last the neighbours will respect me'.[20] Vanessa and Duncan did not attend the wedding, but two days beforehand, Angelica thanked Duncan for a letter which 'has made me much happier, and I am glad that you see that I am not marrying for superficial motives'.[21] Bunny thought Vanessa opposed the marriage because she misguidedly believed that he married Angelica to 'revenge some imaginary slights received in the past – that I was acting because of some psychological chip on my shoulder'. He did not understand why Vanessa could not perceive what was blindingly obvious: 'One look at Angelica would have been enough to convince any normal person that it was natural that I should be in love with her and wish to marry her.'[22]

Later that afternoon Bunny and Angelica, together with

[19] David Garnett, ed., *Carrington: Letters and Extracts from her Diaries* (London: Jonathan Cape, 1979; paperback edition, Oxford University Press, 1979), p. 11.

[20] Quoted in Partridge, *A Pacifist's War*, p. 133.

[21] AVG/D. Grant, The Central Institute of Art and Design, National Gallery, London, TS, 6 May 1942 [copy or unsent letter?] [KCC].

[22] DG, 'Burst Balloons', unpublished TS [c. 1970] [RG].

William and Richard (who now joined them on his first day of leave) took the train to Northumberland, where they stayed at the Crown Inn, Stannersburn, near Hexham. It was a strange honeymoon, for it encompassed not only Bunny's sons but also a farm which had been bought in memory of Ray. Called Ridley Stokoe, it was located in the hamlet of Tarset, near Hexham. Bunny had purchased it only a few weeks previously for £2,200.

For many years Bunny had benefited from the financial advice of Maynard Keynes and Ralph Partridge, both astute players of the stock market. He was able to buy the farm having sold investments bought on Maynard's advice, though prevailing upon Richard to lend him money to secure a mortgage. Ridley Stokoe comprised three-hundred-and-thirty acres of moor and crag, wild wood and river, fields and a farmhouse. Bunny had not bought it so much to make profit (it was hard land to farm and any profit would go to the tenant farmers), but more because he had a romantic attachment to that craggy, remote countryside, an attachment inherited from Ray. As a girl, she loved walking those wild moors and Bunny thought that Ridley Stokoe would enable Richard and William to share their mother's pleasure. He contemplated burying Ray's ashes there, telling Tim White that she had stayed a little way down river in the same valley and often talked about it.[23] Richard and William were immediately captivated by the landscape, and for William it would become an important refuge and focus in years to come. Bunny observed that his younger son was 'a completely different animal here',

---

[23] Ray's ashes remained in a cupboard at Hilton Hall until Richard found them when he took over the house. After being buried under a mulberry tree until it blew down, they found a final resting place in the shadow of a crag at Ridley Stokoe.

and that Richard, once he had sloughed off the formal carapace of the RAF, was 'plodding slowly along, good tempered & amused'.[24]

Bunny's marriage was made public in an announcement in *The Times* on 11 May, a conventional notice recording that Angelica was the 'only daughter of Clive Heward Bell & Vanessa Bell'. That particular untruth could not be publicly revised, although Clive, staying with Frances and Ralph, 'became suddenly unbuttoned, as if released from a vow, and for the first time dropped all pretence that Angelica was his daughter'. He told the Partridges that he was 'devoted to old Bunny', and according to Frances, gleefully referred back to 'the days when both Vanessa and Duncan were always telling him what a fascinating character Bunny was'.[25]

In the summer of 1942, Bunny became Secretary to an Agricultural Committee overseeing propaganda expressly aimed at peasants in enemy and occupied countries, propaganda intended to cause a reduction in the overall output of food. Bunny was also involved in supplying the BBC with material to broadcast in their 'Dawn Peasants Programme', a subversive prototype of BBC Radio Four's *Farming Today*. The interdepartmental problems which had dogged the PWE at its inception continued, particularly between the Agricultural Committee of the PWE and the BBC. Bunny was in an especially frustrating position as he was expected to ensure the Agricultural Committee vetted the BBC's scripts, although the latter continually failed to submit them. As Bunny observed, this lack of cooperation could prove disastrous, for instance when 'tagged on to an item designed

---

[24] DG/FP, Crown Inn, Stannersburn, Tuesday 12 May 1942 [KCC].
[25] Partridge, *A Pacifist's War*, diary entry for 20 June 1942, p. 139.

to encourage the sabotage of threshing machinery was the report of the death sentence being inflicted on a Poznan farmhand for agricultural sabotage'.[26] In August, Bunny was sent to the Directorate of Plans to assist the journalist and social reformer Ritchie Calder, who occupied a new post, as Director of Plans and Campaigns. As well as drafting propaganda leaflets, Bunny was involved in writing strategic papers on subjects including Anglo-American Co-operation. With the US now in the war it was important to address how planning and training could be integrated between the two allies.

In early 1943, Bunny and Angelica moved from Clifford's Inn to James and Alix Strachey's London house at 41 Gordon Square, one of many London squares which had sacrificed its handsome railings to the war. Angelica was pregnant, expecting a baby in the autumn. Richard warmly approved of the situation, but as Bunny told Tim White, 'William more silently regards it as our business'.[27] William had passed the entrance exam to King's College, but contrary to his father's and brother's advice, he was thinking of joining the Navy. As Bunny commented, the silent William 'would never give a command in a loud voice'.[28] Bunny persuaded him to enrol as a miner, as what would become known as a 'Bevin Boy' after Ernest Bevin, the Minister for Labour and National Service. Although Bunny was deeply protective of William, he thought that working with miners would broaden his mind. And so in October 1943 William began work at the Old Louisa pit at Stanley, near Durham, working

---

[26] DG, *The Secret History of PWE*, p. 113.
[27] DG/THW, 41 Gordon Square, 2 July 1943, in DG, ed., *White/Garnett Letters*, p. 124.
[28] DG/RG, Ham Spray, 22 August 1943 [RG].

seven-and-a-half hour shifts loading coal onto a conveyer. Bunny despatched regular packages of provisions and wrote nearly every day.

On 17 October at 41 Gordon Square, Angelica gave birth to a baby girl weighing eight-and-a-half pounds. 'What is very interesting', Bunny wrote to Richard, 'is that the birth of a child, which has been intentionally begotten, & which one has talked about for 9 months, <u>comes as a surprise.</u>'[29] The baby was called 'Virginia', but after a while her parents settled on the name 'Amaryllis Virginia', giving her the same forename initials as her mother and her great-aunt, Virginia Woolf. A few weeks after the birth, Angelica went down to Charleston, from where she wrote to Bunny: 'Our life together has been so full: and nobody else has an idea of what we are to each other or how much we have felt together – they do not know what our real life <u>is</u> at all.'[30] When Bunny briefly joined her there, he wasn't exactly welcomed into Vanessa's or Duncan's arms, but they became more friendly & agreeable after Amaryllis's birth.

At the PWE Bunny was privy to information which he was not at liberty to impart. Early on he had taken the line that as secrecy wasn't his forte he would make it a policy to say nothing at all outside the office. On one occasion, writing to Richard stationed in Sierra Leone, Bunny tore the letter up as it contained indiscreet remarks. In fact Bunny's correspondence gives only the most superficial information about his work. To Richard, eager for news of the war, he wrote cryptically: 'I am doing extremely interesting & valuable work – using my imagination in a most concrete manner: visualising the future & building plans on my

---

[29] DG/RG, 41 Gordon Square, 17 October 1943 [RG].
[30] AVG/DG, Charleston, 'Thursday' [late November 1943] [KCC].

362

visualisation.'[31] Frances Partridge was bemused by his generally knowing air.

But at the end of October Bunny knew something that made him fear for the safety of Angelica and Amaryllis if they remained in London. He wrote to Frances and Ralph asking whether his wife and baby could go to stay at Ham Spray, stating that he was unable to discuss the reason behind his request. Thus Bunny inadvertently opened a Pandora's Box. If he could intimate to the Partridges that London was unsafe, should the Partridges tell their London friends? As Frances reflected in her diary, 'had he the right to hand over this piece of explosive to me, to load me up with gun-powder and then say: Don't go off.'[32] It was the kind of ethical dilemma Bunny had hitherto managed to avoid. In the event the reason for Bunny's request evaporated, so Angelica and Amaryllis remained in London. Frances speculated that Bunny knew about the huge air raids inflicted upon Berlin, and probably believed the Germans would retaliate. As he told Richard in September 1943, 'I get all the information going – so I can discuss nothing'.[33]

In January 1944 Bunny was promoted to Director of Training. With promotion came a large office, a slight salary increase, a secretary, Ann Hopkin, and work until eight o'clock in the evening. 'I am really trying to put my shoulder to the wheel', he told Tim White.[34] The PWE School was opened in February 1944 at Brondesbury in north-west London, the opening having

---

[31] DG/RG, 41 Gordon Square, 1 July 1943 [RG].

[32] Partridge, *A Pacifist's War*, p. 172, diary entry for 1 November 1943.

[33] DG/RG, 41 Gordon Square, 6 September 1943 [RG].

[34] DG/THW, 41 Gordon Square [January 1944], in DG, ed., *White/Garnett Letters*, p. 143.

been delayed for four months by an inter-departmental battle over domestic staff, necessitating the personal intervention of Churchill. Bunny's was an important job, coordinating the training of PWE 'black' saboteurs involved in working on the ground with members of the resistance in occupied countries.

In January 1944 the Luftwaffe returned to London in what became known as the Little Blitz. As Bunny told Richard, 'the Luftwaffe resumed the bombing of London with rather more determination than we have known for a long time', adding, 'the display in the sky was notable'.[35] The last serious attack occurred in April, but between times the London Library was hit, losing 20,000 books. Bunny watched the fire service dowse the flames engulfing 27 Brunswick Square, the house in which Richard was born.

The doodlebug or V1 was an even more perfidious threat, which noisily announced its trajectory but silently stopped above its target. To get out of London, Bunny and Angelica moved into an ugly, yellow-brick, castellated, furnished bungalow called Scearnbank, located close to The Cearne. Bunny commuted to London each weekday, but enjoyed being in the countryside, spending his free time raising geese, making marmalade and emptying the earth closet. He and Angelica slept on the roof in the middle of raids, watching the buzz-bombs passing overhead, which Angelica likened to 'an infernal invention of Dante's, put into action by Leonardo da Vinci'.[36] Frances and Ralph were shocked to find great chasms nearby, left by incendiary bombs amid the bluebells. Realising that Scearnbank was beneath the main doodlebug route to the capital, they returned to Gordon Square.

---

[35] DG/RG, 25–28 February 1944 [RG].

[36] AVG, 'Connie', 1986, TS [Northwestern].

When Groves gave Bunny the complete plan for Overlord, the proposed Normandy landings, Bunny was horrified that 'anything on which so many lives depended should be read by anyone of so little importance as myself'.[37] Mainly he worried lest he should inadvertently blurt out any detail: he was almost paranoid in this respect. On one occasion, in the summer of 1944, Leonard Woolf told Bunny he had heard the Germans had a new secret weapon, a powerful rocket. Bunny's blood ran cold, for the weapon was the V2, a long-range rocket which had yet to be deployed. Leonard recounted that when he casually asked Bunny about the rocket, Bunny's 'hair and hackles rose upon his head and he told me furiously that I had no right to be in possession of – far less talk of – what was a top secret'.[38] Bunny feared that if Leonard spread the story, people would assume that he was the source.

In July Bunny was elected a Fellow of the Royal Society of Literature, an event which seemed like something from another life. He was more excited about the prospect of joining William on leave at Butts Intake. Arriving there with Angelica and Amaryllis in early August, he marvelled at how everything was just as they had left it – a tin of flour hermetically sealed and 'various forgotten delicacies such as skipper sardines, tinned peas'. As he told Constance, 'We have forgotten there are such things as sirens, or bombs, or ruined houses & broken glass. In Swaledale all is unchanged.'[39]

---

[37] DG, 'Burst Balloons', unpublished TS [c. 1970] [RG].
[38] Leonard Woolf, *The Journey Not the Arrival Matters: An Autobiography of the Years 1939 to 1969* (London: Harcourt Brace Jovanovich, 1975), pp. 138–9.
[39] DG/CG, Butts Intake, Saturday 5 August 1944 [HRRC].

Digging a hole in which to bury the entrails of the rabbits which he had shot, Bunny was seized by a violent cramp which made him feel as though the muscles and tendons were being drawn out of his legs, rather as he had eviscerated the rabbits. In agony and unable to move, Bunny clung helplessly to his spade. He had been intermittently dogged by what he called 'lumbago' for five or six years. The pain was on the left side, occupying his buttock and when it was particularly bad it ran down the back of his thigh towards his knee. In January 1942 and again in January 1943 Bunny underwent treatment under the orthopaedic physician James Cyriax, a pioneering clinician who recognised the new concept of referred pain.[40]

After several agonising days in bed where Bunny had to hold his leg into position to reduce the pain, the local doctor was summoned. Despite his ministrations (aspirins), Bunny remained in agony, unable to move. One day Angelica had to go out, leaving ten-month old Amaryllis crawling on the bedroom floor in Bunny's charge. The baby pulled a drawer out of a wash stand and levering her weight upon it, brought the whole thing down on top of herself. Somehow Bunny managed to get out of bed and scoop Amaryllis up, but he screamed more than she did. To compound matters, Bunny's incapacity came at a particularly difficult time for Angelica. Not only was she isolated up a remotely located and steep track several miles from the nearest town, but the cottage made no concessions to twentieth century conveniences, or even to those of the nineteenth century. She had a baby to care for and, following a series of what Bunny described as 'rash acts', was in the early stages of pregnancy.

---

[40] Cyriax's mother, Dr Annjuta Cyriax, was a friend of Constance, and the sister-in-law of Antonia Almgrem, Bunny's first lover.

Unable to endure the pain, Bunny sent a telegram to Cyriax requesting advice. Concluding that there was a piece of broken cartilage jammed against Bunny's sciatic nerve, Cyriax sent an ambulance. Later, Bunny could reflect on the farcical scene of the ambulance men carrying a screaming man atop a wooden chair down a narrow and almost vertical staircase, but at the time he could only feel the pain. On 1 September Bunny arrived back in Gordon Square. Cyriax confirmed his diagnosis and gave Bunny a stark choice: he could wear a permanent truss, and forgo all those physical activities in which he took pleasure: digging, rowing, diving and chopping wood. Or he could have a difficult and dangerous operation with a 50 per cent success rate. If the operation failed he could end up wheelchair bound and impotent.

Bunny was operated on by Mr Harvey Jackson at Imperial College Hospital on 7 October 1944. William took leave in order to be near his father, and Barbara Bagenal looked after Amaryllis to help an exhausted and very worried Angelica. Bunny was fit – particularly so for a fifty-two-year-old man of his generation. Nevertheless, as the days passed and as his legs remained numb, he worried that he had made the wrong decision. When, a week after the operation, he could wriggle his left toes, it was a good sign. Movement gradually returned to his legs and with a combination of physiotherapy and determination he began to recover strength. Amaryllis had learnt to say "Oh! Dear" because her mother exclaimed it so frequently during Bunny's incapacitation.

Chapter Twenty-Five

'I could give a whole list of writers [...] who are now being squeezed dry like oranges in some official job or other [...]. They will come out of the war with nothing to show for their labours and with not even the stored-up experience that the soldier gets in return for his physical suffering.' (George Orwell)[1]

When Bunny left Butts Intake, he could have had no idea that it would be three months before he would return to his office. When he did eventually return, it was to a different job. He would become an historian and write the official history of the PWE, a role which would take him through to the end of the war and beyond. He had been invited to take on this job by Major General Kenneth Strong, who succeeded Robert Bruce Lockhart as Director-General of PWE although Groves, with his soft spot for Bunny, was probably behind the appointment.

As 1944 came to a close, patriotic red-white-and-blue streamers appeared in the British shops, signalling a new optimism that

---

[1]   As I Please', *Tribune*, 13 October 1944, quoted in Hewison, *Under Siege*, p. 85.

war would end and Britain would be the victor. Freedom beckoned and Bunny yearned to return to imaginative writing. As he ruefully commented, 'One of the tiresome things to which I must accustom myself is that the [end of the] war will not mean for me, a release from the world of <u>MOST SECRET</u> & <u>TOP SECRET</u> papers & ideas [...]. And while I moulder & live & think the whole war over again, my friends will be writing & reading new books, seeing new plays, adapting themselves to live in a new world.'[2]

In many respects Bunny was lucky to have this job. He would have a guaranteed income, a financial cushion shielding him from competition with all the other writers returning to civilian life. The situation would initially be bleak for writers: the war brought many changes, not least the introduction of paper rationing, which radically reduced publishers' outputs. Several literary magazines had folded, including the *Cornhill* and *Criterion*. It was not just a matter of starting again with a blank page: networks and literary milieus would need to be reconstructed; the framework of publishers, distributors and booksellers re-established.

The Secret History carried Bunny past VE Day, 8 May 1945, and on into the following year. He had not published a novel for a decade and had latterly spent almost as much of his career not writing novels as he had previously devoted to writing them. Such concerns preoccupied many writers emerging from six years of war, but Bunny worried that he had changed from novelist to jack-of-all-trades: biographer, journalist, critic, editor, propagandist and now historian. Bunny was in danger of becoming forgotten, fading in the wake of a new generation of writers.

---

[2] DG/F Partridge, 41 Gordon Square, 18 May 1945 [KCC].

One such writer placed Bunny firmly in the past, an emblem of an earlier era. Evelyn Waugh's novel *Brideshead Revisited* was published in the month which saw Victory in Europe declared.[3] The narrative concerns the recollections of its protagonist, Charles Ryder, looking back to the 1920s and 1930s from the vantage point of the Second World War. It is not so much a nostalgic yearning for better times than an acknowledgement that war had made even the recent past seem like another age.

In the 1920s, when Waugh's fictional aesthetes Charles Ryder, Sebastian Flyte and Anthony Blanche were at Oxford, they whiled away their university years in carefree hedonism. Waugh gave them books to read: Roger Fry's *Vision and Design* (1920), Lytton Strachey's *Eminent Victorians* (1918), Clive Bell's *Art* (1914), Aldous Huxley's *Antic Hay* (1923) and David Garnett's *Lady into Fox*.[4] For Waugh, these books exemplified the excitement of the 1910s and 1920s, a new aesthetic, an invigorating modernity which contrasted with the old-fashioned set-texts his young creations were expected to read. Fry, Strachey, Bell, Huxley and Garnett epitomised the promise of that earlier post-war age: they had each broken with tradition, crafting a new kind of art criticism, art history, biography and literature. But from the vantage point of the Second World War, all this took place in another time, a period locked in Charles Ryder's memory, irrevocably lost, if not forgotten.

Bunny's scrupulous and painstaking research enabled him to present the kind of clear and concise analysis of the PWE that he had brought to the Lawrence *Letters*. In keeping with his

---

[3] Evelyn Waugh, *Brideshead Revisited* (London: Chapman & Hall, 1945; Penguin 1981).

[4] Ibid. p. 71.

remit, Bunny presented a series of succinct and considered conclusions, suggesting where improvements could have been made. Rigorous and objective, his *Secret History* did not flinch from telling the truth, from chronicling the paralysing inter-departmental conflict of the PWE's early days. Bunny achieved this with irony and humour, throwing into sharp relief the absurdity of the bureaucratic process. In contrast to *War in the Air*, *The Secret History* is a substantial book. Moreover, it differed from propaganda in that it was addressed to a different audience: future political warriors rather than the contemporary general public. Above all, it is a testament to Bunny's wide-ranging capabilities and intellectual acuity that he could write such an incisive account simultaneously documenting the inspired stratagems of political warfare and the absurd intrigues of political infighting.

On 15 May Angelica gave birth to a second daughter at Gordon Square. Bunny, who could always recognise such things, announced that she had his mouth, Angelica's hands and a Greek nose. The baby was named Catherine Vanessa, but, as with Amaryllis before, her parents changed their minds, re-naming her Henrietta Catherine Vanessa. The name appealed to Duncan, who had a dotty Aunt Henny, but Bunny had really named his daughter after Henrietta Bingham.

Two months after Henrietta's birth, Bunny moved back to Hilton with his new family. He had been away for the best part of five years, although he often longed to return. Even so, he approached the move with 'A good deal of despair mixed up with all sorts of plans & activities'. Bunny's despair centred on returning to the house he had shared with Ray in what now seemed another life, and to the memories which would doubtless surface. In the event, Bunny was delighted that the 'natives of Hilton have been obviously

& oddly glad to see me'.[5] People stopped to shake his hand, Amaryllis was approved of, Henrietta cooed over. It must have been strange for all those people who had last seen Bunny shortly after Ray's death, to encounter him now with a new wife and two little girls. With great sensitivity Hilton's new chatelaine decided she did not want to change the house from the way Ray had made it, resolving that any changes would be wrought gradually.[6]

Bunny no longer had either the inclination or need to compartmentalise his life and was so content that even when he encountered Frances Partridge's beautiful young friend Janetta Jackson at a party given by Cyril Connolly, he did not feel the urge to over-amplify his blue-eyed charm, reflecting, 'Ten years ago it would have been <u>fatal</u> to have seen her at all'.[7] He kept his London sojourns as brief as possible, hating to be away from Angelica. 'It seems inconceivable', he wrote to her in October 1946, 'that I should have parted from you only this morning. Somehow today has seemed like a week.'[8]

Bunny's social life carried on much as it had done when Ray was alive. This was largely down to Angelica, who seamlessly took hold of the reins of hospitality, making Hilton as welcoming as before. Many of Bunny's old friends wandered back through Hilton's doors as if they had only been momentarily away. Ray's siblings and their families returned: Judy and Dick Rendel, Horace and Rachel Marshall, Tom and Nadine Marshall and Frances and Ralph Partridge. Even Duncan and Vanessa became regular visitors, enchanted by their granddaughters,

5   DG/F Partridge, Hilton, 18 July 1945 [KCC].
6   AVG interviewed by the author, Forcalquier, France, 3 January 2008.
7   DG/F Partridge, 41 Gordon Square, 18 May 1945 [KCC].
8   DG/AVG, The Reform Club, 10 October 1946 [KCC].

tacitly reconciled with Bunny. There were many friends whom Bunny had not seen during the war, including John Hayward, one of the first post-war visitors to Hilton, now much less mobile, having to be carried from the car to the house in an armchair. Charles Prentice re-entered Bunny's life, no longer a publisher, but still a firm friend. Mina and Bunny resumed their transatlantic correspondence which had faltered during the war.

Bunny had not seen Tim White since that fateful holiday at Sheskin Lodge in 1939. He decided that Tim would be a good companion to take grouse-shooting at Ridley Stokoe, where William, still un-discharged, was on leave. Bunny had allowed himself to forget that Tim was not the easiest companion. In the intervening years he had become more selfish and he had not recovered from the death of his beloved Setter, Brownie ('my wife, mother, mistress & child').[9] As the days in Northumberland passed, Bunny's tolerance dwindled. He reported to Richard, 'There has been a certain amount of wrangling between Tim & me with William silently sitting in judgment on us. I am afraid Tim sometimes makes me very irritable.'[10] But even William's patience was stretched when Tim commandeered his precious gun. Unable to pot a grouse, Tim complained petulantly that Bunny had taken him, there on false pretences. In fact Bunny had taken him there en route to Butts Intake where, currently homeless, Tim would spend the winter living rent-free.

In 1943 Leonard Woolf had invited Bunny to become his partner in the Hogarth Press. Bunny declined at the time, but having learnt that Leonard was dissolving his partnership with John Lehmann,

---

[9] THW/DG [Doolistown], [?25 November 1944], in DG, ed., *White/Garnett Letters*, p. 179.

[10] DG/RG, Crown Inn, Stannersburn, 1 October 1945 [RG].

he wrote in February 1946 to ask Leonard whether he would consider selling him the Press. He was interested in making the purchase because, as he told Leonard, 'I am setting up with Rupert Hart-Davis as a publisher and I hope this justifies my asking'.[11] (In the event, the Hogarth Press was acquired by Chatto & Windus.)

Bunny had known Rupert for many years, initially through Edward and Jamie Hamilton, latterly because Rupert was a director of Jonathan Cape. Though not bosom friends, they respected one another. Rupert was fifteen years Bunny's junior, an Old Etonian who had dabbled with a stage career before turning to publishing. Approaching his fortieth year, he retained the moustache he had adopted in the army during the war, which, together with the pipe clamped permanently between his teeth, gave him a rather formidable militaristic air.

Bunny first mooted the idea of a joint publishing venture in 1941, when Rupert was serving in the Coldstream Guards. 'After the war', Bunny wrote perceptively, 'there will be a burst of intellectual curiosity of all kinds. Thousands of soldiers will feel they have missed a lot and will turn eagerly to reading books and some of them to writing them.' 'Of course', he added, 'I don't really know that I want to be a publisher: what I do know is that I don't want to be a journalist.'[12] Rupert replied enthusiastically, telling Bunny his idea was 'the first thing that has excited me for months'. 'Between us', he reflected accurately, 'our literary 'connection' is considerable, and we have the advantage [...] of being really interested in books.'[13]

---

[11] DG/L Woolf, Hilton, 19 February 1946 [Sussex].

[12] DG/RH-D, Claverham Farm, Berwick, 10 February 1941, TS [Northwestern].

[13] RH-D/DG, as from Bromsden Farm, Henley-on-Thames, 15 February 1941 [Northwestern].

In March 1946 Rupert Hart-Davis was formally registered as a Limited Company. Rupert and Bunny were joined by Teddy Young, an outstanding book designer responsible for Penguin Books' first penguin logo of 1935. Initially the three directors met once a week for lunch when they would make plans. Bunny was still tied into the completion of his *Secret History* and Rupert was finishing a life of Hugh Walpole for Macmillan. Although they hoped to get out their first books for the Christmas market, they were hampered by the fact that they could obtain hardly any paper. Paper remained rationed, allocation based on a percentage of a publisher's pre-war usage. As Hart-Davis had not existed before the war, they were assigned a miniscule six tons per annum. Nevertheless, in August 1946 they moved into their offices at 53 Connaught Street, off the Edgware Road. This was adorned with a splendid sign painted by Angelica, a fox on both sides, a loose adaptation of the fox colophon, which Reynolds Stone had designed for the business. They had chosen a fox partly because Bunny was identified with *Lady into Fox*, but also, according to Rupert, 'because this animal might be said to represent both the author's and the bookseller's traditional view of the publisher'.[14] Bunny had, of course, set foot in all three camps during his career.

Their premises harked back to the early days of the Nonesuch Press: there was a ground-floor room for secretaries, but most of the business was conducted in the basement, where Rupert occupied a small room at the front and Teddy Young was housed in a larger room at the back. Bunny perched somewhere in between, but he had no desire to be involved in the day-to-day running of the business. Instead, he intended to read manuscripts at Hilton,

---

[14] Quoted in Richard Garnett, *Rupert Hart-Davis Limited* (London: The Book Collector, 2004), p. 8.

coming up to London once a week to attend Director's meetings, establish editorial policy, see authors and comment on manuscripts. As far as possible, he wished to be removed from routine administration and finance. Given his experience as literary editor of the *New Statesman*, Bunny knew he was unsuited to office work.

Bunny and family members put up £10,000 starting capital, one-third of the firm's working capital, worth £259,500 in today's terms.[15] Of this Bunny invested £5,000, Richard £2,350, Angelica £900 and William £250. In addition Angelica and Richard purchased preference £1 shares amounting to £500 each. Richard recollected that Angelica probably had help from Clive Bell, and that he and William might have been able to contribute as a result of proceeds from the sales of the Oxford *Seven Pillars of Wisdom* and *The Mint*, both legacies from Edward. In June Bunny benefited from the sale of Edward's books, and in October he sold some land to the local council, but £5,000 was a considerable sum to raise and he had to mortgage Hilton Hall to do so.

Rupert invested £3,000 and various friends, including Geoffrey Keynes, Arthur Ransome, Peter Fleming, Eric Linklater and H.E. Bates contributed the rest. Even with a working capital approaching £30,000, the firm was seriously under-funded. None of the three partners had any proper knowledge of finance. According to Rupert's biographer, Philip Ziegler, the company 'never had the resources that would have allowed him to pay the sort of advances demanded by most established authors, to risk printing large quantities and holding substantial stocks, to spend freely on advertising and promotion'.[16]

---

[15] www.nationalarchives.gov.uk/currency/results.asp-mid.

[16] Philip Ziegler, *Rupert Hart-Davis: Man of Letters* (London: Chatto & Windus, 2004), p. 133.

In normal circumstances Bunny might have turned to Maynard Keynes for advice. But Maynard, who had suffered ill health for some time, died of a heart attack on 21 April. Bunny was always struck by what he described as Maynard's 'emotional loyalty', commenting that he 'never went back on the people to whom he had given his affection or love'.[17] Bunny had greatly benefited from his astute financial guidance and from his generosity over the years, paying for bees in the First World War, helping to establish Birrell & Garnett, funding Richard's and William's education.

Bunny commemorated Keynes's life by publishing two of his Memoir Club papers, 'Dr Melchior' and 'My Early Beliefs'. In his Introduction Bunny explained that the memoirs were printed 'with the allusions and personal jokes which were immediately understood by the circle to which they were read'. The reader, he felt, was privileged, for 'He is hearing what was written only for the ears of those to whom the writer could speak entirely without reserve, and who would never mistake his meaning'.[18] Bunny alluded to an earlier age: with Maynard's death, he recognised that those old Bloomsbury values, the shared humour, understanding, allegiances and beliefs, were passing. Lytton Strachey, Carrington, Roger Fry, Virginia Woolf and now Maynard, were all gone. A few years previously, when Vanessa Bell painted a group portrait of the *Memoir Club* Roger, Lytton and Virginia were represented by portraits on the wall, as *memento mori*.[19]

---

[17] DG/Roy Harrod, Hilton, 7 March 1947 [BL].

[18] John Maynard Keynes, *Two Memoirs*, Introduced by David Garnett (London: Rupert Hart-Davis, 1949), p. 8.

[19] (c. 1943), National Portrait Gallery, London.

While Bunny mourned the latest in a line of lost friends, he could not allow himself to dwell on his own age and mortality. If ever it was imperative to live in the present, it was now. In the month that Rupert Hart-Davis was registered as a company, Angelica discovered she was pregnant. Her hands were already full with a two-and-a-half-year-old and a baby of ten months. She and Bunny discussed the implications of her pregnancy and Bunny recorded in his diary, 'Told her my views'.[20] Bunny's 'views' centred on his aversion to abortion, at least in terms of his own potential offspring. In a later notebook, in which he sketched out Volume 4 of his memoirs, he recorded: 'The conception of twins. A[ngelica] with difficulty persuaded to have them.'[21]

From Angelica's perspective, if the pregnancy went smoothly, by Christmas she would be the mother of four children, the eldest three years old. It wasn't the kind of life she had envisaged. She had assumed she would be able to enjoy a life similar to her mother's, with painting and creativity at the fore. Times, however, were very different in 1946 to the 1920s, when Angelica was a child and Vanessa benefited from servants, especially the stalwart Grace Higgens. Although Bunny employed a part-time home-help, after the Second World War it was difficult to obtain live-in staff; to a large extent war-work had liberated women from domestic service. Anyway, Bunny could not afford a full-time nanny or housekeeper. The pregnancy went ahead, but Angelica spent much of that summer concerned about how she would manage.

In the autumn Bunny handed over his completed *Secret History*. He was enormously relieved, feeling he was no longer torn

---

[20] DG, Pocket Diary, entry for Thursday 28 March 1946 [Northwestern].
[21] DG, Notebook, 'Volume 4', unpublished MS [Northwestern].

between this Herculean endeavour and the demands of a new publishing venture. According to the historian Andrew Roberts, the *Secret History of PWE* remains 'the most important document we have concerning the multifarious activities of this vital branch of Britain's wartime propaganda arm'. It did not, however, see the light of day for more than fifty years, remaining unpublished (as intended) during Bunny's lifetime. Lodged in the Cabinet Office, Bunny's manuscript was disinterred in the summer of 1952 by someone in the Information Research Department, who declared it a '*chronique scandaleuse*'. As Roberts observed, 'David Garnett was always likely to have been an odd choice for bureaucrats to make if they wanted a safe banal official history written, let alone a white-wash'.[22]

On 21 November 1946, Angelica gave birth to twins, each weighing a little over seven pounds. Although Bunny and Angelica had hoped for a boy they were delighted with the baby girls, who they named Frances and Nerissa. Bunny felt immensely proud of them, and as he told Frances Partridge, he had fallen 'madly in love with their whimpering charm'.[23] Meanwhile, Amaryllis and Henrietta were at Charleston, being cared for by Vanessa, who wrote acerbically to Jane Bussy: 'you can imagine that the news of two and both female was not received with unmixed joy in this house, though apparently the father at least was quite content'.[24]

William, however, had been a great cause of anxiety. Now twenty-one, he had laboured in the Durham mine long after the

---

[22] Roberts, Introduction in DG, *The Secret History of PWE*, p. xv.

[23] DG/FP, 51 Gordon Square, 22 November 1946 [KCC].

[24] VB/Jane Bussy, Charleston, 20 December [1946] in Marler, ed., *Selected Letters of Vanessa Bell*, p. 509.

end of war and his application for release had been refused. When his appeal against this decision was turned down, in October, accompanied by Daniel Hopkin, MP, Bunny went in person, to canvas Ness Edwards, Parliamentary Secretary to the Minister of Labour & National Service. Hopkin was the father of Ann Hopkin, Bunny's former secretary at the PWE, and it was his influence which led to William's eventual release. Bunny received the good news the day after the twins' birth: William would be free by the end of the year and would join Richard (who had been discharged in September) at King's College, Cambridge.

Having returned to Gordon Square for the twins' birth, it was from there a few days later that the babies were rushed to Great Ormond Street Hospital, owing to sudden and dramatic weight loss. They both had pyloric stenosis, a narrowing of the passage between the stomach and small bowel, which prohibits the passage of milk into the bowel, causing dehydration and malnutrition. After several anxious days when Bunny felt that 'Nothing matters suddenly but to keep them alive', their condition stabilised.[25]

Throughout Angelica's pregnancy Bunny had also been preoccupied with Constance's health as she had become perceptibly weaker. He and Nellie took turns to look after her, Nellie staying at The Cearne for extended periods. In November George Barnes, Director of the Third Programme at the BBC, wrote to ask Bunny whether Constance could be persuaded to join in a discussion on translation, to be broadcast early the following year. Bunny knew she was too frail to participate, but he raised the subject one evening, noting down his mother's

---

[25] DG, Notebook 'Volume 4', unpublished MS [Northwestern].

comments, so they could be discussed by those who did take part. Constance did not live to hear the broadcast: she died on 17 December 1946, two days short of her eighty-fifth birthday. Poignantly and in retrospect, Bunny scribbled in his pocket diary against 13 December: 'Last talk with CG.'[26] Bunny attended the cremation on the 19th, taking Nellie with him. Afterwards he buried his mother's ashes under a walnut tree at The Cearne. With Constance's parting an era had come to a close. H.G. Wells had died in the summer, and now there were very few remaining of Bunny's parents' pioneering generation. Constance had lived to hear of the birth of her twin granddaughters, and although she had not seen them, she died knowing that her beloved son was happy and fulfilled.

Bunny adored all his children, and was delighted when Richard commented upon the four little girls, that 'the remarkable thing about them compared with other children' was 'their good looks'. Bunny loved Amaryllis's and Henrietta's exuberantly high spirits and relished everything about the twins, now returned to health, even enjoying the occasions when he and Angelica were 'woken up & sit up side by side in bed, each with a small, wide-eyed creature, to be given breast & bottle & patted until the wind is expelled'.[27] Mina Curtiss, writing to congratulate him on the latest additions to his family, commented, tongue in cheek: 'I am absolutely enraptured with the picture of you as the father of four daughters – a patriarch. How wonderful! It is obviously what you were always meant to be.'[28]

26 DG, Pocket Diary 1946 [Northwestern].
27 DG/FP, Hilton, 6 February 1947 [KCC].
28 MCurtiss/DG, The Ritz-Carlton, Boston, 19 January 1947 [Northwestern].

Chapter Twenty-Six

'Well my heart is in this place – in making butter & cheese – curing my own bacon up the chimney. It is rather a big undertaking really to keep it all going.'[1]

It was not until a year after the establishment of Rupert Hart-Davis Ltd that their first two books were published, on 1 February 1947.[2] *Fourteen Stories* by Henry James was selected and introduced by Bunny. Rupert Brooke's hitherto unpublished essay 'Democracy and the Arts' came with an introduction by Geoffrey Keynes. Despite the thin quality of rationed paper, both books received critical praise for the high standard of production. But the book which really launched Hart-Davis was Stephen Potter's *Theory and Practice of Gamesmanship*, which amused the partners so much that they gambled their paper ration, printed 25,000 copies and thus launched a new word and concept into the English language.

Bunny threw himself enthusiastically into the new venture. He enjoyed the weekly directors' meetings, reading manuscripts,

---

[1] DG/Elizabeth Frost, Hilton, 4 January 1949 [Northwestern].
[2] Despite the date 1946 on the title pages.

correcting proofs and even meeting booksellers. Most importantly, his new role conferred upon him the status and trappings he had enjoyed at the Nonesuch Press and the *New Statesman*: he was a bookman again, inhabiting the clubbable London world of publishers and writers. Moreover one of Bunny's novels was back in the limelight. On 30 May *The Times* announced a new ballet for Sadler's Wells, based on *The Sailor's Return*. Sally Gilmour, who had shone in *Lady into Fox*, played Tulip.

Mina Curtiss came to Hilton, bringing sardines and olive oil to counter the effects of rationing in Austerity Britain. But she was served champagne and ham, for conscious of the need to provide for a young family, Bunny had extended his husbandry beyond the vegetable patch. A pair of pigs, fattened and butchered, now hung in the chimney as hams.

With four young children, it was difficult for Bunny and Angelica to travel abroad together. For this reason, at the end of June, Angelica took a month's holiday with a friend in Sweden. This established a pattern whereby Bunny and Angelica would take off separately at different times, so that one parent remained at home. On this occasion, Amaryllis and Henrietta were delivered to Charleston, Bunny caring for the twins, now seven months old. Bunny missed Angelica desperately, lamenting, 'I have really no conviction that you exist & cannot believe you will return to me'.[3]

At both the Nonesuch Press and *New Statesman* Bunny had been instrumental in helping to establish writers' careers, not only by publishing their work or writing positive reviews, but also because he gave sound critical advice. Sylvia Townsend Warner told him 'it was you, dear Bunny, who made a serious writer of

---

[3] DG/AVG, The Cearne, 11 July 1947 [KCC].

me. You were my godfather, you held me at the font'.[4] John Lehmann recalled that Bunny gave him excellent advice about writing prose. 'I went away', he commented, 'rather chastened by his advice, given in the most sympathetic and friendly manner, and soon decided to go on writing poetry.'[5] At Hart-Davis Bunny continued in this vein, championing, among others, Nicholas Mosley. In 1948 Bunny recommended they publish Mosley's first novel, *Spaces in the Dark* (1951), but not before asking the author whether he intended to publish under his own name, alluding to the unpopularity of Mosley's father, Sir Oswald. Mosley replied that he had experienced no problem with his surname in the army, to which Bunny retorted, 'The literary world is not like your nice soldiers'.[6]

This literary world was superficially genial, but publishers were running businesses, and the old boys' network could work both ways. On the one hand it might encourage the kind of good humoured cooperation which enabled Hart-Davis and Chatto & Windus to toss a coin rather than outbid each other for Mina Curtiss's latest book; on the other it did not discourage publishers from trying to poach one another's authors. Bunny was not averse to such casual pilfering, writing to Clive Bell to say that he hoped his next book would be brought to Hart-Davis, rather than the Hogarth Press.

Bunny was editing and annotating a single-volume edition of the novels of Thomas Love Peacock, to be published by

---

[4] STW/DG, Maiden Newton, 24 January 1962 in RG, ed., *Sylvia and David*, p. 66.

[5] John Lehmann, single page of [incomplete] TS re DG, n.d. [Princeton].

[6] Quoted in Nicholas Mosley, *Efforts at Truth: an Autobiography* (London: Secker & Warburg, 1994; Dalkey Archive, 1995), p. 17.

Hart-Davis. Here he took the opportunity to publish a corrective to Dr Richard Garnett's published views on Peacock, in which, as Bunny explained, his grandfather made 'violent and quite unjustified attacks' on Peacock's character.[7] Like others of his generation, Dr Garnett could not contend with what he considered to be immoral flaws in Shelley's character. Dr Garnett was subject to the patronage of the poet's son and daughter-in-law, Sir Percy and Lady Jane Shelley, keepers of the Shelley flame who had a vested interest in keeping the flame pure. In upholding the myth that Shelley left his wife Harriet following an irreparable breach, only subsequently falling for Mary Godwin, Dr Garnett sanitised the reputation of Sir Percy (Mary's son) who remained the product of a pure liaison rather than of adultery. Dr Garnett thus implied that Shelley favoured monogamy, even though he wanted to continue with Harriet while starting with Mary. Peacock came under fire because he had remained loyal to Shelley, maintaining a 'disinterested truthfulness' in relation to the poet's love-life.[8]

Although Peacock was one of Bunny's favourite authors, Shelley was a kindred spirit. As Bunny pointed out, with some sarcasm, all that Shelley had been guilty of was being 'blind to the enormous moral importance of being off with the old love before he was on with the new.' And so, between the lines of his thoughtful and often humorous introductions to Peacock's novels, there lodges a discourse on Bunny's belief in free love, that it is possible to have 'two emotions at once'. In particular, his assertion that Shelley 'loved Mary passionately and Harriet

---

[7] David Garnett, ed., *The Novels of Thomas Love Peacock* (London: Rupert Hart-Davis, 1948), p. xii.

[8] Ibid., p. xiii.

tenderly', mirrored his own feelings about Angelica and Ray during the years 1938–40.

The year 1948 saw Bunny making a conscious shift from London to Hilton. He continued to spend a day or two in London mid-week, but his pocket diary reveals a growing preoccupation with what would become an all-consuming passion: farming. Just as flying had swept Bunny off his feet in the late 1920s, now farming became an obsession. If butter and cheese were rationed, Bunny reasoned, the best way to circumvent shortage was by owning the means of production. And so on 19 March 1948 he recorded in his diary 'News of cow'. When Oakdale Milky Way arrived the children kissed her, Bunny milked her, they churned their first pound of butter and, as Bunny optimistically informed Frances Partridge, 'We are already thinking of rearing one of her calves'.[9]

Though Richard was to start at Rupert Hart-Davis the following January, William had no specific career plans and Bunny partly turned Hilton into a farm to provide occupation for him. In addition to William, the farm was managed by Harry Childs, so, in theory, Bunny could focus on literary work. But he couldn't resist getting involved. While the farm expanded – more Jersey cows purchased – piglets born – sugar beet sown – fodder crops produced – Angelica began to withdraw. An inveterate record-keeper, Bunny's pocket diaries invariably marked the occasions when he and Angelica had sex. The records are mere hiero-glyphs celebrating an act central to Bunny's well-being. But as milk yields improved, congress declined, replaced with cursory notes of long-drawn-out discussions. In the summer of 1948, following a 'long talk with AVG' Bunny miserably recorded:

---

9 DG/FP, Hilton, 25 April 1948 [KCC].

'Depressed & sleepless night. Felt completely isolated & on the brink of disaster.'[10]

Bunny felt besieged from all sides. At home Angelica blew hot and cold: sometimes she was warm and cheerful, at others frosty and remote. At work, Hart-Davis was experiencing financial difficulties. The firm had been under-capitalised from the beginning, and Rupert realised that it would not become profitable without increased capital. Bunny tried to buoy him up, stating, 'if we can survive we shall do brilliantly well and I am personally convinced that we shall survive'.[11] This was not strictly true: Bunny was nervous about the business, and had written some months previously to Charles Prentice, inviting him to purchase shares, perhaps in the hope that as a shareholder his publishing experience could be tapped. No longer involved in publishing, Prentice declined, telling Bunny 'publishing is a job you have willy-nilly to be in or out of'.[12]

Bunny preferred to be away from the office, working at home, but as Rupert's biographer Philip Ziegler commented, the 'somewhat ambiguous division of responsibilities between the usually-absentee Garnett and the omnipresent Rupert was always a potential cause of friction'.[13] Bunny sometimes felt marginalised, a situation to which he contributed by his determined absenteeism, but there was an unspoken symbiosis between the two men, for it suited their personalities to occupy their elected positions. Rupert 'was a man of strong likes and

---

[10] DG, Pocket Diary 1948, entry for Saturday 3 July [Northwestern].

[11] Quoted in Ziegler, *Rupert Hart-Davis*, p. 142.

[12] C. Prentice/DG, Piper's Barn, Penpol, Near Truro, 29 May 1948 [Northwestern].

[13] Ziegler, *Rupert Hart-Davis*, p. 142.

dislikes and the dislikes were more easily defined than the likes'.[14] He had given the company his name and it was appropriate for him to take on the role as the company's figurehead, a role which Bunny anyway did not want. But both partners believed in 'standards', as Bunny told Rupert, 'I could not agree more about keeping up a high standard. It is the only possible policy for us – because it is the only thing we can be sure of and can do better than other people.'[15] High standards did not guarantee successful books.

Beleaguered by business concerns, Bunny also felt compromised at home when in early September Angelica took off again for the best part of a month to Italy with Duncan and Vanessa. Bunny felt bereft, writing dejectedly to Angelica that he depended on her 'too much: everything I think & do, is in relation to you & when you are gone, the bottom rather falls out of things'.[16] He went to stay with Frances and Ralph Partridge at Ham Spray, from where he set off to a cattle sale and purchased a young cow, driving all the way back to Hilton with her on the back seat of the car.

That was part of Angelica's problem. She had married a writer, and as an artist, she expected they would achieve the same sort of creative harmony which her parents enjoyed. One of the things Angelica appreciated about Bunny was his work as a novelist, and throughout her childhood this is what he had been. At Charleston she had been in the company of painters and writers, or people like Maynard with great intellectual capabilities and aesthetic sensitivity. But now her husband was driving

[14] Ibid., p. 135.

[15] Quoted in ibid., p 137.

[16] DG/AVG, Hilton, 9 September 1948 [KCC].

around with a cow in the back of his car. When she read his letters, detailing the second visit of the Man from the Ministry of Agriculture, she was reminded that Bunny had changed. He was writing a novel, but instead of telling her about that, he remarked that Topsy had given a record amount of milk. It was not surprising that Bunny felt Angelica seemed very far away and wondered whether, perhaps, she would go 'further & further away', even after she came back.[17]

With the exception of a week staying with Tim White on Alderney, Bunny had not been abroad since his trip to Paris with Angelica in 1938. He was consequently looking forward to a holiday in Paris with Mina in the New Year, but over Christmas illness descended on Hilton. First Bunny became ill with flu, then all four little girls went down with whooping cough, then William was admitted to hospital with pneumonia. Bunny soon followed, diagnosed with atypical pneumonia. Although Mina kept open her invitation, Angelica was so exhausted that Bunny decided to stay at home. He eventually caught up with Mina at the end of March 1949, at Juan les Pins on the Côte d'Azur, where she rented a villa overlooking the sea. This was Mina's solution to the problem of their different sized pockets. Mina was wealthy and expected to stay at the best hotels, but Bunny explained that if she wanted to stay at the 'Ritz-Carltons' his money would run out in a few days.

The two friends spent their time working on their respective projects. Bunny was re-writing *Elephant Bill*, a book by Lieutenant-Colonel J.H. Williams about his wartime experiences with elephants in Burma. Although the story was exciting, Williams could not write, and Bunny spent considerable time ghosting the

[17] DG/AVG, Hilton, 15 September 1948 [KCC].

book. 'There is a certain charm', he reflected, 'in being a "ghost" writer. One has so very little responsibility.'[18] Actually, Bunny took this work seriously, devoting the best part of five months to the task.

As Bunny and Angelica began to realise, the problem with separate holidays was the heightened demarcation between liberty and sacrifice, with one person enjoying freedom while the other remained trapped twixt cowshed and nursery. They resolved to spend part of August together in France, taking their older daughters and leaving the twins (now aged nearly three) at Hilton in the care of a nanny who had worked for friends. In the event Angelica departed on 3 August, taking only Amaryllis. Bunny remained at Hilton, for Henrietta could not travel, having contracted measles. He hoped this would cause only a temporary delay, but a few days later it was obvious that both Nerissa and Fanny had been infected. Nerissa developed pneumonia and was admitted to hospital, seriously ill. Although she rallied as a result of the new wonder-drug, penicillin, Bunny couldn't leave the twins, as all his 'latent love & feeling of responsibility' had surfaced.[19] He eventually left for Paris, with William and Henrietta, three weeks after Angelica's departure. After a few days, Bunny set off on a tour with William, leaving Angelica in Paris with Amaryllis and Henrietta. There they remained while Bunny and William returned home. The twins were delighted to see Bunny, although, as he told Angelica, they said, ' "Mummy gone" – & apparently think it's final'.[20]

In early 1950 Bunny revived the Cranium Club, which had

---

[18] DG/M. Curtiss, Hilton, 22 February 1949 [Berg].
[19] DG/AVG, Hilton, 11 August 1949 [KCC].
[20] DG/AVG, Hilton, Thursday 8 September 1949 [KCC].

lapsed as a result of the war. 'It is very pleasant', he told Mina, 'to meet some old friends – though going through the list of members I saw that out of 51, thirteen are now dead.'[21] Adrian Stephen had died two years previously, but the most recently departed was Charles Prentice, the publisher who had taken Bunny on at Chatto and had been devoted to Ray as much as to him. Prentice died in Kenya after an overdose of barbiturates, having been ill for some months. He had fallen in love with his sister-in-law, Lynn Adamson, with whom he lived for several years, causing opprobrium in some quarters. Bunny had remained loyal, and had last seen Prentice on the eve of his departure for Kenya in 1949. Lynn Adamson gave Bunny Prentice's ring.

Despite Bunny's fears that he would end up on the literary scrap heap, he remained very much in the public eye. The previous year, the publication of *The Novels of Thomas Love Peacock* was marked by a live BBC radio broadcast, in which Bunny entered into a discussion with 'Dr Richard Garnett', played by the actor Felix Aylmer; a young Welsh actor, Richard Burton, took the role of Shelley. Bunny's short stories, *Purl and Plain* were broadcast by the BBC that year. In January 1950 *A Rabbit in the Air* was broadcast on BBC radio and in March 'New Books and Old' concerned *A Man in the Zoo*. *Elephant Bill* was published in May, a best-seller, which sold out a fourth impression by Christmas. (Bunny received no royalties, his ghosting all in a day's work at Hart-Davis.) He was also still working as an occasional reader for Jonathan Cape, for whom he was editing *The Essential T.E. Lawrence*.

Having outgrown its cramped offices at Connaught Street, in July 1950 Hart-Davis moved to 36 Soho Square. This had the

---

[21] DG/M. Curtiss, Rupert Hart-Davis Ltd, 53 Connaught Street, 4 January 1950 [Berg].

benefit of an enormous basement suitable for keeping stock, a ground floor reception room occupied by typists, a large first-floor office for Rupert and smaller offices for production and publicity. In theory Bunny shared Rupert's office, but still the absentee partner, he worked mostly at Hilton. By now Rupert's mistress, Ruth Simon, had been brought in as an editor, and she occupied a cubby hole off Rupert's office and shared with him an apartment at the top of the building.

According to Philip Ziegler:

> The atmosphere in the office was as carefree as in the flat above. 'It was great fun to work there,' Teddy Young remembered, and the word 'fun' is one which recurs repeatedly in descriptions of the daily routine. A lot of work in fact got done, but there was always time to joke or gossip. The directors took long and usually bibulous lunches and nobody complained if the junior staff from time to time indulged themselves as well.[22]

Bunny's bibulous lunches were confined to mid-week, but he enjoyed his work, obtaining the same sort of pleasure from reading manuscripts that Edward had done. But Bunny remained concerned about the state of Hart-Davis finances, believing that although they anticipated a small profit in this third year of trading, the business required more investment. He had put in all he could, mortgaging not only Hilton but also The Cearne. Just when he persuaded Mina to invest £700, the company had a piece of luck. As Richard Garnett explained, 'Dr Henry Goverts, a wealthy bibliophile based in Liechtenstein, but with a taste for

---

[22] Ziegler, *Rupert Hart-Davis*, p. 161.

all things English, was tempted to invest in a British publisher.'[23] Hart-Davis fitted the bill.

In June 1950, when Angelica presented her first Memoir Club paper, Frances Partridge noticed that Bunny 'beamed out upon the rest of the company from within a warm blanket of absorption in his own affairs'. She recalled that afterwards they 'walked in a body through the hot dark night to Duncan's rooms, passing James [Strachey] standing on his doorstep in a white silk suit. It was as if all London had shrunk to Bloomsbury and was peopled only by those human portents.'[24] Even in its diminished state, the Bloomsbury Group carried on its traditions in its time-worn territory as if little had changed. But changes were taking place, especially in the Garnett household, where Bunny and Angelica tried to negotiate a *modus vivendi*. Angelica was increasingly restless and dissatisfied with life. Bunny understood her need for space, her craving for time to paint, but life with four daughters and a muddy farm always seemed to impinge. In July, when Angelica spent a fortnight in France she wrote to Bunny: 'We will both turn over a new leaf when I return.'[25]

In November Bunny added another fifty acres to his farm, having purchased Kidman's Farm at Hilton. He reported to Mina that he was 'becoming a farmer as well as all my other occupations', and that 'the fields, animals, plans of growing crops makes me extremely happy'.[26] Just as he liked to dress the part, don the uniform, carry the immaculately rolled umbrella, he now carried the 'Farmer and Stockbreeder' diary in his inside

23 RG, *Rupert Hart-Davis*, p. 17.
24 Partridge, *Everything to Lose*, diary entry for 6 June 1950, pp. 116–17.
25 AVG/DG, Cézy, Wednesday [July 1950] [KCC].
26 DG/M. Curtiss, Hilton, 18 November 1950 [Berg].

pocket. Here a new name began to appear, against his one or two days each week in London. It was then that he saw Ann Hopkin, his former secretary at the PWE. The affair probably began in April 1951, when Ann wrote to Bunny stating that she was very fond of him.[27] It was Bunny's first defection from Angelica.

[27] A. Hopkin/DG, The Office [c. April] [1951] [Northwestern].

Chapter Twenty-Seven

'It is a miracle to recreate yourself when you have been changing for nearly sixty years, and living with yourself all the time.'[1]

In the autumn of 1951 Bunny started writing his autobiography. He had been toying with the idea for several years, thinking he might write something about a single period, perhaps Sommeilles or living at Charleston during the Great War. As far back as 1938 Maynard Keynes had encouraged him to write his memoirs: 'I am not one of those who have acquaintance with the past, but you are, and you should use it.'[2] Of course Bloomsbury's Memoir Club promoted 'acquaintance with the past', stirring up a potent mix of nostalgia, introspection, ribaldry and what Bunny summed up as 'an almost gourmet-like love of the foibles of old and intimate friends'.[3] Bunny

---

[1]   DG/L. Woolf, 20 November 1961 [Sussex].

[2]   JMK/DG, 7 February 1938 [KCC].

[3]   David Garnett, 'Forster and Bloomsbury', in Oliver Stallybrass, ed., *Aspects of E.M. Forster: Essays and Recollections Written for his Ninetieth Birthday* (London: Edward Arnold, 1969), p. 34.

found he could easily recall his past, could view his life 'as a whole & get an impression of the periods & changes'.[4]

If he could look back with objectivity, he did not approach the present with such detachment. Ann Hopkin's father had recently died, and Bunny, always a reliable listener and good comforter, provided a level of consolation to which she responded by falling in love. Ann was half Italian and half Welsh, an attractive olive-skinned, dark-haired woman of thirty-two. She had been called to the Bar in 1948 and was now working at Somerset House in the Solicitors' Office of the Inland Revenue. She told Bunny she had already been wounded in love and couldn't bear to be hurt again. He promised not to make her unhappy.

Bunny had also formed an intense friendship with Rosemary Hinchingbrooke, the thirty-six-year-old wife of his neighbour, the Conservative MP Victor Montagu, Viscount Hinchingbrooke. According to Bunny, Rosemary was 'a big attractive woman with short fair hair which contrasted strikingly with her light brown eyes which were so often expressive of a surprised sincerity'. Their friendship got going one day when he was on his tractor, ploughing. Rosemary drew up in her car, got out, and asked if she might drive the tractor. She climbed up, her skirt pulled up to her thighs. 'That', Bunny said, 'was the beginning of my personal friendship with her'. He employed the word 'personal' to distinguish between her friendship with Angelica, for, as he put it, the 'friendship with Rosemary was not one but two. Her friendship with me was one thing; that with Angelica was another.'[5] Rosemary was a good listener, the recipient of both Bunny's and Angelica's confidences. She was also a keen artist,

---

4 DG/M. Curtiss, Hilton, 23 September 1951 [Berg].

5 DG, Notebook, 'Rosemary Peto', unpublished MS [Northwestern].

often painting with Angelica. Indeed, the two women and their children were in and out of each other's homes. As Henrietta Garnett observed, the Garnetts and Montagus became 'a kind of clan'.[6]

Bunny turned sixty in March 1952, an event which passed without celebration. He spent Easter week with Mina Curtiss in Paris, where she had taken an apartment on the prow of the Isle St Louis, with views of both banks of the Seine. During the 1950s Mina travelled from America to France on an almost annual basis, where she undertook research and translated works by Degas, Halévy and Proust. Throughout the 1950s Bunny would spend a week or two with her there most years. Knowing that Bunny was hard up, Mina offered her patronage diplomatically, telling him that as the apartment was paid for, he would need only to fund his passage across the Channel. In Paris Bunny had a taste of the high life to which Mina was accustomed, dining in the best restaurants, entertained by Parisian intellectuals and *haute societé*, engaged in a ceaseless round of exhibitions, dinners and afternoon tea. Invited to tea by Alice B. Toklas, Bunny was particularly taken by her 'vigorous chestnut moustache'.[7]

This taste of good living was a momentary respite from difficulties at home. When Bunny returned he found Angelica absent, at Charleston with the children. He wrote telling her, 'I long to see you darling & feel as though I should never do so again'.[8] She returned to Hilton only to leave a fortnight later for a painting holiday with Rosemary. Bunny worried she might not return,

---

6 HG/SGK [personal communication].
7 DG/AVG, 45 Quai Bourbon IV, Good Friday [11 April] 1952 [KCC].
8 DG/AVG, Hilton, Saturday 19 April 1952 [KCC].

that she was immersed in other relationships and found him old and uninteresting. His letters to her were full of anxiety: 'Don't do anything you may regret', he urged, 'Darling I long to see you: will you love me when you come back?'[9]

Bunny was also worried about Hart-Davis Ltd. Not only had the company experienced a bad spring, but Bunny found his attitude to the business progressively at variance to that of Rupert. Their gentlemanly manner of dealing with contradictory opinions had given way to frayed tempers and loud verbal exchanges. The firm was losing money, economies had to be made: Teddy Young went half-time and then left; standards were subsumed by cheaper type and bindings. Having already agreed to a substantial cut to his expenses allowance, Bunny now agreed to waive his salary for a whole year. Rupert made no such sacrifice.

Bunny believed he could afford this gesture as he anticipated receiving payment for the rights to *A Man in the Zoo*, again the subject of a putative film. Mina had introduced Bunny to 'an old beau', 'one of the few intelligent Hollywood producers', a man of 'excellent taste' who had been educated in England.[10] This was presumably John Houseman, with whom Mina had been in love at one time, and with whom she worked at the Mercury Theatre in the 1930s. By 1953, however, the treatment was in the hands of Howard Koch, a left-wing scriptwriter blacklisted by Hollywood and resident in London. Whether the payment was down to Houseman, Koch or someone in between, it was not forthcoming in 1952 when Bunny needed it badly.

It was obvious that Hart Davis urgently required further investment. In April 1952 Herbert Agar, a wealthy Anglophile

---

[9] DG/AVG, Hilton, 24 May 1952 [KCC].

[10] M. Curtiss/DG, The Ritz-Carlton, Boston, 19 January 1947 [Northwestern].

American, offered to contribute substantially on condition that Milton Waldman, another American and former chief editorial advisor to the British publisher William Collins, be brought in as joint managing director with Rupert. Bunny greeted this prospect with dismay. Rupert would not make up his mind and retreated to bed with flu. As Philip Ziegler observed, with Rupert 'It seemed always to be a case of jam tomorrow'.[11]

Bunny wrote to Angelica on 10 May to say the investors had dropped out. It was a mixed blessing. He also mentioned that he was to be made CBE in the Queen's Birthday Honours List, the 'outsider' now apparently irrevocably within. On 15 July Bunny was awarded the CBE at Buckingham Palace, with Angelica and Richard in attendance. The artists Lawrence Gowing and William Coldstream and the actor Michael Redgrave were also made CBE, along with Bunny's old friend, Arthur Waley. Dennis Proctor, a fellow Cranium Club member, wrote to congratulate Bunny, but expressed what must have touched a raw nerve: 'Since you have been my favourite living writer for quarter of a century, I was delighted that your work has at last been recognized by the powers that be. (Perhaps even it might encourage you to give us some more of it?)'[12]

In August it was Bunny's turn for a holiday. He took Ann to Venice, hoping it would help her recover from lingering depression. They were lovers, but this made Bunny yearn all the more for Angelica, and for the passionate love she had once felt for him. He feared that his absence with Ann, far from being a cause of regret, would merely be a liberation & relief to Angelica. While Bunny and Ann travelled through the Dolomites into

[11] Ziegler, *Rupert Hart-Davis*, p. 164.
[12] Dennis Proctor/DG, 46 St Mary Axe, London, 6 June 1952 [Northwestern].

Italy, Angelica tackled an errant pig, only to find all the goslings had escaped. She wrote to tell Bunny that Lady had given birth to a bull calf; the milk had been TB tested, and that she hoped he was enjoying himself. There were no endearments at the end of the letter.

At Hilton, Angelica was unstinting in her efforts to provide a happy and fulfilled childhood for the children, creating memorable Christmases and participating in family word-games while, as Richard put it, 'up to her elbows in domesticity'.[13] She cooked delicious meals, encouraging her daughters to learn to cook, usually against a background of the pigs' potato peelings stewing on the Aga. Somehow she found time to paint, create mosaics and play the violin and piano, but she rarely had time to devote herself properly to anything beyond the domestic sphere. She began to resent the repetitive nature of housework and the muck brought in from the farm.

Life had changed, and with the expansion of the farm Bunny had changed too. He was putting in more and more hours and despite advertising for a second man, could find nobody to support Harry. The attraction of early mornings and milk pans was beginning to wane. 'I get awfully tired', Bunny told Mina, '& seem to do nothing only because I do so many little things. It would be so delightful to be able to lie in bed in the morning instead of getting up at 7 o'clock.'[14] But farming was a commitment, and just as Prentice had remarked about publishing, a job you have willy-nilly to be in or out of. Bunny always took pride in his strength, in his fitness and stamina, enjoying productive physical labour: digging, building things, planting seeds and

[13] RG, 'For Angelica 17 July 2009' [RG].
[14] DG/M. Curtiss, Hilton, 10 January 1953 [Berg].

pruning trees. But he had forgotten just how relentless farm work was in winter when the weather was bad and daylight short. As a twenty-five-year-old, he had hated dung-carting for Hecks: now aged sixty he was carting dung again. Then there was the tedious bureaucracy, quite contrary to Bunny's romantic view of farming: filling in forms recording milk yields and percentages of butter-fat. Henrietta Garnett remembers this as a solemn weekend ritual carried out at the dining table, 'like Gladstone saying his prayers'.[15]

At Hart-Davis there was cautious reason for optimism. Teddy Young's *One of Our Submarines* proved a best-seller, a thrilling book about his war-time naval career when he escaped from a sunken submarine. But then, against all Bunny's instincts, Milton Waldman and Herbert Agar joined the board in December 1952. Bunny did not trust Waldman's judgement: he had reviewed *The Sailor's Return* dismissively when first published, and had turned down *Gamesmanship* while at Collins, not finding it funny. Bunny lunched with him several times in an effort to reach some sort of understanding, but did not succeed.

Meanwhile, Bunny's relationship with Ann had become problematic. After the holiday in Venice, she was finding it difficult to accept she could only play a part-time role in his life. He was fond of her, but from the outset had made it clear that he could be only an intermittent lover. She wanted more and came close to a breakdown, recognising that Bunny's love for Angelica was overwhelming. Ann acknowledged that it was physical love which Bunny sought from her, and she was right: Bunny had turned to her when the physical side of his marriage began to wane. But he loved Angelica more than he could love any other woman.

---

[15] HG/SGK [personal communication].

From Paris Angelica wrote: 'Really Paris is the only place to live in you know, it's the only place you can do what you like in and enjoy it all at the same time. If one could only live here modestly in some studio & bring the children up to speak French.'[16] Angelica recalled her own childhood, when she travelled regularly to Cassis with Vanessa and Duncan, stopping in Paris en route. She longed to provide her daughters with similar experiences, but more, she longed to be free like her mother, to paint and travel at will. Angelica once told Bunny, 'I'm not at all good at accepting things I don't like'.[17] That was part of the problem. In many respects she was similar to Bunny: as children they were both used to getting their own way. But from the perspective of greater age and experience, having lived through Ray's death and cared for his sons, Bunny had, to some extent, overcome this selfish instinct. The problem between Bunny and Angelica was that they were at different stages of their lives, with differing expectations and needs.

In May 1953 Hart-Davis reached a crisis. The new investors, with Rupert's agreement, demanded a financial reconstruction which involved writing down the ordinary shares to 50 per cent of their value, in order, as Bunny put it, to attract 'new money purely at the expense of the old shareholders'.[18] Bunny sought advice from Leonard Woolf, among others, who counselled against acceding to the proposal. Bunny believed Rupert had betrayed him – going off for a holiday with Ruth at Butts Intake – 'after arranging the whole plan & pretending to me that it came as a shock to him on his return'.[19] Bunny felt particularly

---

[16] AVG/DG, Hotel d'Angleterre, 'Monday' [c. 4 May 1953] [KCC].

[17] AVG/DG, Charleston, 'Saturday' [17 February 1940] [KCC].

[18] DG/M Curtiss, Hilton, 27 May 1953 [Berg].

[19] DG/M Curtiss, Hilton, 27 May 1953 [Berg].

wounded because he had struggled to put up his initial capital and had invested more heavily than Rupert. With a smaller shareholding, Rupert stood to lose less, especially as the Board was considering a proposal to increase his salary. When Rupert complained that he could not fund his children's school fees Bunny replied: '*I* had to borrow money last autumn and winter. *My* children go to the Council school because I cannot afford to send them elsewhere.'[20] According to Richard Garnett, Rupert was not 'a deceiver and swindler, except in deceiving himself. He had an unfortunate capacity for shutting out what he didn't want to know.'[21]

Bunny eventually realised 75 per cent of his original investment. 'This means', he told Mina, 'that I am free of the incessant compromises & discussions – and that I can now write without being asked to read manuscripts.'[22] He felt years younger. Unfortunately, Bunny had only recently handed in the manuscript of his first volume of memoirs to Hart-Davis. He felt unable to withdraw it, as it would mean delaying publication, but realised that it could prove problematic with regard to subsequent volumes. In this respect Rupert behaved like a gentleman, asking Ian Parsons at Chatto & Windus to take it on. This had the additional benefit of returning Bunny to his original publisher without losing face as a result of his defection to what had been his own publishing house. As for the new deal at Hart-Davis, Richard Garnett explained: 'For three years, from 1953 to 1955, the firm had two managing directors, and they went their separate ways, so separate that there is no mention of Milton Waldman in

---

[20] Quoted in Ziegler, *Rupert Hart-Davis*, p. 165.
[21] RG/SK.
[22] DG/M. Curtiss, Hilton, 27 May 1953 [Berg].

Rupert's autobiography.'[23] Fortunately Richard had been away at the height of the crisis; he remained at Hart-Davis, where his abilities in both editorial and design had already made him invaluable. Bunny never sought to influence him otherwise.

Bunny's relief at leaving Hart-Davis was enhanced by a letter from Mina, telling him her charity, the Chapelbrook Foundation, was to award him a grant of $2,500 in support of his writing. Mina had established the Foundation to provide funds for writers over the age of forty and to enable them to complete work in progress. As one of the first beneficiaries, it seems likely the Foundation was formed with Bunny in mind. Lincoln Kirstein and Bunny's old friend Archie McLeish were fellow trustees. 'You mustn't think of this in terms of a gift', Mina told Bunny, 'because all the happiness it gives me to know that you are free to write things that give me such pleasure makes the whole thing an uneven exchange, any debt being on my side.[24]

Bunny was also delighted when in July 1953 Richard brought his girlfriend, Jane Dickins, to Hilton. She was a stage designer and Bunny found her 'extremely pretty: indeed a lovely creature', admiring her 'exquisite figure', and 'violet blue eyes'. 'She comes', Bunny informed Mina, 'from a family of Professors: her father is Professor of Anglo-Saxon at Cambridge and her grandfather is old Sir Herbert Grierson [...] the editor of Donne'.[25] Bunny immediately put Jane at her ease when he told her that it was her grandfather who had given him the James Tait Black Memorial prize for *Lady into Fox*. Coming from what she described

---

[23] RG, *Rupert Hart-Davis Ltd*, p. 22.

[24] M. Curtiss/DG, Chapelbrook, 30 November 1953 [Northwestern].

[25] DG/M. Curtiss, Hilton, 21 March 1954 [Berg].

as 'a more conventional background', to Jane Dickins, Hilton Hall 'seemed wonderful and free'.[26]

In August 1953 Bunny and Angelica achieved the impossible: they went on holiday together to the French Riviera. William was in tow, and the three of them joined Harold Hobson and his wife Maggie on a boating holiday. It was a carefree break, Bunny and Angelica feeling closer than they had for some time. Back home, Bunny found a letter waiting from Ann, desperate to see him. As Bunny told Angelica, 'The dreadful thing is that <u>when</u> I see her I like her very much – in fact more than that. But when I don't see her, I don't want to see her ever again.'[27] Nevertheless, he carried his own key to her house.

That autumn Bunny travelled down to Mappowder in Dorset to visit Theo Powys, who was dying. Theo reminisced about Tommy and Ray and thanked Bunny for all he had done for him. Bunny had been a stalwart friend. He helped Theo to become a published author, lobbied for his civil pension and in 1925 had written an appreciation of him in *The Borzoi*. There he commented: 'To Powys death is the only thing which will not fail him, until then he knows he is at the mercy of life.'[28]

Professionally, it was an exciting time: with the exception of editorial and propaganda work, Bunny had not produced a book in two decades. On 16 November his first volume of autobiography, *The Golden Echo*, was launched at a party at Chatto & Windus. Raymond Mortimer told Bunny that his new book 'makes me think of you more admiringly and affectionately than ever. You

26 Jane Garnett, 'Notes on Bunny', unpublished TS [personal communication].
27 DH/AVG, Hilton, 'Sunday night' [c. July 1953] [KCC].
28 David Garnett, 'T.F. Powys' in *The Borzoi 1925: Being a Sort of Record of Ten Years of Publishing* (New York: Alfred A. Knopf, 1925), p. 90.

have never written better, I think indeed never so well; and you so treat the remarkable persons and circumstances of your childhood and boyhood that one's sense of yourself becomes overwhelming.'[29] In a subsequent letter, Raymond could not resist pointing out a few inaccuracies: 'though I don't pretend to know better than you how to spell your dog's name, the German philosopher had a Z in the middle of his name – Nietzsche'.[30] In his *Sunday Times* review Mortimer hailed *The Golden Echo* as the 'most absorbing and best written' of all Bunny's books[31], while *The Times* pronounced it 'entrancing'.[32] *Time* magazine commissioned a photograph of a dapper, be-suited Bunny with his Siamese cat perched on his shoulder. But some reviews located Bunny's autobiographical life in a former age. The *Listener* invited the reader to see how Bunny's world 'looks as a detached historical phenomenon',[33] while James Stern, in *The New York Times Book Review*, placed him in 'the last decade of Europe's Golden Age'.[34]

The Golden Echo covers Bunny's life to the beginning of the First World War. He took the book's title from Gerard Manley Hopkins' poem of the same name, which celebrates the loveliness and everlastingness of youth, whilst recognising, in its companion poem, *The Leaden Echo*, that 'nothing can be done / To keep at bay / Age and age's evils'.[35] In his 'Intimations of

---

[29] R. Mortimer/DG, Long Crichel House, 7 November 1953 [Northwestern].

[30] R. Mortimer/DG, Long Crichel House, 13 November 1953 [Northwestern].

[31] Quoted in Chatto & Windus advertisement, 1953.

[32] Saturday 28 November 1953.

[33] 24 December 1953.

[34] 7 November 1954.

[35] Quoted in DG, *Echo*, p. ix.

Mortality By Way Of Preface', Bunny explained that he had no belief in God, but that what can survive, after death, is the written word, and what does survive are permutations of ancestral genes, so one 'may be given a few moments of vicarious existence' in one's descendants.[36] *The Golden Echo* wonderfully evokes childhood and youth, capturing the textures of time and place and the people who formed the fabric of Bunny's young life. It is an almost painterly portrait of a bygone era, of trams and gaslight, roads devoid of cars, of writers long dead, like Conrad, Lawrence and Galsworthy. As Sylvia Townsend Warner perceptively commented, 'children do live in the suburbs of their parents' lives'.[37]

Eddy Sackville-West wrote enthusiastically, recognising 'in every paragraph the tone of voice of my old friend, B.G.' adding that he looked forward to volume two, 'but I imagine that a certain amount of evasion – so foreign to your nature – will be inevitable'.[38] Here he alluded to Bunny's love-life during the First World War. Already writing volume two, Bunny told Mina: 'The rocks & shoals are immense: I shall have to be extremely adroit if I am to succeed in saying anything worth saying.'[39] Duncan told Bunny how much he enjoyed volume one, while confessing that he was a little nervous about the next volume.

Bunny rehearsed volume two at the Memoir Club, reading what Frances Partridge considered an admirable paper, 'partly

---

[36] DG, *Echo*, p. x.
[37] STW/DG, Maiden Newton, 17 December 1955, in RG, ed., *Sylvia and David*, p. 58.
[38] E. Sackville West/DG, Long Crichel House, 23 November 1953 [Northwestern].
[39] DG/M. Curtiss, Hilton, 23 October 1953 [Berg].

about his relations with Duncan, Lytton, Frankie Birrell & Clive' 'and partly some unpublishable episodes illustrating his attitude to sex'.[40] Bunny approached the meeting with some trepidation, as he wanted to ensure that Duncan, Clive and Vanessa approved of what he said about them. He found it went down surprisingly well. Frances advised him to cut nothing, although Clive was worried about the sexual references, stating: 'If you think you can publish things of that kind today my dear Bunny [...]'[41]

Mina advised Bunny to keep his sex life out of the text, an impossible undertaking for a man with the double-handicap of a compulsion to speak the truth and an overriding libido. He informed her he had introduced his sex life 'where it arises naturally as one of the results of my visit to Lytton's cottage at Christmas', referring to the time when he fell in love with Duncan Grant in 1914.[42] By and large, Bunny was careful to consult those who appeared in his memoirs, although his idea about what constituted matters of a sensitive nature might diverge from that of his friends.

In March 1954 Bunny and Angelica threw a party at Hilton in joint celebration of Bunny's sixty-second birthday and Richard and Jane's engagement.[43] Frances Partridge observed there were quite a lot of 'good grey heads and white ones too hinting at the last volume of Proust',

Angelica's four little girls, wearing their party dresses and highly excited, revolved among us with dishes of caviare

---

[40] Partridge, *Everything to Lose*, p. 200, diary entry for 23 April 1954.

[41] DG/M. Curtiss, Hilton, 10 May 1954 [Berg].

[42] DG/M. Curtiss, Hilton, [?12 November 1955] [Berg].

[43] They married on 18 April 1954, at Shirehall Register Office, Cambridge.

and smoked salmon. Looking down one saw an angelic face looking up enquiringly from waist level, munching hard. There was music: William and Angelica played an oboe sonata: Leslie Hotson sang American songs; the little girls played solemnly on recorders. Duncan and Morgan greeted each other like survivors on the same raft.[44]

In September Angelica returned to Paris, this time staying with a new friend, the Italian artist Giovanna Madonia, to whom Angelica and Bunny had been introduced by Rosemary Hinchingbrooke. Earlier that year she had been involved in a love affair with the American poet Robert Lowell. According to Bunny, Giovanna was 'extraordinarily beautiful with a classic beauty – very brown & thin'.[45] Like Rosemary, Giovanna's friendship was not one but two, as she maintained separate friendships with Bunny and Angelica, while remaining friends with them as a couple. From their Paris hotel Angelica wrote to Bunny, 'The great virtue is that the bed is soft & comfortable and as we both sleep without kicking we can manage very well'.[46] Bunny replied provocatively: 'It occurred to me last night that you & I are behaving over Giovanna rather as Shelley & Mary behaved over Emilia Viviani [...]. I wish Giovanna would inspire me to write something as wonderful as Epipsychidion!'[47]

Bunny's moral code had often mirrored those lines in Shelley's autobiographical poem: 'I never was attached to that great sect, / Whose doctrine is, that each one should select / Out of

[44] Partridge, *Everything to Lose*, p. 196, diary entry for 11 March 1954.
[45] DG/F. Partridge, Panarea, 4 August 1958 [KCC].
[46] AVG/DG, [Paris], 22 September [1954] [KCC].
[47] DG/AVG, Hilton, 26 September [1954] [KCC].

the crowd a mistress or a friend, / And all the rest, though fair and wise, commend / To cold oblivion.' It was the beautiful Emilia Viviani who inspired Shelley to write these lines. Shelley sought a triangular relationship with Emilia and his wife Mary, much as Bunny and Angelica were involved in some form of triangle with Giovanna. As Bunny wrote volume two of his autobiography and as he penned a casual 'Note on Sexual Life', *Epipsychidion* was much on his mind. 'Sexual love is', he recorded, 'apart from anything else, an infallible means of judging character. When one has been a woman's lover the veils of illusion are torn down – one sees her naked:- and loves her forever.'[48]

---

[48] DG, 'Notes on Autobiography: Volume 2', unpublished MS [Northwestern].

Chapter Twenty-Eight

'Truth and wit are felt by many to be rather shocking virtues which should appear in public only if they are decently veiled.'[1]

With the exception of an occasional short story and the ill-fated *Castle Bigod*, Bunny had written no fiction in twenty years. His autobiography had eased him back into the habit of writing and he began a short story which soon took on a momentum of its own. Bunny could not leave it and became intrigued by the characters, wanting to let them develop further. He soon found himself writing a novel. The story was set in France, so when, in the autumn of 1954, Mina invited him to join her there, it seemed the perfect opportunity to position his characters in an authentic landscape.

Bunny and Mina travelled in an enormous chauffeur-driven Buick and stayed at the most expensive hotels. Uncomfortable with such extravagance, Bunny was relieved when in one town they found the best hotel closed, having to accept second-best. They spent a couple of days as guests of Baron Philippe de

---

[1] DG, 'Introduction', in Keynes, *Two Memoirs*, p. 8.

Rothschild and his wife Pauline at Château Mouton-Rothschild, touring the vineyards and consuming vintage wine at every meal. Although Mina was generosity itself, Bunny was discomfited by her patronage, particularly as he thought everyone regarded him as her lover, which he was not.

Bunny felt guilty at leaving Angelica to cope at Hilton. 'I long to be close to you', he wrote to her, 'Shall I ever succeed in being? Darling, I don't ask anything.'[2] He wrote again in a similarly anxious vein, 'Darling Catt, I love you far too much. But please tell me that you can be happy in some ways.'[3] He promised change. He would reduce the number of pigs; spend less on the farm and work harder at writing. 'You see I <u>can</u> write and it is idiotic that I should so easily be dismayed & distracted.'[4]

Angelica had heard all this before. It was easy for Bunny to make promises in France away from the farm, but he had only recently spoken of buying another field. It wasn't only the farm which Angelica found oppressive. She hated domestic chores, complaining that the children were undisciplined and unhelpful. At thirty, William was a kindly and dutiful older brother who often released Bunny and Angelica from childcare. But he also came in for criticism: 'William also is somehow just like another bigger child it seems to me. He does everything required on the farm [...] but he is extraordinarily unwilling to take responsibility and seems to expect meals to appear as though by magic. I feel more than ever that he ought to make some effort to take life by the horns.'[5] Bunny replied, melodramatically, that he

---

[2] DG/AVG, Hotel Pujols, Albi, 'Friday evening' [15 October 1954] [KCC].

[3] DG/AVG, Hotel de France [?Pau], 'Tuesday' [October 1954] [KCC].

[4] DG/AVG, Grand Hotel, Toulouse, Wednesday 20 October 1954 [KCC].

[5] AVG/DG, Hilton, 'Monday breakfast' [October 1954] [KCC].

wanted to love Angelica 'with love that liberates & does not strangle & hold you down like the wet ploughland'.[6]

When Bunny told Angelica he had visited George Sand's château, she seized the opportunity to explain how far she felt life had shifted from her expectations. 'Your letter about George Sand's château arrived [...]. How near one feels to all those people [...]. Just think of the dinner party with Turgenev & Pauline & Flaubert all together [...]! That is the sort of life we ought to be leading instead of being isolated by our hard work.' 'Hasn't your holiday', she reasoned, 'made you see that in many ways its such a terrible waste of time for you to do anything except write – you have only one life and there is only one of you with your gifts and delightful though other occupations may be they have no importance beside this.'[7] Angelica had married a writer: in France he was writing a novel, the first for many years. She feared that when he returned to Hilton, he would be tethered to the farm, in the process tethering her, too.

Meanwhile, nervous of prosecution, Chatto & Windus delayed the publication of Bunny's second volume of memoirs. The firm's solicitor had identified a number of potentially libellous points, particularly regarding Betty May's heroin addiction. Only the previous year Sylvia Townsend Warner had been required to modify a passage in *The Flint Anchor*, in which one man declared love for another. Bunny refused to delete the offending passages and instead set about tracing Betty May. He placed an advertisement in *The Times* seeking the author of *Tiger Woman*, Betty May's autobiography. Within four days the *Daily*

---

6   DG/AVG, 7 Rue de Lanneau, Paris 5e, 'Tuesday morning in bed', 26 October 1954 [KCC].

7   AVG/DG, Hilton, 'Wednesday' [October 1954] [KCC].

Express discovered her whereabouts, and after a passage of thirty-five years, Bunny and Betty May were reunited in a pub at Chatham. He found her 'most charming; not much changed – white hair, very alive'.[8] Betty gladly signed a letter endorsing what Bunny had written, but it was not long before she wrote to him asking for money. He sent her a five pound note: 'I just hated asking you', Betty wrote, 'but I went out & bought some nice things to wear.'[9]

Bunny carried out what he called 'a last séance' with Duncan and Vanessa to double-check they had no objections to their inclusion in volume two. He read them the passages in which they appeared, afterwards feeling reassured and happy, because Vanessa laughed at his jokes, and Duncan seemed genuinely pleased by what he heard and exuded warmth towards Bunny. It came as a surprise, therefore, when Bunny received an anxious letter from Vanessa, who had heard from Leonard Woolf that he might have quoted from one or two of her letters without reading the passages to her.

This was not the only contentious literary matter in which Bunny was involved. The *New Statesman* had invited him to review Richard Aldington's *Lawrence of Arabia: A Biographical Enquiry* (1955), heralding his review on the front page with the legend 'DAVID GARNETT on Aldington's Lawrence'. In January 1955 Bunny spent two full days reading the biography carefully. He concluded that Aldington was 'a disappointed man, full of hatreds and jealousies', and that he had written the book 'to cause a scandal and so make a lot of money'. What Bunny found

8   DG/M. Curtiss, Hilton, 5 April 1955 [Berg].
9   Betty May/DG, Osborne House, 26 Star Hill, Rochester, 8 [March] 1955 [Northwestern].

most objectionable was Aldington's revelation of Lawrence's illegitimacy, which he considered shameful as Lawrence's mother was still alive. Bunny's review vigorously defended Lawrence against Aldington's character assassination and the 'sneer on almost every page'.[10] Ironically, Aldington had written to Bunny about the biography in 1950, when Bunny responded with good advice, suggesting Aldington should stay on the right side of Lawrence's mother, should listen to A.W. Lawrence and refrain from treating T.E.L. as a victim. This advice had apparently fallen on deaf ears.

Aldington naively hoped his book would be reviewed by impartial critics, and that A.W. Lawrence, Bunny, Basil Liddell Hart and Robert Graves, among others, would be disbarred from the job.[11] His hopes were in vain, as they all either opposed the book or mounted a concerted defence of T.E.L. Bunny, Liddell Hart and A.W. Lawrence briefly considered publishing a booklet refuting Aldington, but it was not a financially feasible proposition.

In April 1955, twelve-year-old Amaryllis was dispatched to stay with a family in Rouen for two months to learn French. Bunny felt apprehensive about leaving Amaryllis in France, but it was part of the education which Angelica believed vital and liberating for her daughters. Bunny missed his eldest daughter, and when, a month later, marital relations suffered a further decline, he decided to visit Amaryllis. On the day of departure he issued a spur of the moment invitation to Ann Hopkin, asking

---

[10] DG, 'Books in General', *NS&N*, 5 February 1955.

[11] See Fred D. Crawford, *Richard Aldington and Lawrence of Arabia: A Cautionary Tale* (Carbondale and Edwardsville, IL: Southern Illinois University Press, 1998), p. 116.

whether she would like to spend a few days with him at the end of the break. She was delighted, although she knew it was a last minute invitation.

Bunny took Amaryllis on a nostalgic tour of Duclair and Jumièges, places he visited with his mother, aged fifteen. He delighted in his daughter's sudden bursts of enthusiasm and spontaneous demonstrations of affection. But when he left, she clung to him, in an agonising parting. Bunny couldn't bear to see Amaryllis unhappy. He spent a restless night in a hotel room beneath a clock tower, the clock chiming every half hour, five minutes ahead of a neighbouring clock. Afterwards he wrote to Angelica, 'I haven't felt life so empty & worthless for the last fifteen years'.[12] Only Ann's arrival at Dieppe lifted his spirits.

Having completed his French novel, *Aspects of Love*, Bunny wrote to thank Mina, saying he owed the book entirely to her. She had supported him with the Chapelbrook grant, had enabled him to write and research in France, and had supplied the original anecdote around which Bunny wove his story. It was a story which she had heard from the poet Alexis Leger,[13] about a young couple alone in a château, who heard the ghostly sound of steps descending from the attic, and on investigating, found only a single green slipper on the stair. Bunny toyed with the idea of naming the book '*Un Souvenir Leger*' in homage to its perpetrator, but settled instead on calling his young man Alexis, although the phrase: '*Ce sera un souvenir léger pour toi*' (it will be a slight memory for you) is a leitmotif in the text.

Bunny composed *Aspects of Love* concurrently with his second volume of autobiography, *The Flowers of the Forest*. It is as if the

---

[12] DG/AVG, Chateau Renault, 'Sunday evening', 15 May [1955] [KCC].

[13] Otherwise known by the pseudonym Saint-John Perse (1887–1975).

process of harnessing and sorting his memories conjured forth a parallel and even more personal book in which, in the guise of fiction, Bunny elaborated upon his emotional life and presented a manifesto of his beliefs. Thus *Aspects of Love* might stand as an extended footnote to his memoirs. It was hardly surprising that Angelica encouraged him to scrap his novel, for she not only encountered herself within its pages at different stages of her life, but also saw herself portrayed from the vantage point of Bunny's particular rationale of love and marriage.

The book propounds Bunny's credo of free love, his ideal of hierarchical passionate love with marriage as the apogee, an apogee only attained in the context of freedom to take other lovers. Bunny's aim was to illustrate 'that the conventional attitude to age is all nonsense',[14] or, as he put it to Mina, 'I found myself in the middle of the fascinating subject of the attraction that men of 60 have for women of 20–30', 'on which', he added, 'I am qualified to write if only because of my marriage to Angelica'.[15] It was not only Angelica who 'qualified' Bunny on this account: Giovanna and Ann were half Bunny's age, and both provided inspiration for characters in the book.

The story concerns four main characters, all wound up in the kind of triple helix in which Bunny was prone to involve himself. It is an interlocking of lovers of different ages, youth in love with age, youth turning into age and then falling in love with youth. As far back as 1918, Bunny had toyed with the idea of writing a story on 'the psychology of a boy of nineteen who is very much upset and shocked because the girl he has sentimental & vague feelings towards falls in love with a much older and more

---

[14] DG/R. Partridge, Hilton, 9 November 1955 [KCC].
[15] DG/M. Curtiss, Hilton, 5 April 1955 [Berg].

417

interesting man'.[16] The plot remains essentially the same, although Alexis, the boy, is seventeen rather than nineteen. So Alexis falls in love with Rose (mid-twenties) who falls in love with Alexis's uncle, Sir George Dillingham (sixty-four); Sir George falls in love with Rose, but has a mistress, Giulietta (mid-twenties) who loves Sir George, but is in love with someone of her own age. Rose marries Sir George, and they have a child, Jenny (who attains the age of fourteen at the end of the book). Rose takes a younger lover; as Jenny matures, she falls in love with Alexis (now circa 40); Alexis loves Jenny, but cannot love her passionately as she is too young, so after Sir George dies, Alexis goes off with Giulietta leaving the door open for his return to Jenny when she grows up.

Even reduced to such a schematic synopsis, it is evident that *Aspects of Love* might equally be called 'Aspects of Bunny'. There he is: gauche youth (Alexis) and elder statesman (Sir George, a poet), with 'his silver hair, wild rose complexion, and blue eyes'.[17] Angelica is there too, as Rose, the beautiful young actress who becomes even more beautiful approaching middle-age; although Amaryllis was a model for Jenny, as Jenny moves from childhood through puberty, she is recognisably Angelica at the same stage. Giulietta is based on Giovanna Madonia, 'small and slim and brown with black hair falling onto her shoulders, an aquiline nose, and black eyes gleaming through beautifully cut narrow eyelids'.[18] Bunny also drew upon his relationship with Ann Hopkin, reflecting in scribbled notes of preliminary ideas, 'The young actress from the Old Vic: Can draw on Ann & DG'.[19]

---

[16] DG/CG, 'Sunday night' [February 1918] [HRRC].

[17] DG, *Aspects of Love*, p. 81.

[18] Ibid., p. 67.

[19] DG, Notebook, 'Aspects of Love', unpublished MS [Northwestern].

Bunny's travels with Mina (the apartment on the Isle St Louis in Paris, Château Mouton-Rothschild and George Sand's château) were all brought into the book, as was Bunny's holiday with Ann in Venice.

It is a deeply personal book, coloured by events from Bunny's life. Sir George finds it difficult to contemplate returning to the house where his wife had died in the spring of 1940, 'it was painful to see the place again; it would be unendurable to be continuously reminded of the past'.[20] Of course this mirrors Bunny's feelings over Hilton and Ray, but was he writing that particular passage at the time when in May 1955 he told Angelica, 'I haven't felt life so empty & worthless for the last fifteen years'?[21] Bunny also deployed his text to settle old scores. When Rose and Sir George are worried about the nature of the relationship between middle-aged Alexis and their adolescent daughter, Rose says to Alexis: 'By the way, I've been meaning to ask what footing you are on with my daughter?'[22] Rose and Sir George have morphed into Vanessa and Duncan, 1938. Even Rupert Hart-Davis comes in for a pasting: he is the 'big man with ugly ears' who bankrupts Sir George; the latter tells Rose, 'I thought I knew him quite well, and all the time every word of this friend and business associate was calculated. Every word was inspired by an ulterior motive.'[23]

Above all, *Aspects of Love* is a bold exposition on male virility, specifically Bunny's. As he told Ralph Partridge, 'When I was thirty I believed the physical relations of people of 40 & upwards

---

[20] DG, *Aspects of Love*, p. 22.

[21] DG/AVG, Chateau Renault, Sunday evening, 15 May [1955] [KCC].

[22] DG, *Aspects of Love*, p. 110.

[23] Ibid., p. 80.

must have grown pretty feeble & that at 50 or 60 it was the vanity which led them to pretend they had any physical desires'.[24] But in this novella Bunny could inform the reader otherwise, from the female point of view: 'George is not a satyr because he is sixty-four', Rose declares, telling Alexis that Sir George 'makes love perfectly. Even better than you did.'[25]

While the novel is ostensibly a hedonistic celebration of inter-generational love, a sense of piquant, proleptical inevitability overshadows the narrative. Sir George must acknowledge that most of his life is behind him, but the past was 'a world only of yesterday which he could scarcely believe had vanished'.[26] As time passes and Sir George lives progressively in the past, the generation gap is no longer a triumph of experience over youth: it cannot be breached. Rose sadly acknowledges that she is no longer the flame that ignites, but 'only the embers on the fire'.[27] When Sir George dies, his credo 'Set down the wine and the dice / and perish the thought of tomorrow', can only apply to those of a younger generation, left behind.[28] Consequently, this most personal of all Bunny's novels, is profoundly moving in the context of his life, specifically in terms of the age gap between him and Angelica and of his own sense of transience in her life. As the novel's dedicatee, Angelica is literally as well as meta-phorically present in the text. As Paul Levy observed, 'When one realizes that David Garnett was present at Angelica Bell's birth, one can appreciate fully the delicacy of the tribute offered so

---

[24] DG/R. Partridge, Hilton, 9 November 1955 [KCC].

[25] DG, *Aspects of Love*, p. 44.

[26] Ibid., p. 30.

[27] Ibid., p. 47.

[28] Ibid., p. 138.

publicly – and courageously'.[29] The book was hailed critically as Bunny's triumphant return to fiction. *The Times* proclaimed it 'a pagan hymn written in praise of physical passion and the delights that go with it'.

Both *Aspects of Love* and the long awaited *The Flowers of the Forest* were published in the autumn of 1955. They sold well, although as Bunny's editor, Norah Smallwood, commented about his autobiography, 'I'm afraid you are right in thinking that in some cases the book is being used as a means of having [a go] at one or two of the Bloomsbury giants'.[30] The reviews were generally positive, many commenting on Bunny's frankness, but some swiped at what they perceived as Bloomsbury's 'elitism'. 'I would not mind being attacked myself', Bunny told Angelica, 'but the hatred of Lytton, Maynard, Roger, Vanessa, Duncan, Clive, is really extraordinary. The book seems to have stirred up a wasp's nest.'[31] The review that stung the most was Harold Nicolson's in the *Observer*. Nicolson, a long-time acquaintance, slated what he considered Bunny's inconsistency:

At one moment we feel like we have got to know and like this cuddly young man with his soft eyes and sensitive mouth. At the next moment we are faced by a skilled and handsome labourer who with his tremendous biceps can heave logs or turnips without rest [...] and who spends his leisure hours tumbling lassies in the bracken [...]. We are never quite sure by the end whether to regard Mr Garnett

29 Paul Levy, 'Profile of David Garnett', for *Books & Bookmen* [c.?1977], TS [Northwestern].
30 N. Smallwood/DG, Chatto & Windus, 11 October 1955 [Northwestern].
31 DG/AVG, Venice, 'Sunday' [October 1955] [KCC].

as a selfless idealist, as a somewhat guiless hedonist [...] or as the artist-egoist.[32]

Nicolson missed the point: Bunny was all these things. If there was one reason why his autobiography succeeded it was in his skilful self-depiction as someone in the process of development, a combination of personae nuanced by age, circumstance and mood. Perhaps Bunny exaggerated when he told Geoffrey Keynes that the reviewers had given the book 'a pasting on moral grounds',[33] but Bunny laid himself open to criticism in his bluntness about loving many women, and in his jubilant passages celebrating his love for Duncan Grant.

Encapsulating the period of the Great War to the early 1920s, this volume celebrated Bunny's Bloomsbury friendships. Here Bunny described Duncan as 'a genius', 'the most original man I have ever known'. Most importantly, he stated that Duncan's friendship was 'a great piece of good luck', for 'it came at a time when I might have succeeded in my ambition of becoming a purely conventional person'. As a result of Duncan's friendship 'I became and for the rest of my life have remained in what I take to be the true meaning of the word, a *libertine*: that is a man whose sexual life is free of the restraints imposed by religion and conventional morality'.[34]

In stating that Duncan saved him from becoming a conventional person, Bunny alluded to the kind of love which remained illegal in Britain until the Sexual Offences Act of 1967. Moreover

---

[32] *Observer*, Sunday 9 October 1955.

[33] DG/G. Keynes, Hilton, 21 December 1955 [KCC].

[34] David Garnett, *The Flowers of the Forest* (London: Chatto & Windus, 1955), pp. 18–19.

he employed the term 'libertine' as a euphemism for someone whose sexual choices were neither constrained by marriage nor confined to one gender. Bunny was extremely brave to place his homosexuality on the page. He did so at a time when the censor prevailed, when not only authors, but their publishers and printers, could be prosecuted and even imprisoned. It is hardly surprising that Bunny's friends were nervous about volume two. They, of course, understood what he meant by the term 'libertine'.

Much of this volume had been rehearsed at the Memoir Club, but in taking these recollections from the inner sanctum of Bloomsbury, and placing them before the public, Bunny laid himself open to the scrutiny of an unfamiliar audience. With one exception there was no immediate precedent for such confessional autobiography, and even his fellow Bloomsberries kept their personal lives close to their chests. Certainly Clive Bell's, *Old Friends: Personal Recollections*, published the following year, by-passed the personal in favour of the general. But there was one notable autobiography which preceded Bunny's, an autobiography ground-breaking in its startlingly honest approach to sexual matters: Stephen Spender's *World Within World*, published in 1951, four years before *The Flowers of the Forest*.[35]

Both men believed in expressing 'truth' and although Spender's propensity for 'truth' was more politically motivated and altruistic, their ideas on matters of sexuality were not dissimilar. 'I believe obstinately', wrote Spender, 'that, if I am able to write with truth about what has happened to me, this can help others who have lived through the same sort of thing. In this belief I have risked being indiscreet, and I have written occasionally of

---

[35] Stephen Spender, *World Within World* (London: Hamish Hamilton, 1951).

experiences which seem strange to me myself, and which I have not seen discussed elsewhere.'[36] For Spender, writing with 'truth' meant he revealed his homosexuality in the same text in which he recalled his courtship and marriage. For Bunny, it meant he labelled himself a 'libertine' while exalting Duncan Grant; he described himself as a womaniser, while recounting his courtship and marriage to Ray. In implicitly advocating that sexuality was not fixed, but a continuum, that it was the person who mattered, rather than gender, Bunny and Spender not only challenged established ideas of 'normal' sexual behaviour, but also challenged the censor, as Bunny had done so often in the past. Seen together, Spender's autobiography and Bunny's volume two established a new kind of life-writing which, in foregrounding sexuality and in its unprecedented degree of honesty, foreshadowed Michael Holroyd's seminal biography of Lytton Strachey, published a decade later.

Where censorship was concerned, the 1950s were no less prudish than the 1920s. Vladimir Nabokov's *Lolita*, published in France in 1955 was banned in England the following year, despite critical plaudits in the British press. It was not until 1959 that Weidenfeld & Nicolson published the book in Britain, following a landmark trial which relaxed the British obscenity laws, opening the door for the subsequent 'Lady Chatterley' trial and eventual publication of D.H. Lawrence's *Lady Chatterley's Lover*. In this context, Spender, Bunny (and their publishers) displayed considerable courage. But seventeen years Spender's senior, and recently awarded the CBE, Bunny was an elder statesman of British literature. Taking risks in fiction was one thing, but it was another matter to display what might have been considered an

---

[36] Spender, *World Within World*, p. viii.

unconventional personal life. In accepting the CBE in 1952, Bunny did something his father would have abhorred. But if, by so doing, Bunny appeared to have joined the establishment, it was short-lived. He could not escape his natural inclination towards non-conformity. He might have said he was genetically predisposed that way.

Chapter Twenty-Nine

'Constance was at all times I believe singularly free from jealousy of any sort – and I am lucky to have inherited from her a certain natural immunity to this painful & unbearable passion.'[1]

Bunny was back in the limelight. He had written a successful novel and the second volume of his autobiography was selling well. *The Golden Echo* and *The Flowers of the Forest* were featured on the BBC radio programme *Talking of Books,* and on the back of his resurgence as a novelist, Chatto & Windus reissued *Go She Must!*

Bunny approached the New Year full of good resolutions. He wanted to focus on writing and as a gesture in that direction stopped farming pigs. Even so, he spent the night of 1 January 1956 in the cow shed, waiting for a Jersey to calve. Ann Montagu, Rosemary Hinchingbrooke's nineteen-year-old daughter, sat up with him, so Bunny named the calf in her honour. Bunny named all his cows after the women in his life. It did not seem to occur to him that there was something rather disconcerting in using his

---

[1] DG, 'Jealousy', in Draft Autobiography Volume I [c. 1951/2] [HRRC].

pocket diary to note 'Rosemary blew up' and 'Inseminate Amaryllis'. Quentin Bell's assertion that Bunny was a 'prize bull in a herd of cows' was not far off the mark.[2]

Early in 1956 Vanessa wrote to Bunny to tell him that 'a rather strange female called Mrs Holtby who lives in Cornwall', an admirer of Virginia Woolf, wanted to know whether he would allow her to take a cast of Tommy's bust of Virginia.[3] They dined together in London, and afterwards Patricia Holtby, a little dazzled by Bunny's literary eminence, wrote to say that she liked him very much. She was tall and thin with very short fair hair, married to Harold, a doctor, and had two children. Bunny thought her 'a rather splendid, wild creature'.[4] They dined together on her occasional forays to London, but Pat soon deflated any expectation of a love affair, explaining that she was a lesbian.

When in February Bunny embarked on volume three of his memoirs he was hampered by tiredness and depression. Henrietta described his rages at this time, which 'could sometimes be quite terrifying. His eyes would bulge and his face would grow brick red and his jowls purple and he would roar at us like a wild beast. But he never laid a finger on us.'[5] Nerissa recounted one such outburst to Leonard Woolf, telling him that their kitten, Apollo, 'does as you say follow one about like a dog, which in this family is a bad thing. For, when Bunny stamps around the house in a bad mood [...] Apollo, following him gets under his feet and then ---- "Miaaowwwwow!" "Oh, get out of my way you blessed

[2] Quentin Bell, *Elders and Betters* (London: John Murray, 1995), p. 81.
[3] VB/DG, Charleston, 4 April [1955] [HG].
[4] DG/EMH, Hilton, 30 May 1961 [Northwestern].
[5] Garnett, 'Aspects of My Father'.

animal!"[6] Olivier Bell thought that she and her husband Quentin were boring compared to Bunny and Angelica, who 'were emotional all the time and had such dramatic emotional feelings'. 'Angelica and Bunny were always having desperate emotional rows; you'd go into a room and find them standing facing each other.'[7]

The underlying problem was Angelica's coldness. Bunny depended on her love and with the bedrock of her love unstable, he found it hard to write or summon up much enthusiasm for anything. Although Ann, Rosemary, Giovanna and Pat intermittently massaged his ego, it was Angelica's love he craved. But Angelica felt imprisoned by Bunny's need for her, by domesticity and Hilton Hall. Daring to look outwards she told Leonard: 'I begin to envisage a time when one may begin to expand a little.'[8] She had taken to disappearing mysteriously to London, or more locally from Hilton for the day.

Bunny's doldrums were lifted by news that he had been elected an Honorary Fellow of Imperial College and that *Aspects of Love* had been in the best seller list for six weeks. As a result he could decline any further grant from the Chapelbrook Foundation. 'I hope now the dog is no longer lame', he wrote to Mina, 'you don't regret enabling him to get over the stile'.[9] He was even more delighted when Richard and Jane's first child, Oliver, was born in March 1956. He adored his grandson, noting the baby's 'great capacity for wonder – like Keats when he got to Scotland'.[10]

---

[6] N. Garnett/L. Woolf [nd] [Sussex].
[7] Ann Olivier Bell, interviewed by the author, 20 February 2007.
[8] AVG/LW, 1 March 1956 [Sussex].
[9] DG/M. Curtiss, 16 May 1956 [Berg].
[10] DG/M. Curtiss, Hilton, 5 September 1956 [Berg].

Despite these pleasures, Bunny could not come up with any ideas for a new novel, turning instead to that old chestnut *Castle Bigod*, now optimistically re-named *Seek No Further*, which he worked on, in a desultory manner, before abandoning it again.

Shortly after his sixty-fourth birthday in March 1956, Bunny stayed with the Partridges at Ham Spray, delighting Frances who commented that the 'visit has been a great success: what one wants a meeting with an old friend to be like, with plenty of easy talk and warmth circulating'.[11] But at Hilton things were distinctly chilly. Despite a successful midsummer party in which the Garnetts exhibited a united front, Angelica needed to get away. In July Bunny noted in his diary that Angelica was in London 'on mysterious private affair'.[12] She had gone to see an artist friend who had stayed at Hilton for a weekend in June. His name was Claude Rogers, and Angelica had known him from the time when in 1938 she studied art at the Euston Road School, which he co-founded in 1937.

At forty-seven, Rogers was ten years Angelica's senior, now a lecturer at London's Slade School of Fine Art, although he lived in Suffolk part of the week with his wife Elsie and their children. He was short, rotund and bespectacled, with dark curly hair. He and Angelica were lovers, and now it was Bunny's turn to remain at Hilton while Angelica went up to London every Tuesday or Thursday to be with Claude. Henrietta, then eleven, sensed something amiss, dreading the 'clank of Angelica's footsteps' on the hall's stone floor, aware her mother was wearing her smart London shoes and would be away 'making merry'.[13] Bunny knew

---

[11] Partridge, *Everything to Lose*, p. 250, diary entry for 12 March 1956.
[12] DG, Pocket Diary, 1956, Sunday 6 July [Northwestern].
[13] HG/SGK [personal communication 2011].

who Angelica was with, for in his pocket diary his notes of her expeditions to London are invariably embellished with the letters 'CP', an oddly thin and rather pointless camouflage of 'CR'.

On 4 August Bunny noted in his diary, 'Talk with Angelica, confessed love for CP; said I would help if I could, felt mixture of pity & tenderness for her'.[14] Despite such bravado, the next day at the Hobsons', Bunny had to turn away in order to obscure the tears welling up in his eyes, when the folk song 'O Waly Waly' played on the record player:

O, love is handsome and love is fine,
And love's a jewel while it is new,
But when it is old, it groweth cold,
And fades away like the morning dew.

Bunny's initial reasonableness soon gave way to feelings towards Rogers of loathing and anger. He worried their friends would find out, that it would be difficult to present a unified front, that the children would be hurt. He was particularly concerned about the possibility of local gossip, for sometimes Rogers met Angelica in Cambridge. As always, Bunny was torn between the need for civilised behaviour and his instinctive jealousy. By and large he behaved honourably, perhaps recalling his promise to Angelica of 1941: 'you can trust me to behave as you would wish if you fall in love with someone else'.[15]

Bunny turned to Pat Holtby for support, explaining he was unhappy though skirting the reason. She chastised him for being evasive, but she was intelligent and insightful and without

---

[14] DG, Pocket Diary, 1956, Saturday 4 August [Northwestern].
[15] DG/AVG, 159 Clifford's Inn, 18 November 1941 [KCC].

knowing that Angelica had been unfaithful, could diagnose the fundamental flaw in the Garnetts' marriage: that Angelica felt resentful. As Pat told Bunny: 'It didn't matter when supreme love made it all feasible, but perhaps the bottom fell out of that when you were unfaithful [...]. So the resentment gathers.' Pat wisely advised Bunny that Angelica needed 'to admire you again – not pity you'. She also warned him: 'you could make two mistakes – to ask for pity [...] or to rush to the ego-massaging embraces of another'. 'Sixty four', she added, 'may be a difficult age, but thirty eight is too'.[16]

When, at the end of August, Rogers left for a fortnight in Holland, Angelica was so upset that Bunny thought she would leave him. Instead, she had time to think, and told Bunny that her feelings for Rogers were less certain. Bunny hoped that the Italian holiday he and Angelica planned would strengthen their relationship and diminish Angelica's feelings for his rival.

The five-week holiday in the autumn of 1956 was mostly successful, although tensions surfaced. Initially they stayed with Giovanna at her family estate at Bertinoro, between Forli and Cesena in Emilia-Romagna. There they had the bizarre experience of being shot at by an invisible person while walking across fields in the dark, the bullet whispering overhead. It was the hunting season, but this was an odd time of day to hunt. Bunny and Angelica moved on from Bertinoro, driving from place to place and visiting art galleries. They returned via France, where they dropped in on Angelica's former drama teacher, Michel St Denis and were then dazzled by luxury at Château Mouton, where they stayed with Pauline and Philippe de Rothschild.

---

[16] P. Holtby/DG, Summerleaze, Bude, Cornwall, 30 August 1956 [Northwestern].

Angelica's affair spurred Bunny to write a new novel which he called 'the jealousy one'.[17] Entitled *A Net for Venus*, the book analysed the destructive nature of jealousy. Bunny was trying to work through his own feelings regarding Angelica, but it was a bit close to home. As he told Mina, the subject of his story was 'the old triangle – husband, wife, lover'.[18] With typical candour he gave his draft to Angelica to read, and she responded unfavourably. It was one thing to be celebrated as the heroine of *Aspects of Love*, another to be flaunted as an adulteress.

On 13 January 1957 Bunny noted in his diary: 'Angelica told me painful things in afternoon: Future in doubt.'[19] He could not sleep, relying on pills, and felt devastated. To compound matters, his farm manager, Harry, was in hospital. As Bunny told Frances Partridge, 'After diminishing my farming interest & vowing to leave all the work to Harry [...], I have suddenly found myself precipitated back onto the tractor & the muck-heap'.[20] He also had the children to look after and dinner to cook, as Angelica had gone to Newcastle to stay with Quentin and Olivier.

Exhausted by farm work, Bunny's emotional state continued to spiral downwards. Baling straw, he noted in his diary 'Baler luckily broke down before I did'.[21] On the same page he recorded that his American editor, John McCallum of Harcourt Brace, had rejected *A Net for Venus*. His manuscript was, meanwhile, lodged at Chatto & Windus, but Bunny became impatient

---

[17] DG/EMH, Hilton, 2 December 1958 [Northwestern].

[18] DG/M. Curtiss, 'St Valentine's Day' [14 February] 1957 [Berg].

[19] DG, Pocket Diary 1957, Sunday 13 January [Northwestern].

[20] DG/F. Partridge, Hilton 11 April 1957 [KCC].

[21] DG, Pocket Diary 1957, Monday 25 February [Northwestern].

waiting for a verdict. He complained that his editor, Ian Parsons, 'doesn't reply, or read what I send him for over a month & I think that I deserve more courteous and efficient treatment. I have been with them for thirty five years [...] have taken other authors to them, they have never lost money on any of my books, and I think I am ill-used, and won't stand it'.[22] Bunny posted a testy letter to Parsons, stating he would not trouble him again. This crossed in the post with a letter from Parsons, rejecting the book. For the first time in his writing career Bunny was without a publisher. At a Memoir Club meeting, Julia Strachey noticed that he was completely absorbed in his own thoughts and seemed absolutely withdrawn.

Bunny had remained in touch with Barbara Ker-Seymer in the twenty or so years since their affair. Now she was living with her lover, the American sculptor Barbara Roett, on Homer Street, Marylebone. The two 'Bars' as they were known, had a room to let, and Bunny took it. It was useful for attending Cranium and Memoir Club meetings, and it enabled Bunny to see Ann Hopkin without having to stay with her. Their sexual relationship had fizzled out, but they remained friends.

Angelica oscillated between chilly detachment and warm demonstrations of affection, leading Bunny to feel alternate extremes of misery and optimism. On the rare occasions when he and Angelica made love Bunny assumed she was being chari-table. In July 1957, having dined alone in London and feeling unhappy, Bunny wrote her a desperate letter. The following day, at an exhibition at the Slade, Bunny narrowly avoided Claude Rogers. Back at Hilton, he handed Angelica his letter, which led to a painful row. Their relationship under duress, it was not the

---

[22] DG/M. Curtiss, Hilton, 29 April 1957 [Berg].

best moment to embark on a family holiday with Quentin and Olivier Bell and their young children Julian and Virginia.[23]

On arriving at Asolo, in northern Italy, they found Quentin and Olivier already established in the rented house. It was too small to accommodate everyone, so William, Amaryllis and Henrietta would sleep in rooms elsewhere in the town. Although it was perfectly reasonable that Bunny's older children should make way for the Bells' infants, Bunny was furious. Quite why he should have been so angry and inflexible is difficult to determine, except perhaps in the context of his current vulnerabilities about Angelica. Quentin thought Bunny's determined adoption of the role of *père-de-famille* embraced his family as well as Bunny's.[24] Bunny became progressively grumpy and isolated, his irascibility culminating at the end of a day-trip to Venice. William was driving with Bunny in the passenger seat. At the turning for Asolo, which Olivier and Will recognised, Bunny insisted Will drive straight on, barking 'straight on' repeatedly. William drove on and on in the wrong direction, Bunny refusing to acknowledge or apologise for his mistake.[25]

Bunny had planned to focus on his new novel during the holiday, but found it impossible to do so. Once again Mina Curtiss came to his aid, inviting Bunny to work on his book at Chapelbrook. With customary diplomacy, she played down her payment for his passage in the guise of giving him space and solitude to write. Arriving on 2 November 1957, Bunny soon fell into a routine where he woke early, bathed, breakfasted, took a walk and then worked all day until dinner. When he climbed

---

[23] Their third child, Cressida, was not born until 1959.

[24] Bell, *Elders and Betters*, p. 81.

[25] Olivier Bell interviewed by the author, 20 February 2007.

Pony Mountain, he could not help thinking about Priscilla Fairchild, with whom he had ascended the hill all those years before.

In mid-November, Bunny went to Harvard, accompanied by his old friend, the poet Archibald McLeish, now Professor of Rhetoric. Having been asked to give an after-dinner speech on D.H. Lawrence, Bunny came armed with a batch of Lawrence letters inherited from Edward, which he hoped the university library might be willing to purchase. As they did not offer what Bunny considered a fair price, he came away with the manuscripts still under his arm.

On 28 November Bunny spent Thanksgiving at the Massachusetts home of George Kirstein, Mina's younger brother, the publisher and owner of the *Nation* magazine. The next day he went to New York, where he stayed at the Beekman Tower Hotel on East Forty-nine and First Street. Mina was also in New York, and although her apartment was too small to accommodate Bunny, they dined together every evening. They also dined with Mina's brother, Lincoln Kirstein, who had recently suffered a nervous breakdown. Apprehensive about how he would find his old friend, Bunny was relieved that Lincoln appeared happy, eager to reminisce about Stephen Tomlin and old times.

On another evening Bunny collected Mina, 'stupendous in a huge mink coat, a string of vast pearls & the largest diamond ring ever seen'.[26] They dined at the Plaza before attending a performance of Lincoln's New York City Ballet conducted by Stravinsky in celebration of his seventy-fifth birthday. The kind

---

[26] DG/AVG, Beekman Tower Hotel, E49th & 1st, New York [November 1957] [KCC].

of high life Bunny enjoyed with Mina in France seemed even more dazzling in New York. Bunny wrote to Angelica, telling her he longed for her, wished she was with him. She replied affectionately, saying she longed to be with Bunny, that he must have faith in his novel, and sending hugs. Writing again to Angelica, Bunny casually mentioned that Shusheila Lall had come to his hotel room on his first morning there, '& we sat & talked for an hour or so'.[27]

Bunny had first met Shusheila in 1950 when she arrived in London, estranged from her husband. At the time Bunny considered her 'the most intelligent woman I have met for a long long time & of (Siamese) cat-like delicacy'.[28] She was a year older than Angelica, exquisitely beautiful, with long dark hair, pale skin, large expressive eyes and a lovely figure clothed in an elegant sari. She told Bunny, at the time, that she felt a foreigner everywhere, and perhaps this, together with her wavering marriage, caused the deep melancholy which often cast its shadow upon her.[29] Bunny had seen Shusheila once or twice since, when she alighted in London. Now she was living in New York, having achieved some sort of reconciliation with her husband Arthur Lall, India's Ambassador to the United Nations.

At lunch one day in New York, Shusheila told Bunny she had been propositioned by a truck driver. Bunny assumed she shared this confidence to encourage him to make a similar proposition. He reasoned that 'If I tell a woman of a love affair I have enjoyed

[27] DG/AVG, Beekman Tower Hotel, E49th & 1st, New York [November 1957] [KCC].

[28] DG/M. Curtiss, Hilton, 13 July 1950 [Berg].

[29] S. Lall/DG, c/o EN Mangat Rai, United Services Club, Simla, 25 May [1950] [Northwestern].

it is usually because I want her to realise that love affairs are possible with me'.[30] And so, three days later, Bunny took Shusheila back to his room where they made love. As he recorded in his journal, a journal created specifically to document the affair, 'I was so excited by the fact of her taking me as a lover – at the age of 65 – that all my love making was shot through with astonishment'.[31] The following day when Mina threw a champagne cocktail party for Bunny, he barely spoke to Shusheila, but 'all the time the thought of her being my lover and a sense of insane triumph and happiness possessed me. Of the 3½ million women in New York I was the favoured lover of the most lovely.'

Lunching with Shusheila the next day at his hotel, Bunny heard someone speak his name. It was Priscilla Fairchild, visiting New York and staying in the same hotel. Bunny hadn't seen her for twenty-five years. She was slender, grey-haired, still handsome and overjoyed to see him. Of course it did his ego a power of good to have his old lover meet the current model, and vice versa. One evening Priscilla went to Bunny's hotel room where they sat and talked for some time. When Bunny embraced her she smiled and disengaged herself. He thought it just as well, but a year later, when he learned she had died from a heart attack, he was pleased that fortune had thrown them together one last time.

It was presumably Shusheila who encouraged her husband to throw an ambassadorial dinner in Bunny's honour. Arthur Lall was as handsome as his wife was beautiful and he impressed Bunny with his way 'of taking his own importance light heartedly for granted'.[32] It was a surreal occasion. Despite the

---

[30] DG Journal, Shusheila Lall [1957] [Northwestern].

[31] DG Journal, Shusheila Lall [1957] [Northwestern].

[32] DG Journal, Shusheila Lall [1957] [Northwestern].

grandiosity of the surroundings and formal attire, dinner turned out to be a buffet which the guests ate on their laps. Bunny became involved in a prickly conversation with Krishna Menon, leader of the Indian Delegation to the UN, who was not as impressed by Bunny's stories of Savarkar as Bunny imagined he would be. Moreover Bunny was pursued all evening by a woman who insisted his books had inspired her to such an extent that she wished to coalesce with him. But the highpoint of the event was Bunny's meeting with Carson McCullers, an author he particularly admired and had asked to meet. She looked sickly and crumpled with pain. Bunny's heart went out to her, and as her hands shook badly, he cut up her food. They established an instant rapport. She wore a green and blue silk kimono, and as they talked Bunny noticed a cockroach dart out of the garment's folds and run across her lap.

Bunny returned from the euphoria of New York to the problems he had left behind in England. Angelica either rejected his advances or accommodated them with evident reluctance. 'What is the point of being tied to a woman who doesn't love me or want me physically', Bunny moaned.[33] Moreover, Bunny realised he had shot himself in the foot in leaving Chatto. After such a long association, he felt 'naked & forlorn'.[34] Leonard Woolf offered to arbitrate with Ian Parsons, but Bunny perceived this as nepotism, reasoning that even if Leonard succeeded on this occasion, the problem would only arise again.

Bunny continued to be irritated by the invisible presence of Claude Rogers, who in June 1958 sent Angelica a bouquet of roses, presumably commemorating their particular anniversary.

---

[33] DG Journal, Shusheila Lall [1957] [Northwestern].
[34] DG/EMH, Hilton, 15 March 1958 [Northwestern].

What rankled most was that they were addressed to 'Miss' Angelica Garnett, as if she were Bunny's daughter. When to his horror, one evening at the Cranium, Bunny found himself sitting next to Rogers, he spoke to him 'just enough to show him I did not want to see him again or to be noticeably cold'.[35] Earlier that day, at the Reform Club, Rupert Hart-Davis had advanced towards Bunny, but seeing his expression of horror, had swerved away.

Bunny was relieved when his agent, Peter Watt, informed him that Longmans would publish both *A Net for Venus* and his new novel, *A Shot in the Dark*. Then the Chicago book dealers, Hamill & Barker, wrote to say that they had found a possible purchaser for his Lawrence letters. Shusheila had taken a job in Geneva and planned to spend a couple of days in England en route. Would Bunny meet her from the ship at Plymouth? Things seemed to be looking up. But Bunny found it exhausting driving all the way to Plymouth for what amounted to a single night together. When Shusheila announced she would be staying with friends in Oxfordshire, leaving Bunny to lodge in a hotel, he suspected her old English lover was on the scene. Bunny had to face the hard fact that Shusheila seemed less ardent than she had been in New York. Perhaps she wouldn't, after all, occupy the gap which Angelica had vacated.

---

[35] DG Journal, Shusheila Lall [1957] [Northwestern].

Chapter Thirty

'To write happily, a writer must love not only the subject but
the audience whom he is addressing.'[1]

A Shot in the Dark was published in the autumn of 1958. In
America it would be published by Little, Brown, having, according to Bunny, been turned down by Harcourt Brace because of
references to 'sapphism'. The story revolves around one of
Bunny's eternal triangles. Robert Harcourt (a dig at the rejecting
publisher?) goes to Italy to escape an unhappy love affair with
Caroline Stephenson, who is subject to 'devastating passions for
her own sex'.[2] There he falls in love with Gemma, the mayor's
daughter, who had once been infatuated with Caroline. Caroline
arrives in Italy and takes up with Gemma leaving Robert to
conquer his jealousy, although he gets Gemma in the end.

While there are similarities between Caroline and Angelica,
Gemma is modelled on Giovanna, with her 'thick black eyebrows

---

[1] DG, 'Books in General', *NS&N*, 18 January 1936.
[2] David Garnett, *A Shot in the Dark* (London: Longmans 1958; Penguin Books
     1962), p. 15.

arched over her large eyes' and 'powerful aquiline nose between high cheekbones'. 'She was not tall, but very slim and high-breasted, with a ridiculously small waist.'[3] Robert, 'strong as a bull' and almost old enough to be Gemma's father naturally resembles Bunny. The book is dedicated to Rosemary Hinchingbrooke.

Part romance, part thriller, the title was inspired by the shot which whispered over Bunny's head while he took a nocturnal walk in Bertinoro. Thematically, the novel explores the conflicts between the new order and the old: tradition versus progress; religion versus paganism; state versus church – themes which allowed Bunny to vent his distaste for organised religion. Robert perceives that the town's Christianity is founded upon an earlier pagan cult of Diana. The cathedral's Madonna altarpiece is a palimpsest, a veiled representation of Diana the huntress, worshipped by the town's womenfolk from time immemorial. As Robert reflects, 'From a rationalist standpoint, there was nothing to choose between a belief in natural magic, and a belief in holy relics and the miracles of the Roman Catholic Church'.[4]

The reviews were not particularly enthusiastic. There was a stinker in the *TLS*, and the *New Statesman* saw little point in the book. John Davenport (an *Observer* critic and occasional dinner guest at Hilton) in a comment elegantly poised between criticism and praise, stated that the virtuosity of Bunny's 'performance would probably shock his early admirers, who enjoyed the restraint of his oblique moralities'.[5]

---

[3] Ibid., pp. 10–11.

[4] Ibid., p. 81.

[5] Publicity blurb, quoted on rear cover of David Garnett, *A Net for Venus* (London: Longmans 1959).

It was a good point. Henceforward and through the 1960s, Bunny's fiction changed. Partly he was interested in expanding his genres. As he commented, 'I have never wished to repeat myself which is perhaps why, though my reviews are almost always favourable, I am not a "bestselling author"'.[6] He was also responding to the fact that the restraints of censorship, which had circumscribed his work for decades, were now loosening and he could write more openly about sex. In his eagerness to embrace a more liberal age and to write more explicitly, he failed to realise that he might come across as slightly seedy to a younger generation of readers. Hitherto, one of Bunny's great strengths was that he found elegant ways to express what could not be stated too boldly. Now, though he still employed verbal economy and textual brevity, Bunny had moved some distance from the restraint of his earlier novels. His messages were no longer oblique but written in Capital Letters.

Bunny was also overly preoccupied with unravelling his personal life in the pages of his books. He had turned from supple and subtle plotting to convoluted themes of jealousy, love triangles and ulterior motives. Moreover, his adoption of what he supposed to be the current vernacular language of youth made him sound like a relic. If he wanted to appeal to younger readers he would need to revise the blurb on the fly leaf of *A Shot in the Dark*, which stated that he was born in 1892 and 'is a farmer as well as an author and includes shooting and fishing among his recreations'. Had Bunny wanted to come across as an old duffer, he could not have expressed it better.

Angelica was bored. She suggested moving to France or Italy and putting the girls in boarding school. Bunny would not entertain such a proposal. He was proud of his daughters' beauty and

---

6 DG/Larry Edgerton, Le Verger de Charry, 28 May 1980 [Northwestern].

high spirits and could not bear to think of them corralled. The children were often described as 'Amazons', an appendage particularly applicable to the twins, who shot and fished and fought as well as any boys. Bunny could not understand why Angelica was so unhappy. She 'has 4 lovely children', he told his diary, 'a house she loves, no money worries – & is quite miserable'.[7] In October, when he went to Geneva for a week to visit Shusheila, she was full of her own preoccupations, talking insensitively of her mysterious English lover. On leaving, Bunny asked himself: 'Goodbye to Shusheila? Forever?'[8]

On 11 March 1959, two days after Bunny's sixty-seventh birthday, Jane Garnett gave birth to a second son, Edward Alexander. 'I feel rather excited', Bunny noted 'at having two grandsons.'[9] That day, he had lunch with Sylvia Townsend Warner. It was the first time they had seen one another for nearly thirty years. There had been a break in their correspondence between 1932 and 1955, which both Richard Garnett and William Maxwell (the editor of Sylvia's *Letters*) believe had something to do with her lover, the poet Valentine Ackland. Sylvia found Bunny hardly changed, though a little deaf. When they talked about Charles Prentice, the years slipped away.

In Bunny's pocket diary references to letters from 'CP' and observations that Angelica returned from London variously 'full of life & power', 'intensely preoccupied with her own affairs' and 'jubilant', suggest that her affair with Claude Rogers had been revived sometime in 1958.[10] The following spring there was a

---

7 DG, Pocket Diary 1958, Saturday 4 October [Northwestern].
8 DG, Pocket Diary 1958, Tuesday 28 October [Northwestern].
9 DG/EMH, 12 March 1959 [Northwestern].
10 DG, Pocket Diary 1959, Thursday 19 and Friday 20 March [Northwestern].

crisis. After her return from London one evening, Bunny slept in the spare room, but in the early hours he confronted Angelica, stating that he could not continue without warmth or tenderness. A few days later when Angelica took the girls to Butts Intake, Bunny wrote explaining that he could not 'live in enemy territory in the arctic circle'.[11] Angelica replied:

> When I seem coldest I am often only clinging to a rock [...] to prevent myself going down [...]. For the first time I've <u>really</u> understood (late though it may seem at the age of 40) that to love well one must be free. But do please understand that it's not exactly from you that I am struggling to free myself – it may seem so at times but I think that its just the first time in my life that I've ever felt truly free – it's a kind of growing up at last simply. Where it concerns our relationship I simply ask you to be patient with me [...] but if you can for a time ask nothing and leave me alone I shall perhaps feel free to love you much more in every way than I have done. You are precious to me and I don't want to hurt you – I'm ashamed of the way I have done so in the past.[12]

Bunny replied, bitterly: 'Time's winged chariot hurrying near. By the time you have decided that you love me & want to hold me in your arms I shall be ashes.'[13]

A Net for Venus was finally published in June 1959. It is a story about Venetia, a beautiful woman in her late thirties, who has a love affair with a younger man (improbably named Carlo Marx)

---

[11] DG/AVG, Hilton, Tuesday 31 March 1959 [KCC].

[12] AVG/DG [Butts Intake], Thursday 2 April [1959] [KCC].

[13] DG/AVG, Hilton, 4 April 1959 [KCC].

while married to Toby, an attractive older man and war-hero. Bunny must have cheered when he read the book's review in the *TLS*, which completely understood what he was trying to achieve: 'He shows us [...] a jealous husband of impeccable dignity and virtue condoning his wife's infidelity and thereby regaining her love.'[14] Bunny had written a wish-fulfilment novel.

It is not surprising Angelica hated it. Some passages are far too close for comfort: 'Must she [Venetia/Angelica] always belong to someone who expected love, as she had belonged during the first nineteen years of her life to her mother [Vanessa]? Then it had been out of the maternal frying-pan into the fire of Toby's [Bunny's] love.'[15] Bunny reproduced aspects of Angelica's affair with Claude Rogers, having Venetia arrive home covered with bits of grass, just as Angelica had on one occasion after a tryst. 'For many years Toby [Bunny] had concealed nothing from Venetia [Angelica]: now it came to him as a shock to realize that he must conceal almost everything. He must try to hide his jealousy, his loathing for Carlo [Rogers], the murderous feeling in his heart, and the pity he felt for her because of her choice of such an unworthy lover.'[16] And so on.

The reviews were more positive than for *A Shot in the Dark*, although several reviewers upbraided Bunny for sloppiness and inconsistency and the *Listener* was not far off the mark in concluding that 'it leaves one with a sense of disappointment, and at moments it even gives one a curious feeling of embarrassment'.[17] Essentially, *A Net for Venus* is a vengeful book, and if Bunny

---

[14] Friday 10 July 1959.

[15] DG, *Net for Venus*, p. 37.

[16] Ibid., p. 62.

[17] 23 July 1959.

thought that by writing it he would emerge triumphant from his jealousy over Claude Rogers, he was wrong. On 24 June Bunny wrote in his diary: 'Will there be roses [for Angelica] from CP, OBE?' The answer, unfortunately, was 'YES'.[18] It was a thorny annual event.

In mid-August the Chicago book dealers Frances Hamill and Margery Barker came to Hilton. Bunny fed them handsomely and arranged with them the sale of a large quantity of material on a commission basis. He was looking after the twins as Angelica and Amaryllis were with Giovanna in Venice and Henrietta, like Amaryllis before, was billeted in France. Bunny enjoyed being alone with the twins, noticing that Fanny, with her dancing eyes and impudent smile, resembled her uncle, Julian Bell. They were to have accompanied William to Ridley Stokoe, but Bunny stayed behind with Nerissa who had stabbed herself in the leg with a hayfork while leaping from an oat stack. Bunny relished physical labour on the farm, 'the pleasure', as he wrote to Angelica, provocatively, 'of feeling one's belly taut and muscular'. She replied: 'Giovanna is divine; very loving & affectionate.'[19]

In October Bunny received an invitation to participate in a symposium on D.H. Lawrence and James Joyce at the University of Southern Illinois, where he would also deliver a series of lectures on English Literature and art. As the University of Texas was mounting a small exhibition on the Garnett family, Bunny arranged to lecture there as well. This was a time when American Anglophilia was at its height and American universities and libraries were acquiring large quantities of modern English literary archives. Young American academics, establishing their

---

[18] DG, Pocket Diary, 1959, Wednesday 24 June [Northwestern].
[19] AVG/DG, Casa Frollo, 'Wednesday' [August 1959] [KCC].

careers by researching twentieth-century English literature, were seeking first-hand testimony. Many of the writers whom Bunny had known – D.H. Lawrence, Joseph Conrad, Ford Madox Ford and Virginia Woolf – were the objects of this focus. As both a successful British writer and the repository of first-hand knowledge, Bunny was an attractive proposition in American academe. He had not so much danced with a man who danced with a girl who danced with the Prince of Wales, but he had performed a Mordkin dance before D.H. Lawrence.

Bunny arrived in New York on 5 November 1959 and flew to Carbondale, Illinois, where he was met by the Lawrence scholar Harry T. Moore and the British diplomat and writer Sir Richard Rees. The following day he attended a cocktail party hosted by Moore, where one of the guests announced she had never read any of Bunny's books '"but I like Mr Garnett. I like his face. I like that tie. I feel crazy about him."'[20] Bunny was surprised to be left mainly to his own devices, installed in an apartment in a new block surrounded by car parks. He found the tiny local supermarket entirely inadequate and that he could only purchase *sliced* bread.

Bunny was resourceful and an excellent cook but he felt like a fish out of water. Southern Illinois was very different from New York, and Southern Illinois *mores* far removed from the worlds of Mina Curtiss and Lincoln Kirstein. Bunny was shocked by the prevailing racism, telling Angelica that white girls couldn't share rooms with black girls and that at nearby Carterville, black people were disbarred from living in the town. Taking the bull by the horns, Bunny gave an unscheduled lecture on Shelagh

---

[20] DG/AVG, Apartment 125–4, Southern Hills, Sunday 8 November [1959] [KCC].

Delaney's play *A Taste of Honey*, in which a white woman and black man have a love affair and resulting child. He found himself shaking throughout.

Bunny lectured to enthusiastic audiences on 'Virginia Woolf & Bloomsbury', Forster, Galsworthy and H.G. Wells, Moll Cutpurse, the Omega Workshop and the two Post-Impressionist exhibitions. On 16 November he delivered the first symposium paper to an audience of over one thousand people, to wild applause. Afterwards Lionel Trilling made 'a most dramatic & subtle speech', but Bunny was bored by long-winded discussions on Christian symbolism and 'Freudian poppycock of all sorts'. He was enormously relieved to have pulled it off and hoped word would circulate in US universities that he was 'good value & eager to meet students'.[21] Bunny found lecturing invigorating, but as the days passed and his lectures fell in the evenings, he became exhausted, especially given the amount of preparation involved.

Bunny spent the day after Thanksgiving in Chicago with Frances Hamill and Marjorie Barker, who were 'full of astoundingly good or hopeful news' which he anticipated would produce a 'nest egg'.[22] This hatched into an offer, from the University of Texas, of $17,500 for some of his manuscripts. Moreover, Hamill & Barker had a proposition for Bunny: would he be prepared to act as a broker or intermediary for the sale of British literary manuscripts in the US? They proposed paying Bunny 10 per cent of the purchase price for an outright purchase or 6 per cent of the sale price for material on consignment. Bunny was being

---

[21] DG/AVG, 125–4, Southern Hills, 20 November 1959 [KCC].

[22] DG/AVG, Pearson Hotel, E Pearson Street, Chicago, 'Thanksgiving Day' [26 November 1959] [KCC].

asked to tout for business among his friends. He received this business offer just before Christmas and must have felt all his Christmases had come at once.

In the meantime, on 5 December he flew to New Mexico, where he lunched with Dorothy Brett, Carrington's friend and a former Slade 'crop-head', now resident in Taos, whom he had not seen for forty years. He found her 'terrifically alive, very happy, & looks almost exactly like a plucked Christmas Turkey.' The next day he set off in a car with four professors to drive to the D.H. Lawrence Ranch at San Cristobal, where he 'felt the ghost of the poor unhappy devil behind every bush.' He saw Lawrence's famous 'indecent' paintings, which he had seen before in 1928, remarking that they were exactly as he remembered them 'not in the least indecent but very bad'.[23]

Bunny delivered his final lecture at Austin, Texas on 17 December. He was exhausted, finding the need for continual superficial cordiality a particular strain. When he viewed the exhibition on the Garnett family at the University Library, he felt 'like the final exhibit'.[24] Then he snatched a few days in New York City, where he dined with Mina Curtiss and George Kirstein and attended the ballet with Lincoln. Afterwards he spent a couple of days with Carson McCullers at her Nyack home. Bunny returned to Hilton on Christmas Eve, where he spent the next night sitting up waiting for a cow to calve.

Bunny had struggled with volume three of his memoirs off and on for four years. It was painful to write, bringing back memories of many lost friends. He felt burdened by the past:

---

[23] DG/AVG, Union, University of New Mexico, Albuquerque, 7 December 1959 [KCC].

[24] DG/AVG, Austin, Texas, 14 December 1959 [KCC].

24 March 1960 was the twentieth anniversary of Ray's death, an event he recorded in his diary. He was also worried about his eldest daughter. While Angelica was away again in France, seventeen-year-old Amaryllis confided to Bunny that she hated her school and was unhappy there. He felt powerless to help her as he could not afford to pay for a private education. 'I wanted to cry', he told Angelica, 'because I love her so much.'[25] But it did not take long before Bunny and Angelica agreed to let Amaryllis spend her final school year at Cranbourne Chase, an independent girls' school in Wiltshire, where she already had a number of friends. When Mina offered to pay the fees, Bunny accepted gratefully. Always the most constant friend, Mina explained that this was a way of showing her gratitude for his earlier declining the Chapelbrook Foundation grant at a difficult time for the Foundation. With one daughter at boarding school, Angelica again tried to persuade Bunny to send the twins away, a proposal which was financially unrealistic and, as far as Bunny was concerned, undesirable.

In the autumn, when Bunny and Angelica stayed with the Partridges at Ham Spray, Frances's 'heart-cockles warmed to dear Bunny, rosy under his white thatch and overflowing with geniality'. But she noticed that Angelica 'radiated a feeling of desperation'.[26] In November, when Bunny and Angelica attended Leonard Woolf's eightieth birthday dinner at the Garrick Club, Bunny spent the night at his Homer Street room, while Angelica stayed in Rosemary Hinchingbrooke's London house.

In December he received an unexpected fillip. Peter Watt telephoned to say that Bunny had been offered 100 guineas

---

[25] DG/AVG, Hilton, 20 February 1960 [KCC].
[26] Partridge, *Everything to Lose*, p. 365, diary entry for 7 November 1960.

(c. £1,600) to comment on the script of a film, *Lawrence of Arabia*, which would be produced by Sam Spiegel and directed by David Lean. Bunny spent a couple of days reading the script and having pronounced it awful was surprised to discover that Spiegel had given him the job of re-writing. Bunny was not alone in this role (Robert Bolt accepted the same job) but he could not afford to turn down the £2,000 (£30,600) on offer. After lunching with Spiegel in early January 1961, Bunny knew it would be an uphill struggle, noting, tersely: 'A dog-fight. Man with hide of a rhinoceros.'[27] He also recognised the quality of the competition when, at the end of the month, he saw Bolt's play *The Tiger and the Horse*. By February Bunny was in despair, telling Frances Partridge, 'I am up to my neck in script writing – about which I know less than nothing'. 'When I have finished the job, there is to be a grand session, I understand, when all the scripts will be cut up with scissors & pasted up like an apotheosis of Heads Bodies & Legs.' 'My chief objective', he added, 'is to get my <u>Head</u> accepted. But I greatly doubt my success.'[28]

Bunny worked on the script throughout the spring, but knew it wasn't his forte. As he had commented to Richard in 1943, 'I never manage to write plays & don't know how to'.[29] He was unsurprised, therefore, when at the end of May, Spiegel turned the script down, pronouncing Bunny's work authentic, but stating that Bolt had done a wonderful job. Bunny could have had no idea, throughout the weeks of writing, that he was involved in a crisis between Spiegel and Lean. While Lean was in Jordan making preparations for filming, he remained ignorant

---

[27] DG, Pocket Diary, 1961, Tuesday 3 January [Northwestern].
[28] DG/Partridge, Hilton, 11 February 1961 [KCC].
[29] DG/RG, Saturday 29 May 1943 [RG].

that any new scriptwriting was being done or that Bunny was involved beyond commenting on the original script. Bolt assumed he was the sole script writer. When he discovered Bunny's involvement, he was furious. It was at this point that Bunny was dropped.

On the 7 April 1961 Clive Bell telephoned to Hilton to say that Vanessa, ill with bronchitis, was dying. Angelica rushed down to Charleston, but Vanessa died just before she arrived. She was buried, without ceremony, in Firle churchyard with Duncan, Angelica, Quentin and Grace Higgens the only mourners. Vanessa had never really been reconciled to her daughter's marriage to Bunny, although she loved their four girls. Nevertheless, she had been one of the central figures in Bunny's life. If Angelica spent subsequent years exploring and analysing her relationship with Vanessa, she could at least reflect that her mother had loved her deeply. In the days following Vanessa's death, Angelica went backwards and forwards to Charleston, sorting matters relating to her mother's estate. Between times, she stayed in London at her parents' *pied-à-terre* in Percy Street. Bunny looked after the girls and cooked meals, a task he enjoyed though it kept him from writing. Grateful for his support, Angelica wrote: 'Darling Catt', 'how you do step into the breach! It's wonderful of you.'[30]

---

[30] AVG/DG, Charleston, 12 April [1961] [KCC].

Chapter Thirty-One

'Bunny loved beauty, and as his daughters were undeniably beautiful, that was enough for him.'[1]

Bunny had reached a stage in his life where he was revered as much for what he remembered as for what he wrote. He was a repository of information about the writers of his parents' generation, as well as of those of his own. He also had impeccable literary credentials as the son of both Edward and Constance Garnett. In February 1961, Bunny was interviewed by the BBC for a radio programme, *Portrait of Frieda Lawrence*, and in the summer Carolyn Heilbrun's *The Garnett Family* was published.

Heilbrun was a young American academic who had earlier written a doctoral thesis on the Garnett family, and who went on to forge a distinguished career as a feminist and literary scholar. Her book placed the Garnetts among an 'intellectual aristocracy', which Heilbrun considered a 'peculiarly English phenomenon'

---

[1] Richard Garnett, 'Tribute to Angelica Garnett', Hilton Hall, 15 July 2009 [unpublished MS] [RG].

originating at the beginning of the nineteenth century when 'families of intellectual distinction [...] began to intermarry'. She thought Bunny's second marriage 'a case in point'.[2] With the exception of this second marriage, linking Bunny via Vanessa Bell to Virginia Woolf and Sir Leslie Stephen, the Garnetts remained singularly free from the intermarriage to which Heilbrun referred. Bunny's inclusion is largely confined to an epilogue, but he was favourably impressed overall, and thought Constance particularly well drawn.

Bunny had been drumming up business for Hamill & Barker who proposed to visit Britain in the summer. Frances Hamill wrote telling him they had high hopes of Mrs Partridge, had received a friendly letter from James Strachey, and wondered whether T.H. White might part with any manuscripts. They had also written to Bunny soon after Vanessa's death, in what seemed undue haste, enquiring whether they could look at her papers while in England. In the event they purchased manuscripts from James and Marjorie Strachey and books from Pat Holtby. Bunny received 10 per cent of the sale price, amounting to £111.00 (c. £1,698 today). The money was very welcome: he still had outstanding mortgage repayments on The Cearne (now occupied by a tenant), a hangover from the Hart-Davis years.

Now in their late fifties, Frances Hamill and Margery Barker became well known for their acquisition of Bloomsbury papers, beginning in 1957 with the purchase of twenty-five volumes of Virginia Woolf's diaries from Leonard Woolf.[3] They were

---

[2] Carolyn G. Heilbrun, *The Garnett Family: The History of a Literary Family* (London: George Allen & Unwin, 1961), p. 15.

[3] They did not receive the diaries until 1970 as Leonard Woolf wanted to retain them for reasons of personal access.

absolutely tenacious in pursuit of rare books and manuscripts, a tenacity softened by an elaborately courteous manner, persuasive charm and plenty of money. If Hamill & Barker were major players in the exodus of literary manuscripts from Britain to the US, then Bunny certainly had a supporting role.

That autumn he was working on volume three, reading his letters from Ray, pondering how to write about her death. When he discussed this with Frances Partridge, she noticed tears welling up in his eyes. Bunny was also reminded of those difficult final months by the arrival of a visitor: Herbert Herlitschka telephoned, asking to come to Hilton. Bunny did not refuse, but was relieved when the visit ended.

At Hilton, the balance had shifted. Now it was often Bunny who remained at home in charge of domestic arrangements, while Angelica stayed in London at Percy Street. Frances Partridge had become a frequent guest following Ralph's death from a heart attack the previous year. Always an astute and close observer, she provides an interesting picture of life at Hilton, conveying an alarming decline in housekeeping, even by regular Garnett standards. She described Hilton as a 'ramshackle, bohemian, improvised, beautiful house full of beautiful things neglected, tattered and thick with cobwebs. Music in confusion and disarray, rolls of dust under the bed, bathroom like a junkshop, the basin leaning out of the wall, furniture propped on books, stains, cracks everywhere, no bulbs in the lights, a smeared single coat of paint on the walls of my room, not enough blankets on the bed.' At the same time she remained impressed by 'delicious meals, plenty to drink', and 'very warm, lovely civilization'.[4] As Bunny recorded in his autobiography, 'Places

---

[4] Partridge, *Hanging On*, p. 77, diary entry for 2 October 1961.

explain people. They become impregnated with the spirit of those who have lived and been happy in them.'[5] It was as though the disharmony between Bunny and Angelica had been absorbed in the fabric of their house.

Amaryllis left her new school prematurely to train as an actress at the Central School of Speech and Drama in London. Although acting was hardly a stable occupation, Bunny did not discourage her, believing he could not 'save her from mistakes & can only provide at best a shoulder for her to weep on'.[6] Henrietta, on the other hand, had been sent to a coaching establishment which she hated. When she came home in a hysterical state, protesting that she only wanted to be happy, Bunny agreed she could go to Dartington College to study drama and art. Henrietta later considered 'it rather strange of him not to have bothered about our education. I don't just mean that he sent us to stiflingly inadequate schools, but that he never evinced any interest whatsoever in our lessons [...]. For if we learned anything at all, it was because we had free rein to read anything we liked from his extensive library.'[7]

Bunny was inordinately proud of his daughters. In January 1962 he wrote to Sylvia Townsend Warner, lovingly describing their individual characteristics: eighteen-year-old Amaryllis was the apple of his eye; 'the most sensitive, intelligent, lovely, understanding creature'. Henrietta was 'stunningly good-looking. A whizzer.' Nerissa was 'very gentle, liable to be embarrassingly unselfish'. Fanny he described as 'defiant, greedy, clumsy, honest as it is possible to be – and with a head on her shoulders'.[8] For

---

[5] DG, *The Flowers of the Forest*, p. 103.

[6] DG/C. Bell, Hilton, 11 February 1961 [Sussex].

[7] HG, 'Aspects of My Father'.

[8] DG/STW, Hilton, 19 January 1962, in RG, ed., *Sylvia and David*, pp 65–6.

Bunny, the 1960s was his daughters' decade. Having enjoyed the swinging twenties, thirties and forties, the sixties offered little that Bunny had not experienced. The women in his life had been sexually liberated decades before. Now seventy, he could watch his daughters from the sidelines, appreciating their beauty and giving them freedom to do as they pleased with whom they pleased.

Angelica was spending more and more time in France. She was there in January 1962, in February and again in May. Bunny wrote to her stating he had been 'going through such emotions about MOBY DICK'.[9] It was not the novel by Herman Melville to which he referred, but a houseboat moored in London, at Cheyne Walk. Bunny thought it a snip at £1,200 (£15,432 today), the perfect solution to Amaryllis's accommodation problems and an ideal London base for himself. It was, however, more like a beached whale than a houseboat, having originally been used in the Dunkirk evacuation and now badly in need of repair.

In a generally buoyant frame of mind, Bunny agreed to go to Alderney at the end of June, to see Tim White, recuperating from heart surgery. Tim's novel *The Once and Future King* had been turned into a highly successful musical, *Camelot*, and as a result he was now both celebrated and wealthy. He had become friendly with the actress Julie Andrews, who starred in the musical, and her then husband, the set-designer Tony Walton. When Bunny met them at Alderney he instantly warmed to them, but as usual he found Tim a strain and was shocked by his emaciated condition.

Later that year, Tim wrote a warm and appreciative letter in which he said that Bunny had been responsible for changing his life. He explained that this occurred late in the 1930s, when he was going through a religious phase. Unaware of Ray's illness,

---

[9] DG/AVG, Hilton, Wednesday 16 May 1962 [KCC].

he had held forth to Bunny on the subject of death and damnation, stating that it was a matter of moral choice whether one ended up in heaven or hell. As he teasingly recalled, 'Very quietly, you said, 'I think (pause) the enormous facts of birth and death (pause) are so *tremendous* (long pause) that all these fairy stories or fables about them are (struggle for the right words) are (long struggle) that they *degrade* them'. 'I am now', Tim announced, 'an agnostic'.[10] He signed the letter, 'your loving TIM'. It was an affectionate tribute, penned fifteen months before his death from coronary heart disease.

In August, Bunny and Angelica went house-hunting in France, focussing on the Lot. Angelica craved distance from Hilton, but it was as though she imagined, or tried to convince herself, that a house in France would supply the fulfilment missing from her life. After viewing a seemingly endless succession of ruined mills, they finally looked around an old *auberge* in the tiny but picturesque village of St Martin-de-Vers, about seventeen miles north-east of Cahors. The house comprised a living room-kitchen, dining room, drawing room, two small bedrooms and a large bedroom; outside a small garden had the benefit of a spring. It belonged to an elderly lady who dismissed any questions about sanitation by pointing to '*une chaise percée*' precariously balanced upon boards over the rubbish heap, which, she informed them, was private and – being in the open air – healthy. Bunny was overcome by the building's charm and he and Angelica decided to buy it, a purchase concluded three months later. This common purpose brought him and Angelica unexpectedly close. What Bunny enjoyed most was 'the freedom

---

[10] THW/DG, Alderney, 12 October 1962, in DG, ed., *White/Garnett Letters*, p. 303.

which for some childish reason I find in buying *paté* from a charcuterie instead of sausages from Mr Anderson'.[11]

The Familiar Faces was published by Chatto & Windus in October 1962. It had taken a long while to write and was, Bunny acknowledged, a painful work. The book came at a fertile period for Bloomsbury memoirs. Leonard Woolf had recently published two volumes, *Sowing* (1960) and *Growing* (1961), and Gerald Brenan published *A Life of One's Own* (1962) which he dedicated to Bunny. Once again Bunny's book was the subject of major reviews, mostly positive. *The Times* concluded that Bunny employed 'all the old skill of pinning a personality to our memory with a single sentence', and that 'the very tones of those years we knew rings true'. Several critics mentioned that Bunny's trilogy (ending in 1940) was already an important reference point for historians of the period. In the journal *Critical Quarterly*, C.L. Mowat singled out Bunny's autobiography for praise. Referring to the spate of literary memoirs which 'draw on a whole set of writers and their friends, and have a value for literary history', he rated Bunny's the 'most delightful and sustained autobiography of this class'.[12]

The *TLS* reviewer, however, complained that Bunny's latest volume was too long and too anecdotal. Raymond Mortimer, in the *Sunday Times* gave a generally glowing review, although he thought that Bunny was too 'occupied with his memories, not with the effect he may make upon his readers'.[13] Mortimer explained to Bunny that he thought he 'seemed to assume in

---

[11] DG/AVG, 'Saturday evening' [8 December 1962] [KCC].

[12] C.L. Mowat, 'From the Edwardian Age to the Thirties: Some Literary Memoirs', *Critical Quarterly*, Vol. 5, No. 2, Summer 1963.

[13] 21 October 1962.

your readers knowledge they cannot have about persons you discuss': a fair point, particularly if the reader had not read the two previous volumes. As a salve, Mortimer praised the 'sweetness with which you speak of your friends', as 'one of the great charms of the book – which makes me love you better than ever'.[14] His main complaint, however, was the omission of an index, which Bunny presumably planned to append to volume four. Other friends wrote similarly appreciative letters. Jamie Hamilton thought it was time they got together to write about their aeroplane. Francis Meynell found the book moving, especially Bunny's portrait of Vera Meynell. Sylvia Townsend Warner praised the book's 'warmth and judiciousness and fortitude', telling Bunny, 'I love you more than ever since this book'.[15] John Hayward, always generous, told Bunny he had 'recaptured & fixed for ever in words [...] the pleasure & pain of loving people & places & of the emotions they once aroused'.[16]

There was one discordant voice: Mina Curtiss could not understand why Bunny felt the need to reveal that she and Henrietta Bingham were undergoing psychoanalysis in the 1920s. She felt it was not only an error of judgement, but a betrayal of trust. She told Bunny his transgression would not affect their friendship, adding: 'in all honesty – and as Proust used to say who wants honesty – I can't help saying that *Familiar Faces* seems to me an extremely self-indulgent book'.[17] Several others drew Bunny's

---

[14] R. Mortimer/DG, 5 Canonbury Place, 19 October 1962 [Northwestern].

[15] STW/DG, Maiden Newton, 17 October 1962, in RG, ed., *Sylvia and David*, p. 68.

[16] JDH/DG, 19 Carlyle Mansions, Cheyne Walk, 3 November 1962 [Northwestern].

[17] M Curtiss/DG, Chapelbrook, 26 November 1962 [Northwestern].

attention to errors of fact, assuming that as with volumes one and two, he would publish errata in volume four. Diana Mosley, a new fan, wrote to tell him how much she liked all three volumes, but that 'Mosleyite fascists' did not exist in the 1920s.

Nellie remained as important to Bunny as ever. She was not interested in material possessions, chastising Bunny for bringing her gifts, wanting only his company, conversation and affection. 'It was so utterly lovely seeing you', she wrote after one visit, 'You bring a world with you that is different from other worlds'.[18] In September 1962, soon after returning from France, Bunny received a letter from Nellie expressing a great longing to see him. 'I want so much to see you', she said, 'I love you and am so happy to think of you'.[19] Nellie was ninety, and having been ill the previous year, remained weak. She had been a mainstay in Bunny's life for so long that it was hard to countenance that she might die. He visited her regularly and was delighted to find her mind undimmed. But this letter of 19 September is the last extant letter from Nellie to Bunny. He did go to see her, and in November was with her just a few days before she died on the 13th. Bunny's cousin Rayne had gone to sit with her and was in the next room when Nellie died in the night. Bunny dealt with her possessions, and also with the disposal of her body, which she left to a teaching hospital. He felt Nellie's loss deeply: he had loved her almost as much as his parents, and had known her almost as long as he knew himself.

On 22 December Henrietta married Burgo Partridge, Frances and Ralph Partridge's son and Bunny's nephew by his marriage

[18] EMH/DG, c/o Dr Wilks, Headley Down, Nr Bordon, Hants, 18 August 1951 [Northwestern].
[19] EMH/DG, Openlands, Headley Down, 19 September 1962 [Northwestern].

to Ray. Henrietta was only seventeen but wildly in love. They made all the wedding arrangements themselves and Frances couldn't help noticing the 'geniality of Bunny', who, with Nellie still on his mind, 'began talking about the necessity of leaving one's body to the doctors'.[20]

Bunny was working on a translation from the French of Victoria Ocampo's psychological investigation of T.E. Lawrence's character *338171 T.E.*[21] This was more to Bunny's taste than the film *Lawrence of Arabia*, which he took Amaryllis to see in January 1963. Although he appreciated the 'marvellous scenes of deserts & camels in colour', he considered that Peter O'Toole's 'impersonation of Lawrence was grotesque & the whole thing really an abomination'.[22] Bunny wrote immediately to Sam Spiegel expressing his gratitude to Spiegel, for not using his script. 'I am indeed fortunate', he added, 'for I have come out of the preposterous affair with clean, though not empty hands'.[23]

The film had been premiered a month previously, at which time A.W. Lawrence charted its inaccuracies in a letter in *The Times*. He also published an article entitled 'The Fiction and the Fact' in the *Observer*, concluding: "I need only say that I should not have recognised my brother".[24] Spiegel published a rejoinder in *The New York Times* in which he skilfully shifted the spotlight from questions of historical accuracy to a personal attack on A.W. Lawrence, whom, he suggested, neither wanted family

---

[20] Partridge, *Hanging On*, p. 139, diary entry for 23 December 1962.

[21] Victoria Ocampo, *338171 T.E.*, trans. David Garnett (London: Victor Gollancz, 1963).

[22] DG/C. Bell, Hilton, 11 January 1963 [Sussex].

[23] DG/S. Spiegel, Hilton, 11 January 1963 [copy] [Northwestern].

[24] Quoted in Crawford, *Richard Aldington*, p. 155.

skeletons rattled nor understood T.E.L.'s narcissistic nature. Spiegel concluded by stating that Lawrence's supporters had profited from selling the film rights, quoting the 'clean, but not empty hands' comment of one biographer.[25] A few months before the film's release, Bunny had taken part in a BBC television documentary entitled *T.E. Lawrence 1888–1935*. As the documentary's producer Malcolm Brown explained, in endeavouring to portray a real person, they deliberately attempted to produce a counterpoint to the David Lean film.[26]

For some time, Bunny's accountant had been pressing him to get rid of the farm at Hilton. It was a drain on resources and Bunny was only too aware that it had placed a strain on his marriage and kept him from writing. It was a hard decision, but in April 1963, while Angelica was in France, Bunny sold his Jersey herd. With Amaryllis pursuing an acting career, Henrietta married and Nerissa at art school in Leeds, only Fanny remained to be settled. But if Bunny hoped that an almost empty nest and no farm would draw Angelica closer or make her feel less tied, he was wrong. Now she usually spent midweek in London where, worried about Duncan, she devoted as much time as she could to him. But there was something to look forward to: Henrietta was expecting a baby, and Bunny rejoiced in the way this would again result in a Marshall-Garnett child. He informed Mina that the baby 'will be curiously related to my other grandsons as his mother will be their aunt and his father their first cousin once-removed'.[27] The baby

[25] Quoted in Crawford, *Richard Aldington*, p. 155.

[26] Malcolm Brown, 'An Introduction to the BBC 1962 documentary *T.E. Lawrence 1888–1935*', *Journal of the T.E. Lawrence Society*, Vol. 1, No. 1, Spring 1991.

[27] DG/M. Curtiss, Hilton, 20 June 1963 [Berg].

would be Oliver's and Ned's half-cousin on the Garnett side and second cousin on the Marshall.

In July, two young Americans, Peter Stansky and William Abrahams, joined Bunny for lunch at Hilton. An historian, Stansky was a graduate of King's College, Cambridge and of Harvard and went on to a distinguished academic career. Abrahams was a poet and novelist, and would become a highly respected literary editor. They were jointly writing a biography of Julian Bell and the poet John Cornford, both of whom lost their lives in the Spanish Civil War.[28] That same month Bunny had tea at the Reform Club with Leon Edel, the great Henry James scholar and biographer. But there was one other biographer, whom Bunny first met that summer of 1963, who would change the face of literary biography and in the process rattle the nerves of the elderly gentlemen of Bloomsbury. The biographer was Michael Holroyd, then embarking on his life of Lytton Strachey.

Bunny's relationship with Holroyd began much as it would continue. The problem with Bunny was that he was 'on the whole in favour of truth in biography – but not at the expense of the happiness of the living & their security'.[29] Like other Bloomsberries, Bunny was caught between a temperamental desire for openness and an instinctive inclination towards caution, as his reply to Holroyd's request for an interview reveals:

(1) 'Naturally I will give you any help I can.'
(2) 'But – as I have experiences of biographers who either impose their own preconceived ideas on their subjects, or

---

[28] Published as *Journey to the Frontier: Julian Bell and John Cornford: Their Lives and the 1930s* (London: Constable, 1966).

[29] DG/J. Strachey, Hilton, 29 June 1966 [BL].

are by nature temperamentally incapable of ever understanding what these subjects were like, I won't make
promises.'

(3) 'Such reservations are really foolish. We had better meet [...]
and I will try to tell you something about the Lytton I knew.'[30]

Having met Holroyd at the Reform Club over tea and buttered
toast, Bunny was sufficiently impressed to invite him to read
Lytton's letters at Hilton. Indeed he was so amiably disposed that
he suggested Holroyd bring his bathing drawers. On 19 June
Holroyd spent the day at Hilton and as a result felt he and Bunny
had 'got on very well'.[31] Bunny thought Holroyd 'a charming
young man'.[32]

Bunny and Angelica spent August at St Martin-de-Vers. It was
an odd time to go away, as Henrietta's baby was overdue.
Henrietta was only eighteen, and it might be supposed that it
would be comforting to have her parents close by. Frances
Partridge, felt 'considerable agitation' at 'this seeming desertion'.[33]
On 9 August Bunny and Angelica received a telegram announcing the birth of their grand-daughter, Sophie Vanessa. She had
been born by caesarean section two days after Henrietta was
rushed into hospital with suspected toxaemia. Bunny felt such
anxiety for Henrietta that going for a walk to garner his thoughts,
he lost his way. In London, Frances was angry with Bunny and
Angelica, writing, tersely, 'I don't know how much you really
want to hear about this agonising week?' although she reassured

[30] DG/M. Holroyd, Menton, 14 December [1962] [BL]; my numeration.
[31] Michael Holroyd, interviewed by the author, August 2010.
[32] DG/M. Curtiss, Hilton, 20 June 1963 [Berg].
[33] Partridge, *Hanging On*, p. 177, diary entry for 1 August 1963.

them that mother and baby were fine.[34] Burgo told Bunny that Henrietta ('simply marvellous, patient & brave') was 'tired but very happy'.[35]

Despite this joyful news and all the hopes pinned on L'Ancienne Auberge, Bunny and Angelica were not getting along. Bunny felt separation inevitable. But on 7 September their problems had to be put aside: they received another telegram, this time stating that Burgo had died. He had suffered an aortic aneurism while Henrietta was in the bath and baby Sophie asleep in her cot. Bunny immediately returned to England to collect his daughter and grand-daughter and bring them to France. Lunching with Frances Partridge, he was unable to express his sorrow for her loss, focussing instead on practical matters, but he wrote afterwards telling Frances he felt 'such love' for her, and wished they could have talked more.[36]

Henrietta and Sophie spent only nine days in France before Angelica put them on a plane for England. Frances could not understand Bunny's apparent lack of sympathy, recording in her diary, 'I feel somehow in spite of all that is endearing in Bunny a certain ruthless selfishness and lack of sensitivity. He simply can't begin to imagine the nature of the shock Henrietta experienced.'[37] Of course Frances also referred to her own pain. But she had responded to Burgo's death with apparent forbearance, insisting

---

[34] F. Partridge/DG, Flat 5, 14 West Halkin Street, Saturday night 10 August 1963 [KCC].

[35] B. Partridge/DG, 35 Cadogan Square, Saturday 10 August [1963] [Northwestern].

[36] DG/F. Partridge, St Martin-de-Vers, 'Tuesday Morning' [16 September 1963] [KCC].

[37] Partridge, *Other People*, p. 16, diary entry for 4 October 1963.

on 'no funeral, no wake, and no grave'.[38] In the circumstances, perhaps Bunny thought it inappropriate to show emotion, or assumed that Frances, who went on holiday to Italy less than a fortnight after Burgo's death, was stronger than she appeared. But a year later, reading the entries for September 1963 in his 'Log Book of the Car', Bunny was 'shocked to find what we left out: Burgo's death'.[39] Perhaps Bunny was insensitive; perhaps he had simply been intent on removing Henrietta and Sophie from the immediacy of the situation. Perhaps, as the Log Book was kept by both Bunny and Angelica, this sad event fell unrecorded, between them.

Bunny and Angelica returned to England in October. Their relationship under considerable strain, Bunny half-heartedly considered moving to New York. But it was Angelica who made a move: in December she decided to take a studio in London. Bunny wrote to tell Nerissa, lodging with Quentin and Olivier in Leeds, that it was 'an enormous & very grand studio', adding 'I don't expect that we shall see much of her in the coming year'.[40] A few days later Fanny was accepted as a pupil at Dartington College. With the exception of William, it appeared Bunny would be left at Hilton, quite alone.

---

[38] Ann Chisholm, *Frances Partridge: The Biography* (London: Weidenfeld & Nicolson, 2009), p. 276.

[39] DG, Log Book of the Car, 25 July 1964 [Northwestern].

[40] DG/N. Garnett, Hilton, 14 December 1963 [AOB].

Chapter Thirty-Two

'I have determined not to feel bitter and only to do so when I lie awake in the early hours.'[1]

Bunny's novel, *Two by Two*, was published in the autumn of 1963.[2] Its sub-title, 'A Story of Survival', gives the game away: ostensibly about Noah's Ark and the Flood, it was actually an evolutionary reinterpretation of the Old Testament story, with a bit of Big Bang Theory for good measure. Reviewers were quick to look for a political message, and some found one in the shape of Noah, whom Bunny portrayed as a drunken despot. David Pryce-Jones, in the *Sunday Times*, congratulated Bunny on his 'courageous publication'. If he was courageous, it was in disparaging the Biblical version of events.

Approaching the subject from a rational and scientific perspective, Bunny stated in the Preface: 'In this scientific age the story of the Deluge raises many scientific questions. How did the plants fare? What did the herbivorous animals eat until the grass

---

[1] DG/STW, Hilton, 2 March 1966, in RG, ed., *Sylvia and David*, p. 100.
[2] David Garnett, *Two by Two: A Story of Survival* (London: Longmans, 1963).

grew again? How did the carnivores manage to wait until their natural prey had obeyed the Divine command to be fruitful and multiply?'[3] Bunny's Ark is surrounded by floating corpses, bloated with gas from the effects of decomposition.

The book is dedicated to Fanny and Nerissa, who are present in the text in the shape of Fan and Niss, twins who stow themselves away in the Ark disguised as monkeys. Fan maintains that the deluge should not automatically be attributed to God: 'just because we are ignorant and can't be bothered to think it out'.[4] Instead, she concludes 'It was because of some big universal change'.[5] Fanny Garnett found her presence in her father's fiction disconcerting because he used 'anecdotes of things that had happened or things that he valued about us', and, as a fabulist, embroidered them. She thought it was all part of his disbelief in the afterlife: 'the only way he could actually continue in any way was either through his children or through his writing'.[6]

The critics liked the novel, although now Bunny was often reviewed in a job-lot with other novelists, rather than as the star turn. Simon Raven, in the *Observer*, was amused by Bunny's 'pleasant little joke';[7] *The Times* commented, tautologically, on the 'two enchanting girl twins', praising Bunny's 'mixture of rationalism and lyricism'.[8] In the *Guardian*, Anne Duchene described the novel as 'a wonderfully robust little fantasy in

---

[3] Ibid., p. vii.

[4] Ibid., p. 65.

[5] Ibid., p. 87.

[6] F. Garnett, interview, 31 May 2008.

[7] 29 September 1963.

[8] 3 October 1963.

marvellously unstrained prose [...]. Not the very best Garnett; but a great refreshment.'[9]

Feeling lonely, Bunny tried to persuade Frances Partridge to accompany him to Spain. Since Ralph's death, she and Bunny had grown closer, partly an outcome of their mutual concerns for Henrietta and Sophie. Frances declined, but Bunny kept to his plan to travel to Malaga to visit Gerald and Gamel Brenan. It was the journey, rather than the arrival, that mattered. He hoped to gain solace from a meandering drive through France, to find happiness in a landscape he loved. Before leaving, he wrote to Angelica, in January 1964, telling her it was not her fault 'that your feelings for me have come to an end', but that it was his 'misfortune that they should have come to an end now'.[10]

Bunny planned to spend six weeks away, a fortnight with the Brenans sandwiched between driving through France and touring Spain. But he found the French countryside almost unbearable to countenance, the memories of earlier tours crowding upon him. He returned to Génainville, where he had stayed with Ray and the boys in 1931 and meandered along the same back roads he had travelled with Duncan in 1927. It was as if too many avenues of memory converged: Ray; Duncan; Angelica. 'Sometimes', he wrote to Angelica, 'the country is so beautiful in its melancholy contours & spinneys & little streams that I feel I could be happy looking at nothing but nature all my life. But if so why this letter? Why try to communicate?'[11] Bunny wrote to Angelica almost every day. He hated being lonely and instinctively turned to her, his letters full of love, sadness and remorse.

----

[9] Friday 4 October 1963.

[10] DG/AVG, Hilton, [January 1964] [KCC].

[11] DG/AVG, 'Beside a beech wood', 31 January 1964 [KCC].

'The thing is', he said, 'however much I try to avoid it, I love you & shall find it impossible to live wholly without you'.[12]

Angelica was businesslike in her replies, abandoning their mutual nickname, 'Catt', addressing him as 'Bunny', and signing off 'Angelica'. Having shed some of the ties which bound, at Charleston Angelica still felt engulfed by an 'awful recognition of the past' in which she could 'no longer feel my own identity; my eyes get full of the colours & patterns I see there, which I long to dissociate myself from – the result is [...] absolute misery'.[13] It was not only family life at Hilton which oppressed Angelica. Her mother, her childhood, her memories were all part of the mix.

At *Casa Brenan*, Bunny enjoyed reminiscing with Gerald, but Gerald's affability soon waned and Bunny was glad to leave. Loneliness engulfed him. Even the possibility of meeting Henrietta in Madrid was too much: he couldn't countenance 'another week on a lonely pilgrimage in this part of Spain'. 'To tell the truth', Bunny wrote to Angelica, 'I am still in despair about my life. I find it too boring to live alone. And pointless to live without intimacy & love.'[14]

During Bunny's absence Angelica lived at her Fulham Road studio, venturing to Hilton for an occasional weekend. With William the sole occupant, Hilton Hall was cold, untidy, empty and sad. It must have been difficult for him, living alone in a house replete with memories, a palimpsest of family life, first with Ray and Richard, later with Angelica and his sisters. Believing 'the sooner we left it', 'all the better', Angelica tried to raise the

---

[12] DG/AVG, Hotel de France, Chateau sur Loire, 5 February 1964 [KCC].

[13] AVG/DG, Studio B, 404 Fulham Road, SW6, Sunday 9 February [1964] [KCC].

[14] DG/AVG, between Avila and Segovia, Spain, 7 March 1964 [KCC].

subject with Will. 'I simply lacked courage however to talk about the future or his ideas about life', she told Bunny. 'I think one must wait for the right moment or he will simply shut up like an oyster.'[15] While Angelica endeavoured to negotiate a diminution of family life, to map an independent existence, Bunny continued to hope that some compromise could be reached. 'Can't we manage to have a bit of everything?' he asked. 'Some months at Hilton, some in France.'[16] 'The trouble is', Angelica replied, 'I am happy here – I don't want to start a full family life again. I suppose it's as selfish as hell – but I've had my whack of it.'[17] For seventeen-year-old Fanny, away at college, Angelica's move to London came as a surprise and a shock; it was settled during her absence, and she returned to a *fait accompli*.

Frances Partridge was saddened by the sudden recognition that Bunny and Angelica were 'two quite disconnected people'. Visiting Hilton, at the end of May, she observed Angelica's 'grey eyes looking at him very coolly now', concluding, 'I would be frightened if I were him'.[18] She noticed Bunny's 'slightly bewildered loneliness because of Angelica's withdrawal, and his kindness and sweetness to his children'. 'Angelica hates this house', she concluded. 'No love for poor old Hilton from her now.'[19] Suddenly comprehending the situation, Jane Garnett wept with shock.

Bunny turned to Rosemary Hinchingbrooke for comfort, believing, perhaps, that she might furnish the intimacy he craved,

---

[15] AVG/DG, Tuesday 4 February [1964] [KCC].

[16] DG/AVG, Hotel de France, Chateau sur Loire, 5 February 1964 [KCC].

[17] AVG/DG, Studio B, 404 Fulham Road, Friday 13 March [1964] [KCC].

[18] Partridge, *Other People*, p. 57, diary entry for 29 May 1964.

[19] Ibid., p. 58, diary entry for 30 May 1964.

as she had left her husband (reverting to her maiden name, 'Peto'). As far as she was concerned, it was one thing to be intimate with Bunny and Angelica as individuals when they were a couple, but the dynamic had changed. She urged him to 'find someone who will be glad to give you everything you want & need'.[20] Bunny wasn't sure anyone would want a man of seventy-two. Anyway, all he wanted was Angelica.

He recognised that Angelica had been torn for a long time, between family on one side and freedom on the other. 'Perhaps', he conceded, 'any attempt to reconcile them is a mistake.'[21] Therein lay the rub. Angelica acknowledged she found it 'difficult to decide between two opposite extremes'.[22] Caught between them, she felt trapped. Nevertheless, Bunny hoped that a planned holiday at L'Ancienne Auberge might bind them again, but with William and Fanny in tow and various guests added to the mix, the holiday was hardly conducive. The atmosphere was not improved by the arrival of a telegram bringing bad news about Clive Bell's health, nor a subsequent letter announcing his death on 18 September. Neither Bunny nor Angelica returned for the funeral.

After alighting briefly in England on 23 October Bunny flew to the United States, for a lecture tour of the Universities of Southern Illinois, Davis, California and Austin, Texas. He would also participate in a D.H. Lawrence symposium at Taos. He hoped to spend Christmas in Mexico and planned to stay in the US until January. Arriving in New York he dined with Shusheila Lall, spent a day with George Kirstein and went to see Carson McCullers at Nyack. At Carbondale, Southern Illinois, Bunny's itinerary was punishing,

[20] R. Peto/DG, Windleshore, Isle of Wight [pmk 4 May 1964] [Northwestern].

[21] DG/AVG, Hilton, 10 July 1964 [KCC].

[22] AVG/DG, Butts Intake, Thursday 2 April [1959] [KCC].

classes starting at eight in the morning and continuing until 9 o'clock at night. His T.E. Lawrence lecture was well attended, but Bunny found it irritating that the audience was interested in Lawrence because they had seen the film. He also found it difficult to gauge his audience: 'One class burst into rounds of applause when I finished. Others sometimes looked baffled.'[23]

Angelica was disappointed to find her legacy from Clive Bell tied up in trust, so she would not be able to spend capital on a new studio. She found her rented studio too cramped to accommodate the children: 'If it wasn't that we all have to live in one room', she complained, 'I should love having them, but as it is I cannot help finding it rather bitter that they have so far taken up about 3 months of this year here when I had hoped to prove to myself that I could work'.[24] She was not, however, entirely open with Bunny, as she was, in fact, in the throes of house-hunting, and had gone as far as to commission a surveyor's report on a property in Islington.

Angelica eventually plucked up courage to write to Bunny about her plans. 'IF I DO buy', she disingenuously reassured him, 'there is no reason why you should not come and live there with me whenever you want to. I shall have the studio separate from the living room, so that we can both work independently.'[25] They both knew this was untenable. Notwithstanding that Angelica no longer wanted to live in the country and Bunny could not face living permanently in London, Angelica wanted freedom. 'I have reached a time of life' she explained, 'which as a man you haven't experienced, when the demands of my own

[23] DG/F. Partridge, Carbondale, 23 November [1964] [KCC].

[24] AVG/DG, Studio B, 404 Fulham Road, London, 6 November [1964] [KCC].

[25] AVG/DG, Studio B, 404 Fulham Road, 25 November [1964] [KCC].

nature have become imperative, and I feel I must satisfy them or go under. It is the last chance for me.'[26]

From America Bunny replied: 'I don't want to be abandoned and you are in fact abandoning me.'[27] He was powerless to stop Angelica, and, it may be assumed, she had chosen her moment carefully. 'Your letter', she wrote, 'seems primarily to be a cry of anguish because you hadn't realised that I wanted to continue living in London most of the time.' She pointed out that she would soon be financially independent: 'a minimum of 700 a year from Clive, and I stand to inherit all Duncan's money and half Virginia's'.[28] The house in France was in Angelica's name. Being financially independent, she was able to do what Ray could not: leave Bunny. But there was a fundamental difference in attitude between the two women. Angelica wanted to be free to pursue an independent life, a life in which Bunny would be welcome only by invitation. Ray, on the other hand, wanted to be with Bunny more than anything, but she wanted him to be faithful. It was as if Angelica had become Bunny's nemesis.

Bunny could do little but focus on his teaching. At Davis, California, he was asked to go over to Berkeley to examine D.H. Lawrence's *Sons and Lovers* manuscript, where he was fascinated to discover that Edward had deleted passages on ninety-three pages, 'not because of improprieties but simply because the book was far too long'.[29] His teaching complete, and

[26] AVG/DG, Studio B, 404 Fulham Road, 25 November [1964] [KCC].

[27] DG/AVG, Denver, Colorado, 29 November [1964] [KCC].

[28] AVG/DG, Studio B, 404 Fulham Road, 4 December 1964 [KCC].

[29] DG/AVG, c/o Professor Wayne Harsh, 32 Oakside Drive, Davis, 5 Davis, 1964 [KCC].

before participating in the Lawrence symposium, Bunny visited the Lawrence Ranch, accompanied by Harry Moore, his host and friend at Carbondale, by David Chambers, the brother of Jessie Chambers, Lawrence's first love, and by his current hosts, Professor E.W. Tedlock and Warren Roberts.

If anything could raise Bunny's spirits, it was the wonder of spending Christmas travelling in Mexico with E.W. Tedlock's son, Dennis, an extremely knowledgeable guide, later a distinguished authority on Mayan literature and culture. Bunny found him an ideal companion. They journeyed by bus to Mexico City which Bunny considered like 'a city in the United States with all its faults but not its amenities'. But Oaxaca and Puebla were altogether different, the latter 'a most delightful heavenly city, brilliantly illuminated, full of masses of gay people & crowded markets'.[30] From Oaxaca they visited the magnificent Mesoamerican stepped pyramids of the Sun and Moon, climbing to the top of the former to enjoy the glorious view. Bunny hoped that one day he would be able to visit Mexico with Angelica. 'Do you think there is still a chance of my doing so?' he asked her.[31] On 6 January 1965 he flew to Texas to deliver his final lecture. Then he spent a week in New York, where he dined with Mina Curtiss and Lincoln Kirstein and with Duncan's former lover, George Bergen. Returning to London on 15 January, he found his family delighted to see him and Angelica unusually affectionate.

Frances Partridge commented that Bunny was 'magnificent – brave as a lion, full of interesting news of America'. She also noticed that he and Angelica 'seem to have re-entered an area of

---

[30] DG/AVG, Puebla Mexico, 31 December 1964 [KCC].

[31] DG/AVG, Hotel Belpra, Ponciano Arriaga, Mexico City, 5 January 1965 [KCC].

mutual warmth and affection most delightful to witness'.[32] To some extent Angelica had overcome that feeling of being trapped between opposite extremes. She had reached a decision regarding not living with Bunny and stuck to it. Even so, she was not immune to guilt. She was forty-six, the very age Bunny had been when she fell in love with him; he was seventy-three. She was not impervious to his concerns about being left alone in old age. She did not want to return to Hilton, but felt she could at least commit to holidays with Bunny.

So, on 18 March Bunny and Angelica embarked on a two-month vacation, driving through France and Italy to Greece. But having lived mainly separately since the previous October, the enforced closeness of travelling together served only to re-activate the fault lines in their relationship. During the first week Bunny's pocket diary is peppered with phrases such as 'Decided on divorce' and 'Despair'. In France they collected Angelica's friend, Marriott Lefevre, who would spend three weeks travelling with them. Thus it was difficult for Bunny and Angelica to either vent their frustration or nurture intimacy.

At Andritsaena in Greece, Bunny awoke from a nightmare in which he was travelling by sea to India with Rupert Hart-Davis, to find an earthquake in progress. Bunny and Angelica held hands and were joined in their room by Marriott and an elderly lady, lost in the black-out. Bunny irritated Angelica with his detached curiosity, but the next day, in Bassae, where many houses were in ruins, he was overcome by the devastation. Seeing how people's lives had been changed overnight, he reflected on the state of his marriage, deciding divorce was the only solution.

After Marriott's departure on 15 April, the atmosphere

---

[32] Partridge, *Other People*, p. 106, diary entry for 18 January 1965.

improved. Bunny and Angelica rendezvoused with Frances Partridge and her friend Eardley Knollys at Orta, in Italy, where they had a delightful time, 'reading, talking, eating, going for a walk & botanising', the latter something which Frances and Bunny would progressively enjoy together.[33] Frances noticed that Bunny and Angelica 'left the bath strikingly dirty', as they had 'evidently been roughing it'.[34] Given Bunny's Spartan tendencies, they had lodged in cheap hotels. Even so, he spent much of the holiday mired in what he called his 'imbecile obsession about money'.[35]

By the end of the holiday everything seemed more positive and Angelica even told Bunny she would return to Hilton, *pro tem*. But she didn't, instead buying the Islington house. Dining with Bunny in June, Frances Partridge's 'heart contracted', hearing 'his sad and quavering voice saying how he hated the idea of living in London, that it tired him dashing up and down and he got melancholy and lonely at Hilton with no one but William'.[36] With the family axis shifting from Hilton to London, the structure of Bunny's life crumbled. There was no work to take him to the capital, no purpose other than to see Angelica, who did not want to see him.

At Hilton, with only William for company, Bunny was working on an edition of his correspondence with Tim White, who had died the previous year. He was also writing a preface for an edition of Tim's American diary, to be published by Putnam.[37]

---

[33] DG, 'Drive Spring 1965', Orta, Casa Forbes, 2 May [Northwestern].

[34] Partridge, *Other People*, pp. 128–9, diary entry for 3 May 1965.

[35] DG, 'Drive Spring 1965', Brindisi, 27 April [Northwestern].

[36] Partridge, *Other People*, p. 137, diary entry for 18 June 1965.

[37] T.H. White, *America at Last: The American Journal of T.H. White with an introduction by David Garnett* (New York: G.P. Putnam's Sons, 1965).

As Bunny told Sylvia Townsend Warner, 'I find that almost all my remarks about Tim are rather disobliging. And I begin to feel as irritated as if he were actually in the house.' 'Both Ray & I loved Tim', he explained, '& he certainly was remarkable. But somehow he always got things wrong.'[38]

Henrietta Garnett described Bunny as 'one of the most generous people I have ever known'.[39] At this time he had little to be generous with, running Hilton, L'Ancienne Auberge and Moby Dick while contributing to the support of all four daughters. Nevertheless, when Angelica's former drama teacher, Michel St Denis, fell on hard times, having suffered ill health, Bunny arranged to pay him £5 a month. He also established modest trust funds for Harry and Rosemary, his former farm workers, and for Betty May.

Late in the summer Bunny and Angelica took their – now regular – holiday at St Martin-de-Vers. Bunny stayed on afterwards, returning to a novel he had abandoned because he could not develop a story-line. Nevertheless, he remained absorbed by the characters, 'And so I write about them although I haven't anything to say – except there is this bunch of people'. Bunny had also embarked on a fourth volume of memoirs, but it was not a propitious time to be looking back to the years immediately following Ray's death, when he and Angelica had been united in love.

Bunny received a luncheon invitation from Angela Derville, the daughter of his old friend Alec Penrose, who lived with her French husband, Joe, a short distance away at the Château de Charry, near Montcuq. Bunny arrived on 24 October resplendent in a new beret which he thought made him look French. He

---

[38] DG/STW, Hilton, 18 February 1965 [Berg].
[39] HG, 'Aspects of My Father'.

was charmed by Angela and Joe. 'They will be a great help to us I feel sure', he told Angelica, adding, 'I suppose you are busy with your Château in St Peter's Street'.[40] Angelica was, indeed, busy overseeing alterations and repairs. Bunny found solitude strange: with no one to occupy the present, he found himself going over and over the past.

Angelica tried to spend weekends with Bunny at Hilton and to maintain a semblance of family life, but by January 1966 the situation had again become untenable. Bunny found her uncommunicative and unapproachable, always scraping away at her violin. He could not understand why she bothered to come back at weekends, as she had nothing to say. Angelica evidently felt as hopeless as Bunny, asking 'is it any good going on as we are? Ought we not to divorce or separate?' 'I always felt', she added, 'that it would be cruel abandonment if I left you; but I see now that this is probably conceited and that it's perhaps crueller to stay in this way, only half and half.'[41] Bunny reluctantly agreed. 'The agony', he told Angelica, 'will be the thousands of little things.' 'When you married me I didn't think it would last for more than ten years. But you aren't too old to find someone with whom you can blossom.'[42] 'There are moments', Angelica told Bunny, 'when I feel terrified of a lonely future – I don't seem to be a very attractive woman.'[43] 'Our whole trouble', Bunny replied, 'is that I find you too attractive & that is the reason for our parting'.[44]

[40] DG/AVG, St Martin-de-Vers, Lot, Lundi 24 October 1965 [KCC].
[41] AVG/DG, 79 St Peter's Street, Thursday [27 January 1966] [KCC].
[42] DG/AVG, Hilton, Friday 28 January 1966 [KCC].
[43] AVG/DG, 79 St Peter's Street, [3 February 1966] [KCC].
[44] DG/AVG, 'Sunday' [January 1966] [KCC].

Frances Partridge could not help but be moved by Bunny's 'sad face and trembling hand', reflecting that at his age 'how cruel to be left suddenly without support'. Reading aloud Henry King's poem on the death of his wife, Bunny almost broke down. Frances thought it 'expressed almost too poignantly his sadness at the loss of his own'.[45] 'Meanwhile', she observed, 'he valiantly takes on the cooking and housekeeping.' When Sylvia Townsend Warner arrived for a weekend at Hilton, she was shocked to see Bunny so changed. 'He is still riddled with shock', she recorded in her diary, 'and talks slower than ever, and though we were all gay at dinner there was a sensation of how well we were keeping it up.'[46]

The ensuing months were an agony of indecision. Should they separate? Should they divorce? Was divorce too final? Should they merely live apart? Having settled on divorce, Bunny panicked. 'I want you to think over what we are doing', he wrote to Angelica. 'It means amputation – your never coming back to Hilton where there is so much that we share. It has arisen because our bodies have grown different ways, but it is madness to let them dictate our whole lives.'[47] Rosemary advised Angelica against divorce and William, protective of Bunny, also tried to steer her away from the idea. But Angelica began to remove her possessions from Hilton: paintings which had long graced the walls, rugs from the floor, the silver Duncan and Vanessa gave her as a wedding gift.

Angelica spent much time discussing the situation with Rosemary Peto, who was undergoing psychoanalysis with Michael Fordham.[48] Under Rosie's influence, Angelica began a

---

[45] Partridge, *Other People*, pp. 201–2; diary entry for 19 February 1966.

[46] RG, ed., *Sylvia and David*, p. 102.

[47] DG/AVG, Saturday 12 February 1966 [KCC].

[48] The brother of Theadora Fordham.

process of self-analysis, trying to understand her motives, past and present. Temperamentally attracted to explanations which shielded her of responsibility (her parents' 'deception' regarding her father; Bunny's 'victory' in taking her from her parents), she suddenly had what she described as a 'flash of truth', a realisation that the sexual difficulties between her and Bunny were 'all on <u>my</u> side' and that, as she told Bunny, 'I was using sex as a weapon against you & was not, as I had been assuming, a <u>victim</u> of bad sex relations, but the <u>originator</u> of them'. Whilst this bombshell might have given Bunny cause for hope, it was only momentary, for Angelica then announced that sex with Bunny would still be difficult, because, early in their marriage 'I was in love with you as a father-substitute, never having enjoyed a full parental relation with a real father. Now that I have fully realised the character of this love, there is mere vacuity instead of sexual desire.'[49]

Then Angelica dropped another bombshell. 'I have arrived', she told Bunny, 'at a new point of view, and I hope you can bear a little more analysis from me.' She now wondered whether 'clinging to the theory of the father substitute' was an 'effort to produce something behind which to hide', that in fact she had 'until now failed to grow up'. Better still, 'if I could grow up', she suggested, 'I might be able to cope with all the difficulties and in all important ways with our relationship'. She added that 'a bird in the hand is worth two in the bush'.[50]

Bunny thought that 'Five months of solitude and heart-searching' had made Angelica even more beautiful.[51] After their

---

[49] AVG/DG, 79 St Peter's Street, 2 April [1966] [KCC].

[50] AVG/DG [May 1966] [KCC].

[51] DG/STW, Hilton, 19 May 1966, in RG, ed., *Sylvia and David*, p. 103.

reconciliation Frances Partridge noted with pleasure that they appeared 'to be as sweetly happy and united as anyone could wish'.[52] As Bunny wrote to Sylvia, 'there may be more surprises in store – probably painful ones. But I am feeling very happy.'[53] For years he had clung to every shred of hope Angelica offered. Now that she seemed to have resolved her own conflicted feelings, could there be lasting harmony between them?

[52] Partridge, *Other People*, p. 222; diary entry for 22 May 1966.
[53] DG/STW, Hilton, 19 May 1966, in RG, ed., *Sylvia and David*, p. 103.

Chapter Thirty-Three

'History repeats itself.'[1]

In the spring of 1966 Bunny finally completed a novel which had occupied him, on and off, for eight years. He called it *Ulterior Motives*, and was delighted that it was accepted by his former American publisher, Harcourt Brace.[2] All the more so when Hiram Haydn, his US editor, complemented Bunny for being 'so graceful & tough minded, so wise & sometimes so ferocious. It is a great blend & I am proud to be your publisher.'[3]

It was a ferocious book, for it had begun as a revenge novel, aimed at Rupert Hart-Davis. Bunny's preliminary notes stated it was about a 'man with a compulsion to deceive and swindle – RHD', 'the man who always has an ulterior motive'.[4] By the time Bunny completed the novel he had moved some distance from his own ulterior motives, although Rollo Kitson, the single

---

[1] DG/FP, St Martin-de-Vers, 11 October 1967 [KCC].
[2] David Garnett, *Ulterior Motives* (London: Longmans, 1966).
[3] Quoted in DG/AVG, Hilton, 21 March 1966 [KCC].
[4] DG, Notebook for 'Ulterior Motives', unpublished MS [Northwestern].

unsympathetic character in an otherwise agreeable cast, resembles Rupert physically, if drawn in an unflattering light. His face was 'enormous and exactly the colour of underdone cold beef and the short hairs of his moustache and the eyelashes and eyebrows were the colour of yellow oatstraw'.[5] Bunny portrayed Kitson as an unscrupulous businessman battening financially on his subordinate business partner.

Set in France and Geneva, the novel concerns an Anglo-French family headed by St Clair de Beaumont, a writer, loosely based on Angelica's former tutor, Michel St Denis. Like St Denis, the fictional St Clair de Beaumont broadcast to the French during the Second World War, encouraging his countrymen to stand fast against their German oppressors. St Clair has two daughters, Pasionara and Alamein, and a son Winston who is strongly attracted to the bluff Captain Kitson. St Clair's nephew, Amadeo, is in love with Alamein, but when Kitson latches onto the family, he endeavours not only to wrench Alamein from Amadeo, but also, for personal gain, to exploit St Clair's wealth and Amadeo's talent as an inventor.

The book contains themes common among Bunny's novels: homosexuality and the blurring of sexual boundaries; young women taking older men as lovers; women's entitlement to financial and sexual independence. But in one respect it differs considerably from his previous work. The blurb summarises the novel as a 'light but far from frivolous story', perhaps because some of the ideas about human relationships therein derive from the sociologist Jacob Moreno. Bunny certainly lifted the word 'telefactor' (the name he gives to Amadeo's invention) from this source. Moreover, Moreno's contention that the underlying and

---

5 DG, *Ulterior Motives*, p. 12.

surface structures of human society are mutually influential and cannot be detached from each other appears to have attracted Bunny, for it is one of the themes he develops in this book.[6]

Bunny, who always saw himself as both scientist and novelist, would have enjoyed the idea that science can explain a deeper reality beneath superficial appearances, just as the novelist, in the words of St Clair de Beaumont, deals with 'truths of the imagination'.[7] But in *Ulterior Motives* Bunny cleverly utilises Moreno's underlying and surface structures in a disquisition on morality which provides a socio-scientific rationale for his own double-standards in marriage. Alamein's uncle explains:

> I am a scientist and I do not believe in sin. But I am telling you that there are two standards of value, or of behaviour. Each of them is equally necessary. Because they conflict we conceal most of our sexual lives and usually hide part of them from our sexual partners [...]. But a double standard about sex is inevitable because the demands of the sex cells are irreconcilable with decent behaviour. And just as their existence as a separate form of human life is scarcely recognised, so their demands are unrecognised and misapprehended.[8]

Bunny dedicated the book to Harold Hobson in 'gratitude for a friendship begun in 1898'.

The novel also contains a sly dig at Michael Holroyd. Bunny had largely forgotten about the impending biography of Lytton

---

[6] See Jacob L. Moreno, 'The Sociometric View of the Community', *Journal of Educational Sociology*, Vol. 19, No. 9, May 1946, p. 540.

[7] DG, *Ulterior Motives*, p. 9.

[8] Ibid., pp. 37–8.

Strachey, but in June 1966 he went over to Frances Partridge's London flat to collect Holroyd's completed manuscript (volume one) left there by Duncan. This Bunny read over the next few days with growing alarm. He objected most to the 'great mischief' he believed the published biography would cause. For Bunny maintained 'the rule should be roughly that physical details be omitted' and that biographers 'should not go into other people's love affairs'.[9] He was particularly concerned about how Lydia Lopokova and Geoffrey Keynes might feel in relation to revelations about Maynard's sexuality, and suggested that these revelations should be 'translated into terms of intimate friendship'.[10]

Bunny's overriding concern was that his friends, Duncan chief among them, would have their sexual lives and sexuality exposed. This was a real concern at a time – before the Sexual Offence Act of 1967 – when homosexual acts remained illegal. Robert Skidelsky, in his biography of Maynard Keynes, succinctly encapsulates the double-lives which homosexuals of the Bloomsbury generation had to maintain, especially if they were in the public eye: 'Much in Keynes's life was coded, hidden from the prying outsider. His extreme reluctance to give interviews testifies to his self-protectiveness. He was not as he seemed, in appearance, habit or thought.'[11] For the elderly gentlemen of Bloomsbury, it was a worrying prospect that their long-drawn shutters of secrecy would be thrown open. Duncan even feared arrest.[12]

---

[9] DG/J. Strachey, Hilton, 29 June 1966 [BL].
[10] DG/J. Strachey, Hilton, 29 June 1966 [BL].
[11] Robert Skidelsky, *John Maynard Keynes: The Economist as Saviour 1920–1937* (London: Macmillan 1992; Papermac 1994), p. 422.
[12] Spalding, *Duncan Grant*, p. 457.

It was a difficult matter to confront, for it undermined Bloomsbury's belief in openness, although this openness was normally directed internally rather than towards a wider world. Bunny allowed the fictional St Clair to ventriloquise his concerns and those of much of Bloomsbury, about having their private lives revealed:

> I have these old fashioned reticences. What I would like to tell my friends – for I conceal nothing – I would frankly dislike to see in print. In spite of all the enlightenment which has burst on us in these latter years, the old fashioned prejudices exist, I do not share them. But perhaps I am still a little afraid of them.[13]

Bunny threw himself into the 'Holroyd Question', firing off anxious letters to James Strachey and Duncan Grant. James admitted, grudgingly, that he found the biography 'quite entertaining, and that in spite of the author's efforts, Lytton's character does […] begin to come through. And it can't be doubted that the young man has taken quite an immense amount of trouble.'[14] Duncan wrote to Holroyd, stating that he could not 'help feeling very much averse to having my most private feelings of so long ago openly described', echoing Bunny's view that 'the feelings of the living should be considered'. Although Duncan tried to be reasonable, to 'take a more objective view', he quoted Bunny's opinion that despite changing attitudes, old-fashioned prejudice still prevailed.[15]

---

[13] DG, *Ulterior Motives*, p. 28.

[14] J. Strachey/DG, Lord's Wood, Marlow, Bucks, 2 July 1966 [Northwestern].

[15] D. Grant/M. Holroyd, Charleston, Monday 4 July 1966 [BL].

Anxious about how he would be represented in Holroyd's second volume, Bunny wrote to James, asking to see it. Having given luncheon, in London, to the Canadian scholar, S.P. Rosenbaum, another chronicler of Bloomsbury, Bunny headed down to Lord's Wood, in Marlow, Buckinghamshire, the home of James and Alix Strachey. There he stayed up until the early hours reading Holroyd's manuscript, afterwards noting in his diary 'ending of 2nd vol – Good'.[16] Even so, Bunny had what Frances Partridge described as a 'heated conversation' with her on the subject. She could not understand his views in the light of his own published memoirs. Bunny retorted that 'I've made it a rule not to make revelations about people who are still alive, or have relatives alive who would mind'. Frances regretted not raising the question of his own lengthy quotations from Ray's 'intensely private and personal letters'.[17]

Holroyd honourably took Bloomsbury's concerns into consideration, writing in more general terms of feelings 'of great friendship rather than love'. But he refused to accept Bunny's view that his book would 'harden people's reaction against homosexuality', explaining that 'if Lytton's homosexual loves were treated not slyly or sensationally, but with openness and truth, using what was emotionally significant just as one would in describing a heterosexual love, then this would only have the effect of increasing tolerance'.[18] It would be another year before Holroyd's first volume was published, and after this flurry of concern, the furore temporarily died down.

Bunny's life was running more smoothly than for some time.

[16] DG, Pocket Diary 1966, Friday 8 July [Northwestern].
[17] Partridge, *Other People*, p. 250, diary entry for 14 July 1966.
[18] Quoted in Spalding, *Duncan Grant*, pp. 457–8.

Not only had Angelica returned to him, at least at weekends, but Rosemary Peto had adopted the habit of joining him for lunch on Moby Dick. Despite letters protesting that the affair must end as she disliked being disloyal to her partner, Renee Fedden, Rosemary regularly returned for more. Angelica dropped Bunny a note, telling him 'I love you – and my chief feeling is one of thankfulness that it has been possible for me to come back to you – & gratitude that you have made it so easy'.[19] Angelica's return meant everything for it restored family life to Hilton. As Bunny gleefully informed Sylvia: 'My daughters arrive today: the garden is full of peas, globe artichokes, spinach, strawberries and raspberries starting. Angelica busy bottling fruit. Hive bursting with honey.'[20] It was his idea of paradise.

In August The Cearne was sold. Bunny had given it to Amaryllis, and although he felt she should be free to do as she wanted, it was a terrible wrench. He spent a miserable couple of days clearing the attics of thousands of books. It was as though he was sweeping the house of memories. Although tenanted since Constance's death, the house had belonged to him, a symbol of his childhood and his parents' singular lives. Amaryllis had no childhood memories of The Cearne and had never lived there. Bunny regretted giving it to her, especially as she used the proceeds to buy a house near Angelica. 'Islington', Frances Partridge noted dryly, 'is now Bunny's idea of hell'.[21]

On 11 November he left for his annual lecture tour in the US. Unusually he felt happy to depart: Duncan had recently exuded warmth and intimacy and there was the delightful

---

[19] AVG/DG, Charleston [31 May 1966] [KCC].

[20] DG/STW, Hilton, 18 June 1966, in RG. ed., *Sylvia and David*, p. 105.

[21] Partridge, *Other People*, p. 255, diary entry for 3 August 1966.

prospect of Angelica joining him in the New Year. From New York he made his customary pilgrimage to Carson McCullers at Nyack, but this was a saddening experience as she was now bedridden, though working on her autobiography. She died the following September.

Bunny's itinerary included additional universities, beginning with Vassar, where he lectured on Bloomsbury. From there he headed to Cornell, speaking about H.G. Wells and tutoring individual students. He met the novelist Alison Lurie, whose then husband, Jonathan Peale Bishop, taught there: it was the beginning of a gentle literary friendship. Having been invited to Cornell by Arthur Mizener, an academic working on a biography of Ford Madox Ford, Bunny was able to give him one of Ford's letters, which he had discovered lodged in the attic at The Cearne.

On 20 November Bunny flew to Toronto where he lectured at Massey College at the invitation of S.P. Rosenbaum. His feet barely touched the ground before he was off again, this time to Chicago, where he was met by Frances Hamill, who drove him to her family estate in Illinois. Bunny was particularly taken with her garage door: 'you press a button in the car & the door opens & you drive in'.[22] From there he took a train to Carbondale, where he dined with Harry and Beatrice Moore, before flying to San Francisco en route to lecture at Stanford. On 5 December Bunny arrived at Davis, California. Angelica wrote telling him she felt nothing but admiration for his stamina. With a gap to fill between lecturing at Davis in early December and at Texas in mid-January, Bunny arranged to stay at the D.H. Lawrence Ranch, San Cristobal. Apart from one or two meals with Dorothy

---

[22] DG/AVG, 5 Hamill Lane, Clarendon Hills, Illinois [KCC].

Brett, who lived nearby, Bunny remained alone, surrounded by snow, pines and silence. He missed his home and family, writing wistfully to Angelica, 'How I wish I could put my nose out at Hilton & look for the first primrose'.[23]

At the end of December Bunny flew to Los Angeles to meet the film-maker Jean Renoir, who wanted to film *Aspects of Love*. The project was hampered by financial considerations and both Renoir and Bunny feared the story would need to be modified to suit American casting. For these reasons they agreed the film should be made in France and Italy with English and French actors. Bunny thought the detour to LA worthwhile just to have met Renoir. While there, he dined with his old friend Elsa Lanchester who now resembled an 'intelligent & kindly Pekinese'. Julie Andrews rang up, but Bunny was out at the time. His chief excitement, however, was the prospect of being with Angelica, to whom he wrote on 4 January 1967, saying how wonderful it was 'to think that tomorrow you will be in New York – on the same continent'.[24]

From New York Angelica wrote telling Bunny she was thoroughly enjoying herself. Duncan's former lover, George Bergen, had taken her under his wing, and was 'devoting himself entirely to my entertainment'.[25] A week later Angelica and Bunny were reunited at Austin, Texas. Their Mexican holiday was generally successful and Bunny relished showing Angelica the places to

---

[23] DG/AVG, D.H. Lawrence Ranch, San Cristobal, Nr Taos, Sunday 17 [December], 1966 [KCC].

[24] DG/AVG, Del Capri Hotel, Los Angeles, Wednesday 4 January 1967 [KCC].

[25] AVG/DG, St Moritz Hotel, 6th Avenue and Central Park South, NY, Monday 9 January [1967] [KCC].

which he had travelled two years previously. When they returned to England on 16 February, Bunny had been away for three months.

After what seemed a honeymoon period things began to cool again. As Bunny told Sylvia, 'I am alone with William and cook our meals. And when I am not alone with him the house is full at week-ends and I dispense drinks.'[26] Bunny wrote Angelica a poem: 'Summer does not come / Wind breaks branches, cancels the sun / [...] Clouds cover you, you are swept away / All warmth cancelled and gone for good.'[27] His self-pity did not last, as there was a more pressing cause for concern: Angelica had a lump in her breast. 'I am to my own surprise not frightfully worried', she said, 'So you must try not to be either'.[28] It seemed like a cruel repetition. Bunny could not sleep for worry, but was a little reassured when Noel Olivier told him that treatment had improved considerably since Ray's time.

In August Angelica was admitted to St Mary's Hospital, Paddington, where she underwent two operations, the second the removal of her ovaries to reduce the likelihood of a recurrence of the tumour. As Bunny told Sylvia, 'I think and hope they have done what ought to have been done when the same thing happened to Ray'.[29] Angelica was in hospital for two weeks, and Bunny visited every day for the first, travelling up from Hilton and back again. To Bunny's consternation, Angelica decided to convalesce at Charleston where Grace Higgens would care for her. It was partly an instinctive desire to return to her childhood

---

26 DG/STW, Hilton, 28 March 1967, in RG, ed., *Sylvia and David*, p. 117.

27 DG, 'To Angelica', 23 May 1967 [Northwestern].

28 AVG/DG, 79 St Peter's Street, London, 'Tuesday' [July 1967] [KCC].

29 DG/STW, Hilton, 2 September 1967, in RG, ed., *Sylvia and David*, p. 123.

home, but it was also a means of evading what she considered to be Bunny's 'over-emotionalism'.[30] Bunny was distraught and Angelica eventually capitulated to his pleas to look after her. In the event she told Leonard Woolf, Bunny had in fact 'restrained himself & has fed me deliciously & I have myself improved considerably'.[31] She made such progress that on 1 September she left, with Duncan and Nerissa, for St Martin-de-Vers.

Bunny took part in a BBC radio broadcast about Virginia Woolf and in a BBC television panel game, *Take It or Leave It*, a literary quiz chaired by Robert Robinson. In respect of the latter, Bunny confessed to appearing much to his disadvantage, hindered, no doubt, by his habit of punctuating his sentences with long pauses in search of an appropriate word. On 17 September he set off for St Martin-de-Vers where he coincided with Angelica and Nerissa for just a week, before they left. Alone, he devoted much of his time to collecting sloes and mushrooms. In early October his solitude was interrupted by Alison Lurie who stopped for a couple of days, as arranged. They got on well, 'in a charming professional way', talking about their families, writers and writing.[32]

Afterwards, Bunny received a letter from Angelica beginning 'Bunny my dear', 'there is something I want to tell you'. 'I must tell you', she continued, '& feel I should have told you before, which makes it all the more difficult. It is not good news for you of course, as you must guess.'[33] In New York, in January, while

---

[30] AVG/L Woolf, Hilton, Monday 21 August [1967] [Sussex].

[31] AVG/L Woolf, Hilton, Monday 21 August [1967] [Sussex].

[32] DG/AVG, L'Ancienne Auberge, St Martin-de-Vers, Sunday 8 October 1967 [KCC].

[33] AVG/DG, 79 St Peter's Street, London, 'not sent on Rosie's advice' [but Bunny did receive it] [KCC].

waiting to join Bunny, Angelica had fallen in love with George Bergen. She had harboured the secret ever since. She could not stop thinking of him and had decided to go to New York for an indefinite period.

Bunny replied that if things did not work out 'you have got a lot to fall back on – Charleston & Hilton & all of us'.[34] He told Frances Partridge he had been ignorant about the affair, 'Angelica never suggested that she was in love with George – I knew she had liked him & that he had laid himself out to be charming […] but no more'.[35] He felt particularly hurt as Angelica had seemed so happy in Mexico. Even so the intervening months had not been good. As he told Sylvia with some bitterness: 'In the early summer Angelica came down to Hilton about once a fortnight – slept in my bed – made love without wanting to – dug up a few weeds in flower beds & disappeared again.'[36]

On the eve of her departure, Angelica wrote to Bunny stating 'you & I should divorce whatever happens'.[37] He was inclined to agree. He could take no more of the comings and goings, her vacillations, her being caught between extremes, her inability to commit to one way of life or another. Emotionally exhausted, he left St Martin on 29 October, staying with Giovanna in Paris on the way home. He was glad to find Henrietta and Sophie at Hilton. Harold and Maggie Hobson rallied round, Duncan invited Bunny to Charleston and Frances Partridge lost little time in asking him to dinner. 'All that I liked most in his character

---

[34] DG/AVG, L'Ancienne Auberge, St Martin-de-Vers, 11 October [1967] [KCC].

[35] DG/F Partridge, St Martin-de-Vers, 23 October [1967] [KCC].

[36] DG/STW, St Martin, 17 October 1967 [Berg].

[37] AVG/DG, 79 St Peter's Street, Tuesday 17 [October 1967] [KCC].

came to the fore. He talked of Angelica without any bitterness but with great sadness.'[38]

Then Angelica dropped another bombshell. She did not, after all, want a divorce although Bunny had instructed his solicitor to start proceedings. The reason Angelica did not want a divorce had nothing to do with Bunny and everything to do with George. Divorce – with Angelica cited as the guilty party – would reveal her relationship with George to his wife, from whom he was separated but not divorced. This, in turn, would enable his wife to divorce him on grounds of adultery, which might adversely affect his access arrangements to his teenage daughter. Bunny would have to hold fire until George's daughter was of age. 'I am as keen on divorce as you are', Angelica told him, 'but we must wait for George's O.K.'[39]

Bunny felt that 'losing the loved one through death is in a way easier to bear than their simply taking themselves off'.[40] He tried not to feel sorry for himself and determined that this time separation would be final. It was then that Bunny and Duncan turned to each other for support. At Charleston, the two men read one another's letters from Angelica, both anxious that she was unhappy and might be hurt. It was evident that she was lonely, knowing few people in New York; that George battened on her for money; that she felt cramped in his small flat; that he was incapable of expressing his feelings although capable of verbal cruelty; that he was withdrawn and elusive.

When Duncan had experienced similar drawbacks with George nearly four decades earlier, he had turned to Bunny for

---

[38] Partridge, *Good Company: Diaries 1967–1970* (London: HarperCollins, 1994), entry for 9 November 1967.

[39] AVG/DG, 791 Lexington Avenue, 10021 NYC, 4 January 1968 [KCC].

[40] Partridge, *Good Company*, p. 83; entry for 19 January 1968.

support. Now Duncan consoled Bunny, reminding him that at least he had the comfort of 'four lovely & devoted daughters'.[41] They were comfort, indeed, rallying around their father. That Christmas, Bunny was surrounded by family and friends: Henrietta, Sophie, Amaryllis, Nerissa, William, Richard, Jane, Oliver and Ned; on Boxing Day they were joined by Rosemary Peto, Renee Fedden and Renee's daughter Katherine. Fanny arrived for New Year, as did Noel's son, Benedict Richards.

Michael Holroyd's long anticipated first volume of his Lytton Strachey biography was published in September 1967.[42] James Strachey did not live to see the published book. The biography arrived in the shops shortly after a momentous piece of legislation: the Sexual Offences Act, which decriminalised homosexual acts between men over the age of twenty-one. Although homosexuals no longer feared imprisonment, what remained of Bloomsbury nevertheless anticipated the biography with trepidation. Frances Partridge recognised 'something impressive about it', though conceding to Bunny that volume two might 'make us all feel unpleasantly naked & exposed'.[43] But when volume two was published in early 1968 the Bloomsbury survivors generally agreed that it was rather good. Bunny acknowledged that Frances's view was right, that 'the book has a lot of merit'.[44] Two decades later, Michael Holroyd shed an interesting perspective on Bloomsbury's attitude to his book: 'Let those who feel tempted

---

[41] D. Grant/DG, Charleston, 14 November 1967 [KCC].

[42] Michael Holroyd, *Lytton Strachey: A Critical Biography, Volume 1: The Unknown Years (1880–1910)* (London: Heinemann, 1967).

[43] F. Partridge/DG, Flat 5, 14 West Halkin Street, SW1, 18 October 1967 [KCC].

[44] DG/F. Partridge, Moby Dick, 12 March 1968 [KCC].

to dismiss the Bloomsbury group as a timid self-regarding coterie ask themselves whether, had their own principles come to be tested in such an awkward practical fashion, they would have passed the test with such style and courage.'[45]

---

[45] Michael Holroyd, 'Foreword', in Hugh Lee, ed., *A Cezanne in the Hedge* (London: Collins & Brown, 1992), p. 11.

Part Five

MAGOUCHE

Chapter Thirty-Four

'I am still in old age a normal male animal.'[1]

When Angelica returned to London in May 1968, seven months after leaving for New York, Bunny could not face seeing her. When he eventually did, he was surprised at how detached he felt. The reason for this detachment was a strikingly beautiful, intelligent, witty and charming American in her late forties. Her name was Magouche Phillips, and Bunny was bowled over when they met as dinner guests of Frances Partridge. Frances could not help noticing Magouche's 'on-coming response' to Bunny, and that it made him 'radiant with pleasure'.[2]

'My life has been rather social lately', Bunny told Sylvia in immense understatement.[3] Between March and May he visited the Bells in Sussex, dined with Barbara Ker Seymer and Barbara Roett, Frances Partridge, Tom and Nadine Marshall, Rosemary Peto, Cyril and Deirdre Connolly, Anna Wickham's son Jim

---

[1] DG/AVG, Hilton, Saturday 26 July 1969 [KCC].
[2] Partridge, *Good Company*, p. 86; entry for 10 February 1968.
[3] DG/STW, Hilton, 7 June 1968, in RG, ed., *Sylvia and David*, p. 142.

Hepburn and with Harry Moore, over from the US. He lunched with Leonard Woolf at Monk's House, stayed at Charleston with Duncan, travelled to Marlow twice to see Alix Strachey and stayed at Biddesden House, Wiltshire at the invitation of Bryan Guinness, Lord Moyne. He lunched with Morgan Forster in Cambridge, took tea with Geoffrey Keynes, fished the Itchen with his cousin Dicky Garnett, attended Cranium Club meetings and a Royal Literary Fund white-tie dinner, to which he arrived an hour late, having lost his waistcoat. Between times, Bunny entertained his daughters and their guests at Hilton. Frances Partridge observed that he 'struggles on with extraordinary gallantry. Nine to dinner on Sunday – I don't know how he does it.'[4]

This renewed vigour was largely due to Magouche. Bunny learned that her first name was really Agnes, and that she had been given the name Magouche by her husband, the artist Arshile Gorky, who committed suicide in 1948 leaving her with two young daughters, and that she had two more daughters by a second marriage which ended in divorce. 'Felt a new man', Bunny noted in his diary the morning after he and Magouche dined *à deux* at her Chapel Street house in Kensington.[5] Magouche was exactly the tonic he needed. Bunny was astonished that she liked him. 'It is the only weakness', he commented, 'in a character otherwise of iron strength'.[6] With many friends in common, Bunny slipped easily into her world, although he soon realised that the two of them would get on best if he did not make undue demands. He recognised that she was very much her own person and that there were times when she did not want him around.

4   Partridge, *Good Company*, pp. 151–2, diary entry for 22 September 1968.
5   DG, Pocket Diary 1968, Thursday 14 March [Northwestern].
6   DG/F. Partridge, c/o Brewster, Gastouri, Corfu, [July 1968] [KCC].

The *White–Garnett Letters* was published by Jonathan Cape in June 1968 to considerable critical acclaim. It came out a year after Sylvia Townsend Warner's biography of White and many critics considered it a companion to the biography. In contrast to Bunny's recent novels, the *Letters* attracted longer reviews, many concerned with unravelling the mysteries of White's psychology and marvelling at Bunny's capacity to remain friends with him. The *Observer* concluded that 'The friendship with David Garnett must have been one of the most satisfying things in his [White's] life. Garnett's letters to him are delightful, candid with plenty of self-revelation but no protestations. The contrast which they point with White's emotional immaturity is almost painfully marked.'[7] Quentin Bell, in the *New Statesman*, declared it 'a most enjoyable book'[8], while Philippa Toomey, in *The Times*, said, 'We can only be grateful to David Garnett for giving us this vivid history of an unlikely friendship'.[9] In the *Sunday Telegraph*, Anthony Curtis pronounced it a 'magical book', stating its beauty resided in 'the well-matched creative weight and striking power of two extremely different literary types'.[10]

Buoyed up by encouraging reviews, Bunny embarked on a month's holiday with Magouche. It was wonderful for him to have a travelling companion again and they adored travelling together. Magouche said that it was Bunny who taught her about France, showing her churches, driving, as he always preferred, along quiet back roads.[11] He found her a delightful companion

---

[7] 16 June 1968.

[8] 21 June 1968.

[9] 15 June 1968.

[10] 16 June 1968.

[11] M. Fielding, interview, 25 February 2010.

and cheerfully adventurous. By Lake Geneva, they trespassed in a private garden where they swam in privacy while a gardener clipped the other side of the hedge. In early July they arrived at Avane, near Siena, where they stayed with Magouche's daughter, Maro, and her husband, the artist Matthew Spender, Stephen Spender's son. Bunny thought their villa an earthly paradise. He liked Matthew, finding him 'intelligent, practical, & easily moved to enthusiasm by ideas'. Maro he found beautiful and with a great sense of humour. After an evening of wine and grappa Bunny awoke feeling thirty years younger. He also felt the urge to start writing again, a sure sign of contentment.

'I feel more & more', Bunny wrote from Hilton to Angelica in December, 'that living here with William & spending energy in weekend parties & the middle of the week in London is an impossible life extravagant of money & energy'.[12] Hilton was an old house which needed to be nourished, to resound in the clatter of footsteps on the hall's stone floor, to the sound of feet climbing the irregular wooden stair. Now Hilton reverberated in a silence which only heightened its air of abandonment and decay. Frances Partridge noted that the house was imbued with sadness, its structure 'crumbling around Bunny'.[13]

From Morocco where she was painting with Duncan, Angelica replied: 'To tell the truth – not to be repeated please – I have grown fond of a boy here whom I intend to bring back with me.' 'My relationship with him', she explained, 'is half lover half filial-maternal.'[14] His name was Abdel-Ali Taïtaï, and according to Angelica, he was aged eighteen. Bunny's response was to

---

[12] DG/AVG, Hilton, 3 December 1968 [KCC].
[13] Partridge, *Good Company*, pp. 151–2; diary entry for 22 September 1968.
[14] AVG/DG, Fes, 7 December 1968 [KCC].

scribble dismissively in his diary: 'Letter from Angelica: Moorish boy lover.'[15] He could be relatively blasé because he was free from resurging concerns about his position in Angelica's life, restored to happiness by Magouche. A few diary pages later Bunny recorded a 'Wish' for 1969: 'as full an emotional & sex life as in '68'.[16] It had been a good seventy-sixth year.

In January 1969 when Bunny attended Duncan's eighty-fourth birthday dinner, he was surprised to see 'the odious Holroyd' had been invited.[17] He was also surprised when Jamie Hamilton, a fellow guest, enquired whether he intended to marry Magouche. Bunny replied that it would be bigamy. 'But what extraordinary people the conventional people are', he exclaimed to Angelica, 'I think only half witted people could think of marrying unless they are having children'.[18]

The chief event in Bunny's working life was that he had been asked by Michael Howard of Jonathan Cape to select and edit Carrington's letters and diaries for publication. Cape would pay an advance of £1,000 and £250 towards the cost of copying and typing the material. It was a job which Bunny could not afford to turn down, although it didn't occur to him that without the 'odious' Holroyd's biography of Lytton Strachey, this particular book would never have been mooted. Bunny's first task was to track down the letters. Those lodged at the University of Texas were not a problem because Frances Partridge held the copyright, so Bunny could work from photocopies of the originals. Carrington's brother Noel was a great help, and Michael Howard took a strong personal

---

[15] DG, Pocket Diary 1968, Friday 13 December [Northwestern].
[16] DG, Pocket Diary 1968, Wednesday 1 January 1969 [Northwestern].
[17] DG/AVG, 21 January 1969 [KCC].
[18] DG/AVG, 21 January 1969 [KCC].

interest in the project. Julia Strachey, Barbara Bagenal, Alix Strachey and Rosamond Lehmann, among others, had retained their letters and Bunny was able to read the originals, or transcripts. Some letters had been lost or destroyed. But there was, anyway, a vast amount of material, and Bunny approached it with relish, telling Angelica: 'May as well make the best of things & embark on every adventure while possible.'[19] He found the process moving and amusing by turns. Carrington's letters to Lytton he thought 'amazing – so frank & improper & devoted to him'.[20] But he worried that they were 'full – almost too full – of jokes about buggery which will shock a lot of people'.[21]

Frances commented that for his age Bunny was 'a model of energy, activity and enthusiasm', and 'in a handsome suit of blue check, steps about as briskly as a young man'.[22] He told her 'Sex begins at fifty'.[23] He was happy, but Angelica's return in March caused mixed feelings. He was pleased to see her, but not with Taïtaï in tow. Bunny met the young man on April Fools' Day, noting in his diary 'Taiti – bored – why get involved?'[24] Who was bored is unclear.

At Hilton, Frances Partridge found the cold deathly and that even in bed, bundled in vest, flannel night-gown, bed-jacket and dressing gown with a smuggled eiderdown over the blankets, she could not get warm. 'But none of this mattered', she observed, 'besides the ghostly melancholy that drips from these walls,

---

[19] DG/AVG, Hilton, Friday 31 January 1969 [KCC].

[20] DG/AVG, Hilton, 3 February 1969 [KCC].

[21] DG/AVG, Hilton, Monday 24 February 1969 [KCC].

[22] Partridge, *Good Company*, pp. 169–70; diary entry for 16 February 1969.

[23] Partridge, *Good Company*, p. 165; diary entry for 22 January 1969.

[24] DG, Pocket Diary 1969, Tuesday 1 April [Northwestern].

apparently unnoticed by its inmates Bunny and William.'[25] All was to change, as William, now forty-four, had fallen in love. The object of his affection was Linda Burt, whom Bunny described as 'a delightful, quick-witted girl of twenty-eight. She is small, dark, with eager eyes, laughs a lot and plays the clarinet.'[26] To Bunny's delight William announced that in July they would be married. In the circumstances Bunny felt he could not remain at Hilton, telling Quentin: 'It needs a stout heart to cook & eat lonely meals at that long table.'[27]

In April 1969 Noel Olivier died. She suffered a stroke after tending a vine, surrounded by her children and grandchildren. Henrietta, who was at Hilton when Bunny received the news, heard him let out an anguished wail of pain. He told Quentin that Noel's death 'leaves an awful gap. I knew and loved her from the time she was four years old.'[28] To some extent, Bunny had raised his daughters with the Olivier sisters in mind, hoping, as Henrietta observed, that 'we should grow up proud and fearless'.[29] But there was another reason for his sadness. Several years later he wrote ruefully in his diary that if only he had asked Noel to 'come to bed with me our lives might have been different'.[30] To what extent this was wishful thinking or sentimental fantasy is unclear. But there is no doubt that she had been a mainstay in his

[25] Partridge, *Good Company*, p. 170; diary entry for 16 February 1969.

[26] DG/STW, Hilton Hall [c. 6 August 1969] in RG, ed., *Sylvia and David*, p. 152.

[27] DG/Q. Bell, Moby Dick, 106 Cheyne Walk, London, 4 November 1969 [AOB].

[28] DG/Q. Bell, 15 April 1969 [AOB].

[29] HG, 'Aspects of My Father'.

[30] DG, Pocket Dairy 1973, 20 February [Northwestern].

life and that he loved her even more than her sisters and had been closest to her as a child.

Still undecided about Hilton, in April Bunny set off for Italy with Frances Partridge, to stay with Magouche at Avane. 'I feel I must be the only female he has travelled with in separate rooms', Frances reflected in her diary, 'and only hope he doesn't feel humiliated before the hotelier.' With Bunny behind the wheel, Frances found the journey somewhat trying as he sped along relentlessly, unwilling to see sights. When they arrived all became clear: 'Magouche was not expecting us before Monday at earliest, and our thundering advance now plainly shows as a valiant and obstinate attempt on Bunny's part to beat the band, and prove that he's not a dead dog yet, but a *man*.'[31]

At lunch, one day, reminiscing about the Noel Olivier–Rupert Brooke–James Strachey triangle, Bunny flew into a rage in response to what he considered a derogatory comment by Maro Spender. According to Frances, 'Bunny did a full, glaring half-turn and burst out in a pressurized voice "*no*, it wasn't like that *at all*"'. He was ashamed of his behaviour, noting in his diary that he had been beastly to Maro and felt upset himself. Frances was surprised later to hear Magouche saying, '"Now everyone's in tears – Maro *and* Bunny"'.[32] Noel was still much on his mind. With the exception of Harold Hobson, she had been the last link with his childhood. 'There is no one', he lamented, 'to whom I can talk about the past without explanations now.'[33]

From Avane, Bunny journeyed alone to St Martin-de-Vers where he found Nerissa, who had been living there for the best

---

[31] Partridge, *Good Company*, p. 184; diary entry for 26 April 1969.

[32] Partridge, *Good Company*, p. 187; diary entry for 1 May 1969.

[33] DG/AVG, Hilton [actually Moby Dick], Tuesday 15 April 1969 [KCC].

part of a year. Together they went to the Château de Charry to view Le Verger, a converted outbuilding which was to let. Comprising one bedroom, a living room, kitchen, bathroom and a studio in a separate building, it was located three miles from the town of Montcuq, half a mile from the Château and commanded a splendid view to the south over a valley, the château turrets visible between trees. Bunny thought it perfect and decided to take it. He would no longer live at Hilton, he couldn't live permanently on *Moby Dick*, Angelica wanted to sell L'Ancienne Auberge and he recognised that Magouche's life was too full for him to share it on a full time basis.

There was one final family event at Hilton before Bunny's departure. It was the venue for a magnificent party following Linda's and William's wedding on 19 July. Bunny cooked a ham and a salmon and tables heaving with food were laid in the garden. Bunny told Sylvia it had been a wonderful party, and that Linda's relations 'come from Islington. So did most of our other guests – including Angelica.' In the same letter he explained that William and Linda planned to move to Yorkshire and that he could not remain at Hilton alone. 'I see', he said 'that my life is uprooted and at a turning point', adding, 'Adventure begins at seventy-seven, and I embark on it doubtfully'.[34]

Before embarking on any adventure, Bunny needed to complete the Carrington letters. In August, while Magouche was away, he occupied her Kensington house, working there with Amaryllis (who had taken a secretarial course) as his assistant. Immersed in long-ago Bloomsbury, Bunny was shocked to learn that Leonard Woolf had died. Leonard had been something of a mentor to Bunny, who often turned to him for advice. Leonard

---

[34] DG/STW, Hilton [c. 6 August 1969] in RG, ed., *Sylvia and David*, pp. 152–3.

appreciated Bunny's qualities, so much so that in 1943 he asked him to be his executor. Bunny now assumed he would have to take on this arduous role, but was relieved to learn that Leonard's companion Trekkie Parsons had been assigned the task.

In October, Bunny took Magouche on a tour of his northern haunts: they stayed at Butts Intake and then went to Ridley Stokoe. It was like a final pilgrimage; for Bunny had resolved to let Hilton even though he could barely countenance the practicalities of such a step. As William and Linda had moved to Yorkshire and Richard and Jane lived mostly in London, Bunny turned to Angelica for help, telling Quentin, afterwards, that she had come down to Hilton Hall 'like the Angel of Death and for almost a week bonfires blazed and the junk and records of 45 years were consumed'.[35] Emotionally exhausted, one evening in London Bunny was knocked down by a car when crossing the road. The driver rushed over to help him, only to receive a resounding punch in the face, followed by two more. A few moments later, Bunny realised that his reaction had been caused by feeling powerless, like a five-year-old at school.

He had been affected more than he cared to acknowledge by the prospect of leaving Hilton. For forty-five years it had been his home, the focus of family life, the locus of all his energy as a gardener and farmer. Returning there a few days after the London accident, Bunny found himself taking a corner too fast. He lost control of the car, charged some cottages and ended up stuck in a front garden. When, in November, Bunny wrote a letter of condolence to Sylvia following the death of her lover, Valentine Ackland, his words were as much a lament for his own

---

[35] DG/Q Bell, Moby Dick, 106 Cheyne Walk, London, 4 November 1969 [AOB].

changing life as for Sylvia's loss: 'I love the visible world so much that it consoles me to know that it is going on: however much we mess it up – day and night, high tide and low tide, summer and winter: forever [...]. But such reflections are no help for pain and loneliness: for that there's no cure, my dear.'[36]

Bunny left Hilton for France on New Year's Day 1970. He stopped, en route, at Charleston, where he found Duncan gentle and charming and Quentin and Olivier as affectionate as ever. The next morning he dropped in on Lydia Lopokova at Tilton, before driving on to Newhaven. Grace Higgens thought he seemed a little confused: he arrived after tea, though expected for lunch, and took Olivier's spectacles to France, having mistaken them for his own. Bunny reached St Martin-de-Vers on 4 January, but it had not been a pleasant drive. The car went out of control on an ice-covered hill and Bunny had to let it slide backwards towards a ditch where it became lodged. Fortunately someone came and helped push it out but the whole experience magnified his sense of isolation.

At L'Ancienne Auberge he cleared cupboards and drawers in preparation for the furniture's removal to Charry. On 9 January he spent his first night in Le Verger alone. He wondered whether he would cope, whether he had the capacity to live alone, whether seclusion would cause him to age. But as he told Angelica, 'I do feel this place is a home I shall cling to'.[37] To Frances he wrote with more resignation: 'For good or ill this place is <u>me</u> – not perhaps the Bunny Garnett known to so many – but the old man I really am.'[38]

---

[36] DG/STW, Hilton, 8 December 1969, in RG, ed., *Sylvia and David*, p. 155.

[37] DG/AVG, Charry, 22 January 1970 [KCC].

[38] DG/F. Partridge, Charry, 25 January 1970 [KCC].

Bunny returned to Hilton a month later to set about finding a tenant. Thus he established the pattern for the ensuing year: periods at Charry alternating with periods in London, an endless succession of journeys between. It was a schizophrenic existence, propelling him from peace and solitude to the frenetic social whirl of London and back again. It was as though he could not relinquish England for France, could not make the final break, could not, perhaps, exchange the 'Bunny Garnett known to so many' for 'the old man I really am'. Partly he could not relinquish Magouche. While he was in London it seemed natural to resume their routine of midweek dinners and nights on *Moby Dick*, but exiled in France no such routine could exist.

On 23 February Bunny arranged for a notice to be placed in *The Times*, advertising Hilton Hall to let. While trying to find a tenant for Hilton, Bunny was simultaneously endeavouring to sell L'Ancienne Auberge, to which he periodically returned. He found the combined processes unbearable, trailing through unfurnished rooms at L'Ancienne Auberge and an uninhabited Hilton Hall. Bunny was relieved when the script writer Johnny Byrne took on the tenancy of Hilton for two years.

At Charry Bunny began to make friends. He instantly warmed to Bysshe and Meg Elstob, who lived about ten miles away, and were both unfailingly kind, with a knack of turning up just when Bunny needed friendly faces. He gradually made other friendships, curiously always with expatriates, rather than the French, although Bunny eventually made friends with his French doctor, Doctor Cano, and his wife. As Bunny settled in, visitors came. In August Richard, Jane, Oliver and Ned arrived; later Angelica spent a few days with Bunny, en route from Morocco, bringing two carpets he had commissioned her to buy. Michael Howard, his publisher at Cape also came, and was fed what Bunny described as 'a most successful dish: sliced lamb's testicles (cold) in a tunny fish mayonnaise'.[39] But the best and happiest event was the birth in September of William's and Linda's first child, Merlin. On receiving William's telegram with the news, Bunny burst into tears.

In late September he flew to Taos to take part in a D.H. Lawrence symposium with James T. Boulton (soon to co-edit Lawrence's *Letters*) and Harry Moore. It was a relatively brief stay and after a couple of days with Mina afterwards, Bunny flew to London. On 5 November *Carrington: Letters and Extracts from her Diaries* was published, the book launch coinciding with an exhibition of Carrington's paintings at the Upper Grosvenor Galleries in Mayfair, where according to Frances Partridge, the 'crush was inconceivable'.[40]

It was not a straightforward book to edit, particularly given Carrington's idiosyncratic spelling and grammar which Bunny wanted to retain to reveal her charm. As ever, Bunny maintained that passages about living people would have to be left out and he certainly edited himself from the text. He excised ten lines about his love affair with Alix; nine about posing naked for Carrington and twenty-six about Frankie Birrell weeping over his marriage to Ray.[41] Raymond Mortimer and Michael Holroyd wrote glowing reviews of the book, although in other quarters the stereotype of elitist Bloomsbury prevailed. Even Gerald Brenan, reviewing the US edition, castigated Bloomsbury for being 'very pleased with itself and inclined to look suspiciously

---

[39] DG/F. Partridge, Charry, 3 September 1970 [KCC].

[40] Partridge, *Life Regained*, p. 98; diary entry for 6 November 1970.

[41] DG/AVG, Hilton, Monday 24 February 1969 [KCC].

on outsiders'.[42] But the book sold well and was chosen by two *Sunday Times* pundits as a Christmas book of the year.

Bunny really wanted a companion to live with him in France and his companion of choice was, naturally, Magouche. 'Why won't she come away from it all and live with me and be my love', he complained, having lost sight of his earlier resolution to make no demands. Frances Partridge tried to make Bunny accept facts, telling him that Magouche's life was very busy with friends, lovers and sociability, and that the only thing he could do was make the most of what he'd got. Bunny had anticipated Magouche spending part of December in France with him, and in his disappointment he wrote a desperate letter to her friend Janetta Parlade. She replied, incisively, 'when you write to insist that someone does what you want in the end they do it more out of loyal obligation than out of love'.[43] Given all the changes in Bunny's life, he clung desperately to the idea of Magouche as the one constant. But he was deceiving himself. In Magouche he had found a lover who behaved, in some respects, much as he had done: she wanted freedom to do as she pleased and to love whomsoever she chose.

Bunny spent Christmas 1970 in Yorkshire with William, Linda and Merlin, moving on to spend several days at Butts Intake over the New Year, surrounded by deep snow. Alone in the silence, he remembered being there with Ray and with Angelica. It was as though he had one foot in the past and the other in an uncertain and lonely future.

---

[42] Gerald Brenan, 'A Hidden Life', *New York Review of Books*, July 1971.

[43] J. Parlade/DG, Torre de Tramores, Benahavis, Provincia de Malaga, Spain, 2 January 1971 [Northwestern].

Chapter Thirty-Five

'This place is really paradise.'[1]

In the New Year of 1971 Bunny threw himself into a social round of family and friends, as if squirreling nuts against a lean winter. He was entertained by his daughters, dined with Harold Hobson, had lunch with George Kirstein at the Savoy and supper with Frances Partridge. He attended Duncan's eighty-sixth birthday dinner, Cape's fiftieth anniversary party, visited Rosie Peto on the Isle of Wight and Giovanna Madonia in Paris. He also stayed at Charleston where he wrote while Duncan painted: an interlude reminiscent of those moments of shared contentment during the Great War. Having achieved some sort of resolution regarding his position in Magouche's life, it was with her that he set off in February for Charry. They had what Bunny described as a 'heavenly' time, Magouche leaving a few days shy of his seventy-ninth birthday.

Bunny was absorbed in writing a novel, waking in the night with a new idea, which he would scribble down lest he forgot it.

---

[1] DG/BK-S and B. Roett, Charry, 20 April 1970 [TGA].

The creative process involved peaks of satisfaction and troughs of despair, and, as usual, he was experimenting with a new genre: It was 'a picaresque story (which goes on & on from adventure to adventure)', he told Angelica, but 'the palette knife is needed to scrub out vast areas of inferior Delacroix – lions springing on stallions etc'.[2]

In April Bunny was joined by Frances Partridge, the two of them spending their time contentedly searching for flowers. They found five species of orchid. One evening they talked of loneliness: a condition they shared. Frances asked Bunny whether he thought he would ever return to Hilton. In 'a tremulous voice' he replied, ' "The truth is I don't want to. I love the house, but it's too full of ghosts".'[3]

Although Bunny returned to England periodically, Charry gradually took possession of him and he began to feel it was home. Family and friends poured over the threshold, a reminder that though exiled in France, Bunny remained in their hearts. He delighted in visits from the children and grandchildren of old friends. As Henrietta commented, 'It is indicative of his temperament that many of the younger generation knocked on his door'.[4] Sometimes he barely had time to change the sheets before another visitor settled into the spare room. Henrietta described her father at this time as being 'surprisingly domesticated' and 'interested in the dailyness of domestic life'.[5] He revelled in the

---

[2] DG/AVG, Charry, 26 March 1971 [KCC].

[3] Partridge, *Life Regained*, p. 151; diary entry for 25 April 1971.

[4] Henrietta Garnett, 'David Garnett'. in S.P. Rosenbaum, ed., *The Bloomsbury Group: a Collection of Memoirs and Commentary* (Toronto: Toronto University Press, 1995), p. 300.

[5] Ibid., p. 301.

textures of routine: washing laundry, taking lunch outside, mending clothes, marketing in Montcuq, bottling wine, foraging for mushrooms and cooking for guests. He gained a reputation as a splendid host and skilled cook, though, according to Henrietta, while 'his cooking was delicious, the small kitchen was exceedingly untidy. The mousetraps, baited with a variety of enticing morsels, were ignored. Instead the little field mice who came in from the cold feasted on the debris that was left lying around.'[6] Bunny liked to work at a wooden table outside beneath an oak, his favoured place for meals as well. 'Everything is perfect', he wrote to Angelica, 'Yet why do I sometimes ask myself: "What are you doing here? What is the point of it?" '[7]

Bunny's eyesight was not what it had been: dining with Grace Higgens he sprinkled his rhubarb & junket with salt thinking it was sugar. Sometimes he did not notice that his food was not particularly fresh, and this, coupled with a predilection for foraged mushrooms, caused gastric upsets among his guests. Richard recollected one occasion when he deftly removed mouldy cheese which Bunny had placed before a pregnant visitor. Diana and Peter Gunn, staying with Bunny in 1972 were both taken ill in the night and reaching for the only receptacles to hand, were sick into Bunny's saucepans. As he explained indignantly to Frances, 'The blame was laid on a risotto of guinea fowl with onions, garlic, rice, tomatoes, peppers & some slices of my preserved cèpes'.[8] Bunny mistakenly assumed all boletes were *cèpes* and therefore safe to eat. But *cèpes* are *boletus edulis* and according to notes in his recipe book, he was picking

---

[6] Ibid., p. 301.
[7] DG/AVG, Charry, 'Evening' 2 October 1971 [KCC].
[8] DG/F. Partridge, Charry, 9 November 1972 [KCC].

boletus erythropus and *boletus luridus*, both of which cause gastric problems. 'I am a bit doubtful about these', he wrote later in his recipe book, 'one made me sick in the night – or I <u>was</u> sick.'[9]

Bunny's latest novel, *A Clean Slate*, was published by Hamish Hamilton that summer. It got off to a good start with positive reviews in *The Times* and *Guardian*. Bunny told Sylvia his novel was 'very sexy, and I use the word cock a good deal'.[10] It was banned for indecency in South Africa. The story concerns Lady Billy Tonson, 'a beautiful extrovert of forty-seven' who falls for David, a schoolboy of seventeen, inducting him in the arts of love.[11] As Bunny pointed out to Frances Partridge, although this bore a superficial resemblance to Angelica's relationship with Ali (as he was now known), most of the book had been written long before Angelica's Moroccan adventure, and the characters were completely different. Bunny was, in fact, experimenting with writing 'entirely from the woman's point of view'.[12]

As an attempt to write about sex from the woman's viewpoint, *A Clean Slate* is a somewhat egocentric act of reflected glory. Ironically, the book's main weakness resides in Bunny's unfettered descriptions of sex, some of which are cringingly anatomical. When Billy gives young David a lesson on female genitalia ('the man in the boat') and sanitises his penis after congress with a prostitute ('she swabbed his parts thoroughly

---

9 DG, Recipe book, unpublished MS [HG].

10 DG/STW, Le Verger de Charry, 2 September 1971 in RG, ed., *Sylvia and David*, p. 159.

11 David Garnett, *A Clean Slate* (London: Hamish Hamilton, 1971), endpaper blurb.

12 DG/STW [Le Verger de Charry, Montcuq; apparently incomplete: September 1970] in RG, ed., *Sylvia and David*, p.157.

[...] and then pressed open the lips of the urethra') it is as though a gynaecologist has run riot in a brothel.[13] Perhaps Bunny hoped for the kind of success which Harold Robbins and Jackie Collins enjoyed at this time. It was very much a late 1960s novel.

In October, Bunny was visited by Alan Maclean his publisher at Macmillan, who hoped to persuade Bunny to accept an invitation to be the guest of honour at a literary luncheon hosted by the formidable bookseller Christina Foyle. The occasion would coincide with Bunny's eightieth birthday the following March, and mark the publication of his novel *The Sons of the Falcon*. It was ironic that living in France, Bunny seemed to be more in demand than ever. In November he learned from his agent, Hilary Rubinstein, that Bernard Smith, the American script editor and film producer, wanted to make a film of *Lady into Fox* with Patrick Garland as scriptwriter and director. The problem was that Smith wanted Bunny to grant him a free option for twelve months to buy time to finance and set up the film. Bunny evidently agreed to this proposal, as almost a year later *The Times* 'Diary' announced that Patrick Garland would direct the film of *Lady into Fox* and had finished the screenplay. Given the fate of so many films of his books (including the Renoir proposal) Bunny did not hold out much hope.

As part of the fanfare for *The Sons of the Falcon* and Bunny's eightieth birthday, Ruth Hall interviewed him for an *Observer* colour supplement spread. He told Angelica, 'She makes me out to be an aged Casanova with a sugary disposition', adding, 'My own fault I suppose'.[14] On 5 March *The Sons of the Falcon* featured on the BBC Radio programme *In View*, and on the 8th the Foyle's

---

[13] DG, *Clean Slate*, p. 28 and p. 35.
[14] DG/AVG, Charry, 14 February 1972 [KCC].

Literary Luncheon took place at the Dorchester. Twenty-five tables accommodated nearly three-hundred guests, the VIPs exhibited at a long table, like a Last Supper, with paying guests seated at smaller tables below. Bunny was joined at the top table by Harold Macmillan, Rosamond Lehmann and Christina Foyle, together with his choice of friends and family including Richard and Jane, the Hobsons, H.E. Bates, Francis Meynell, Stephen Spender and Bryan Guinness.

Macmillan delivered the opening address to which Bunny responded self-deprecatingly by thanking him for his compliments, even though he did not agree with them all. Bunny said he still hoped to improve as a writer: he was a slow developer. His speech dwelt upon the key people in his life, in particular his parents, Frankie Birrell, Francis Meynell, Duncan and Vanessa. He finished by reading a poem on the subject of his own mortality. If not the most uplifting reflection on eighty years, it was characteristically rational.

William could not attend as Linda gave birth that day to Bunny's fifth grandchild, Romany. But most of those dear to Bunny who had missed the literary luncheon were present that evening at a birthday party hosted by Magouche. The throng included Duncan, Angelica, Henrietta, Sophie, Nerissa and Fanny; Quentin, Olivier and their three children; Frances Partridge, Richard, Jane, Ned and Oliver. William arrived beaming with happiness. Bunny was absolutely in the bosom of his family and it had been a long while since it had gathered around him like this.

The Sons of the Falcon was a resounding critical success. The *Financial Times* commented 'David Garnett has never been predictable. He has produced a large and varied *oeuvre*, and *The Sons of the Falcon* is a new departure [...]. It is first and foremost a "rattling good yarn".'[15] The *Sunday Times* considered it 'admirably written and immensely readable', and that Bunny displayed 'that gift of empathy with a distant, and to most of us unimaginable, way of living that is worth a hundred times more than the most painstaking historical reconstruction'.[16] The *Guardian* called it 'A high piece of old-fashioned melodrama [...]. Fierce, scarlet, unforgettable stuff.'[17]

Set in the Caucasus in the 1860s, the novel was inspired by a story Bunny had been told in 1920, concerning a family icon which worked miracles. When the family split, the icon was retained by one branch though coveted by the other. During an annual pilgrimage when the icon was paraded, the subordinate branch laid ambush to claim it. Hearing of this, the head of the family thrust his sword through the belly of his youngest child, afterwards concealing the icon in the corpse.

The story fascinated Bunny, who tried to imagine a culture in which a man could kill his child to save a religious symbol. The book was also coloured by Bunny's recollections of Ray's tales of her travels in the Caucasus in 1913. 'The Caucasians are picturesque people' she had written to her brother Tom, 'they have killed and robbed several people [...] already this season'.[18] The novel's gestation was comparatively rapid, written almost entirely

[15] Quoted in David Garnett, *The Sons of the Falcon* (London: Macmillan 1972; Quartet paperback edition, 1973), blurb.

[16] Quoted in ibid., blurb.

[17] Quoted on verso of David Garnett, *Plough Over the Bones* (London: Macmillan, 1973).

[18] RAG/Tom Marshall, Kislovodsk, Caucasus, Tuesday [16/19 July 1913], in Ray Marshall, 'Ray in Russia 1913', unpublished journal and letters compiled and edited by Richard Garnett [RG], p. 32.

during the winter of 1970–71. For the first time, Bunny, who usually wrote relatively short novels, composed on an epic scale. As the *Guardian*'s critic observed: 'The narrative thunders along at a fantastic rate.'[19]

Bunny's career was undergoing something of a renaissance. Chatto & Windus re-issued *Beany-eye* and *The Grasshoppers Come* in a combined volume. *The Times* republished Bunny's *The Appendix*, first published in the *New Statesman* in 1938. Ian Parsons was curious as to when volume four of Bunny's memoirs might appear. Bunny remained under contract to produce it and in anticipation Chatto had reprinted *The Golden Echo* the previous year.

Bunny encountered persistent problems with this volume. It was conceived in four parts: the war; the Rupert Hart-Davis years; farming at Hilton; the years since his separation from Angelica. Bunny proposed to 'deal with the first of these in some detail' but would 'say little about the second, because it is impossible for fear of libel to tell the truth and hateful to rake it up. Nor shall I say much about my experience as a farmer.'[20] The canvas was rather limited. Bunny told Sylvia: 'Everyone tells me to write a fourth volume of my memoirs. But nothing is interesting except truth, and truth can be painful [...]. If I attempted a book a large part of it, all bitterness, hatred and unforgiveness would have to be left out and a very expurgated version of my heart produced [...]. I could not say that by farming I slowly lost Angelica and arrested the growth of William.'[21] Despite several attempts, Bunny could not progress beyond the end of the war.

---

[19] Quoted in DG, *Sons of the Falcon* (Quartet paperback edition, 1973).

[20] DG, Notebook [c. 1972], unpublished MS [Northwestern].

[21] DG/STW, Le Verger de Charry, 8 June 1976, in RG, ed., *Sylvia and David*, p. 211.

After ten weeks in England, Bunny returned to Charry where he shooed away the peacocks which had flown over from the Château. When a few days later Bunny was joined by Rosemary Peto, she recorded in his visitors' book: 'Memorable peacock and octopus stew.'[22] Bunny asked whether she would accompany him on a longer touring holiday in France. She gently declined, though acknowledging: 'I am so fond of you & we still have such a strong physical passion.'[23] But Bunny rarely wanted for company. In August he was joined by Henrietta and Sophie, and by William, Linda and their 'Peregrine Wind Quintet'. Ann Hopkin arrived accompanied by her husband Robin Boyd. Henrietta cooked for the assembled multitude, and Bunny felt very close to her. A few weeks later Frances Partridge came, bringing the music critic Desmond Shawe-Taylor, whom Bunny initially took against, but discussing George Moore, they discovered they liked one another after all. Frances was 'full of admiration for Bunny's determination, philosophy and appetite for life'.[24] He remained redoubtable. Fishing with his cousin Dicky Garnett in Wales during a gale, he thought nothing of climbing a tree to retrieve his tangled line.

That autumn Bunny anticipated an impending visit from Angelica with mixed feelings. She was coming to finalise the sale of L'Ancienne Auberge, and had written to Bunny telling him he was 'necessary' to her and their daughters. For Bunny, this statement represented a lifeline to which he clung, hoping it signified that all was not lost between them. 'You know my dear', he

[22] 'Visitors Book of the Ancienne Auberge, St Martin-de-Vers & Le Verger de Charry, Montcuq 1963–72', 13–19 June 1972 [Northwestern].

[23] R. Peto/DG, 'Saturday' [pmk 29 May 1972] [Northwestern].

[24] Partridge, *Ups and Downs*, p. 75; diary entry for 23 September.

replied, 'my arms are always open. Only I have no claims on you.'[25] When Angelica sent a telegram saying she would arrive accompanied by the art historian Richard Shone, Bunny's hopes were dashed. It was not that he anticipated any resumption of their former relationship, but he had hoped to be able to talk, as he would say 'intimately', especially about their daughters. Bunny wrote a note which, on arrival, he handed to Shone, asking him to make himself scarce. In the circumstances, Shone did the honourable thing and left. Bunny was particularly aggrieved to discover that he was only 'necessary' to Angelica 'to take part in digging up the most painful parts of the past'.[26] He could understand well enough psychoanalytical shorthand, but he had little time for it, believing instead 'that as a metaphor from mining, we imagine what is buried is worth dragging up – whereas perhaps it is best buried'.[27]

Geographically distanced from Magouche, Bunny's time with her was all the more precious. They spent part of the summer in Greece and at Avane, and she stayed with him for ten days in the autumn. Afterwards, he found solace in a four legged companion, a tabby tomcat whom he named Tiber, after Carrington's cat. As Bunny told Sylvia 'He has turned out to be handsome beyond belief, affectionate – he loves to lie in my arms, purring'. 'I am', Bunny concluded, 'his slave'.[28] Bunny lavished his affection on Tiber, feeding him tit-bits, ministering to his wounds

[25] DG/AVG, Charry, 5 October 1972 [KCC].

[26] DG, Pocket Diary 1972, 'Notes', between September and October [Northwestern].

[27] DG/AVG, Charry, 27 October 1972 [KCC].

[28] DG/STW, Le Verger de Charry, 2 November 1972, in RG, ed., *Sylvia and David*, p. 170.

after encounters with the Wood Cat, and presenting him with a 'Mouse for morale'.[29]

In January 1973 Bunny told Frances: 'I determined the other morning to live to be 100 – at least', explaining that 'the sun was warm & the sky blue and the bare poles of the trees & the thick leaves underfoot were so incredibly beautiful that I feel very strongly that I never wanted to stop looking at the world'.[30] Bunny was particularly happy because Amaryllis had arrived unexpectedly. He had not seen her since the previous spring and initially found her rather changed, but as they settled into one another's company, he thought her more self-assured and less self-conscious than before.

Bunny's contentment derived largely from Charry. Just before his eighty-first birthday, he wrote to Sylvia, saying 'It is a blessing not to be in England' as he had found it upsetting there the previous year, returning to old haunts, dipping into the lives of friends and family which only served to remind him that his life had changed immeasurably, and he could not now call upon them at will. Telling Sylvia that Tiber had survived two bad fights with the Wood Cat, Bunny added: 'He has to lead his own life. It's like my children.'[31] But he worried about his daughters. He did not hear from them often, and as he told Angelica, 'When I don't hear anything I'm always afraid I shall hear of some disaster'.[32]

Bunny was working on his memoirs and on a novel based on his experiences at Sommeilles. In March 1973 his short stories were published as *Purl and Plain*. They had been written over a

---

[29] DG, Pocket Diary 1973, 3 February [Northwestern].

[30] DG/F. Partridge, Charry, 27 January 1973 [KCC].

[31] DG/STW, Charry, 1 March 1973, in RG, ed., *Sylvia and David*, p. 173.

[32] DG/AVG, Charry, 31 January 1973 [KCC].

period of more than fifty years, so he dedicated them to Sylvia Townsend Warner, for their friendship had lasted almost as long. Bunny explained that some stories were 'written in fancy stitch; the rest of them are straightforward knitting'.[33] The critics preferred the plainly stitched stories and generally also the earlier ones. Russell Davies, writing in the *Observer* Review concluded that 'The best pieces are probably the oldest, or at least those which, reaching back into the author's memory, have a sepia-tinted quality of age'.[34] Together they span Bunny's creative life. Reading them is like dipping into his novels and into the subtly differentiated times in which they were written. *Colonel Beech's Bear*, written during the Great War, harks back to an even earlier time, 'the happy days before motor-cars' when Bunny was a boy at The Cearne. 'I lived with my father and mother in a lonely cottage overlooking a great sweep of blue valley and shut in on all sides by a big wood in which I spent my childhood, creeping among the dry bracken like a serpent and imagining myself to be one of Fenimore Cooper's noble redskins.'[35] Bunny had written this in another age.

That spring Bunny enjoyed a holiday with Magouche first in Venice and then at Avane. There, towards the end of April 1973, Bunny received a telegram from Angelica stating she would arrive that afternoon. He noted in his diary that the purpose of her visit was surely 'to announce tragedy'.[36] He was right. Amaryllis had drowned in the Thames. The coroner brought an

---

[33] David Garnett, *Purl and Plain and Other Stories* (London: Macmillan, 1973), p. 24.

[34] 1 April 1973.

[35] DG, *Purl and Plain*, p. 24.

[36] DG, Pocket Diary 1973, 27 April [Northwestern].

open verdict. There was no trace of drugs or alcohol in her body. Perhaps she had slipped off a gang plank near *Moby Dick*. Angelica was certain it was 'a deliberate act, horribly courageous',[37] 'perhaps not premeditated in a conscious way for long beforehand but a step to which she had felt magnetized for some time'.[38] Richard recollected receiving a phone call from Amaryllis, shortly before she died, asking about working for the Samaritans. He wondered, afterwards, whether she really wanted help *from* them.[39]

Bunny believed it was 'either an impulse or an accident', but added 'what does it matter? Death matters. Not how or why it comes.'[40] His initial response was to be alone, to withdraw. He found Magouche angelic in her compassion and consideration, but he really only wanted Tiber. He could not keep Amaryllis from his mind, and in the following months went over and over whether there was anything he could have done. He wondered whether she was constitutionally strong enough for an acting career; whether he had failed her by not 'formulating rationalism' in her.[41] Inevitably, he felt 'shame & bitterness' because he 'might possibly have been able to prevent her action & enable her to live another fifty years enjoying happy daily life'.[42] Magouche thought Bunny 'absolutely magnificent', telling Frances 'you see how he will deal with it, struggle with it naked as it were'.[43]

---

[37] AVG/DG, 57 Ellington Street, 12 May 1973 [KCC].

[38] AVG/DG, Charleston, 5 May 1973 [KCC].

[39] RG/SK, 30 January 2012.

[40] DG/AVG, Charry, 8 May 1973 [KCC].

[41] DG, Pocket Diary 1973, 10 May [Northwestern].

[42] DG/AVG, Charry, 29 May 1973 [KCC].

[43] Quoted in Partridge, *Ups and Downs*, p, 150; diary entry for 8 May 1973.

Amaryllis's body was cremated on 3 May. Bunny did not attend the simple service in London; instead he went to Sommeilles as planned. There he visited the cemetery and gazed upon the old family graves bearing the names so familiar to him. Georges Rawoit had died but several of Bunny's huts endured. Returning to Charry, Bunny was 'glad & yet not glad to be alone for a bit – to return to the routine of daily life & be in my own little house'.[44] There a letter from Frances was waiting, in which she told him that Alix Strachey had died. He reminded Frances that after someone's death, Alix had once remarked, 'Our ranks grow thinner.' 'Well', he observed, 'they are scarcely ranks today'.[45] The ranks were further depleted with the death of Harold Hobson, whom, Bunny sadly told Frances, was 'honest & incorruptible as few men are'.[46] 'I had known him all our lives', he reflected, 'and there was a delight in finding him the same at seventy as he had been at seven.'[47]

'May has been a beautiful but unhappy month', Bunny wrote in his diary, 'I feel older & wonder how long I can keep on alone'.[48] But in June he signed an agreement giving him a life tenancy of Le Verger de Charry. A few days later Giovanna arrived, bringing warmth and affection and lifting Bunny's spirits. When Henrietta and her boyfriend Michel turned up later in the month, Bunny wept with joy. Then Magouche came, helping him transform the studio into habitable quarters to accommodate guests. Richard and Oliver arrived to occupy

[44] DG/AVG, Le Verger de Charry, 8 May 1973 [KCC].

[45] DG/F Partridge, Charry, 7 May 1973 [KCC].

[46] DG/F Partridge, Charry, 19 June 1973 [KCC].

[47] DG/Maggie Hobson, Charry, 3 April 1979 [RG].

[48] DG, Pocket Diary 1973, notes between May and June [Northwestern].

these new quarters, shortly followed by William, Linda, their children and the Peregrine Wind Quintet. After the emotional upheaval of Amaryllis's death, Bunny now began to feel that some sort of stability might be restored. Inspired by Tiber he returned to the long abandoned 'Puss in Boots', now renamed 'The Master Cat'. But he could not progress with his memoirs. He had been reading his 1938–9 diary, written when he was in love with Angelica. He knew now that he would never write volume four.

Chapter Thirty-Six

'I wear my beret & old fishing jacket & talk French so
perfectly that everyone thinks I am some distinguished
person with an English accent.'[1]

Plough Over the Bones was published in October 1973. Of all
Bunny's novels it was the longest in gestation and the most
biographical, but the biography is of place rather than people.
Bunny's first attempt at the book occurred in early 1916, shortly
after his return from Sommeilles. Working with the Quakers in
France had affected Bunny so profoundly that nearly sixty years
later he could vividly recall people and place. He dedicated the
novel to the memory of Francis Birrell. It is not the story of the
British who built huts (they are peripheral figures), but of Dorlotte
(Sommeilles) and its inhabitants, of the effects upon them of the
Battle of the Marne and its aftermath. It is a story of collective
courage and the importance of place in people's lives. But
Frankie Birrell is recognisably there, in a minor role, as Bruce, 'a

---

[1] DG/AVG, The Roadside beyond St Yrieuse, Thursday 6 December
[KCC].

small unkempt figure, in spectacles' who charmed everyone.[2] If the book has a central character it is Georges Roux, closely modelled on Georges Rawoit. But it is the French countryside and country life which occupy centre stage in some of Bunny's most lyrical descriptive writing.

It was well-received. Bunny would have enjoyed the review in the *Listener*, which proclaimed his realism 'as sharp as a September apple: yet the whole has the mellowness of moss'd cottage trees'.[3] The Scotsman declared the novel 'a work of powerful verisimilitude' and 'testimony to Mr Garnett's love of the French countryside and its people'.[4] *The Times* reviewer found the book 'intensely moving', observing that Bunny 'clearly shares a love for the things his villagers value as emblems of continuance – the home, the sturdy produce of the vegetable garden, the satisfactory zither of bees in an orchard'.[5] But it was Peter Ackroyd, the twenty-four-year-old *Spectator* critic, who really understood what Bunny was about:

> Garnett's manner is generally a quiet one, and his prose has a lucid transparency through which the facts of his narrative shine. It is almost wisdom, for it allows him to narrate the social struggles of the villagers with exactly the same tone and emphasis as he details the atrocities and savagery of battle. This makes for a kind of solid truthfulness, and a generosity of spirit that does not emphasise one aspect of life at the expense of all others.[6]

---

[2] David Garnett, *Plough Over the Bones* (London: Macmillan, 1973), p. 89.

[3] 18 October 1973.

[4] 20 October 1973.

[5] 18 October 1973.

[6] 20 October 1973.

He concluded that Bunny's prose 'suggests that each man – whether in battle or in love – is essentially alone'.[7]

Bunny knew what it was like to be alone. He tried to model himself on Duncan, who lived so admirably in the present, but as Bunny told Frances Partridge, 'My difficulty is that I cannot help loving although I know that it is inappropriate to do so. If I get a letter or even a postcard, I can banish the past … But after a month or six weeks [of] silence old feelings begin nagging like a hollow tooth.' Bunny felt particularly cut off from events when William's third child, Jessica, was born in January 1974.

Having completed *The Master Cat*, Bunny wondered what to write next. 'You know how uneasy one feels', he told Frances Partridge, 'when there is no bit of work for one to neglect.' He also confessed to committing a folly: he had arranged to buy a hive and a swarm of bees. 'No fool like an old fool', he declared.[8] He reasoned that he ought to be reducing his responsibilities and that French bees were bad-tempered, but against such practical considerations he simply liked bees and knew they would make him happy. Frances exclaimed that Bunny 'goes from strength to strength and almost makes one believe in immortality'.[9]

He returned to England that summer, primarily to see his new granddaughter and research his latest book, a historical novel based on the life of his maternal great-grandmother, Clementina Carey. Bunny was happy because for the first time in several years he saw something of his daughter Fanny. They travelled together first to Wales to see Dicky Garnett then to Boughrood to stay with the publisher Michael Howard, and finally up the

---

[7] 20 October 1973.

[8] DG/F. Partridge, Charry, 30 March 1974 [KCC].

[9] Partridge, *Ups and Downs*, p. 299; diary entry for 5 July 1974.

east coast of Scotland to research his book. Even so, Frances Partridge observed a disquieting animosity towards Bunny on the occasion of Sophie's eleventh birthday, when Angelica and Fanny 'ganged up' against him. Frances was astounded at their apparent inability to appreciate Bunny's 'courage, the value and splendidness of his love', his 'sanity' and 'lack of self-pity.'[10] Many people admired Bunny for these very qualities and the extraordinary parade of visitors of all ages who made their way to Charry later that summer, testifies to the fact that he was appreciated and loved.

Although Magouche parcelled up the time she could spend with Bunny, he had spent most of March with her and with Janetta and Jaime Parlade at their villa, Tramores, in the hills near Marbella. Magouche was restoring a farmhouse in Andalusia, and Bunny looked forward to joining her there in November. He was suffering from sciatica and hoped the Spanish sun would act as a balm. In his customary haste, he set off having received no confirmation that she expected him at the time he elected to arrive. On 1 November he arrived at the farmhouse, Rosalejo, to find it deserted. Having booked into a hotel for the night, he woke in the early hours with a sudden realisation that Magouche had in fact tried to put him off. No letter had arrived because of a French postal strike, but Joe Derville had conveyed a verbal telephone message from Magouche, which was obviously inaccurately relayed.

Bunny went on to Gerald Brenan's where he received a telephone call from Magouche suggesting they meet at Rosalejo a week later. Meanwhile Bunny's sciatica worsened and he obtained cortisone pills from a local chemist. When he

---

[10] Partridge, *Ups and Downs*, pp. 316–17; diary entry for 12 August 1974.

was eventually reunited with Magouche they stayed in a rented apartment rather than at her house. Bunny saw little of her as she spent her days overseeing the builders and in the evenings she returned late, exhausted. Although surprised to receive an invitation from Janetta Parlade to stay at Tramores, Bunny accepted as Magouche seemed preoccupied. He was touched by Janetta's sweetness and consideration towards him, all the more so as he soon felt very unwell with flu-like symptoms, a temperature, trembling and depression.

On 14 December Magouche called a doctor, who instructed Bunny to stop taking the steroids. It took him almost a fortnight to recover sufficiently to be taken to Gerald's to make room at Tramores for Frances Partridge. It was only gradually that it occurred to Bunny that he was not wanted and had come to Spain at the wrong time. When Magouche brought Xan Fielding to Tramores Bunny was too ill to attach any significance to the event, but on a subsequent tour of Rosalejo it was obvious that Magouche and Fielding were sharing a bed.

It was not that Bunny objected to Magouche's lovers but he did expect to be the centre of her attention when he was with her. He also felt Magouche should have told him about Fielding. Bunny reasoned that such openness would not have changed his feelings for her. Instead it would have shown that she valued him as a friend as well as a lover. But like the Bunny of yore Magouche was adept at compartmentalisation. She had not anticipated that a postal strike and inaccurately relayed message would cause her compartments to conflate.

Bunny felt cuckolded and hated appearing foolish before Gerald, Janetta and Frances. He realised that Janetta and Gerald had colluded with Magouche in an elaborate scheme to keep him and Fielding apart. Frances, who arrived late on the scene,

534

considered the plot to separate Bunny and Fielding 'rather too overt'.[11] Fielding's relative youth and heroic stature did not help. Twenty-six years Bunny's junior, Fielding had been a war hero, leading the resistance in Crete, fighting alongside Cretan guerrillas and narrowly escaping execution by the Gestapo in occupied France.

Bunny had been away from Charry for two months, but still felt too weak to manage the journey home. Fanny came to his rescue, arriving on 3 January to drive him to France. Once home, Bunny determined never again to see Magouche. 'Love is only valuable if one can return it', he wrote to Frances Partridge, 'And I shall not feel love of any kind for Magouche again'.[12] Frances suggested Bunny should not be hard on Magouche, should remember that she loved him and not reject her affection.

Magouche wrote to Bunny stating he was her 'nearest and dearest friend of the last eight years'.[13] She explained that she had not tried to deceive him, that when she had endeavoured to bring the subject of Fielding into their conversations Bunny seemed not to want to hear. In a frenzied act of excavation, Bunny went back through all Magouche's letters, and in an unsent letter to Frances Partridge, catalogued each reference to Fielding. 'You see', he said, 'she believes she can keep afloat by keeping her affairs in watertight compartments. She is quite right in this: the trouble arises when she tries to mix them.'[14] If Bunny didn't recognise the pot calling the kettle black, he also failed to

---

[11] Partridge, *Ups and Downs*, p. 340; diary entry for 30 December 1974.

[12] DG/F. Partridge, Charry, 14 February 1975 [KCC].

[13] Quoted in DG/F. Partridge, Charry, 17 February 1975 [KCC].

[14] DG/F. Partridge, Charry, 20 February 1975, in DG's hand at top: 'NOT SENT', TS, [Northwestern].

acknowledge that the whole situation had been caused by his own neglect to check whether she had been expecting him.

Over the ensuing weeks Bunny spent all day and most of the night unable to escape from what he called 'this obsession'.[15] It was not until 27 February that Bunny's mind seemed to clear and he was able to write to Frances: '*Le brave Lapin est dans son assiette*' ('Good old Bunny is feeling well').[16] At dinner, one evening, seated beside a doctor, Bunny asked about the effects of cortisone, explaining that he had taken a high dosage in Spain. The doctor replied that cortisone may have made Bunny vulnerable to infection, hence the flu-like symptoms. He was horrified that Bunny should have been given the drug, which had, he felt certain, contributed to his heightened emotionalism. Perhaps Bunny had suffered from *steroid psychosis*, a condition which can affect people on high doses. Abruptly stopping the treatment may have exacerbated the situation: the dosage should be gradually reduced otherwise irritable or delusional behaviour can ensue. Bunny's behaviour over Magouche was certainly uncharacteristic. He had not reacted hysterically like this when Angelica left him. Bunny kept his word and did not see Magouche again. In 1978 she married Xan Fielding.

The Master Cat: The True and Unexpurgated Story of Puss in Boots was published in December 1974 while Bunny was in Spain. He was delighted with the illustrations: he had searched for someone who could achieve a similar directness to Ray and settled on his daughter Nerissa. Visually, it is a charming book with Nerissa's fine and appealing illustrations heading every chapter. It is written in the style of a fairy tale, but as Paul Scott warned

---

[15] DG/F. Partridge, Charry, 23 February 1975 [KCC].
[16] DG/F. Partridge, Charry, 27 February 1975 [KCC].

Country Life readers, it certainly wasn't a children's book.[17] It has a Roald Dahl-like quality and is full of the macabre and grisly. Reviewers found it original, ironic and plausibly feline.

The Master Cat is a testament to Tiber who 'made some minor corrections and […] agreed to certify it as the tradition of his race, and believed by him to be true in all particulars'.[18] Tiber's paw print is the seal of approval. But the cat makes another appearance, for he is present on the back cover of the book, photographed sitting on his master's lap. Bunny admired his independent spirit but found it unsettling when Tiber would disappear, returning dilapidated from another altercation with the Wood Cat. In early 1975, just a few months after his immortalisation in print, Tiber disappeared again, this time for good.

'You know', Bunny wrote to Frances Partridge in March 1975, 'when I look back on my life there are only two women I have been completely in love with – Ray and Angelica'.[19] A week later he received a letter from a stranger – a twenty-five-year-old Australian environmental science student – proposing to visit him. She was the ex-girlfriend of a fan who had been corresponding with Bunny. Her name was Marie Harvey and she told Bunny she had light brown hair, would be wearing jeans and carrying a back-pack. He collected her from the station and she spent a week with him at Charry in April. Bunny told Frances the visit had been 'wonderful', that he and Marie 'became as thick as thieves & as close as the ivy & the oak & the longer we talked the more we liked each other & the barrier between 25 &

---

17 19 December 1974.

18 David Garnett, *The Master Cat: The True and Unexpurgated Story of Puss in Boots* (London: Macmillan, 1974), p. 134.

19 DG/F. Partridge, Charry, 14 March 1975 [KCC].

83 vanished'.[20] Afterwards, Marie wrote to say how much she valued his friendship and affection. He had evidently impressed upon her the importance of sharing a bed in getting to know someone. '*Le brave Lapin*' was most certainly '*dans son assiette*'.

Marie spent two successive Christmases with Bunny. Together they made Christmas puddings and spent their evenings reading Carson McCullers, Conrad, Hudson and others of Bunny's favourite authors. Bunny enjoyed sharing his literary and culinary knowledge with her. Marie was genuinely fond of Bunny and if an intimate friendship between March and November seems unusual, then Bunny was an unusual man. As ever Frances Partridge can be relied upon to provide a window into his robust old age: 'The athletic figure of his youth', she said, 'retained considerable dignity even in his eighties [...]. He was still ready and eager to dive into a pool of cold water [...]. He was a happy, remarkably sane and lovable man.'[21]

Bunny was still in demand. David Korda and the actress Jeanne Moreau were independently interested in filming *Aspects of Love* and Moreau visited Charry to discuss the matter. Peter Ackroyd and Claire Tomalin sought occasional reviews from him for the *Spectator* and *New Statesman* respectively. Reviewing Virginia Woolf's autobiographical essays *Moments of Being* in the *New Statesman* ('Lady into Woolf'), Bunny commented that like D.H. Lawrence 'she will be interpreted *ad nauseam* instead of being enjoyed. So, ignoring interpreters, it is good to read what she says about herself.'[22] In August Bunny was the subject of a celebratory feature in the *Illustrated London News*, entitled 'A

---

[20] DG/F. Partridge, Charry, 18 April 1975 [KCC].

[21] Partridge, *Everything to Lose*, p. 119.

[22] DG, 'Lady into Woolf', Summer Books, *New Statesman*, 11 June 1976.

Survivor of Bloomsbury'. He was evidently one of the fittest to have survived so long. Frederic Raphael also wanted to write an article on Bunny, and having contacted him, was invited to lunch at Charry. The article, which appeared some years later in *PN Review*,[23] is curiously inaccurate, stating that Frankie Birrell (rather than Francis Meynell) founded the Nonesuch Press, and that a few months after the interview, Bunny was found lying dead among his grape vines. Bunny did not possess any grape vines at the time. Despite his willingness to help the biographers and researchers who came to his door, Bunny was sometimes irritated by superficial questions along the lines of ' "Do you remember any anecdotes about Lytton Strachey" '.[24]

'One gets tired of being an exile', Bunny told Angelica, 'not from the country but those one loves'.[25] He planned to visit England in July, to receive an honorary D.Litt. from Birmingham University, but in March 1977 Bunny rushed to London on an unscheduled visit. Henrietta had fallen thirty feet onto concrete smashing most of the bones on her right side and breaking her pelvis. She was in Charing Cross Hospital, lucky not to be brain-damaged or paraplegic. Staying with Angelica, Bunny was surprised by the way she seemed both intensely familiar and strangely foreign to him. 'We had known each other almost too well', he said, '& have each changed so much that one sometimes feels as though one of the steps in the staircase has disappeared.'[26]

Up She Rises was published in March 1977. It is the story of Bunny's maternal great-grandparents Clementina Carey and

[23] Frederic Raphael, 'Aspects of Garnett', *PN Review*, 115, May–June 1997.
[24] DG/AVG, Charry, '2 am' [18 February 1977] [KCC].
[25] DG/AVG, Charry, 24 February 1977 [KCC].
[26] DG/AVG, Charry, Saturday evening 9 April 1977 [KCC].

Peter Black, of his great-grandfather's sea-going adventures and Clementina's heroic trek from Scotland to the south coast of England to see her husband, in port for one day. Bunny's second-cousin, Jane Gregory, undertook much of the family research. Bunny thanked her in an author's note, but dedicated the book to the memory of Constance, 'Translator of Russian'. As Bunny told Angelica, 'In the past I despised reviews and if I thought the book good I didn't mind a damn [...]. But I have a low – I suppose it is low – desire for recognition while I am alive! I get so tired of people who say they have read *Lady into Fox*.'[27] The reviews were less widespread than for his previous books, but they were good. Peter Tinniswood, in *The Times*, declared it 'a joy to read'[28] and Susan Kennedy, in the *TLS*, thought it a 'warm and affectionate portrait of a courageous woman'.[29]

In September, when Bunny underwent his annual medical test to renew his driving licence, he was given only a six-month permit. He blamed it on his spectacles, through which, he said, he could see no better than with the naked eye. 'All I need', he reasoned illogically, 'is a very powerful pair to read the letters in the test.'[30] As his sight deteriorated, his driving became even more idiosyncratic. When Rosie Peto visited, she insisted on doing the driving because Bunny drove so fast it terrified her. Quentin and Olivier's daughter, Virginia Nicholson, recalls Bunny's habit of accelerating as he approached a junction, his eyes fixed ahead as he enquired whether anything was coming

---

[27] DG/AVG, Charry, 24 February 1977 [KCC].

[28] 24 March 1977.

[29] 25 March 1977.

[30] DG/AVG, Charry, 24 September 1977 [KCC].

while he sped across the road.[31] On one occasion Henrietta leapt from the car rather than endure the horror of his driving. Bunny would no more concede his sight had deteriorated than stop climbing ladders high into trees to collect his bees.

Neither David Korda's projected *Aspects of Love* nor the Patrick Garland film had got off the ground, but in 1975 *A Man in the Zoo* was dramatised for BBC Television. Reviewing the programme in *The Times*, Alan Coren commented that Bunny was 'a man who fenced literature off into a small perfection'.[32] It was a nice accolade. In September 1977 *The Sailor's Return* was shot on location in Dorset. It was directed by Jack Gold, with Tom Bell and Shope Shodeinde in the principal roles. Having relinquished the film rights to the book Bunny made no financial gain. The film was a critical success, but did not attract a significant audience, mainly because, as George Moore had observed, the ending was too bleak. A young Australian film-maker, Joanne Lane, had bought the rights to *Lady into Fox*, hoping to shoot the film with a cast of real foxes. Despite months attempting to train them, like Sylvia Tebrick, they preferred to be wild.

Bunny was engaged in another literary project, compiling an anthology of essays on the writers and artists he had known. It was, he told Sylvia, a sort of 'brief lives', with Bunny as the catalyst. Alan Maclean thought the book would be so popular it would make Bunny rich, but as Bunny told Sylvia,' I don't very much want to be rich'. 'I have all I need and enough tomato chutney for two years.'[33] He had given Hilton Hall to his grandsons Oliver and

[31] V. Nicholson, interview, 12 October 2010.

[32] 12 March 1975.

[33] DG/STW, Le Verger de Charry, 22 October 1977, in RG, ed., *Sylvia and David*, p. 232–3.

Edward and had long ago handed Ridley Stokoe to William. Bunny owned no property in France and the sale of L'Ancienne Auberge had largely benefited Angelica. He paid for an expensive steel hull to encase the leaking Moby Dick, before giving the boat to Fanny.

After years of silence, Bunny heard from Shusheila Lall, now living on a remote farm in Kulu province, India. She invited Bunny to stay, and remarkably, given the rigours of the journey, he said yes. But then he heard nothing from her. 'As you see', he wrote to Sylvia, 'I am not in Cashmere, or even Kashmir, and I am rather worried because my dear Shusheila, who sent me the warmest of invitations [...] has not replied to two letters suggesting that I accept it'.[34] Shusheila was in no position to follow through her invitation, having been murdered by her servants.[35] It is doubtful Bunny ever knew this dreadful fact.

On 1 May 1978 the ranks, now extremely thin, were further depleted by Sylvia's death. She and Bunny had corresponded to the last. Twelve days later Bunny received sad news from Angelica. Duncan had died on 9 May, following a short illness. He 'led a full & happy life and is a model to us all', Bunny replied, advising Angelica to follow Duncan's example and 'live in the present'.[36] Alone at Charry, Bunny did not follow his own advice, taking out Duncan's letters and reading them over and over again.

[34] Ibid., p. 232.

[35] www.tribuneindia.com/2003/20030215/windows/above.htm.

[36] DG/AVG, Charry, 12 May 1978 [KCC].

Chapter Thirty-Seven

'He remained almost heroically active to the last.'[1]

Bunny worked on his 'lives' throughout 1978, but as the months passed he had to admit that his eyes were not what they had been. He consulted his optician who confirmed cataracts and booked Bunny into Moorfield Hospital, London, where he had the cataract removed from his right eye on 16 June. As he had to wait a month before being fitted with glasses to correct his sight, he utilised the time visiting friends and family in England. He was delighted to be made Companion of the Royal Society of Literature, alongside Stephen Spender and Philip Larkin.

Bunny spent much of his time at Hilton, now occupied by Richard and Jane. Jane's talent as a stage designer had transformed Hilton Hall into an elegant setting for paintings, pottery, textiles, sculpture and books. Bunny could not quite believe it was the same house he had inhabited. In July it was the backdrop for a *South Bank Show* feature on Bunny. Presented by Melvyn

---

[1] Quentin Bell, Obituary of David Garnett, *Royal Society of Literature: Reports for 1979–80 and 1980–81* (London: Royal Society of Literature, 1981), p. 46.

543

Bragg, it was a pioneering television arts programme which eventually ran for thirty years. As Kim Evans, the show's producer, explained to Bunny, the programme would tie in with the release of the film *The Sailor's Return*, focussing on Bunny as the author of the original novel, of *Lady into Fox* and the prospective book of memoirs.

Bunny was filmed in Hilton Hall and in the garden, resplendent in an enormous pair of thickly glazed spectacles with his beret perched jauntily on his head. He noted in his diary, 'Got on well with Melvin Bragg; drank wine all the time'.[2] The careful observer may have noticed that the level of wine in the bottle of red placed on the table between them was able to rise, as well as fall. It was evidently replaced several times during the course of the day's filming.

Returning to Charry in early August, Bunny was relieved to be back. But he thought it was time to have a companion to live with. Earlier in the year, when Quentin's and Olivier's daughter Virginia stayed for two months, he felt a weight had been lifted. It was not that he could not cope alone, but he enjoyed companionship and found Virginia particularly engaging company. They had what she describes as a bond over food, both enjoying cooking, devising menus and marketing.[3]

In the meantime there was the usual stream of visitors to keep him occupied. Frankie Birrell's nephew, Hallam Tennyson (the poet's great-grandson) also came to interview Bunny for a BBC radio programme, and in December *Lady into Fox* was BBC Radio 4's *Book at Bedtime*. Bunny had finished his book of memoirs, which Richard had dissuaded him from calling 'On

---

[2]   DG, Pocket Diary 1978, 21 July [Northwestern].

[3]   V. Nicholson, interview, 12 October 2010.

the Lips of the Living', instead opting for *Great Friends*. Richard also persuaded his father to have a telephone installed at Charry and to buy a 'Super-Comtesse', a sort of mobile invalid carriage, as insurance against failing his next medical. In October Bunny had been given a 'Pi-jaw' on his age by a locum doctor, who only granted him a three-month driving permit. The 'put-put' lurked, a malevolent presence, signalling what might lie ahead.

Bunny's hoped-for companion arrived on Christmas Day 1978, in the shape of his daughter Fanny. As he told Frances Partridge, 'We have settled into an absolutely truthful, intimate and amused relationship'.[4] In the ensuing months Fanny busied herself by forging a garden for Bunny, driving iron wedges into unforgiving rock. She knew he longed to grow vegetables again, something which would give him enormous pleasure. She completed the garden on Easter Sunday 1979, having planted asparagus, carrots, bay, rhubarb, tomatoes and vines. Bunny planned it all on paper, drawing up planting schedules and purchasing seeds with the same enthusiasm as for his vegetable garden at Wissett Lodge in 1916.

Great Friends was published by Macmillan in June. It was a handsome book, containing not only Bunny's descriptive 'Portraits of seventeen writers', but also reproductions of photographs, paintings and sculptures of each. Bunny was present on the front cover, dapper in his Savile Row sky-blue tweed suit. He quoted Samuel Butler on the title page: 'Yet meet we shall, and part, and meet again, / Where dead men meet, on lips of living men.'[5] The portraits range from the writers Bunny had known as

---

[4] DG/F. Partridge, Charry, 21 February 1979 [KCC].

[5] David Garnett, *Great Friends: Portraits of Seventeen Writers* (London: Macmillan, 1979).

a boy, like Galsworthy, Conrad and Edward Thomas, to those of his own generation and social milieu, including Virginia Woolf, E.M. Forster, Maynard Keynes, Lytton Strachey and T.H. White.

Great Friends had come about because Richard (working for Macmillan) recalled how well Bunny had previously written about other writers, including D.H. Lawrence. He gave Alan Maclean various passages to read and the book was commissioned. It was well received and widely reviewed, so much so that *Gay News* focussed on Bunny's memoir of D.H. and Frieda Lawrence, in which he quoted Lawrence's 'black beetles' letter in full. Characteristically torn between the need for truth and what he perceived as potentially problematic revelations about his own sexuality, Bunny again came close to revealing his bisexuality in print. Post-Holroyd, he could now admit 'my friends were homosexuals', but in relation to his own sexuality, he accused Lawrence of 'barking up the wrong tree'. With his children and grandchildren in mind, Bunny could not quite make it through the confessional door, lingering instead on the threshold.

In a review inevitably entitled 'Bloomsbury Survivor', C.P. Snow singled out Bunny's 'cheerful impartiality', that even in his late eighties he could 'still keep his disinterested interest active and fresh'.[6] In the *New Statesman*, Jonathan Raban perceptively observed the paradox in Bunny: 'His pedigree is purest Bloomsbury, but his temperament is much closer to that of Buchan and Kipling.'[7] Bunny enjoyed the review, but did not care to be compared to Kipling, an 'Imperialist'. Raban explained that the similarities were located in what he perceived to be a

---

[6] *Financial Times*, 16 June 1979.
[7] Jonathan Raban, 'Broad Church', *New Statesman*, 15 June, 1979.

shared 'poetic tenderness and detailed attention to machines, to the outdoors, to the precise naming of landscapes', and that it was 'as one of the heroes of a kind of exactitude in writing', in which he saw parallels between Kipling's and Bunny's work.[8] Raban recognised there was more to Bunny's craft than fantasy and fable alone, that his writing was underpinned by the land on which he had laboured and the earth which he dug.

Bunny planned to spend June in England, but before leaving, Giovanna visited and stayed a night. Fanny tactfully made herself scarce. In England Bunny undertook his usual rounds. Visiting Angelica at Charleston he found her 'friendly but restrained', pondering 'Can we ever have been happy & married?'[9] Due to return to France on 2 July, Bunny was confined to Hilton for an additional week. A nightmare in which he was attacked by a chow caused him to fall out of bed, leaving him with a black eye and cracked rib. He had never much liked dogs.

Back at Charry Bunny was visited by Rosie Peto and her partner Renee Fedden, and in quick succession by Anna Wickham's son, Jim Hepburn, Geoffrey Keynes's son Stephen, Francis Meynell's son Benedict, and by Dicky Garnett and his younger sister, Anne Lee Mitchell. Bunny's grandson Ned came to help bottle wine. The garden was full of courgettes, beans, leeks, tomatoes, peppers and aubergines, but such abundance did not deter Bunny from frugally resurrecting some ancient cold chicken which he disguised in a curry. He was so ill afterwards that he spent hours on the bathroom floor. His powers of recovery were such that when, a week later, he needed stitches for a wound in his arm, he insisted on receiving no anaesthetic,

---

8 J. Raban/DG, 145 Felsham Road SW15, 27 June 1979 [Northwestern].
9 DG, Pocket Diary 1979, Monday 11 June [HG].

to satisfy his curiosity as to whether he could bear the pain.

In May 1980 Bunny received a letter from an American Professor of English, Matthew J. Bruccoli, who was completing a biography of F. Scott Fitzgerald and particularly wanted to know whether Bunny could provide information derived from his correspondence with Fitzgerald. Bruccoli continued to say that the only available evidence of their correspondence was Fitzgerald's inscription to Bunny in *Tender is the Night*. He hoped Bunny might still have the book.[10] Bunny had never even seen it. This was the first he had heard of such an inscription. In fact, Bunny did not much admire Fitzgerald, and was unimpressed when he read *Tender is the Night* back in 1952.

It transpired that the inscription had been quoted by Alan Ross in a 1948 *Horizon* article: ' "Dear David Garnett" it read, 'Notice how neatly I stole and adapted your magnificent ending to LADY INTO FOX which I know practically [...] by heart" '.[11] Bunny assumed Fitzgerald had sent him the book care of *Horizon*'s editor, Cyril Connolly, assuming Connolly would forward it. He was probably right, as the inscribed book remained on Connolly's bookshelves until it was sold at Sotheby's as part of the 'Cyril Connolly Collection', eventually residing in the University of Tulsa, Oklahoma. A bibliophile, Connolly took great care of his library even if he did not care to whom the contents actually belonged. According to John Sutherland, Connolly misappropriated at least two collector's items from among Stephen Spender's books. Fitzgerald's inscription was a

---

[10] Matthew J. Bruccoli/DG, Jefferies Professor of English, University of South Carolina, Columbia, 1 May 1980 [Northwestern].

[11] F. Scott Fitzgerald, quoted in DG/F. Partridge, Charry, 23 May 1980 [KCC].

nice accolade, and Bunny was glad to learn of its existence.

In June he made his annual pilgrimage to England where he visited Angelica, took tea with Barbara Bagenal and saw his children and grandchildren. But as he wrote to Mina Curtiss, 'I am 88 and beginning to depend on other people to do things like changing the wheel of a car.'[12] He decided that the time had come to have a companion. Fanny had been with him for much of the previous year, and it was a great comfort to know that she had bought a cottage nearby, but he did not want her to feel tied. He had recently experienced bouts of dizziness and wanted to have someone on hand in case these returned. He composed an advertisement entitled 'WOMAN WANTED', stipulating the candidate should be well educated, healthy, middle or upper class, not religious, dog-free, independent, have work to occupy her, should speak French, drive a car and have no lover or children on the scene.

Bunny's agent, Hilary Rubinstein, knew just such a woman, and on 23 July Joan O'Donovan arrived for a preliminary meeting. She was a writer, at one time the lover of the writer Frank O'Connor (whose real name was Michael O'Donovan), with whom she had a son. (She changed her name to O'Donovan by deed poll.) As Bunny told Frances, 'She is sixty-five, has a cap of grey hair' and 'eats and drinks everything and likes cooking'.[13] Having agreed that Joan would arrive in October for a trial period until Christmas, Bunny quickly found that they got on well and shared similar tastes. While Joan tapped away on her electric typewriter, Bunny sorted through his correspondence with Sylvia Townsend Warner (his letters to her having been

---

[12] DG/M. Curtiss, Le Verger, 1 September 1980 [Berg].
[13] DG/F. Partridge, Charry, 7 August 1980 [KCC].

returned after her death). He was thinking of editing the correspondence for publication, though he told Frances that his letters 'will want a good deal of pruning as I find to my surprise that I wrote to her freely about Angelica. They are not discreditable but private.' 'There is too little privacy nowadays', he lamented, adding, 'There soon will be not one of my friends or acquaintances whose biography has not been written'.[14] Joan left for Christmas, as arranged, although she would return in the New Year. Expecting a lonely Christmas, Bunny was surprised and delighted when Henrietta arrived on Christmas Eve.

In January 1981 he worked on his selection of Sylvia's letters; Joan returned, and they continued harmoniously as before. On the 29th Bunny cooked a particularly good dinner for Meg and Bysshe Elstob: stuffed eggs followed by roast pork and red cabbage with apple; baked pears for pudding. Bunny noted in his diary that the following day was like a 'fine spring day'.[15] He bought eighty litres of wine which he set aside to bottle later. That was the final entry in his diary, the last words he wrote. The following day he had a stroke and was left more or less paralysed. Joan called Henrietta, who came straight away. She was soon joined by Richard, William, Nerissa, Sophie and her fiancé, Wenzel Gelpke. Fanny did not come. Henrietta commented that when she saw Bunny at Christmas, she noticed he had aged, and had a 'faraway look in his eyes'. He told her how much he loved her and of his hopes for Sophie. 'He spoke of all the people whom he loved. It was a kind of requiem.'[16]

Joan told Richard that Bunny had initially reacted to being

---

[14] DG/F. Partridge, Charry, 24 November 1980 [KCC].
[15] DG, Pocket Diary 1981, 30 January [Northwestern].
[16] HG, 'Aspects of my Father'.

incapacitated with 'violent fury'. Richard sat up with his father, talking late – 'a sort of farewell'.[17] While the others remained, Richard returned to a publishing deadline in London. On 17 February Bunny had another stroke, 'decided that this sort of life was not for him', and died, a few weeks short of his eighty-ninth birthday.[18] According to his wishes, his body was removed to the School of Anatomy in Bordeaux. As he earlier remarked to Frances: 'no funeral, no black ties, no cold feet, no horrors'.[19] Bunny had so loved the physical world around him that he could not contend with the concept of any kind of afterlife, except that of his books and those who lived on to carry his genes. The last letter he received was from Rosemary Peto. 'Darling Bunny', she wrote, 'Thank you for your existence'.[20]

[17] RG/SGK, 4 October 2011.
[18] RG/SGK, 4 October 2011.
[19] DG/F. Partridge, Charry, 11 December 1975 [KCC].
[20] R. Peto/DG, Le Rocher de la Mere, Le Vigan, 8 February [1981] [Northwestern].

Afterlife

Bunny had an immense capacity for friendship. Frances Partridge described him as a 'first-rate-friend', 'staunch, warm and appreciative'.[1] His brother-in-law Quentin Bell wrote, 'In a friendship which lasted for sixty-five years I do not remember that we ever had a real quarrel'.[2] His childhood friend, Harold Hobson, moved to the village of Hilton simply to live close by. Both Sylvia Townsend Warner and Mina Curtiss were lifelong friends, his correspondence with each spanning half a century.

Although Bunny was loved and respected in his lifetime, a very different figure appeared in print after his death. In contrast to the lovable character found in Frances Partridge's published memoirs and diaries, in other quarters Bunny emerged as an unsavoury, predatory male with 'unnatural' sexual appetites. The book that marked a watershed in his representation was *Deceived with Kindness*, a memoir written by Angelica Garnett,

---

[1] Partridge, *Everything to Lose*, p. 119.
[2] Bell, Obituary of David Garnett.

published in 1984, three years after his death.

Angelica spent seven years writing the memoir, which she said represented 'an emergence from the dark into the light'.[3] It was written, ostensibly, to unravel the motives behind her parents' deception concerning the identity of her father, whom she believed to be Clive Bell until, aged seventeen, she was disabused of this fact by Vanessa. Although Angelica originally intended the memoir to encompass only her childhood and youth, in the event it contained a chapter chillingly entitled 'Bunny's Victory', where she portrayed him as a predatory older man, intent on ensnaring an innocent young victim. Whilst acknowledging 'It is dangerous to talk only of people's secret motives [...] because one may so easily be wrong', Angelica stated that Bunny's 'self-ishness and perhaps revenge [...] led him to make a victim of an ignorant and unsuspecting girl who was unable to defend herself'.[4]

It is true Bunny was twenty-six years Angelica's senior, but in *Deceived with Kindness* she depicts him as consciously and strategi-cally exploiting her youth and innocence, in order to exact revenge upon Vanessa for rejecting his advances at the time of the Great War. There is no evidence of any such advance, and even if an advance had been rejected, it was out of character for Bunny to be vengeful in this context: his fifty-year friendship with Mina Curtiss was founded upon her refusal to go to bed with him. The youthful Bunny was inclined to be demonstrative, as Vanessa noted in 1916: 'He's always very nice to me, and he

---

[3] Angelica Garnett, *Deceived with Kindness* (London: Chatto & Windus 1984; Oxford University Press paperback, 1985) p. 175.

[4] AVG, *Deceived*, p. 157.

likes I think to be demonstrative to everyone he likes, but he's not in love with me.'[5]

Angelica had the advantage of hindsight: she spent much of the 1960s and 1970s trying to make sense of the past and her place within it. Such introspection inevitably involved the ordering of events, exploration of motives and examination of emotions. Moreover memory is not infallible and there are many inaccuracies in Angelica's narrative, not least that she long remained ignorant of the fact that Bunny and Duncan had been lovers. Bunny had informed her of this in June 1939 three years before their marriage.[6] As her brother, Quentin diplomatically stated, 'To say that this is an honest narrative is not to say that it is accurate'.[7]

Deceived with Kindness is framed by Angelica discovering the works of Karen Horney, a Neo-Freudian psychoanalyst. Although Angelica did not undergo psychoanalysis, she was heavily influenced by Horney's books, in particular their emphasis on the effects of parental influence upon the child *as experienced* by the child at the time. According to Horney, a child's need for parental approval can be so pronounced that in adulthood it seeks out a partner to resolve the problems experienced in childhood, thus perpetuating the dependent and compliant relationship.

---

[5] VB/R. Fry, Eleanor Farm, West Wittering [Chichester], Sunday [?9 May] [1916] [TGA], quoted in Marler, ed., *Selected Letters of Vanessa Bell*, p. 179.

[6] DG, Pocket Diary 1939, entry for Friday 2 June [Northwestern]: 'after dinner told her [Angelica] about Duncan & myself which she did not know'.

[7] Quoted in Regina Marler, *Bloomsbury Pie: The Making of the Bloomsbury Boom* (London: Virago Press, 1997), p. 238.

It is obvious why Angelica was attracted to this rationale. But her perspective of her relationship with Bunny contrasts markedly with the evidence of their correspondence during their courtship and early years of marriage. Her memoir is highly subjective, created in response to Duncan's death, to an ensuing emotional break-down and to the form of self-analysis which Angelica felt most answered her needs. It reflects the vantage point of a particular moment and is the outcome of the cumulative narratives Angelica shaped to explain and rationalise her life.

Once in print, Angelica's authoritative portrayal of Bunny became enshrined as 'truth'. In a review of the book in *The New York Review of Books*, the journalist Janet Malcolm acknowledged Angelica's severity regarding her parents, but seemed to entirely accept her portrayal of Bunny. If anything, Malcolm wrote about Bunny in even more venomous language than Angelica had done.

Angelica stated she did not 'understand how incestuous my relationship with Bunny was'.[8] Such comments have reverberated through subsequent biographies of Bunny's friends and contemporaries, where he has become tarnished with the taint of incest and sex-addiction. He is typically described as 'the libidinous novelist', 'the Don Juan' and 'a noted connoisseur of feminine charms'.[9] Such short-hand is, of course, true – he could be constructed as each of these – but also very much more. In *The Neo-Pagans*, a group-biography of Rupert Brooke and his

---

[8] AVG, *Deceived*, p. 156.

[9] In, respectively: Miranda Seymour, *Robert Graves: Life on the Edge* (London: Doubleday, 1995), p. 166; Anthony Curtis, *Lit Ed: on Reviewing and Reviewers* (Manchester: Carcanet, 1998), p. 206; Nigel Jones, *Rupert Brooke: Life, Death & Myth* (London: Richard Cohen Books, 1999), p. 72.

circle, Paul Delany referred to Bunny's 'epic amorous career' and implied that Daphne Olivier was the only Olivier sister he was 'able to ensnare'.[10] Dismissive perhaps, but the language of blame and entrapment echoed Angelica's.

If Angelica saw herself, in hindsight, as a victim, it is extremely unlikely that Bunny's other women lovers would have cast themselves in this mould. Indeed, the view of Bunny as a predatory womaniser is hardly fair to the women he is alleged to have conquered. Bunny wasn't keen on the one-night stand. He was interested in women for their intelligence as much as their beauty. According to his daughter Frances Garnett, he 'actually valued the intellect of a woman – he knew that women could be equally intelligent and equally intellectual.'[11] With the exception of a few youthful dalliances, Bunny's women lovers were characterised by independence, intelligence and education. It is a mistake to assume that Bunny spent his time seeking out innocent virgins. The women he loved chose him as much as he chose them. Moreover, Bunny maintained long friendships with former lovers, and in some cases, the sexual relationship continued for years or even decades.

Today the 1960s is seen as the era of women's sexual emancipation. In Bunny's circles women were sexually emancipated many decades earlier. For example, in 1915 when Bunny and Frankie Birrell called on James Strachey, they found the twenty-three-year-old Noel Olivier visiting. As Bunny recorded in his journal, 'When Noel came in she dropped French letters out of

---

[10] Paul Delany, *The Neo-Pagans: Friendship and Love in the Rupert Brooke Circle* (London: Macmillan, 1987), p. 69 and 230.

[11] Frances Garnett, interview, Cambridge, 31 May 2008.

her bag […]. Noel laughed & coloured a little.'[12] Noel typifies the independent women of Bunny's social milieu: she went on to become a consultant paediatrician.

With the passage of time Angelica's perspective shifted. In a new preface to the second edition, published in 1995, she no longer perceived her marriage to Bunny as entrapment by him, but as an 'ill-judged' 'act of rebellion' on her part against her parents. She even went so far as to say: 'I must discard the self-protective role of eternal victim.'[13] However the damage had been done. After all, with Bunny's three volumes of memoir long out of print (and they ended in 1940 with Ray's death) we only have Angelica's word for it. The reviewer in *The Economist* perceptively described *Deceived with Kindness* as 'an absorbing though deliberately one-sided and somewhat hostile tale', adding, 'One hopes that it serves its therapeutic purpose'.[14]

Angelica's version of Bunny not only eclipsed all others, but in tarnishing him, marginalised his published work and diminished his reputation. Only *Lady into Fox* and *Aspects of Love* remain in print. This is a shame, as he was an original writer of courage and distinction. Moreover, as a publisher, literary critic, editor, historian and bookseller, Bunny was an influential and important figure in the twentieth-century British literary landscape. Ironically, during the 1980s and 1990s when British literary biography was at its apogee, Bunny's ground-breaking autobiography was perceived, in some quarters, as evidence of his moral ignominy. At a time when biographers were mining Bunny's memoirs for information about their own subjects, his self-depiction as a

---

[12] DG, Journal 1914–18, entry for Tuesday [19 January 1915] [Northwestern].
[13] AVG, *Deceived with Kindness* (Pimlico edition with new preface, 1995), p. viii.
[14] Marler, *Bloomsbury Pie*, p. 238.

'libertine' appeared to add credence to Angelica's text. In more recent years, Bunny has appeared in biographical fiction hovering over Angelica's cradle ready to snatch her.

In the 1920s the Nonesuch Press was largely responsible for bringing Restoration drama back into print. Bunny was passionate about Restoration drama; he formed the Caroline Club specifically to read these plays. While Bunny, versed in Restoration literature, could identify the different types of libertine and could distinguish between a libertine and a rake, it was perhaps unrealistic for him to expect his readers to share his scholarly familiarity with the subtleties of seventeenth-century cultural terms and distinctions. Bunny recognised Libertinism as an *intellectual* movement which elevated the pursuit of pleasure. There was more than one kind of libertine: the dissolute and licentious character, and the 'philosophical libertine', a freethinker. It was with this second, more cerebral version that Bunny identified.

In his autobiography, Bunny deliberately dissociated himself from the 'dissolute' and 'licentious', stating: 'I am not, and had little impulse ever to become, a *rake*: that is a man whose loose life is the result of a reaction against the restraints imposed by his upbringing, or one who has a psychological craving for self-destruction and seeks it in the brothel, or the gutter.'[15] Bunny stated that in being the 'lover of very many women', he had always been driven by sensuality and the need to give sexual satisfaction. Moreover, he bravely intimated, as explicitly as he dared, his love for men and women. Even so, his attempt at truth has been misconstrued. The term 'libertine' has been taken up as shorthand to dismiss Bunny as exactly what he said he was not: a rake. It is interesting that Stephen Spender's autobiography

---

[15] DG, *Flowers*, p. 19.

caused similar revilement. His biographer John Sutherland remarked that Spender's 'frankness, far from disarming critics, has given some of them ammunition with which to attack him'.[16]

Bunny was not perfect. He espoused honesty but lacked self-awareness. His need for diversion was often destructive. He was cruel to Ray. Perhaps he was selfish in loving Angelica and marrying her. But as an imperfect example of humankind he created courageous stories, wrote beautiful prose, supported his friends, helped other writers, remained true to his convictions and loved his family. It is as though Bunny's literary achievements, all the good that he did and all the love people felt for him have been obscured by the palimpsest of a single, courageously written but ultimately harmful book.

---

[16] John Sutherland, *Stephen Spender: The Authorized Biography* (London: Viking, 2004; Penguin 2005), p. 2.

Edward Garnett

Constance and Bunny

The Cearne

Bunny as a boy, in The Cearne porch

Nellie Heath

Sommeilles Equipe 1915, Frankie Birrell seated middle row, second left; Bunny front right

Duncan Grant, c.1918, Vanessa Bell (1879–1961) © Tate, London 2015

Photograph of Angelica and Vanessa Bell, 1928, artist unknown
© Tate, London 2015

Ray

Hilton Hall,
1920s

Bunny and Stephen Tomlin, 1920s

DG climbing into a window, La Bergère, Cassis, 1920s

The writer in his study, 1930

Richard, c.1928

William, Bunny and cat in back garden,
Hilton Hall, 1929

Ray, Yorkshire, 1939

Bunny, T. H. White and peregrine falcons, 1939

Angelica at Butts Intake, 1940

Bunny and babies, 1946

Henrietta

Amaryllis

Fanny and Nerissa

Angelica and Bunny in the 1960s

Picture credits: all courtesy of the Estate of David Garnett and Tate Gallery Archives.

Acknowledgements

First of all, my thanks go to the late Richard Garnett for his unstinting encouragement, for sharing his formidable knowledge and for allowing me unrestricted access to his father's papers at Hilton Hall (these now reside at Northwestern University). Although Richard read this book in draft, my only regret is that he didn't live to see it published. I am also grateful to Jane Garnett for her warm hospitality and her valuable insights into the family environment at Hilton.

Henrietta Garnett has been extremely generous in giving me access to the papers of Duncan Grant and those papers of David Garnett in her keeping. I am grateful for her illuminating conversation, her kind hospitality and unceasing encouragement and enthusiasm.

I am indebted to the late Angelica Garnett for allowing me to read her correspondence with David Garnett which is in the Archives of King's College, Cambridge. This was particularly generous given that she would inevitably feature in my account of his life. I am grateful for her kindness in allowing me to interview her and for her hospitality.

For granting interviews, allowing me to read letters in their possession (or both) I particularly thank Anne Olivier Bell,

575

Frances Garnett, Michael Holroyd, Stephen Keynes, Virginia Nicholson, Joan O'Donovan, the late Magouche Fielding and the late Hilary Rubinstein.

I am also grateful to the following for help in various ways: Elizabeth Belsey, Emily Bingham, Monika Buchell, Anne Chisholm, Jan Dalley, Phil Davies, Richard Denyer, Larry Edgerton, Claire Flay-Petty, Susan Fox, Edward Garnett, Oliver Garnett, Jonathan and Nicky Gathorne-Hardy, Janet Gill, Crauford and Nancy Goodwin, Olga Grlic, John Harriss, Diana Hopkins, Claire and Geoffrey Kiddy, Mr and Mrs J. Kirkwood, Nicola Lacey, Andrew Lambirth, Jawaid Luqmani, Catherine MacGowan, David Marshall, Marina Martin, Stephen Massil, David McKitterick, Neil McWilliam, J. Lawrence Mitchell, Judy Moore, Paul Morrison, Tom Morrison, Amanda O'Shea, Bill Rau, Anthony Rudolph, Elaine Shaughnessy, Ceinwen Sinclair, John Smart, Matthew Spender, Peter Stansky, Tilli Tansey, Ann Thwaite, the Lord Walpole, Norma Watt and Denis and Hazel Wilkinson. Thanks also to John Sutherland for responding so promptly to a last minute query.

I have been greatly assisted by archivists and librarians, first among them, Patricia McGuire, the Archivist at King's College Cambridge, who has been unstintingly kind and helpful during the years of my research. I also extend grateful thanks to the archivists and librarians of the following institutions: the HRHRC at Austin, Texas (Richard Workman, Jean Cannon and Kurt Johnson); the Berg Collection, New York Public Library (Isaac Gewirtz and Anne Garner); the Bodleian Library, Oxford (Colin Harris); the British Library Manuscript Rooms and Sound Archives; the University of Delaware (Iris Snyder); Imperial College Archives (Anne Barrett and Catherine Harpham); Princeton University Library (Margaret Sherry); Jean Rose of

Random House Group for permission to consult publishing records at the University of Reading Library; the University of Reading Library; Smith College Archives; the University of Sussex Library (Dorothy Sheridan); Tate Gallery Archives; the University of East Anglia Special Collections Library (Bridget Gillies); Ulster Museum (Martyn Anglesea); Wellcome Library (Richard Aspin and Sharon Messenger; with particular thanks to Sir Mark Walport for facilitating access to as yet un-catalogued material there).

Although I have been fortunate in the wealth and breadth of primary material, I am immensely grateful to those biographers and historians whose work I have consulted. In particular, Frances Spalding's biographies of Vanessa Bell and Duncan Grant have been invaluable. Richard Garnett's biography of his grandmother, Constance Garnett, saved me much time in researching David Garnett's forebears. Edward Garnett's biographer, Helen Smith, has been both a great ally and generous source of information.

This book began life as a doctoral thesis. I am indebted to the UK Arts and Humanities Research Council which made my doctoral research possible through the provision of a scholarship. I am grateful to my examiners, Frances Spalding and Giles Foden, for their invaluable constructive criticism. At the University of East Anglia, I owe an immeasurable debt to Jon Cook whose guidance and scholarship considerably enhanced my work.

I would also like to thank my agent Maggie Hanbury and, at Bloomsbury, Stephanie Duncan and Miranda Vaughan Jones. I have benefited enormously from their expertise and enthusiasm for the book.

Finally I thank my son Rafael and husband Tony Barnett for their forbearance during this long project. They have tolerated my physical and mental absences and lived with David Garnett, on occasions, almost as closely as I have. Tony has not only accompanied me on research trips, but has been a constant and loving support. I thank him for all this, and for applying his intellectual scrutiny to every word I have written.

Needless to say any inaccuracies or mistakes are my own.

For permission to quote David Garnett, Constance Garnett, Edward Garnett and Nellie Heath I am indebted to the Estate of David Garnett. I am also indebted to Julian Bell and the Estate of Angelica Bell for permission to quote from her published writing and unpublished letters and to Henrietta Garnett for giving me permission to quote Duncan Grant, Vanessa Bell and Burgo Partridge.

For other permissions to quote I gratefully acknowledge: Peter Ackroyd; Virginia Allen (Noel Olivier); Victoria Bacon (Edward Hyams); the Bertrand Russell Peace Foundation; Betty May courtesy of a family member who wishes not to be named; Anne Chisholm; the Estate of John Dreyfus; the *Financial Times*; the Executors of the Estate of Michael Fordham; Guardian News & Media Ltd (*Guardian* and *Observer*); Adrian Goodman (Ottoline Morrell); Alastair Hamilton (Hamish Hamilton); Duff Hart-Davis (Rupert Hart-Davis); Anne Harvey (Eleanor Farjeon and Herbert Farjeon); David Higham Associates Ltd (the Estates of John Lehmann and T. H. White); Michael Holroyd; Lawrence James c/o the Andrew Lownie Literary Agency; Professor Simon Keynes (Geoffrey Keynes); Paul Levy; Desmond MacCarthy (Desmond MacCarthy); Susie Medley (Francis Birrell); the Executors of the Estate of Alix Meynell; the Executors of the Estate of Francis Meynell; Paul Morrison and Tom Morrison (Barbara Mackenzie-Smith); the *New Statesman*; News Syndication (*The Times, Sunday Times* and *The Times Literary Supplement*); Mark

Norton (H.T.J. Norton); Dr Henry Oakeley (John Hayward); Janetta Parlade; the Arthur Ransome Literary Estate; Professor Stephen Rhys (Theadora Fordham); Andrew Roberts c/o Capel & Land Ltd; the Lord Sackville (Edward Sackville-West); the Earl of Sandwich (Rosemary Peto); the Scotsman Publications Ltd; the Seven Pillars of Wisdom Trust (A.W. Lawrence and T.E. Lawrence); the Sophia Smith Collection, Smith College (Mina Curtiss); the *Spectator*; the Estate of Adrian Stephen; the Estate of James Stern, c/o Imrie & Dervis; the Society of Authors as the Literary Representatives of the Estate of Julian Bell; the Society of Authors as the Literary Representatives of the Estate of Quentin Bell; the Society of Authors as agents of the Strachey Trust (Alix Strachey, James Strachey and Lytton Strachey); Tanya Stobbs (Sylvia Townsend Warner); Telegraph Media Group Limited (*Sunday Telegraph*); the University of Sussex and the Society of Authors as the Literary Representative of the Estate of Leonard Woolf; Mrs R. Vellender (Edward Thomas); Caroline White (Rayne Garnett/Nickalls); John Worthen c/o the Andrew Lownie Literary Agency; Philip Ziegler (for *Rupert Hart-Davis: Man of Letters*, Chatto & Windus, 2004) c/o The Random House Group and United Agents.

Quotes from Olive Garnett's Diaries are property of Caroline White, Tabb House, 7 Church Street, Padstow, Cornwall; extract from *John Maynard Keynes: The Economist as Saviour* by Robert Skidelsky reprinted by permission of Peters Fraser & Dunlop [www.petersfraserdunlop.com] on behalf of Robert Skidelsky; the information in the Parliamentary Recruiting Committee Circular is re-used under the terms of the Open Government Licence; Judith Mackrell *Bloomsbury Ballerina* © Judith Mackrell 2008, the Orion Publishing Group, London; Jonathan Raban © Jonathan Raban c/o Aitken Alexander Associates; unpublished

Select Bibliography

David Garnett: Fiction

Burke, Leda [pseudo.] *Dope Darling* (London: T. Werner Laurie, 1919)

Lady into Fox (London: Chatto & Windus, 1922)

A Man in the Zoo (London: Chatto & Windus, 1924)

The Sailor's Return (London: Chatto & Windus, 1925)

Go She Must (London: Chatto & Windus, 1927)

The Old Dovecote and Other Stories (London: Elkin Mathews & Marrot, 1928)

No Love (London: Chatto & Windus, 1929)

The Grasshoppers Come (London: Chatto & Windus, 1931)

Pocahontas or the Nonparell of Virginia (London: Chatto & Windus, 1933)

Beany-Eye (London: Chatto & Windus, 1935)

A Net for Venus (London: Longman, 1951)

Aspects of Love (London: Chatto & Windus, 1955)

A Shot in the Dark (London: Longmans, 1958)

Two by Two (London: Longmans, 1963)

Ulterior Motives (London: Longmans, 1965)

A Clean Slate (London: Hamish Hamilton, 1971)

The Sons of the Falcon (London: Macmillan, 1972)

Plough Over the Bones (London: Macmillan, 1973)

Purl & Plain & Other Stories (London: Macmillan, 1973)

The Master Cat: The True and Unexpurgated Story of Puss in Boots (London: Macmillan, 1974)

Up She Rises (London: Macmillan, 1977)

David Garnett: Non-Fiction

The Battle of Britain: August–October 1940 (London: HMSO, 1941)

The Battle of Britain, abridged by permission from the Air Ministry Account of the Great Days, August to October 1940 (Puffin Picture Book, Harmondsworth/New York: Penguin Books [1941])

War in the Air: September 1939–May 1941 (London: Chatto & Windus, 1941)

The Campaign in Greece and Crete (London: HMSO, 1942)

The Secret History of PWE: The Political Warfare Executive 1939–1945, with an introduction by Andrew Roberts (London: St Ermin's Press, 2002)

David Garnett: Autobiography & Memoirs

A Rabbit in the Air (London: Chatto & Windus, 1932)

'War Victims' Relief' in Julian Bell, ed., *We Did Not Fight: 1914–18 Experiences of War Resisters* (London: Cobden-Sanderson, 1935)

The Golden Echo (London: Chatto & Windus, 1953)

The Flowers of the Forest (London: Chatto & Windus, 1955)

The Familiar Faces (London: Chatto & Windus, 1962)

The White/Garnett Letters, edited with a preface by David Garnett (London: Jonathan Cape, 1968)

Great Friends: Portraits of Seventeen Writers (London: Macmillan, 1979)

Works by Other Authors

Baldick, Chris, *The Modern Movement: Volume 10: 1910–1940* (Oxford: Oxford University Press 2004)

Bates, H E, *Edward Garnett* (London: Parrish, 1950)

Baynes Jansen, Diana, *Jung's Apprentice: A Biography of Helton Godwin Baynes* (Einsiedeln: Daimon Verlag, 2003)

Bell, Anne Olivier, (ed.), *The Diaries of Virginia Woolf 1915–1935* (London: Hogarth Press, 1976–82)

Bell, Julian, ed., *We Did Not Fight: 1914–18 Experiences of War Resisters* (London: Cobden-Sanderson, 1935)

Bell, Quentin, *Bloomsbury* (London: Weidenfeld & Nicolson, 1968)

Bell, Quentin, and Virginia Nicholson, *Charleston: A Bloomsbury House and Garden* (New York: Henry Holt Company, 1997)

Bradbury, Malcolm, and James McFarlane (eds), *Modernism 1890–1930* (London: Penguin, 1991)

Cave, Roderic, *The Private Press* (London: R.R. Bowker Company, second edition revised and enlarged, 1983)

Chisholm, Anne, *Frances Partridge: The Biography* (London: Weidenfeld & Nicolson, 2009)

Crawford, Fred D., *Richard Aldington and Lawrence of Arabia: A Cautionary Tale* (Carbondale and Edwardsville, IL: Southern Illinois University Press, 1998)

Cruickshank, Charles, *The Fourth Arm: Psychological Warfare 1938–1945* (London: Davis-Poynter, 1977)

Curtis, Anthony, *Lit Ed: On Reviewing and Reviewers* (Manchester: Carcanet, 1998)

Curtiss, Mina, *Other People's Letters: A Memoir* (Houghton Mifflin, 1978; London: Macmillan, 1978)

Dakers, Caroline, *The Countryside at War 1914–18* (London: Constable, 1987)

Deghy, Guy, and Keith Waterhouse, *Café Royal: Ninety Years of Bohemia* (London: Hutchinson, 1955)

DeGroot, Gerard J., *Blighty: British Society in the Era of the Great War* (London: Longman, 1996)

Delany, Paul, *The Neo-Pagans: Friendship and Love in the Rupert Brooke Circle* (London: Macmillan, 1987)

Dreyfus, John, *A History of the Nonesuch Press* (London: Nonesuch Press, 1981)

Farjeon, Eleanor, *Edward Thomas: The Last Four Years* (Oxford University Press 1958; paperback edition 1979)

Feather, John, *A History of British Publishing* (London: Croom Helm, 1988)

Gardiner, Juliet, *The Thirties: An Intimate History* (London: Harper Press, 2010)

Garnett, Angelica, *Deceived with Kindness: A Bloomsbury Childhood* (London: Chatto & Windus, 1984)

Garnett, Richard, *Constance Garnett: A Heroic Life* (London: Sinclair-Stevenson, 1991)

Garnett, Richard, ed., *Sylvia & David: The Townsend Warner/Garnett Letters* (London: Sinclair-Stevenson, 1994)

Goodall, Felicity, *A Question of Conscience: Conscientious Objection in the Two World Wars* (Stroud: Sutton Publishing, 1997)

Harman, Claire, *Sylvia Townsend Warner: A Biography* (London: Chatto & Windus, 1989; Minerva edition 1991)

Harris, Pippa, ed., *Song of Love: The Letters of Rupert Brooke and Noel Olivier, 1909–1915* (New York: Crown, 1991)

Hewison, Robert, *Under Siege: Literary Life in London 1939–45* (London: Weidenfeld & Nicolson, 1977)

Holroyd, Michael, *Lytton Strachey* (London: William Heinemann 1967 and 1968; revised edition, Chatto & Windus, paperback, 1994)

Holroyd, Michael, ed., *Lytton Strachey by Himself* (London: William Heinemann, 1971; Abacus, 2005)

Hyams, Edward, *The New Statesman: The History of the First Fifty Years 1913–1963* (London: Longmans, 1963)

James, Lawrence, *Raj: The Making and Unmaking of British India* (London: Little, Brown, 1997)

Jones, Nigel, *Rupert Brooke: Life, Death & Myth* (London: Richard Cohen Books, 1999)

Jefferson, George, *Edward Garnett: A Life in Literature* (London: Cape, 1982)

Johnson, Barry C., ed., *Tea and Anarchy! The Bloomsbury Diary of Olive Garnett 1890–1893* (London: Bartletts Press, 1989)

Johnson, Barry C., ed., *Olive and Stepniak: the Bloomsbury Diary of Olive Garnett (1893–1895)* (Birmingham: Bartletts Press, 1993)

Kohn, Marek, *Dope Girls: The Birth of the British Drug Underground* (London: Lawrence & Wishart, 1992)

Kynaston, David, *Austerity Britain 1945–51* (London: Bloomsbury, 2007)

Lee, Hermione, *Virginia Woolf* (London: Chatto & Windus, 1996)

Levy, Paul, ed., *The Letters of Lytton Strachey* (London: Viking, 2005)

Marler, Regina, ed., *Selected Letters of Vanessa Bell*, introduction by Quentin Bell (London: Bloomsbury Publishing, 1993, paperback 1994)

Marler, Regina, *Bloomsbury Pie: The Making of the Bloomsbury Boom* (London: Virago Press, 1997)

May, Betty, *Tiger Woman: My Story* (London: Duckworth, 1929)

Meisel, Perry and Walter Kendrick, eds, *Bloomsbury/Freud: The Letters of James and Alix Strachey (1924–1925)* (London: Chatto & Windus, 1986)

Meynell, Francis, *My Lives* (London: Bodley Head, 1971)

Meynell, Francis, A.J.A. Symons and D. Flower, eds, *The Nonesuch Century: An Appraisal, a Personal Note ... 1923–1934* (London: Nonesuch Press, 1936)

Moorehead, Caroline, *Troublesome People: Enemies of War 1916–1986* (London: Hamish Hamilton, 1987)

Nicholson, Virginia, *Among the Bohemians: Experiments in Living 1900–1939* (London: Viking, 2002)

Nicolson, Nigel, and Joanne Trautmann, eds, *The Letters of Virginia Woolf*, vols 2–6 (London: Hogarth Press, 1976–80)

Overy, Richard, *The Morbid Age: Britain between the Wars* (London: Allen Lane, 2009)

Partridge, Frances, *A Pacifist's War* (London: Hogarth Press, 1978; Robin Clark paperback, 1983)

Partridge, Frances, *Memories* (London: Victor Gollancz, 1981)

Partridge, Frances, *Everything to Lose: Diaries 1945–1960* (London: Victor Gollancz, 1985)

Partridge, Frances, *Hanging On: Diaries 1960–1963* (London: William Collins, 1990)

Partridge, Frances, *Other People: Diaries 1963–1966* (London: HarperCollins, 1993)

Partridge, Frances, *Good Company: Diaries 1967–1970* (London: HarperCollins, 1994)

Partridge, Frances, *Life Regained: Diaries 1970–1972* (London: Weidenfeld & Nicolson, 1998)

Partridge, Frances, *Ups and Downs: Diaries 1972–1975* (London: Weidenfeld & Nicolson, 2001)

Pugh, Martin, *We Danced All Night: A Social History of Britain between the Wars* (London: Bodley Head, 2008)

Seymour, Miranda, *Ottoline Morrell: Life on a Grand Scale* (London: Hodder & Stoughton, 1992)

Skidelsky, Robert, *John Maynard Keynes: Economist, Philosopher, Statesman* (London: Macmillan, 2003)

Smith, Adrian, *The New Statesman: Portrait of a Political Weekly 1913–1931* (London: Frank Cass, 1996)

Spalding, Frances, *Vanessa Bell* (London: George Weidenfeld & Nicolson, 1983)

Spalding, Frances, *Duncan Grant* (London: Chatto & Windus, 1997)

Spender, Stephen, *World Within World* (London: Hamish Hamilton, 1951)

White, Jerry, *London in the 20th Century* (London: Viking, 2001)

Worthen, John, *D.H. Lawrence: The Early Years (1885–1912)* (Cambridge University Press, 1991)

Worthen, John, *D.H. Lawrence: The Life of an Outsider* (Allen Lane, 2005)

Ziegler, Philip, *London at War 1939–1945* (London: Sinclair-Stevenson, 1995)

Ziegler, Philip, *Rupert Hart-Davis: Man of Letters* (London: Chatto & Windus, 2004)

Reference Abbreviations

AS-F	Alix Sargant-Florence
AVG	Angelica Garnett
Berg	Berg Collection, New York Public Library
BK-S	Barbara Ker Seymer
BL	British Library
Bodleian	Bodleian Library, Oxford
CG	Constance Garnett
DG	David Garnett
DHL	D.H. Lawrence
EG	Edward Garnett
EMH	Nellie Heath
Eton	Eton School Library
GLS	Lytton Strachey
HG	Henrietta Garnett
HRHC	Harry Ransom Humanities Research Centre, University of Texas at Austin
Imperial	Imperial College Archives, London
JDH	John Hayward
JMK	John Maynard Keynes
KCC	King's College, Cambridge

Northwestern	Northwestern University Library
NS&N	*New Statesman and Nation*
pmk	postmark
Princeton	Princeton University Library
RAG	Ray Garnett
Reading	Reading University Library
RG	Richard Garnett
STW	Sylvia Townsend Warner
Sussex	University of Sussex Library
TEL	T.E. Lawrence
TGA	Tate Gallery Archives
THW	T.H. White
VB	Vanessa Bell

Material formerly belonging to the Estate of David Garnett was consulted at Hilton Hall, the former home of Garnett's executor, Richard Garnett. Most of this is now at Northwestern University and cited as such.

Index

604

608